T0354359

# The Dark Heart of Utopia: Sexuality, Ideology, and the Totalitarian Movement

## By Kirk Rodby

iUniverse, Inc.

New York   Bloomington

# The Dark Heart of Utopia
## Sexuality, Ideology, and the Totalitarian Movement

*iUniverse books may be ordered through booksellers or by contacting:*

*iUniverse*
*1663 Liberty Drive*
*Bloomington, IN 47403*
*www.iuniverse.com*
*1-800-Authors (1-800-288-4677)*

*Because of the dynamic nature of the Internet, any Web addresses or links contained in this book may have changed since publication and may no longer be valid. The views expressed in this work are solely those of the author and do not necessarily reflect the views of the publisher, and the publisher hereby disclaims any responsibility for them.*

*ISBN: 978-1-4401-3144-8 (sc)*
*ISBN: 978-1-4401-3853-9 (ebook)*

*Printed in the United States of America*

*iUniverse rev. date:04/06/2009*

# Table of Contents

# 1. Introduction

By the time of her arrest, faux trial, and horrific murder at the hands of French revolutionaries during the massacres of September, 1792, it had been supposed for some time that Princesse Therese de Lamballe was the lesbian lover of Queen Marie Antoinette. Not content to leave things at vague rumors or whispers of indiscretions, anti-royalist pamphleteers offered up vivid though fictional descriptions of their lovemaking, which, they alleged, continued even while the two were in custody. Lamballe was hardly alone among the French aristocracy in being accused of libertinage. The Jacobin strain of revolutionary thought, and its bloodthirsty disciples, posited a firm division between the sexual aristocrat and the asexual commoner. Excessive sexuality was a political crime, on a par with treason, and thus itself a sufficient condition for extermination. Apart from her high-profile though fictional affair with Marie Antoinette, Lamballe was an insignificant figure, timid and socially awkward, and hardly the kind of aristocrat one would expect to be singled out for a prelude of the terror to come. She certainly displayed deep reserves of courage when pressed, having returned to France from England to be with the Queen post-revolution, and later being sentenced to death ostensibly for her refusal to condemn the Queen at trial. The more pleasant version of the story has her dragged out into a courtyard immediately after her 'conviction', dispatched quickly, and her head cut off, placed on a pike, and paraded through the streets of Paris. The less pleasant version, attested to by numerous eyewitnesses, has her stripped, raped, her breasts cut off, her heart cut out and devoured, her genitals cut out, her limbs cut off and fired from cannons, and her head cut off, placed on a pike, taken to a hairdresser

1

for attention, and then paraded around the streets of Paris. An early victory for the self-appointed guardians of 'virtue'.

The totalitarian campaign of extermination is a singularly spectacular phenomenon, virtually synonymous with totalitarianism for some, and not without reason the one thing above all others for which these movements are known. Victims, interestingly enough, are routinely defined by totalitarians in terms of their sexual excess and depravity, or very simply by a desire for sexual pleasure. Those to be spared or even perpetrate the act of extermination are defined in turn by a sexual desire limited to procreative purpose, perhaps a longing for asexual methods of reproduction, or even outright asexuality. This basic dichotomy held in Nazi Germany, Bolshevik Russia, Jacobin France, and elsewhere we find these seemingly inexplicable cases of mass slaughter. Correlation is not causation, of course, and yet sexual and reproductive considerations invariably form the core rationale for totalitarian violence. According to the totalitarian, it is the potential for sexual 'infection', of becoming sexual through contact with the demonic other, that necessitates the latter's destruction. Totalitarians see a causative relationship between sexuality and violence, which does itself suggest that the underlying psychology of this phenomenon might have something to do with sexuality generally.

The connections between sexuality and totalitarianism are in fact much broader and deeper, as will be made clear in the following chapters. The core concepts of the totalitarian ideology, its blueprint for the utopia to come, are all built around sexual considerations. The objective of the totalitarian movement, most simply and fundamentally, is to form a metaphysical and quasi-biological (or 'ideo-biological') collective with a single consciousness. The control of sexuality and reproduction is *always* thought by the totalitarian to be essential to the accomplishment of this central goal. Sexual collectivity constitutes a part of the non-negotiable, intransigent aspects of the totalitarian ideology, and any attempt to trace the whys and wherefores of the totalitarian ideology back to its first principles will arrive at this point. As the sexual aspects of the totalitarian ideology are a constant, the pre-totalitarian society is also a constant in terms of its sexual sociology. With a bit of work, the sociology can actually be shown to be causative of the ideology. Changes in the sexual environment are in fact what drives totalitarians to attempt total psychological and metaphysical collectivization.

An investigation of the sexual aspects of totalitarianism will have to come second, however, to a discussion of the precise version of 'totalitarianism' to be explored here.[1] This book is about ideological mass movements, including, but not limited to, those that have been previously designated 'totalitarian' (e.g., Bolshevism, National Socialism, and Jacobinism). All the movements discussed herein are totalitarian in the sense that they develop ideological systems which are intended to stand as total explanations of human nature and destiny. Thus they form the basis for the total control of the individual, which is thought to be instrumental to the perfection of humanity in general. These individuals have been labeled totalitarians, ideologists, true believers, fanatics, political paranoids, and (confusingly) authoritarians, but the essential psychological makeup is a constant. In contrast, the term 'totalitarian' is also used to describe political systems characterized by extreme centralization, highly invasive surveillance, the extralegal application of force against their own citizenry, and unlimited executive authority. In this conception, totalitarianism is primarily a political rather than social phenomenon, with an ideology as one component part, perhaps applied cynically and without genuine belief. Again, this work is concerned with movements, their ideas and objectives, the social conditions which create them, and the underlying psychology of their members. Institutional aspects are discussed only to the extent they relate to an analysis of the foregoing.

The terms 'ideological' and 'totalitarian' are thus used more or less interchangeably here, though ideology is a controversial term in its own right. As with totalitarianism, there is no generally accepted definition of ideology, and the term can, in popular usage, be used to describe anything as broad as one's basic belief system.[2] This work is concerned with a series

---

1    As Richard Shorten writes, "to speak in terms of a *debate* about totalitarianism is to a large degree problematic at the most fundamental level, in the sense that both supporters and adversaries of the idea are by no means in agreement as to precisely which historical phenomena merit the label 'totalitarian'; or, indeed, the time-span over which the label is applicable to, say, a given regime." Richard Shorten, "Francois Furet and Totalitarianism: A Recent Intervention in the Misuse of a Nation" in Totalitarian Movements and Political Religions, Vol. 3, No. 1, Summer 2002, 10. Shorten also points out a tendency among scholars to shape the concept based on cultural and philosophical orientations. The set of movements included herein are, at a minimum, intended to constitute a relatively expansive though by no means exhaustive study of the totalitarian phenomenon. Many more movements could have been included.

2    Good introductions to the subject include Michael Freeden, *Ideology: A Very Short Introduction* (Oxford: Oxford University Press, 2003), and *Terry Eagle-*

of systems of thought which feature commonalities in terms of structure, substance, scope, logic, and attitudes toward empiricism. The subject here is both more comprehensive in structure and more specific in substance than a generic philosophy or baseline set of ideas. In scholarly usage, the study of ideology is concerned either with defective epistemology, the sociological basis of knowledge, or some combination of the two. This work is intended to show the sociological forces behind the defective epistemology of the totalitarian ideology, which is itself a theory of how sociological forces can impair the cognition of non-totalitarians. And yes, this brings us to a bit of an impasse, there being no neutral point between totalitarian and non-totalitarian theory from which to critique the one or the other. In any case, ideology meaning literally the logic of an idea, and this work being concerned with the logic of and behind totalitarian ideas, the term should be unobjectionable here. The next two chapters may be taken as an extended and detailed definition or explanation of what a totalitarian ideology is, though certainly no attempt is made to explain or define ideology as a general matter. The basic theoretical model presented here is based in large part on investigation into totalitarian source material, and is intended to give the reader the totalitarian's view of totalitarianism.

The methodology of this book is as follows. With heavy emphasis on National Socialism and Bolshevism, the basic characteristics of totalitarian thought are distilled from numerous primary and secondary sources. Fundamental principles and recurring patterns are identified; other movements and ideologies are designated as totalitarian based on their consistency with these principles and patterns. These basic characteristics are then systematized and presented in an organized form (Chapter 2.1). The sexual aspects of these ideologies are then investigated (Chapter 2.2), leading to two fundamental conclusions. First, the sexual theories of totalitarian movements are not only perfectly consistent with their ideological systems as a whole, but are in fact integral to such systems. Second, as with the basic structure of the totalitarian ideology, there is very little variation between the sexual theories of these movements, suggesting a common psychology behind all of them. Next, we turn to previous theories of totalitarian and authoritarian psychology and sociology, systematize several partial solutions and match them with the basic structure of the ideology outlined previously (Chapter 2.3). With this basic model in mind, sexual dynamics are then established as the causative

---

*ton, Ideology: An Introduction* (New York: Verso, 2007).

force behind the rise of the totalitarian movement (Chapter 2.4).

The movements discussed herein are intended to provide a broad sample both temporally and geographically. We begin with a recent movement, the Chinese Cultural Revolution (1966-76). Next are two Christian variants on the totalitarian theme, the millennialism of the First Crusade (1096-99) and the demonology of the witch hunts of the early modern era (1560-1660), both French and German affairs. Following these is the French Revolution of 1789, though this work will focus on the Jacobin variant of Enlightenment thought specifically, and cover the year of the Terror (1793-94) in particular. From there, on to India and the slow-burning Hindutva movement, which spans most of the twentieth century and continues to this day. The rise of communism in late Imperial Russia (1861-1917) comes next. We conclude with perhaps the greatest force of destruction in the history of the world — National Socialism and the Third Reich (1933-1945).

Some further clarifications are in order. This work is concerned more with the reasons totalitarian movements come into being, and less so the reasons they eventually manage to gain power. For example, the collapse of the Weimar economy in 1929 may explain why millions of German voters turned to National Socialism in 1930, and political miscalculations on the part of conservatives in 1932-33 provided the direct cause of Hitler's accession to power. The concern here is with the millions of National Socialist voters who turned out in 1926 and 1928 before the economy failed; even more specifically, with the several thousand who signed up in the earliest years of the Weimar republic and remained loyal even during the years the party was banned. A further clarification – none of this analysis is intended to suggest that everyone who becomes involved in such a movement is driven by the same motives. The concern here is with the ideologist, the hardcore fanatic, the 'true believer', the man on the leading edge of the movement. Adventurers, criminals, losers, cynics, and people looking only to play the angles, gain personal power, or make a profit through involvement are largely absent from this work. Hitler will thus be featured prominently, while Goering will not; Lenin, Trotsky, and Bukharin are all included while Stalin has been left out; Robespierre and St. Just, in, Danton, out.

Totalitarianism involves a constellation of attitudes and behaviors, and not all of them are entirely unique to the totalitarian personality. Such individuals are, for example, incredibly fond of somatic metaphors for human organization, particularly in the area of diseases and cures. The mere fact that someone uses somatic metaphors does not thereby make them a totalitarian. On the other hand, someone who designates some group of people as a virus or infection, and then advocates a 'cure' in the form of genocide is much closer to the individual with whom we are concerned. This work does also concern itself with a weak form of the totalitarian personality, an individual who develops similar totalistic and utopian theories, apparently for similar reasons, though one that stops short of embracing every aspect of the totalitarian ideology as outlined here. In this category we might place someone like a St. Augustine, a Jean-Jacques Rousseau, or even an Alexandra Kollontai. Certainly their theories are used as the basis for fully-formed totalitarian ideologies, though their intensity level is lower, as is their tendency to advocate full implementation of their theories, and they often display a revulsion to violence. Calling them 'utopians' would, in this context, fail to provide any meaningful differentiation. All totalitarians are utopians in the sense that they are trying to create some sort of perfect, all-encompassing society.

In the end, the totalitarian impulse toward collectivity is simply an extreme along a continuum of collective impulse. It is anything but modern, having expressed itself in the context of religious systems for thousands of years, and perhaps even in the context of tribal organization predating civilization. The impulse is primitive and atavistic, but protean and capable of expressing itself in new ways as human thought evolves and becomes more complex. It is unlikely to disappear in the future.

## 2.1 The Immovable Mind Meets the Irresistible Force

**A totalitarian ideology is a** system of ideas, and one with a predetermined guiding structure. It is best understood as a certain pattern of thought, as an impulse looking for its own explanation, rather than in terms of the distinguishing ideas and explanations contained in any particular ideology. An ideology will generally incorporate some existing set of nonideological ideas to give itself a coherent form and provide its superficial rationale, though its basic character is determined in advance of any contemporary concepts so absorbed. Certain first principles are necessary to complete the system, and the likelihood that any particular set of ideas will be absorbed is dependent on the preexistence of essential ideas, ease of adaptation, and the absence of a serious conflict between foundational ideological maxims and nonideological superstructure.[3] A similar pattern of absorption, distortion, and addition is evident in all such systems, as in the shift from Darwin's theory of evolution to National Socialism, from witch folklore and Christianity into Demonology, and even from Marxism to Marxism-Leninism.[4] Ideological systems thus tend to look remarkably similar across continents and across centuries, and, in point of fact, have more in common with each other than with their own nonideological precepts.[5]

A totalitarian ideology requires a comprehensive set of interdependent axioms in order to function. These axioms are considered absolute and universal truths which, in concert, provide the foundation for the entire sum of possible knowledge, past, present, and future. Lewis Feuer points out that the 'totalistic' social-political control of the totalitarian movement is mirrored by its 'totalistic' explanation of reality, and that "ideologists

---

3    According to the Berkeley Group, "once the central or nuclear ideas are formed, they tend to 'pull in' numerous other opinions and attitudes and thus to form a broad ideological system." T.W. Adorno, Else Frenkel-Brunswick, Daniel J. Levinson, R. Nevitt Samford, *The Authoritarian Personality*, abridged ed. (New York: W.W. Norton & Co., 1982), 93; see also Andre Haynal, noting that "fanaticism appears in many guises; it is Proteus with a hundred faces, but it always retains essential traits making possible its identification." Andre Haynal, Miklos Molnar, and Gerard de Puymege, *Fanaticism: A Historical and Psychoanalytic Study*, trans. Linda Butler Kezdoglou (New York: Shocken Books, 1983), 82.

4    Note Savarkar on the difference between Hinduism and Hindutva: "Hindutva is not a word but a history. Not only the spiritual or religious history of our people as at times it is mistaken to be by being confounded with the other cognate term Hinduism, but a history in full. Hinduism is only a fraction, a part of Hindutva." V.D. Savarkar, *Hindutva: Who is a Hindu?* (Poona: S.P. Gokhale, 4th ed. 1949), 3.

5    Norman Cohn finds the similarities going back centuries: "Between the revolutionary eschatology of the later Middle Ages and modern totalitarian ideas, there is of course one obvious difference. Where the former borrowed the language Judeo-Christian prophecy, the latter have drawn upon nineteenth-century speculations in the fields of history, biology, and sociology. ... Beneath the pseudo-scientific terminology one can in each case recognise a phantasy of which almost every element is to be found in phantasies which were already current in medieval Europe." Norman Cohn, *The Pursuit of the Millennium* (New Jersey: Essential Books, 1957).

pride themselves above all on what we might call their 'totalism'."[6] An ideological system is, as Eric Hoffer describes it, "a net of familiarity spread over the whole of eternity. ... All questions have already been answered, all decisions made, all eventualities foreseen."[7] Virtually any truth may be ascertained through axiom and exegesis, while the universal nature of the truth contemplated means that truth can *only* be ascertained by reference to the system. The system of truth is either accepted or rejected as a whole, while the embrace of any important untruth positions one firmly in the realm of untruth.

Ideological systems proceed under the aegis of spontaneously-formed axioms which are then nominally subject to the constraints of logic. The deduction of more specific ideas from basic axioms is permitted and even demanded so long as no contradiction occurs, with induction considered a valid methodology to the extent that it confirms the truth of the system. The reexamination of first principles is an impossibility, however. As Hannah Arendt explains:

> As soon as logic as a movement of thought — and not as a necessary control of thinking — is applied to an idea, this idea is transformed into a premise. ... The purely negative coercion of logic, the prohibition of contradictions, became 'productive' so that a whole line of thought could be initiated, and forced upon the mind, by drawing conclusions in the manner of mere argumentation. This argumentative process could be interrupted neither by a new idea (which would have been another premise with a different set of consequences) nor by a new experience.[8]

M.S. Golwalkar, by way of example, explains that "we will not seek to prove this axiomatic truth, that the Race is the body of the Nation, and

---

6    Lewis Feuer, *Ideology and the Ideologists* (New York: Harper & Row, 1975), 130.

7    Eric Hoffer, *The True Believer: Thoughts on the Nature of Mass Movements* (New York: Harper & Row, 1966), 77.

8    Hannah Arendt, *The Origins of Totalitarianism* (New York: Harcourt Inc., 1973) 469-70. Note also Robins and Post on the 'political paranoid': "The scientist tests his hypothesis, ready to disconfirm it if the evidence does not support it. The paranoid, in contrast, knows the truth already and searches for confirmation. His is a fixed conclusion in search of evidence." Robert S. Robins and Jerrold M. Post, *Political Paranoia: The Psychopolitics of Hatred* (New Haven: Yale University Press, 1997), 8.

that with its fall, the Nation ceases to exist."[9] Or as Dr. Walter Gross, head of the Third Reich's Office of Racial Policy, explains, "race stands as the new controlling value in the picture of history — not as a controversial concept of scientists, but rather as an *inviolable fact of all historical life* and as the ultimate basis out of which the effects and achievements of nations originate."[10]

The result is a closed system of thought which is not only impervious to logical challenge, but also, and to an almost astonishing degree, resistant to any factual challenge brought from the experiential world.[11] In order to maintain a minimal degree of plausibility, an ideology does seem to require some basic amount of common, undisputed fact.[12] Beyond that, the ideologist has a tremendous capacity simply to ignore facts in conflict with his theory. Failing that, inconsistent facts are reconciled to the theory by emphasizing their temporal (and thus transitory) quality, and by assuming what Gerhard Niemeyer refers to as "an Archimedian point beyond the realm of experience from which the world of experience can be surveyed, criticized, and even declared a nothingness."[13] Which is to say that in a very particular way an ideology denies the validity of the reality one experiences with the five senses.

The ideologist's factually-challenged sense of reality is rationalized by presupposing an entirely different way of perceiving reality. The totalitarian ideology posits that truth can only be reached through a particular kind of instinct, one having a quasi-biological foundation and inherent to a select group of people (e.g., communists, and 'Nordic' Germans). This instinct is

---

9    Quoted in Chetan Bhatt, *Hindu Nationalism: Origins, Ideologies and Modern Myths* (New York: Oxford/Berg, 2001), 128.

10   Speech of Walter Gross, *Reichstagung in Nürnberg 1933*, ed. Julius Streicher, (Berlin: Vaterländischer Verlag C.A. Weller, 1934)(emphasis added), 147.

11   Arendt, 471.

12   "If ideology were only a species of myth, it would scarcely have the power of attracting the intellectuals of the modern world. The Mosaic myth is an all-essential ingredient in ideology, but the myth, in modern times, must be embedded in scientific, empirical as well as philosophical arguments. An ideology must therefore enlist a certain minimum of sociological argument; it must at least avail itself of a minimum perception of social reality, some empirical facts which will lend at least partial credence to its assertions ... a myth altogether detached from reality can never do service in an ideology." Feuer, 96.

13   Gerhard Niemeyer, *Between Nothingness and Paradise* (South Bend: St. Augustine's Press, 1998), 78.

subject to social and cultural amplification and development, or, alternatively, subject to suppression and extinguishment in the wrong kind of social environment. It is generally understood by ideologists, though, that this type of instinct cannot be created where it does not exist, only brought forth where it is latent. The instinct is developed through societal thought control, leading one to ideological consciousness, or an awareness of the true nature of reality. National Socialism, for example, is built on the 'racial instinct' (*Rasseninstinkt*) of the German man, which could be developed into 'racial consciousness' (*Rassenbewußtsein*) and 'racial thought' (*Rassengedanke*).

Instinct is a precondition for the totalitarian mode of thinking, which bears only superficial relationship to more familiar modes of comprehension. In this respect, ideology transcends the division between science and religion, in truth relying neither on empiricism nor faith, yet claiming foundational legitimacy through both. In spite of their claims to a hidden, instinctual form of knowledge, ideological systems virtually never condemn science outright. Anything tending to prove the system will be embraced regardless of the methodology, but ideologies do frequently claim scientific legitimacy. Not scientific in the sense of employing some form of empirical method, rather scientific in the sense of being 'super-scientific,' or scientific in a way that refuses to recognize any of the limits of, or do any of the actual work of, traditional science.[14] From an ideological standpoint, science is fundamentally deficient in that it tends to deal in incremental rather than universal truths, and that it deals in probabilities rather than absolutes.[15] Scientific theories, unlike ideologies, change as evidence is brought to light. Thus we have Dr. Gerhard Wagner, medical chief of the Third Reich, explaining the pseudo-scientific nature of National Socialism as follows:

---

14 As John Plamenetz explains, the designation 'scientific' does not refer to "a set of assumptions and principles that serve to relate to one another hypotheses that have been confirmed by experiment or some other kind of appeal to the facts.... They think of it as an interpretation of history, of the course of social and cultural change, which brings out its 'significance' in a way that the theories of the mere sociologist and the explanations of the mere historian cannot do." John Plamenetz, *Ideology* (New York: Praeger, 1970), 80.

15 Note Feuer at 131: "The scientist is prepared to entertain the alternative that 'totalism' is unworkable. ...the discipline of suspended judgment, the postponed accumulation of evidence, the weighing of alternative hypotheses, is felt as repressive."

Our genetic and racial thinking stems in the end not from our scientific, but rather from our National Socialist convictions, and ... it was not learned scientists, but rather our Führer Adolf Hitler, and he alone, who made genetic and racial thinking the center of our National Socialist worldview and the foundation of the rebuilding of our people's state.[16]

To the extent involved, ideological 'science' is very much in line with totalitarian logic generally, which means that truth is formed axiomatically and then proven empirically. A failure to establish the truth of the axiom proves the deficiency of the science, not the axiom.

As totalitarianism gives us scientists hostile to scientific methods, so it gives us religious fanatics hostile to faith. Faith is belief in the absence of proof. It is a belief that provides no degree of certainty, is held in spite of its logical and evidentiary deficiencies, and is inherently subjective. Ideology, on the other hand, always insists on its objective truth, certainty, and rationality.[17] It is precisely the removal of faith that allows a religion to be transformed into a totalitarian ideology. The resort to faith is an attempt to shield the ideology from any form of conceptual challenge, an attempt bolstered by the assertion that knowledge is fundamentally a matter of instinct. For the totalitarian, ideological faith is simply a counterpoint to ideological science, the latter thought to give the theory conclusive proof and the former rendering it impossible to disprove. Every totalitarian movement, whether ostensibly religious or otherwise, establishes the absolute certainty of its theory in this way. There is then a tendency to refer to ideologies absorbing secular theories as 'quasi-religious,'[18] but it

---

16    Speech of Gerhard Wagner, *Reichstagung in Nürnberg 1936*, ed. Hanns Kerrl, (Berlin: Vaterländischer Verlag C.A. Weller, 1937), 148.

17    This generally goes without saying, though one Nazi educator explained that "National Socialism is an ideology which makes a total claim to validity and refuses to be a matter for random opinion-formation." Quoted in Hans Peter Bleuel, *Sex and Society in Nazi Germany*, ed. Heinrich Frankel, trans. J. Maxwell Brown John (Philadelphia: J.B. Lippincott Co., 1973), 103.

18    According to Waldemar Gurian, "energies and forces which formerly had their outlet and expression in religion ... are now driving forces behind and in the new despotic regimes of the 20th century. The totalitarian ideologies replace and supercede religion. ... The objection that there can be no religion where there is no belief in God, and where transcendence is swallowed up by immanence, seems to me only a terminological one." Waldemar Gurian,

should be noted that ideologies employing religious concepts are 'quasi-religious' in precisely the same way.[19]

The end to which this super-scientific and hyper-faith instinct is directed is less the differentiation of the real relative to the unreal as it is a differentiation between realities. As Arendt explains, "ideological thinking becomes emancipated from the reality we perceive with our five senses, and insists on a 'truer' reality concealed behind all perceptible things... requiring a sixth sense that enables us to become aware of it."[20] Specifically, ideological systems posit the existence of a distinct 'true reality' set against a 'false reality.' Both are true in the sense that they exist, though only true reality is true in the sense that it constitutes the original design for experiential reality. False reality is true only to the extent that it represents a present, experiential reality, conformity to experience constituting a lesser form of truth at best to the ideological mind.[21] True reality lies just below the surface of the present reality, the latter, as Eric Hoffer describes it, a "faded and distorted reflection of a vast unknown throbbing underneath and beyond us."[22]

The nonconforming nature of this experiential reality means that the truth of the original or ultimate design can never be reached through logic or experience alone. One simply must possess the ideological instinct in order to differentiate between the two realities. As noted before, the

---

"Totalitarianism as a Political Religion," in Carl Friedrich, ed., *Totalitarianianism* (New York: Grosset & Dunlap, 1964), 122-23.

19    On the interchangeability of religious and political concepts in the totalitarian context, see Emilio Gentile, Politics as Religion, trans. George Staunton (Princeton: Princeton University Press, 2006), 44-67. Jaroslaw Piekalkiewicz and Alfred Wayne Penn write also that "when fundamentalist religions come to dominate political systems, their drive to create an earthly utopia that prepares the heavenly for salvation, establishes them as variants of democracy, with characteristics closely related to regimes traditionally labeled *totalitarian*." Jaroslaw Piekalkiewicz and Alfred Wayne Penn, *Politics of Ideocracy* (Albany: State University of Albany Press, 1995), 20.

20    Arendt, 470-71.

21    Note Indira Chowdhury on ideological thought in colonial India: "The indigenous historical narrative often struggled between the post-Enlightenment conceptualization of historical truth as a description of facts or 'things as they actually happened' and universal truth as perceived by the mythic consciousness." Indira Chowdhury, *The Frail Hero and Virile History: Gender and the Politics of Culture in Colonial Bengal* (Delhi: Oxford University Press, 1998), 47.

22    Hoffer, 67.

ideological instinct is thought to require some form of cultural reinforcement in order to develop as designed. Conversely, the existence of false reality is thought to suppress the ideological instinct and to induce something frequently referred to as 'false consciousness.' This is a state wherein the person predisposed to think in an ideological manner fails to grasp this universal truth, owing to a delusion-inducing intellectual environment characterized by non-ideological modes of thought. The totalitarian movement is thus the product of a great awakening, a spontaneous recognition of universal truth by some select group of those predisposed to do so. The rest of those in the relevant population (or in-group) will require help in the form of a comprehensive and invasive scheme of thought control.

Thus totalitarian thought control is thought of by the totalitarian as a matter of helping the individual discover his or her true, uniform, and collective self. As there is some small group aware of this truth and a much greater one remaining unaware, it falls to the former to educate the latter. Robespierre, for example, explains the consciousness-raising to be undertaken by the enlightened revolutionaries of France: "Half the revolution of the world is already accomplished; the other half must be achieved. Man's reason still resembles the globe he inhabits; half of it is plunged in darkness when the other is enlightened."[23] M.S. Golwalkar finds that in India, "there has been a great awakening, a growing political consciousness among our people. Awakening is knowledge and knowledge is the capacity for unity in diversity.... The tendencies of fission should therefore disappear giving rise to the urge for unity."[24] Dr. Gross notes the importance of the consciousness-raising aspect of National Socialism:

> And so follows today, with the totality of our idea corresponding to the totality of our claim, the second wave of the great German revolution: The battle, after the conquest and securing of the state, for the penetration and reformation of the German mind. Where yesterday our battlefields were in the streets and political gatherings, today they are in the places of the mind, in the quieter world of our colleges and research institutions, in all the areas where men work and battle for the worldview of a Volk and its people. And we know well that because of

---

23    Paul H. Beik ed. trans., *The French Revolution* (New York: Walker & Co., 1970), 300.

24    Golwalkar, *Bunch of Thoughts* (Mangalore: Sharada Press, 1966), 29.

it the struggle between an old and new era has entered its decisive stage.[25]

Chinese communist Lin Biao explains that "the decisive factor prompting us to launch a revolution in the sphere of social consciousness is the fundamental change that has occurred in the economic base of society."[26]

Totalitarian movements see themselves as movements of liberation,[27] as reactions against a tyrannical and insidious force enslaving those who would otherwise be enlightened and therefore free. The movement sets out to destroy free will in the name of free will, given that truth is singular and absolute, and would be embraced by all those able to recognize it for what it is. A refusal to embrace the ideological system by those theoretically possessed of the ideological instinct is itself held as proof of the individual's lack of free will. In this conception of freedom, free will must be restrained so that people trapped in nonideological modes of thinking can be freed to embrace the system of thought they would have embraced had their will truly been free. True freedom is the freedom to understand why the party is right, the 'recognition of necessity', or, alternatively, free will is a will that corresponds to that of God. Freedom is not the freedom to do what one desires, but rather the freedom to desire what one truly desires, which is the manifestation of true reality within the experiential reality. If one is in possession of an absolute truth, notes Louis Halle, "then I would not believe in tolerance; for any departure from the unquestionable truth would unquestionable error, and there would be no justification for tolerating it."[28]

---

25    Walter Gross, *Rasse, Weltanschauung, Wissenschaft: Zwei Universitätsreden* (Berlin: Junker und Dünnhaupt Verlag, 1936), 9.

26    Lin Biao, "Why a Cultural Revolution?", in Michael Schoenhals, ed., *China's Cultural Revolution: Not a Dinner Party* (New York: M.E. Sharpe, 1996), 12. According to Marx, a change in economic conditions would itself alter the consciousness of the masses.

27    "[S]upporters of totalitarian ideas believe that man does not, in most cases, act on rational grounds. They maintain that, in general, due to factors of emotion or personality, he is not master of his own actions, thus he cannot control them. Therefore, he must be led or, in some way, have his course of action illuminated by what is conceived to be a better group of men." J. Lucien Radel, *Roots of Totalitarianism: The Ideological Sources of Fascism, National Socialism, and Communism* (New York: Crane Russak, & Co., 1975), 19.

28    Louis Halle, *The Ideological Imagination* (Chicago: Quadrangle Books, 1972), 135.

To the ideologist, there is no paradox in enforced freedom because there is no true individual in any case. According to J.L. Talmon, the French revolutionaries believed that "all the evils, vices and miseries were due to the fact that man had not consulted his true nature, or had been prevented from doing so by ignorance, which was spread and maintained by vested interests. Had man probed his true nature, he would have discovered a replica of the universal order."[29] A. James Gregor finds the same political essentialism in Italian fascism,[30] as does Chetan Bhatt in Hindutva. This political essentialism is not necessarily limited to those representing the natural order. As Yao Wen-yuan, 'Gang of Four' member and ideologist of the Cultural Revolution, explains:

> There is only freedom in the concrete, no freedom in the abstract. In class society there is only class freedom; there is no freedom above class. … There is no such thing as 'free' literature and art detached from class politics, nor can there be any. Whatever their particular form of expression, the ideas of person, including those of any writer, are not isolated ideas 'of his own'. They are a manifestation of the ideas, interests and aspirations definite classes and the reflection of class relations in a given society. Do the 700 million Chinese people have 700 million kinds of 'ideas of their own'? Certainly not. Fundamentally they fall into only two kinds - one is the world outlook of the proletariat, or Mao Tse-tung's thought; the other is the world outlook of the bourgeoisie, or bourgeoisie individualism of every kind.[31]

To the totalitarian mind, those outside the ideological system will never be free in any real sense. True freedom involves the meta-preferential

---

29     J.L. Talmon, *The Origins of Totalitarian Democracy* (London: Secker and Warburg, 1955), 28.

30     A. James Gregor, *The Ideology of Fascism: The Rationale of Totalitarianism* (New York: The Free Press, 1969), 204. According to Gregor, Italian fascism was directed to the 'true ends of human existence,' with the nation conceived of as "an organic or functional whole in which individuals find their place, in which they 'define' themselves. The state is understood to be the express will of such an organic whole, representing the will of the whole people as opposed as distinct from the immediate and empirical will of the individuals composing it." Ibid., 219.

31     Yao Wen-yuan, *Comments on Tao Chu's Two Books* (Peking: Foreign Language Press, 1968), 24.

regulation of desires so as to bring about the utopian society conforming to the original design for experiential reality. Those prone to individualism and egoism have only the freedom to act on desires constructed by a false reality, which either distorts the ability to control preferences or creates them entirely. True individualism is not only an impossibility, as Lin Biao explains, but also a clear marker of ideological deviation: "In class society, each person belongs to a specific class. ... There is no such thing as an abstract, independent individual. To care about oneself is a purely bourgeois worldview."[32]

The truth, according to the totalitarian, is that what we take for the individual is merely an undifferentiated part of the great totalitarian collective. This is one of the most fundamental principles of totalitarian thought, and, in fact, anti-individualism (and pro-collectivity) may be the single most ubiquitous theme in totalitarian ideology generally. St. Just puts the matter bluntly: "Indifference towards one's country and love of self are the source of all evil; indifference to one's self and love of one's country are the source of all good."[33] According to Robespierre, "There are two kinds of egotism: one, base and cruel, which isolates a man from his fellows...; the other kind, generous and beneficent ... which attaches our glory to that of the country."[34] The individual does exist, but only as an individual part of a collective, such as the one found in the Third Reich, for example:

> The earthly prerequisite of all culture and all spirit lies not in the individual-I and lies not in a fantastical humanity, but rather entirely in the sole organic unity and totality that we call Volk. Here is the root of our spiritual life and creation, here is the solid ground out of which our strength grows. Surely there is the multitude of other

---

32    Biao, 18. "What is the essence of old culture and old ideology? We can use a great many words to express it and call it old culture, old ideology, poisonous weeds, ox-monsters and snake-demons, reactionary authorities, old academia, old morals, old art, old laws, old educational systems, old world outlook etc. The most essential aspect of these things lies in them being old in one particular respect, namely as parts of the system of private ownership. In short, they are old in one word and that word is 'self' (*si*). What, then, is new about new things and new ideology? They are also new in one word and that word is public (*gong*)." Ibid., 17.

33    Quoted in Norman Hampson, *Saint-Just* (Cambridge: Basil Blackwell, 1991), 47.

34    Beik, 300.

nations outside the Volk; surely there is the fullness of the individual personality within the Volk. But all life of men rests within the Volk. Out of it comes, often unconsciously, the strength to work on his own I, that finds its objective and fulfillment in the service of the Volk.[35]

Golwalkar suggests also that the Hindu is instinctually collective: "Our view of the relation between individual and society has always been, not one of conflict but of harmony and co-operation born out of a consciousness of a single Reality running through all the individuals. The individual is a living limb of the corporate social personality."[36]

Collectivity may then be thought of as the most basic and direct objective of the totalitarian movement. This is the collectivity which defines man in his natural state, and the end to which his latent collective instincts, properly developed, will bring him. Totalitarian thought control is the corrective that will ostensibly return mankind to its natural, utopian state — one that existed prior to the rise of false consciousness. Totalitarian movements presuppose three distinct stages in a cycle, stage one finding mankind in some kind of innocent and harmonious social arrangement. For Christians, this is Adam and Eve in the Garden of Eden, for communists the era prior to the creation of surplus value and capitalism. Stage two is the fall from grace and descent into false reality, which is always occasioned by the separation of the individual will from the collective will reflecting the original design for reality. It is here that the movement sets itself temporally, at the end of phase two and transitioning into the Apocalypse and phase three, the restoration of true reality within experiential reality. Society as it stands will be wiped away completely, as Roger Griffin explains:

> At the heart of palingenetic ['born anew'] political myth lies the belief that contemporaries are living through or about to live through a 'sea-change', a 'water-shed' or 'turning point' in the historical process. The perceived corruption, anarchy, oppressiveness, iniquities or decadence of the present ... are perceived as reached their peak and

---

35    Walter Gross, *Rasse, Weltanschauung, Wissenschaft: Zwei Universitätsreden* (Berlin: Junker und Dünnhaupt Verlag, 1936), 11.
36    Golwalkar, *Bunch of Thoughts*, 20.

interpreted as the sure sign that one era is nearing its end and a new order is about to emerge.[37]

This is to be the final, everlasting stage of the cycle.

The process of establishing experiential conformity with the original design for reality is seen as inexorable. Totalitarians see themselves as enforcing something like an immutable law of physics, rendering one just as powerful, even omnipotent, if only the decision is made to link the individual will to the collective.[38] Thus 'political messianism,' as historian J.L. Talmon calls it, "postulates a preordained, harmonious and perfect scheme of things, to which men are irresistibly driven, and at which they are bound to arrive."[39] In Augustine's *City of God*, men link their will to that of God's, whose will is fixed and destined to remain so until the end of times. The designs of Augustine's God, as with the laws of nature cited by other totalitarians, are irresistible and immutable: "For certainly He would not be the perfect worker He is, unless His Knowledge were so perfect as to receive no addition from His finished works."[40] Dr. Gross gives a similar account of the National Socialist objective:

> When today in Germany a man defends himself against the uninhibited mixing of foreign blood with that of our Volk, then ... we speak of the clear reverence for the great laws of nature. We have neither created the world nor prescribed its course. A greater power has done so, knowing the necessity of these laws and the ends to which

37    Roger Griffin, *The Nature of Fascism* (New York: St. Martin's Press, 1991), 35.

38    Thomas Blom Hansen refers to this phenomenon as the 'paradoxical dual teleology' of the movement. "On the one hand, history is invoked to justify the movement and its objectives. The movement is but a realization of inevitable historical development.... On the other hand, the founding myth almost always revolves around a notion of self-birth and self-celebration, depicting the founding of a movement in an extraordinary situation by farsighted individuals...." Thomas Blom Hansen, *The Saffron Wave: Democracy and Hindu Nationalism in Modern India* (Princeton: Princeton University Press, 1999), 91.

39    J.L. Talmon, *The Origins of Totalitarian Democracy* (London: Secker and Warburg, 1955), 2.

40    Saint Augustine, *The City of God*, trans. Marcus Dods, intro. Thomas Merton (New York: Random House, 1950), 364.

they are directed. It is only proper for the man to learn and implement these great laws respectfully.[41]

Of course, man in his true state is himself merely a reflection or expression of these forces of nature, as we learn from St. Just: "It has always seemed to me that the social order was in the very nature of things ... if man be given laws which harmonize with the dictates of nature and of his heart he will cease to be unhappy and corrupt...."[42] Once the decision is made to link oneself to the collective, the fulfillment of its destiny is assured. As Lin Biao explains, "The revolutionary movement of the masses is naturally right. While there may be segments and individuals among the masses who deviate ... the main current of the mass movement always accords with the development of society and is always right."[43]

Totalitarian movements are perhaps best known for their staggering body counts, generally thought to be instrumental to the attainment and consolidation of political power. Violence is invariably the preferred method for resolving disputes of any kind, and even nominally democratic movements are apt to accentuate their electoral successes with lethal force. It should always be remembered, though, that for totalitarianism, political power is simply a means to achieve utopian ends. The first prerequisite to the attainment of those ends is widespread acceptance of the ideological system. The irrational idea needs an irrational environment in which to survive, and in this respect violence is employed as an adjunct to the proselytizing efforts of the movement. Relevant individuals are killed or converted, with terrified silence taken as informed assent. This is as close to utopia as ideological mass movements have ever come.

From there, the character of ideological violence becomes more difficult to decipher. As Arendt notes, "terror increased both in Soviet Russia and Nazi Germany in inverse ratio to the existence of internal political opposition, so that it looked as though political opposition had not been the pretext of terror ... but the last impediment to its full fury."[44] The full

---

41    Speech of Walter Gross, *Reichstagung in Nürnberg 1933*, 157-58.

42    Quoted in Geoffret Bruun, *Saint-Just, Apostle of the Terror* (Hamden: Archon Books, 1966), 47-48. As Bruun paraphrases St. Just: "Nature, he believed, had established rational laws to govern men in society no less than stars in space; the legislator was a sort of Newton of the social order had merely to discover the basic principles of his science and the millennium would be achieved." Ibid., 45.

43    Biao, 21.

44    Arendt, 393.

fury of totalitarian terror is inevitably directed to some unfortunate group of otherwise ordinary people thought to be responsible for the individualistic, anti-collective nature of reality as it stands. This group is assigned responsibility axiomatically, with the totalitarian's understanding of his enemy among the most obviously delusional and nonsensical aspects of the ideological system. The chosen group is often marginalized if it exists at all, and would never be in possession of any obvious power to create or alter societal consciousness.[45] Nevertheless, the categorical extermination of this group does provide the movement with its highest operational imperative, standing as an absolutely essential precondition of the utopian future to come.

The mystery deepens as one proceeds into the specifics of totalitarian violence, and in particular how the target group is defined. Three peculiarities emerge. First, the totalitarian tends to rationalize violence in the form of self-defense.[46] He inhabits a nightmare world in which his existence is in mortal danger at all times, threatened by an unseen conspiratorial force bent on his destruction. His reality is defined by a cataclysmic battle between civilizations and ideologies, a battle of light and darkness, from which only one group or the other will emerge. Thus mercy is weakness and weakness is suicide, as Hitler explains at length in *Mein Kampf*.[47] According to Savarkar:

> If that alien religion is also tolerant of our own religion, our tolerance towards it can be a virtue. But the Muslim and Christian religions, which boldly proclaim it to be their religious duty to destroy most cruelly the Hindu religion and to eradicate from the face of this earth the kafirs

---

45    Adorno and the Berkeley Group explain that "hostility resulting from frustration and repression and socially diverted from its true object, *needs* a substitute object (300) through which it may obtain a realistic aspect and this dodge, as it were, more radical manifestations of a blocking of the subject's relationship to reality, e.g., psychosis," and further that "the content of the examples of stereotyped fantasy which we collected has to do predominately with ideas of excessive power attributed to the chosen foe. The disproportion between the relative social weakness of the object and its supposed sinister omnipotence is itself evidence that the projective mechanism is at work." Adorno et al., 299-300, 305.

46    Erich Fromm, *Escape From Freedom* (New York: Henry Holt, 1994) 143-44.

47    Adolf Hitler, *Mein Kampf*, trans. Ralph Manheim (New York: Houghton Mifflin, 1971), 284-329.

and heathens, can never be described as tolerant of other religions.[48]

Life and death are defined collectively, and if an innocent life or several are extinguished in the course of self-defense, it is incidental. According to St. Just, "You are not concerned with the civic aspect but with public safety, which is the prime consideration for us all. ... You have not to decide what refers to this individual or that, but what concerns the republic."[49]

Second, it should be noted that the totalitarian's enemy is very familiar to him, and in many cases indistinguishable from him but for the ideological assertion of difference. Murdered and murderer are closely connected here. Sociologist Gordon Allport once noted that "throughout history human prejudice has had little to do with race. ... For the most part prejudice and persecution have rested on other grounds, often on religion."[50] He adds that "the law of inverse relation between knowledge and hostility fails to hold at the extreme degree of hostility. We are not wholly ignorant of our worst enemies."[51] Ideologists always find their victims very close to home. At the extreme degree of hostility we do in fact find Catholics persecuting Cathars and Protestants, demonologists keeping their witch-hunts fairly local, French commoners killing French commoners during the revolution of 1789, Russian communists killing Russian 'counterrevolutionaries', Chinese communists killing Chinese counterrevolutionaries, Europe's master race killing European Jews rather than Asians or Africans, and Indian Hindus killing Indian Muslims on racial grounds. 'Biological' differences are cited in all cases.

Third, totalitarian extermination is ultimately directed to some other end than the mere annihilation of some target group. A new target group will be substituted if the initial one begins to decline, or else the target group will simply find itself perpetually regenerating its membership. Note Robespierre on the bloody successes of the French Revolution of 1789:

> How shortsighted it would be to regard a few victories achieved by patriotism as an end to all our dangers. Examine our real situation, and you will see that your vigilance and

---

48    V.D. Savarkar, *Six Glorious Epochs of Indian History*, trans. ed. S.T. Godbole, (New Delhi: Radjhani Granthagar, 1971), 169.

49    Quoted in Norman Hampson, *Saint-Just* (Cambridge: Basil Blackwell, 1991), 174.

50    Gordon Allport, *The Nature of Prejudice* (Massachusetts: Addision-Wesley Pub. Co., 1954), xv.

51    Ibid., 226.

energy are more necessary than ever. A secret opposition everywhere hinders the operations of the government; the fatal influence of foreign courts, though hidden, is no less active and no less damaging. One senses that crime, intimidated, has only covered its tracks with more cunning.[52]

The ideologist, moreover, conceives of his conflict in zero-sum terms, his gain coming only at the expense of his defeated enemy.[53] No one killed, nothing gained, as Yao Wen-yaun explains:

> Tao Chu says that this 'socialist ideal' of his is 'beneficial to everybody', including the bourgeoisie. Socialism must eradicate the bourgeoisie through the dictatorship of the proletariat. How can it be beneficial to them? The socialism which is beneficial to everybody is phoney socialism.... It is the reactionary theory of the 'party of the entire people', the 'state of the whole people' and the 'socialism of the whole people' which abandons the class struggle and abolishes the dictatorship of the proletariat.[54]

At a minimum, the ideologist, having picked a fight with reality, seems to require that the fight never reach a point of decision. The process of extermination is to continue indefinitely.

## 2.2  Kinky Sex Makes the World Go 'Round

**The totalitarian ideology divides the** world into two realities, one true and one false. True reality is characterized by sexual purity and asceticism, while false reality is distinguished by sexual degeneracy and pleasure seeking. The transformation of the one reality into the other is to be effected through the control of sexual desire, which constitutes a threat to the natural and/or

---

52   Beik, 285.

53   Jay Gonen, *The Roots of Nazi Psychology* (Lexington: University Press of Kentucky, 2000), 155.

54   Yao Wen-yuan, 9-10. Note also Robespierre: "How tenderly oppressors are treated and how pitilessly the oppressed! Nothing more natural; whoever does not abhor crime cannot love virtue. Yet one or the other must be crushed. Indulgence for the royalists, cry certain people. Mercy for the villains! No! Mercy for innocence, mercy for the weak, mercy for the unfortunate, mercy for humanity! The protection of society is due only to peaceable citizens: there are no citizens in the republic except the republicans." Beik, 284.

divine order. This threat comes by way of the sexual distortion of the thought processes of the in-group member, which then frustrates the development of his or her instinctive asexuality and collectivity, compromising the foundation of true reality as experiential reality. This distortion of true reality comes at the hands of the out-group member, who not only implements a program of sexual domination and destruction, but is the personification of sexuality itself. Thus the totalitarian movement sets out to restore true reality through the control of sexuality, and the control or even extermination of the sexual out-group member. This is the totalitarian movement in brief.

Given the active hostility to all things sexual, there is a tendency to think of these movements as 'conservative'. An ideology differs from a traditional moral code in several important respects, though. In the first place, an ideology is thought to provide a blueprint for a radical transformation and perfection of society, whereas a simple behavioral codex might be thought of in terms of providing stasis and order, or even as having no larger political significance whatsoever. Sexual morality tends to exist on its own level, largely devoid of rationalization, though perhaps backed by an occasional *ex cathedra* pronouncement of its validity. Ideological thinking brings sexuality into its core constructs, turning it into a question of true or false rather than a question merely of right and wrong. The moralist is generally forced to avoid logical contradictions, while the ideologist can always fall back on his other-worldly instincts which transcend the limitations of logic. Ideology is discovered intuitively rather than learned. Morality, moreover, is generally thought of as a guide to behavior. An ideological legal system is not based on any premise of deterrence or even retribution, but rather identification. The totalitarian legal system does not seek to punish sex offenders so as to deter specific sexual behaviors, but rather to identify the offender as part of a group which is thus ultimately proven to be sexual in nature (and hence a mortal threat).

The differences are subtle, and difficult to spot in cases where a moral code is based in whole or in part on an ideological system. Religious movements have, in effect, a back door left open to them at all times; the ideological modifications of Christianity and Hinduism, for example, tend to remain close enough to traditional sexual doctrines that their adherents will not necessarily appear manifestly delusional. Ideologies filled out with progressive doctrines, on the other hand, are at a considerable disadvantage when attempting to explain the novelty of their sexual restrictions vis-à-vis the 'reactionary' sexual morality they are overthrowing.[55] The Soviet sexual revolution of the 1920s experienced the contradiction, with Lenin himself offering a fairly unconvincing explanation of the difference.[56] In the case of National Socialism, which at times intimated a restoration of traditional sexual mores, the challenge was to explain its consistency with those value systems. In spite of its radical, materialist, and pseudo-scientific character, the movement was able to win the support of the more traditional German Nationalist People's Party (DNVP), the Catholic Center Party (Zentrum), and even the support, if inconsistent and wavering, of the Catholic Church itself. Sexual propriety was cited as a specific reason for that support.[57]

In all cases, the totalitarian ideology posits a fundamental division between sexual individualism and collective asexuality. One of China's culture warriors once explained that "falling in love at [an] early age is bourgeois and individualistic."[58] Another, Lin Biao, noted that "the kind of people we need to foster are what Chairman Mao called people who are divested of base interests.... Their opposites are the people centered on 'self'.... To care about oneself is a purely bourgeois worldview."[59] Harriet Evans offers the following observation in her study of women in mid- to late 20th century China:

> Expressions of individualistic interest in appearance or
> romance ... were to be contained by an ethic that stressed
> the superiority of selflessness and collective commitment.

---

55   Note, for example, the apparent contradiction cited by Red Guard member Rae Yang as far as the Chinese Cultural Revolution's position on sexuality: "Only years later did I realize that such an attitude toward sex in a woman had another name, an ancient name. It was chastity.... This notion undoubtedly belonged to the 'four olds'. Yet somehow instead of breaking it, my fellow Red Guards and I had defended it as if it were a sacred teaching of Chairman Mao." Rae Yang, *Spider Eaters: A Memoir* (Berkeley: University of California Press, 1997).

56   See Lenin's conversation with Clara Zetkin reprinted in *The Emancipation of Women: From the Writings of V.I. Lenin,* preface by Nadezdha Krupskaya (New York: International Publishers, 1966).

57   Uta Ranke-Heinemann, *Eunuchs for the Kingdom of Heaven: Women, Sexuality, and the Catholic Church,* trans. Peter Heinegg (New York: Doubleday, 199), 331-32.

58   Gao Yuan, *Born Red: A Chronicle of the Cultural Revolution* (Stanford: Stanford University Press, 1987), 31.

59   Lin Biao, "Why a Cultural Revolution?", in Michael Schoenhals, ed., *China's Cultural Revolution: Not a Dinner Party* (New York: M.E. Sharpe, 1996), p.18.

Throughout the Cultural Revolution, any suggestion of sex in fiction, poetry or drama was enough to have the offending work removed from circulation and its author punished.[60]

The concept was far from novel. Crusade propagandist Eudes of Chateauroux contrasts love which exists for the sake of God with love which exists for the convenience of the individual, "and here we are talking about lustful love which is illicit, not about natural love which is licit."[61] Sex, it is thought by the ideologist, tends to exert a gravitational pull on the interests and attentions of the individual, pulling him or her away from the collective and into the realm of personal satisfaction. Love and pleasure are to be strictly collective affairs. Martyn Liadov, rector of Sverdlov Communist University, reassured everyone that in the future:

> In each of us inhibitive centers will be developed by life itself, by the force of collective creativity. I will not be able to experience pleasure if I see that beside me someone else cannot experience it. I will be capable of experiencing only the general pleasure, the general satisfaction, the unlimited pleasure that will reign all around me.[62]

As sex leads to individualism, individualism leads to sex, according to Dr. Walter Gross of the Third Reich's Office of Racial Policy:

> We can follow the history of all times with shock, as the penetration of foreign blood undermined sexual decency, belief, the value of character, and circumvented morality, and because of that the basic principles of society were destroyed, upon which the building of a thriving and flourishing culture had once been erected.[63]

The penetration of foreign blood, presumably through sex, is in turn the result of a spirit that "sets the destiny of the individual higher than the thoughts of the totality ... out of a virtually fatal, and at the same time false and unnatural viewpoint."[64] Similarly, Bolsheviks Aron Zalkind and N.P.

60　Harriet Evans, *Women and Sexuality in China: Female Sexuality and Gender Since 1949* (New York: Continuum, 1997), 7.

61　Christoph T. Maier, *Crusade Propaganda and Ideology: Model Sermons for the Preaching of the Cross* (Cambridge: Cambridge University Press, 2000), 131.

62　Quoted in Eric Naiman, *Sex in Public: The Incarnation of Early Soviet Ideology* (Princeton: Princeton University Press, 1997), 93.

63　Speech of Walter Gross, *Reichstagung in Nürnberg 1933*, ed. Julius Streicher, (Berlin: Vaterländischer Verlag C.A. Weller, 1934), 150

64　Ibid., 154

Brukhansky both cited the Soviet Union's capitalist (hence individualist) New Economic Policy (NEP) of the 1920s as a causative factor in the 'unnatural' increase in sexual desire.[65]

The in-group member is, of course, naturally asexual, whereas the out-group member is prone to pleasure-seeking. Lust and aimless desire then become markers for the enemy. To illustrate the point, *Der Stürmer* ran a cartoon entitled 'Jewish Culture,' with the subtitle 'From the Natural to the Unnatural.' The cartoon features a young, attractive German couple in the countryside staring off into the distance (not at each other) on the left half of the frame, juxtaposed on the right with a Jewish man sitting next to a woman in a theatre while watching a pornographic movie.[66] Rae Yang, a member of the Red Guard during the Cultural Revolution, offers the following observation from the time:

> Sex was bourgeois. No doubt about it! In my mind, it was something very dirty and ugly. It was also extremely dangerous. In the books I read and the movies I saw, only the bad guys were interested in sex. Revolutionaries had nothing to do with it. When revolutionaries fell in love, they loved with their hearts. They didn't even touch hands.[67]

The imposition of the true ascetic values of the proletariat would require a purge led by 'sexually untainted youth.'[68] Robespierre had also previously explained that "virtue is natural in the people, aristocratic prejudices notwithstanding,"[69] the aristocrat being hereditarily predisposed to 'vice.' According to historian Maurice Lever, "Nothing disgusted the

---

65 Naiman, 125-27.
66 Dr. Gerhard Wagner, after explaining that the Third Reich's Nuremberg Laws were "issued not only for the protection of German blood, but also German honor," explained to the crowd at the 1937 Nuremberg Rally that they "will have fulfilled their purpose when a new generation has grown up in Germany, that out of a self-evidently pure National Socialist viewpoint instinctively rejects the Jews, and has become immune to the Jewish virus." Speech of Gerhard Wagner, *Reichstagung in Nürnberg 1937*, ed. Hanns Kerrl, (Berlin: Vaterländischer Verlag C.A. Weller, 1938), 122.
67 Rae Yang, *Spider Eaters: A Memoir* (Berkeley: University of California Press, 1997).
68 Neil J. Diamant, *Revolutionizing the Family: Politics, Love, and Divorce in Urban and Rural China, 1949-1968* (Berkeley: University of California Press, 2000), 286.
69 Paul H. Beik ed. trans., *The French Revolution* (New York: Walker & Co., 1970), 282.

Incorruptible more than libertinage. There was no better token of the aristocracy's decadence, and nothing more alien to the aspirations of the people."[70]

The distinction and division are critically important because the entire totalitarian enterprise is predicated not only on general ideological conformity, but on conformity in the sexual sphere in particular. Robespierre notes the sexual underpinnings of republican government:

> Since virtue and equality are the soul of the republic, and your aim is to found and to consolidate the republic, it follows that the first rule of your political conduct must be to relate all of your measures to the maintenance of equality and to the development of virtue.... Hence all that tends to excite a love of country, to purify moral standards, to exalt souls, to direct the passions of the human heart toward the public good must be adopted or established by you. ... In the system of the French revolution, that which is immoral is impolitic, and that which tends to corrupt is counterrevolutionary. Weaknesses, vices, and prejudices are the road to monarchy.[71]

The very same preconditions exist for the creation of a distinctly inegalitarian master race, according to Hitler. In order to "be categorized as a higher lifeform, the man must remove the beast from within himself. Otherwise he would remain purely within the boundaries of primitive needs in his aspirations, and would never raise himself up out of the sphere of the animalistic."[72] The very same preconditions exist for the successful crusade, and for the successful communist system as well. Utopian collectivity, in short, requires drastic constraints on sexuality.

The totalitarian ideology conceives of its adherents as a single and greatly extended family, or even as a collective organism, comprising the great number of biologically-desirable, nuclear families as its undifferentiated cells. The indefinite survival of the greater organism is dependent on the productivity, survival, and replication of these cells, hence the totalitarian

---

70    Maurice Lever, *Sade: A Biography*, trans. Arthur Goldhammer (New York: Farrar, Strauss and Giroux, 1993), 461. The presumption of aristocratic debauchery was widespread at the time. Lynn Hunt, *The Family Romance of the French Revolution* (Berkeley: University of California Press, 1992), 105.

71    Beik, 280-81.

72    Speech of Adolf Hitler, *Reichstagung in Nürnberg 1933*, ed. Julius Streicher, (Berlin: Vaterländischer Verlag C.A. Weller, 1934), 79.

movement is very much pro-family in the sense of wanting to encourage the arrangement. Dr. Walter Gross, head of the NSDAP's Office of Racial Policy, explained at the 1933 Nuremberg Rally that "the new state sets the family at the center of its reconstruction work, and thus prepares those legal measures that should give protection and care to the family and the mother in particular."[73] This was shortly after he had explained his theory of national survival:

> Over the long run, this world of struggles and dangers would have annihilated life, if nature had not found a protection in the fertility of its creations. Every autumn, billions of seeds spread out all over the world; perhaps millions of them will be annihilated, it remains still ever enough that the roots strike out and new bearers of life grow up. … Like the nations of the world struck by some terrible fate, that in a moment has annihilated such a great part of the living, they have recovered in a few generations so long as the will to live was found and their fertility was thus undiminished.[74]

Stability in the domestic sphere is national stability, and marriage a political arrangement. Dr. Gerhard Wagner, speaking at the 1935 Nuremberg Rally, notes a dramatic increase in marriages from 1932 to 1934, concluding that it "means virtually an unintentional coordination with the government of the new Reich, the marriage ceremony then being not merely a question of trust between the engaged, but rather a question of trust in the economic and political future of the land."[75] Marriage officially became a patriotic act in service of the collective in revolutionary France,[76] with one commentator noting that "a bachelor is like a foreigner in society."[77] In China, a brief marriage campaign in 1957 explained that pre-marital sex and unregistered marriages were "irresponsible towards the

---

73  Speech of Walter Gross, *Reichstagung in Nürnberg 1933*, 152.

74  Ibid., 148.

75  Speech of Gerhard Wagner, *Reichstagung in Nürnberg 1935: Der Parteitag der Freiheit*, ed. Hanns Kerrl (Berlin: Vaterländischer Verlag C.A. Weller, 1936), 130.

76  James F. Traer, *Marriage and Family in Eighteenth-Century France* (Ithaca: Cornell University Press, 1980), 132.

77  Jennifer Ngaire Heuer, *The Family and the Nation: Gender and Citizenship in Revolutionary France*, 1789-1830 (Ithaca: Cornell University Press, 2005), 47-48.

spouse, the children and society and are derived from bourgeois thought."[78] Gregory Carleton finds that in Bolshevik Russia, "physical intimacy had no other purpose than the 'creation of healthy, robust descendants.' One's choice of partner, method, frequency of relations were issues of truly strategic significance, since choices made at the personal level were joined in a common pattern of behavior that affected human evolution."[79]

The family, in turn, is based on the ostensibly natural subordination of the ascetic and perhaps even virginal, though extremely fertile, in-group female. Tanika Sarkar, in her study of the emergence of Hindu nationalism, finds an ideological parallel being drawn between the Hindu man's absolute sexual control of his wife (conjugality) and control of his political destiny generally: "The politics of women's monogamy ... is the condition of the possible Hindu nation: the one is often explicitly made to stand in for the other. Woman's chastity, then, has a real and stated, and not merely symbolic political value."[80] The totalitarian ideology approaches women with a curious mix of reverence and hostility. In the ideological world, women exist either as breeders or as sexual threats. The mother is celebrated in no uncertain terms while the wife, who combines the properties of reproduction and sexual allure, occupies a relatively uncertain position, even to the point of ideological invisibility.[81] The sexualized woman is acknowledged only to demonstrate the threat she poses.[82] Totalitarian art,

---

78    Meijer, 142.

79    Gregory Carleton, *Sexual Revolution in Bolshevik Russia* (Pittsburgh: University of Pittsburgh Press, 2005), 61-62.

80    Tanika Sarkar, *Hindu Wife, Hindu-Nation: Community, Religion, and Cultural Nationalism* (Bloomington: Indiana University Press, 2001), 41. Chetan Bhatt notes also that the paramilitary wing of the Hindu nationalist movement, the RSS, cited the traditional Hindu family as its organizational template. Chetan Bhatt, *Hindu Nationalism: Origins, Ideologies, and Modern Myths* (New York: Oxford/Berg, 2001), 120.

81    See, for example, Klaus Theweleit's work on the proto-nationalist Freikorps movement in interwar Germany, whose membership divided the world into sexually-threatening 'red' women, innocent and pure 'white' women, and their own rarely-mentioned, 'invisible' wives. Klaus Theweleit, *Male Fantasies Vol. 1: Women, Floods, Bodies, History*, trans. Stephen Conway with Erica Carter and Chris Turner, fwd. Barbara Ehrenreich (Minneapolis: University of Minnesota Press, 1987).

82    See, for example, Frances Lee Bernstein, *The Dictatorship of Sex: Lifestyle Advice for the Soviet Masses* (Dekalb: Northern Illinois University Press, 2007), 111: "In the visual language of [health education] posters, the depiction of Soviet society as an all-male world suggests not so much the exclusion of real women

iconography, and propaganda are employed to desexualize the in-group female, even to the point of rendering her sexless while stripping her bare. According to Patrice Higonnet, "women clearly belonged to a second sex whose first duty was chastity. ... In Republican allegorical painting, women -- when not fully clothed -- bared shapes and breasts that were more nurturing and maternal than seductive and erotic."[83] Hans Peter Bleuel finds the same artistic sensibility on display in Nazi Germany, Hitler himself displaying a fondness for the asexual nude.[84]

Motherhood is idealized not only in a kind of quasi-spiritual way, but as a form of emancipation and equality for the woman herself. In this context, women are deemed equal in the sense of their sphere of activity (reproduction and child-rearing) having equal importance to the male sphere of activity (power and violence). There is a trace of sincerity to be found here, insofar as reproduction is considered a prerequisite both to collective immortality and to the indefinite campaign of violence sought by the ideologist. Tanika Sarkar, for example, notes Hindu Nationalist imagery showing the warrior-goddess Durga holding a baby and standing over the dead body of a demon she has just killed.[85] "Reproduction and mothering are reviewed primarily as acts of anger..." in Hindutva ideology, she explains, which holds that a woman "conceives and nurtures her sons as instruments of revenge...."[86] Dr. Wagner draws a very similar link between reproduction and violence on behalf of the NSDAP: "The German *kinderreich* [child-rich] mother should receive a special place of honor in national society alongside the frontline soldier, as the boundaries of her love for nation and fatherland were the same as the frontline soldier in the thunder of battle."[87] To whatever extent women are allowed off their backs and into the operational aspects of the movement, we find a pattern of

---

from the fizkul'tura movement or from the working class but more the symbolism of woman *as* sexuality. Having sublimated their sexual energy through exercise, the men have no need for that particular amusement, or for the consequent threat to collectivism represented by [a sexually attractive] woman."

83    Patrice Higonnet, *Goodness Beyond Virtue: Jacobins During the French Revolution* (Cambridge: Harvard University Press, 1998), 92-93.

84    Hans Peter Bleul, *Sex and Society in Nazi Germany*, ed. Heinrich Frankel, trans. J. Maxwell Brown john (Philadelphia: J.B. Lippincott Co., 1973), 184-85.

85    Sarkar, 256.

86    Ibid., 284. Sarkar is here paraphrasing the ideas of Sadhvi Rithambara.

87    Speech of Gerhard Wagner, *Reichstagung in Nürnberg 1937: Der Parteitag der Arbeit*, ed. Hanns Kerrl (Berlin: Vaterländlischer Verlag C.A. Weller, 1938), 126.

'controlled emancipation' as Thomas Blom Hansen calls it.[88] This is true regardless of the progressive doctrines to which a totalitarian movement might lay claim. Thus Higgonet finds that in revolutionary France, "When women were invited to participate in Jacobin *fetes* or celebrations, it was usually to serve the food or clean up."[89] Even Lenin's view of female emancipation went more in the direction of an alleviation of domestic duties rather than a formalized equality between men and women: "Public catering establishments, nurseries, kindergartens -- here we have everyday examples of ... the simple, everyday means, involving nothing pompous, grandiloquent or ceremonial, which can *really emancipate women...*"[90] The point was to facilitate a basic level of ideological organization, though by this minimal standard even the National Socialists could claim to be progressive with the formation of their own women's organization, the *NS-Frauenschaft*.

It would be a mistake, however, to see simple patriarchal control in the totalitarian movement. The totalitarian movement is to be masculine, but in a collective and specifically militaristic sense. Neither the family nor its head is intended to have any real degree of autonomy, and there is to be no personal sanctuary for anyone. According to M.J. Meijer, "There really is no clear picture of the family based on communist morality. One finds only conflict situations.... In fact, if one goes by the publications, the normal functioning family hardly seems to exist in China."[91] The totalitarian movement displays a considerable degree of hostility and distrust toward the family, as it does toward anything that might foster interpersonal affection or loyalty. Crusade propagandist Balderic of Dol writes that one should "let neither property nor the alluring charms of your wives entice you from going,"[92] and fellow propagandist James of Vitry suggests taking the crusade in public because "the devil often extinguishes a good proposal through the spouse or worldly friends."[93] The Chinese communist was also

88    Thomas Blom Hansen, *The Saffron Wave: Democracy and Hindu Nationalism in Modern India* (Princeton: Princeton University Press, 1999), 99.

89    Higgonet, *Goodness Beyond Virtue*, 92.

90    V.I. Lenin, *The Emancipation of Women: From the Writings of V.I. Lenin*, fwd. Nadezdha Krupskaya (New York: International Publishers) (emphasis in original), 64.

91    Meijer, 276.

92    August C. Krey, ed. trans., *The First Crusade: The Accounts of Eye-Witnesses and Participants* (Gloucester: Peter Smith, 1958), 36.

93    Christoph T. Maier, *Crusade Propaganda and Ideology: Model Sermons for the Preaching of the Cross* (Cambridge: Cambridge University Press, 2000), 123.

advised to beware "motherly love, the sugar-coated cannon ball to corrupt your mind and prevent you taking the road of the revolution."[94] The dueling priorities are, of course, to ensure a consistent and reliable pattern of reproduction without generating emotional bonds between the individuals involved. Reproduction without love or sex would be optimal for this purpose. The family would wither away entirely in the Soviet utopia to come, according to Bolsheviks like Alexandra Kollontai.

In the totalitarian utopia, family members are expected to relate to one another through the ideological system, correcting each other if necessary.[95] Intra-familial denunciation is encouraged in cases of nonconformity.[96] Ideologists are especially eager to see that parents are relieved of any responsibility for educating their own children. In St. Just's utopia, "Children belong to their mother, if she has breast-fed them, until they are five, and to the republic from then until their death."[97] According to the October 28, 1958 issue of *Chinese Youth*:

> Children will be sent to nurseries and kindergartens to begin collective life early and board in primary schools through to colleges, to rid themselves at an early age from mental development due to the influences of backward and selfish concepts born with the old family institution.... We do not want to imbue their children with the narrow family concept which knows only the home and not the country.[98]

Liadov explained that the conscientious parent "should say: If I want my child to be free of the petty bourgeois characteristics that lie deep within each of us, he must be isolated from us."[99] Modern movements also display a penchant for the formation of ideologically-oriented organizations affiliated with the movement, with something to cover every member of the family, thus relieving them of the need to spend time together.

The totalitarian family is designed to channel the sex drive into

---

94    Meijer, 277.

95    Ibid., 140.

96    Neil J. Diamant, *Revolutionizing the Family: Politics, Love, and Divorce in Urban and Rural China, 1949-1968* (Berkeley: University of California Press, 2000), 309.

97    Quoted in Norman Hampson, *Saint-Just* (Cambridge: Basil Blackwell, 1991), 233.

98    Quoted in Meijer, 267.

99    Quoted in Naiman, 88.

reproduction exclusively, thereby facilitating the latter and destroying the former. One National Socialist marriage pamphlet felt compelled to explain that if "the continuation and enlargement of the nation has been secured by the production of a sufficient number of children, then, from the point of view of the nation, there is no objection to the further satisfaction of the sexual urge."[100] Set in context, if a German couple had, over the course of their marriage reached their target of 8 or more children, and still had some lingering sexual desire, then no harm would befall them if they did something about it (which is still not to say that they should, necessarily). Those movements that favor a more explicitly pro-reproduction ideology tend promote early marriage. They also tend to display a pronounced, even lethal hostility directed at those claiming to be celibate, in large part because they doubt the possibility of such a thing. Robespierre once explained that the Jacobins "do not claim to model the French Republic after that of Sparta; we wish to give it neither the austere manners nor the corruption of a cloister."[101] Communist movements tend to favor the sublimation of sexual energy directly into collective work,[102] living in constant fear of an 'energy drain' from individual sexual activity.[103] Religious movements operate under a dual-level system, where asceticism is considered desirable and marriage acceptable for want of a better alternative. 'Better to marry than to burn,' as the admonition goes. As with communism, religious movements seek to direct sexual energy into collective work. For example, the ideology of the RSS is, according to Thomas Blom Hansen, "psychologically based on the sublimation of sexual energy to patriotic devotion and work."[104] Ultimately, the differences are not very great here, and it is always expected that the vast majority of the appropriate population will reproduce and perpetuate the totalitarian organism.

Love is frequently cited as the force binding the cells of the organism, as when Savarkar explains that Hindus are united "by the tie of the love we bear to a common fatherland and by the common blood that courses through our veins and keeps our hearts throbbing and our affections

---

100 Quoted in Dorothee Klinksiek, *Die Frau im NS-Staat* (Stuttgart: Deutsche Verlags-Anstalt, 1982).
101 Beik, 281.
102 Evans, 7.
103 Carleton, 63-64; Bernstein, 132.
104 Thomas Blom Hansen, *The Saffron Wave: Democracy and Hindu Nationalism in Modern India* (Princeton: Princeton University Press, 1999), 97.

warm...."[105] One finds this love as one abandons all others, according to crusade propagandist Eudes of Chateauroux, "and when his love of God grows, so that it becomes zeal, then his renouncement [is turned into] tedium, so that he cannot stand this world any more and casts it off altogether."[106] Love should always be ideological in nature, never an affirmation of individual characteristics, and this is nowhere more true than in marital relationships. Ideological love supersedes erotic love entirely. Elizabeth Croll explains that, "In the new [Chinese] ideology, desirable or preferential mates were defined according to their state of political consciousness. The ideal marriage partners were those who were politically compatible and in ideological agreement...."[107] Chinese revolutionary and 'Gang of Four' member Yao Wen-yuan asks incredulously:

> Did not Tao Chu say to some young people excitedly, 'There are males and females in the world and they will naturally have love affairs'? ... In class society, people are differentiated according to their class and are linked according to their class relations. The relations between man and woman are no exception.[108]

Lenin spoke of 'objective class relations' in the same context. As the relation is purely ideological, selection of a partner should be based definitively on ideological criteria. The National Socialists promulgated a list of 'Ten Commandments for Choosing a Spouse,' with number 8 urging Germans to "marry only for love," followed by an explanation that "sensual passion is not true love!"[109] Commandment nine advises one not to "look for a playmate, but a life-partner," which involves finding someone racially similar, the reason being that "every race has its own soul. Only similar souls can understand one another."[110]

---

105 V.D. Savarkar, *Hindutva: Who is a Hindu?* (Poona: S.P. Gokhale, 4th ed. 1949), 74.

106 Maier, 131.

107 Elizabeth Croll, *The Politics of Marriage in Contemporary China* (Cambridge: Cambridge University Press, 1981), 83.

108 Yao Wen-yuan, *Comments on Tao Chu's Two Books* (Peking: Foreign Language Press, 1968), 18-19. "'Real love,' according to one newspaper article, 'cannot exist between a feudalistic [person] and a progressive person.'" Diamant, 7.

109 Arthur Gütt, Herbert Linden, and Franz Maßfeller, *Blutschutz- und Ehegesetz* (München: J.F. Lehmans Verlag, 1936), 14.

110 Ibid.

Sexuality, perhaps most importantly, is found at the core of the immortality system of the totalitarian movement. Psychologist Otto Rank found that in primitive societies, men often limited themselves to having sex for pleasure because they thought of the normal process of reproduction as the eventual replacement of, and hence termination of, the self. Thus some primitive immortality systems were based on the idea that if one refused to procreate, one would remain immortal.[111] "Whereas primitive man resisted procreation that he might live on himself, civilized man, realizing the futility of such a wishful conception of life, accepted immortality collectively, that is, through his children in the tribe, community or nation."[112] The system of immortality found in the totalitarian ideology creates a national or supranational organic collective which is defined and defended biologically. The continuation of the whole depends on the reliable and continual reproduction of the individuals within the collective, hence the extraordinary level of concern in matters that would ordinarily be considered personal and private. Anything that constitutes a threat to the collective reproductive system of the totalitarian movement constitutes a threat to collective immortality.

The biological collective is held together through the reproduction of elements deemed biologically similar, though 'biological' similarity and dissimilarity are determined ideologically. Totalitarian movements practice a kind of manufactured racism, generally excluding and exterminating people with whom they have the most in common physically. According to Gerhard Wagner, "Every measure that promotes health and abilities socially, can only be valid as selection in a biological sense if it simultaneously creates the possibility of early marriage and a large family for the individual."[113] This is to be done within bounds, of course: "Interracial sex is racial treason and is to be judged and punished as treason to the nation!"[114] Hindutva takes more or less the same stance with regard to Indian Muslims. "We Hindus are all one and a nation, chiefly because of our common blood...,"[115] explains V.D.

---

111 According to Rank, "Because of his inner resistance to biological procreation, primitive practically tabued sex; or, at least, had to be induced by 'law' to marry and produce children -- a practice similar to that of the totalitarian states in our day which still feel compelled to do so on the basis of their tribal ideology...." Rank, 223.
112 Rank, 227.
113 Speech of Wagner, *Reichstagung in Nürnberg 1935*, 122.
114 Speech of Wagner, *Reichstagung in Nürnberg 1937*, 122.
115 Savarkar, Who is a Hindu?, p.31.

Savarkar, noting further that "an organic growth that has its roots embedded deep in a common land and a common culture. ... The lion's seed alone can breed lions."[116] As the French revolutionary Carrier was adding children to barges to be scuttled in the Loire, he rejected the pleas of their 'counterrevolutionary' mothers by noting that "wolflings grow to be wolves."[117] According to China's culture warriors, "A dragon begets only dragons, a phoenix begets phoenixes, and a mouse's children can only dig holes."[118] In spite of the structural theories of consciousness put forward by communism, the children of ideologically unstable or reactionary parents were generally thought to be similarly inclined, and hence inadmissible. One man, whose parents had been labeled rightists in China, attempted to challenge the theory publicly, and was executed in a stadium before a chanting crowd of tens of thousands.[119]

As we find the totalitarian movement, it is perpetually situated on the precipice of apocalyptic destruction, and this destruction is to come in a specifically sexual form. The reproductive harmony and metaphysical-organic cohesion of the movement are under threat from the forces of hedonism and individualism. It is here that we find three of the most basic and universal axioms of the totalitarian ideology: (1) sex equals death; (2) the out-group equals sex, and; (3) the out-group equals death. Each one can be taken in turn and established independently.

Sex, firstly, is death if had for pleasure. Ideologists are unanimous about this. Crusade propagandist Gilbert of Tournai makes the connection between sex and death quite directly:

> Those given to bodily lust and pleasures are also signed
> with the sign of the devil.... These are signs of death: just
> as small fish hide beneath rocks, so they escape the storm
> and are not swept away by the current ... so crusaders are
> saved, so to speak hiding in a foreign and unknown land,
> whereas lovers of this world are swept away, while playing

---

116  Savarkar *Who is a Hindu*, p.105. Marriage and conversion were to be rare exceptions.  Note also Golwalkar: "In fact, we are Hindus even before we emerge from the womb of our mother." M.S. Golwalkar, *Spotlights: Guruji Answers* (Bangalore: Rashtrotthana, 1974), 114.

117  Otto J. Scott, *Robespierre: The Voice of Virtue* (New York: Mason & Lipscomb, 1974), 210.

118  Gao Yuan, *Born Red: A Chronicle of the Cultural Revolution* (Stanford: Stanford University Press, 1987), 84.

119  Anne F. Thurston, *Enemies of the People* (New York: Alfred A. Knopf, 1987), 111.

in the many eddies of worldly things, and die in their own country.[120]

Robespierre sets the 'social' and 'republican' concept of immortality against individual pleasure, suggesting that the former will inspire "more contempt for death [and] sensuality."[121]  One of China's revolutionary converts explains the sex/death connection as follows:

I fell into the abyss of love. I pursued happiness. Hypnotized by the clutch of love, I was wasting my youth away. ... I felt alone, I felt the pressure of solitude. ... Through education by the League I have come to recognize clearly the two divergent roads. One road leads to decadence and decline, filled with lifeless atmosphere, darkness, and death. The other leads to happiness, activity, hope, light, and new life....[122]

Death here means death in terms of sexual individualism as a threat to the life of the collective. Dr. Gerhard Wagner explains that where "the will to one's own individual advantage and pleasure is set against them, a Volk slides inexorably towards its *völkisch* death, because it is weak in terms of its will to live...."[123]  Golwalkar also takes the sex/death dichotomy to an explicitly collective level, explaining that "no nation can hope to survive with its young men given over to sensuality and effeminacy."[124]  He adds that "[the] history of countries the world over has time and time again shown that sex-dominated literature has been an unfailing precursor to the ruin of nations and civilizations."[125]

120  Maier, 195.
121  Beik, 304-5.
122  Quoted in C.K. Yang, *The Chinese Family in the Communist Revolution*, fwd. Talcott Parsons (Massachusetts: Technology Press, 1959), 126.
123  Speech of Wagner, *Reichstagung in Nürnberg 1935*, 128-29. Conversely, a belief in collective mortality leads to sexual pleasure, according to Dr. Walter Gross: "The conviction that the lifespan and life-strength of nations and their works may be limited in the same way as the individual man, and that therefore growth and development inevitably prefigure decay, that youth and creative manhood must be followed by aging and downfall, led to theory of the downfall of the western world, and at the same time became the internal prerequisite for the decline of character and sexual morality of the postwar period that we have all experienced with shock." Speech of Walter Gross, *Reichstagung in Nürnberg 1933*, 146.
124  Golwalkar, *Bunch of Thoughts*, 229.
125  Ibid., 230.

As sex is equivalent to death, sex is also equivalent to the out-group. As Diamant writes: "According to party propaganda, sexual behavior was directly related to class status. An attack on the culture of 'capitalists' or the bourgeoisie might also, simply by way of association, imply condemnation of the sexual practices of those classes."[126] On behalf of the Third Reich, Dr. Gerhard Wagner offers a three-dimensional account of supposed Jewish sexual perversion:

> It is also interesting that one frequently finds with Jews in particular, a comparable rise in the signs of sexual degeneration, manifesting themselves in a blurring of the physical and psychological secondary characteristics. The Jewish Professor Pilz has also declared the relative frequency of homosexuality in Jews. When Gunther, in his well-known 'Racial Study of the Jewish People' writes, 'the globally painful sensitivity of the male Jew would, with respect to Jewish women, frequently set off unfeminine characteristics and unrestrained efforts for more personal validity in public life, which might also be to declare the domination of the Jewish woman under the influence of revolutionary female movements,' we can only just agree fully. ... It is also interesting that Dutch and German statistics indicate that the circulation of obscene materials is Jewish, and based on official documents, the trafficking in girls is absolutely a Jewish domain.[127]

Jews, as we might have guessed, are thought to be heavily involved in the abortion trade: "It is known that Russia, following its Marxist theories, is the avowed land of Jewish abortion practice."[128] Crusade chroniclers such as Albert of Aachen and Guibert de Nogent deemed Muslims, and even their own Byzantine allies, particularly sexual.[129] The 'sexually predatory Muslim male' is now a generally accepted stereotype in Hindu nationalist circles.[130] Savarkar, describing Muslim incursions into India,

---

126  Diamant, 286.
127  Speech of Gerhard Wagner, *Reichstagung in Nürnberg 1935*, 118.
128  Speech of Gerhard Wagner, *Reichstagung in Nürnberg 1935*, 126.
129  James Brundage, "Prostitution, Miscegenation, and Sexual Purity in the First Crusade," in *Crusade and Settlement*, Peter Edbury ed. (Cardiff: University College Cardiff Press, 1985), 60.
130  Amrita Basu, "Feminism Inverted: The Gendered Imagery and Real Women of Hindu Nationalism," in *Women and Right-Wing Movements: Indian Experi-*

explains that "it was a religious duty of every Muslim to kidnap and force into their own religion, non-Muslim women. This incited their sensuality and lust for carnage...."[131] Gregory Carleton summarizes the Bolshevik position on bourgeois sexuality as follows: "Ideological sin and sexual deviance were the result of bourgeois influence. ... In fact, the indigenous sexual identity of the proletariat was diametrically opposed to that of the bourgeoisie. Mixing the two was akin to violating natural law."[132]

The out-group is also equivalent to death, an agent of mortality. The demonological aspects of the totalitarian ideology are designed in part to explain this phenomenon. It is here we find an enemy existing nowhere in the reality-based world. In their more anthropomorphic incarnations, we find them as horrid monsters and demons with mind-control powers, which are generally employed in the sexual domain. The Chinese Cultural Revolution was brought about with a headline calling for an assault on 'ox ghosts and snake demons,' a pantheon of spirits which includes the 'fox spirit,' thought to use her beauty to prey on sexually inexperienced men.[133] We find the following reference to it in the interrogation of one Zhimei Zhang: "'You're an immoral woman, a fox spirit!', he screamed. 'How many men have you had? Tell us everything! You've corrupted party cadres, and now you've got your hands on one of the revolutionary teachers. Do you really think you can get away with this?'"[134] *Der Stürmer* frequently ran caricatures of Jews as vampires, in one cartoon shown performing recreational vivisection on a beautiful, naked young woman. Soviet demonology is slightly more complex. Eric Naiman's study of fiction in the 1920s finds a preference for the gothic genre, in which an "endangered protagonist yearns for the society of safe, nonthreatening friends and dreads contact with an evil villain who may in some respects be herself."[135] The protagonist is generally found trapped in the villain's castle, which features doors unable to lock or that only lock from the wrong side,

*ences*, Tanika Sarkar and Urvashi Butalia ed. (London: Zed Books, 1995), 163; Tanika Sarkar, "Heroic Women, Mother Goddesses: Family Organisation in Hindutva Politics," in *Women and Right-Wing Movements: Indian Experiences*, Tanika Sarkar and Urvashi Butalia ed. (London: Zed Books, 1995), 185.

131 V.D. Savarkar, *Six Glorious Epochs of Indian History*, trans. ed. S.T. Godbole (New Delhi: Radjhani Granthagar, 1971), 175.

132 Carleton, 57.

133 Diamant, 286-87.

134 Zhimei Zhang, *Foxspirit: A Woman in Mao's China* (Montreal: Vehicle Press, 1992), 145-46.

135 Naiman, 153.

separating "the heroine from the presexual world of her childhood and of a community uncontaminated by lust...."[136] The terror in gothic fiction comes from the inability to shut out the sexualized villain, the self on some level, which is a theme the totalitarian mind would find especially compelling. More directly, Zalkind equated sexuality to both the bourgeoisie and to a giant, parasitic spider, sucking the life of out of the collective body.[137]

The out-group is more frequently thought of in terms of filth, rot, decay, poison, infection (bacterial or viral), and death itself. This element, foreign to the collective body, is highly infectious, a contaminant that spreads itself out throughout the collective organism, violating its health and purity. Peter of les-Vaux de Cernay's *Historia Albigensis*, aside from condemning their sexuality, explains that Cathar heretics were "infected by the leprosy of heresy," that the city of Toulouse was "the chief source of the poison of faithlessness which had infested the people," that "their listeners had abandoned life and were determined to cling to death. Infected and diseased with a worthless animal cunning," that "treacherous Toulouse has rarely if ever been free of this detestable plague, the sin of heresy," that "the neighboring cities and towns ... became infected with the dreadful plague," and that "the limbs of the Antichrist ... the seducers of simple hearts, had infected almost the whole of the Province of Narbonne with the filth of their perfidy."[138] NSDAP [National Socialist German Workers' Party, or Nazi for short] philosopher Alfred Rosenberg, having had the advantage of several centuries of scientific advancement, compares the Third Reich to ancient Rome in the following manner:

> One day Rome saw opposite itself on the Mediterranean a dangerous Syrian epicenter of plague. Carthage was at that time a center where the whole Middle East had settled and begun to dispatch its powers of decomposition to Rome. The stability of the Roman state allowed it to at least wipe out this forward position. Rome achieved a cultural accomplishment, but could not extract the biological consequences for it to be a great empire, because, observing the actual foundations of its state bloodwise, it

---

136 Ibid.
137 Carleton, 73; Naiman, 128.
138 Peter of les Vaud de Cernay, *Historia Albigensis*, trans. W.A. and M.D. Sibly (Rochester: Boydell Press, 1998) 6-12.

was already too weak. National Socialism has beat back this same Syrian-Jewish decay politically....[139]

Lenin opines on the death of bourgeois, capitalist society as follows: "When the old society dies, its corpse cannot be shut up in a coffin and placed in the grave. It decomposes in our midst; the corpse rots and infects us."[140] Hindutva ideologist Sadhvi Rithambara finds a similar quasi-biological impact from Muslims within the Indian collective body:

> Wherever I go, I say, 'Muslims, live and prosper among us. Live like milk and sugar. If two kilos of sugar are dissolved in a quintal of milk, the milk becomes sweet!' But what can be done if our Muslim brother is not behaving like sugar in the milk? Is it our fault if he seems bent upon being a lemon in the milk? He wants the milk to curdle. He is behaving like a lemon in the milk by following [Muslim fundamentalists] like Shahabuddin and Abdullah Bukhari. I say to him, come to your senses. The value of milk increases after it becomes sour. It becomes cheese. But the world knows the fate of the lemon in the milk. It is cut, squeezed dry and then thrown on the garbage heap.[141]

And Robespierre would add that "a nation is truly corrupt when, after having, by degrees, lost its character and liberty, it passes from democracy to aristocracy or monarchy; this is the death of the political body by decrepitude."[142]

The transmission of this infection, or insertion of this poison or pollutant into the collective organism, can come in one of three ways: hereditarily, sexually, or ideologically. The distinction is largely a formality, because the effect (interference with the collective instinct) is precisely the same in all cases. On the hereditary front, the *Historia Albigensis* teaches us that "the poison of superstitious unbelief was passed from father to son one after another," the son inevitably born with an "inborn disposition to embrace heresy."[143] Dr. Gerhard Wagner conflates heredity with ideology

139 Speech of Alfred Rosenberg, *Reichstagung in Nürnberg 1937: Der Parteitag der Arbeit*, ed. Hanns Kerrl (Berlin: Vaterländlischer Verlag C.A. Weller, 1938), 100.
140 V.I. Lenin, quoted in Naiman at 160.
141 Quoted in Sudhir Kakar, *The Colours of Violence* (Viking: New Delhi, 1995), 205.
142 Beik, 282.
143 Peter of Les Vaux-de-Cernay, *Historia Albigensis*, 9-10.

when, after attempting to prove statistically that sexual degeneracy (e.g., homosexuality, circulation of obscene materials, and trafficking in women) is the product of Jewish instincts, he explains that the raw data "should prove only the indisputable fact, that in all things *völkisch*, the corrosive effect of racial mixture is disastrous for the bodily, spiritual, and moral health of the individual man."[144] Hindus, according to Golwalkar, can be distinguished from members of other religions in that the Hindu "gets his samskaar when he is still in the mother's womb.... In fact, we are Hindus even before we emerge from the womb of our mother."[145] This may be the reason that the child bride must be taken sexually prior to her first menstruation, otherwise the "garbhas [wombs] of hundreds of girls will be tainted and impure. And the thousands of children who will be born of those impure garbhas will become impure."[146]

As noted earlier, sexuality leads to individualism and individualism leads to sexuality. The sexual-ideological subversion of in-group instincts can then come from either direction. The intent, or perhaps merely the instinctual drive, of the out-group is to contaminate and subvert the ideological collective sexually. Robespierre explains that the monarchy "could not enslave the French people by force or by their own consent, and they tried to enchain them by means of subversion, revolt, and corruption of their morals."[147] The solution:

> The masterpiece of society would be to create in [man], for questions of morals, a swift instinct which, without the tardy aid of reasoning, would impel him to do good and avoid evil; for the individual reason, led astray by the passions, is often merely a sophist who pleads their cause, and the rule of conduct prescribed by man can always be attacked by man's self-love.[148]

Crusade propagandist James of Vitry explains that sexuality is not only false, but impairs one's ability to discern true and false generally: "A preacher is called blind if he stays in the darkness of sins even though he has eyes, that is reason and intellect; he is considered to be blind as *he has a blemish* in the eye, when his mind's eye is drawn towards the filth of carnal

---

144   Speech of Gerhard Wagner, *Reichstagung in Nürnberg 1935*, 120.
145   Golwalkar, *Spotlights*, 114.
146   Sarkar, *Hindu Wife, Hindu Nation*, 224.
147   Beik, 303.
148   Beik, 305.

pleasure...."[149]   According to Golwalkar, India's increasingly sexualized atmosphere had come into the home, "And in such homes, where children grow without a cultural background they fall an easy prey to Christian propaganda also."[150]   Bolshevik Aron Zalkind also argued that sexuality was an instrument of the 'deceiving class', which  interfered with man's natural tendency to identify with his social class.[151]

The result is an ideological 'sickness' for the in-group member, which is of the same quasi-biological nature as the forces binding him or her to the collective. As the sickness is ideological, the treatment is ideological. Dr. Gerhard Wagner explains the need for preventative ideological remedies:

> [In the past] one waited until the man was sick, one waited on national insurance until cases of disease for medical and -- what was perhaps still more important -- juridical attempts to remedy or to improve the damage that was occurring.  ... We will not wait until the injury and the sickness have set in. Rather we will act preventatively, identifying deviation from the norm before it has come as a sickness of the consciousness of the person affected.[152]

Russian futurist Aleksei Kruchenykh suggested that the work of the sexually-dissolute poet Sergei Esenin might contaminate the reader, and another critic noted that "if Esenin is an 'infection,' then a 'revolutionary, communist, Marxist inoculation, particular among students, is needed.'"[153] The sexually-transmitted disease (STD) thus forms an interesting parallel to the spread of the sexual-ideological disease. Ideologists frequently link out-group members to certain STDs. In the Middle Ages, heretics were linked to leprosy, then thought to be transmitted sexually, and the Nazis linked Jews to syphilis. The ideologist, though, never attempts to treat the STD in its own right, but proceeds instead to 'treat' the sexual-ideological disease. It is as though the STD were merely a symptom of the sexual-ideological disease, or perhaps even a metaphor for the metaphysical actuality existing in the ideological reality.

The sex-death-outgroup triangle is attacked at every angle, accounting for some of the more persistent and striking aspects of totalitarian social

149   Maier, 103.
150   Golwalkar, *Spotlights*, 135.
151   Naiman, 126-28.
152   Speech of Gerhard Wagner, *Reichstagung in Nürnberg 1937*, 128.
153   Carleton, 111.

legislation. Sexual censorship is among the highest priorities for any such movement, and there is virtually no variation between them on this point. The ideological position is to be left unchallenged. Sexual behaviors are legally proscribed, and socially discouraged to the extent that non-procreative sex is considered the province of the out-group and those infected by its members. Sexual unions between in-group and out-group members are discouraged, often with violence.

The endgame is the ongoing extermination of the sexual/mortal out-group. This is designed, most directly, to eliminate any future possibility of the sexual-ideological contamination of the in-group member. Indirectly, there is a metaphysical process of expurgation, whereby sexuality and mortality are removed from the collective organism entirely. To whatever extent these things may be said to exist still within the collective body, the totalitarian ideology situates them in some group, draws a hard and fast line of division, and proceeds to annihilate anyone and everyone on the other side. Totalitarian violence is usually framed conceptually in terms of a medical operation, as the removal of some unwanted part of one's own body, rather than as an assault on something entirely alien to the collective. Crusade propagandist Humber of Romans explains that the Church persecutes heretics "just as a wise physician uses a blade to cut off a putrid limb which infects other parts, when lighter remedies do not work. It is better to let a limb be destroyed with a blade or with fire than to let the healthy parts be infected."[154] Golwalkar agrees that violence "should be used as a surgeon's knife. Even as a surgeon uses his knife to perform an operation to get rid of an infected portion to save the patient, so also violence in certain extraordinary circumstances can be used to cure the society...."[155]

The process of sexual expurgation is reinforced through the sexual character of totalitarian violence. Very often, the victim, whether thought to be intrinsically sexual or merely infected, is humiliated, assaulted, tortured, and perhaps even killed in a sexually-tinged manner. The reasons for this are generally unstated, but the pattern is unmistakable. National Socialists, for example, were fond of performing horrific sexual experiments on women and homosexuals sent to concentration camps. Demonologists often opted to 'interrogate' suspected witches vaginally with sharp or heated metal instruments. Crusade chronicles allude to sexual assaults.[156]

154  Maier, 225.
155  Golwalkar, *Spotlights*, 110.
156  Brundage, 61.

The women of Hindutva, while decrying the sexual objectification of women,[157] have encouraged and participated in violence against Muslims, up to and including "informed assent to such brutalities against Muslim women as gang rapes and the tearing open of pregnant wombs in Bhopal and Surat in December 1992 and January 1993."[158] Diamant points to a desire among the Red Guards "to prove themselves as 'real men' by humiliating class enemies in sexual ways," combined with a "bizarre voyeurism about sex, a curiosity that could be satisfied by forcing others to engage in sex in public view."[159] The fact that these atrocities are carried out by people who consider themselves devoid of sexual impulses or desires strongly suggests an attempt to reinforce the sexual-biological-mortal nature of the ideological counterpart. The counterpart is eliminated, sexuality and mortality put to an end, and utopia thus delivered.

## 2.3 Hell is Other People

**How to account for this** phenomenon? With difficulty, it seems, given the lack of any pre-existing consensus as to what totalitarianism is, let alone the impulses driving it. Experimental forays into the world of illiberal political psychology have typically concentrated on the individual's seemingly excessive deference to authority ('authoritarianism') and how to explain it. It should be noted, though, that not only are totalitarian movements noticeably absent in societies characterized by widespread deference to authority, such movements are found exclusively in societies in a state of modernization and liberalization, those experiencing a breakdown in traditional authority. Neither political nor social repression provides a satisfying explanation, nor does economic adversity provide an explanation. Norman Cohn, for example, notes in his study of medieval fanaticism that "if poverty, hardships and an often oppressive dependence could themselves generate it, revolutionary chiliasm would have run strong amongst the peasantry of medieval Europe.

---

157  Basu, 166.

158  Tanika Sarkar, "Heroic Women, Mother Goddesses", 189-90. Savarkar provides an explanation: "A serpent, whether male or female, if it comes to bite must be killed. The enemy women who enforced conversion and heaped all sorts of humiliation on our mothers and sisters, had by that very devilish act, lost their womanhood, and their right to chivalrous treatment, and deserved nothing but only the most stringent punishment for their atrocious crimes." V.D. Savarkar, *Six Glorious Epochs of Indian History*, 175.

159  Diamant, 303.

In point of fact it was seldom to be found at all."[160] Much the same could be written of most of the movements discussed herein, and if anything, one finds a loose correlation between ideological movements and economic prosperity.

As the totalitarian movement has, seemingly, no rational reason to exist in the first place, it is directed to no rational objective in the end. The movement has as its initial aim the total control of culture and society, with political power viewed only as a means to social ends. The ultimate goal of the totalitarian movement is, quite seriously and explicitly, the perfection of mankind. This perfection being difficult if not impossible to achieve, the ideologist quickly resorts to two of the more conspicuous methodologies of such movements, namely proselytization and thought control. Ostensibly, this is to achieve universal conformity between actual consciousness and true consciousness; the effect is simply to give the irrational idea the irrational environment it needs to survive. Dr. Walter Gross, head of the NSDAP's Office of Racial Policy, explained the importance of National Socialist thought control in 1936:

> And so follows today, with the totality of our idea corresponding to the totality of our claim, the second wave of the great German revolution: The battle, after the conquest and securing of the state, for the penetration and reformation of the German mind. Where yesterday our battlefields were in the streets and political gatherings, today they are in the places of the mind, in the quieter world of our colleges and research institutions, in all the areas where men work and battle for the worldview of a Volk and its people. And we know well that because of it the struggle between an old and new era has entered its decisive stage.[161]

As outlined in the previous two chapters, this deep-seated hatred of reality expresses itself uniformly and with a particular logic. Totalitarian ideologies are all structurally identical — in every century and on every continent in which they appear. This suggests that their salient attributes are not the product of culture or coincidence, but rather generated by some

---

160 Norman Cohn, *The Pursuit of the Millennium* (New Jersey: Essential Books, 1957), 24.

161 Walter Gross, *Rasse, Weltanschauung, Wissenschaft: Zwei Universitätsreden* (Berlin: Junker und Dünnhaupt Verlag, 1936), 9.

very basic personality trait or traits. From whence the totalitarian hatred of reality, then?

## *Totalitarian Psychology — Empirical Models*

**The rise and fall of** National Socialism, along with its undeniably substantial level of popular support in Germany, seems to have provided the impetus for a new conceptualization of illiberal political systems. Contrary to ordinary political intuition, then as now, the psychological disposition of ordinary individuals, a significant portion of them at least, was implicated in the ascendance of tyrannical government. The first major scientific attempt to identify this personality type came from a team of Berkeley researchers, who, with the use of questionnaires issued to volunteers, set out to find the "potentially fascistic individual, one whose structure is such as to render him particularly susceptible to anti-democratic [or fascistic] propaganda."[162] The Berkeley group issued its findings in a study entitled *The Authoritarian Personality*, having identified the following nine characteristics of said individual:

a. Conventionalism. Rigid adherence to conventional, middle-class values.

b. Authoritarian submission. Submissive, uncritical attitude toward idealized moral authorities of the ingroup.

c. Authoritarian aggression. Tendency to be on the lookout for, and to condemn, reject, and punish people who violate conventional values.

d. Anti-intraception. Opposition to the subjective, the imaginative, the tender-minded.

e. Superstition and stereotypy. The belief in mystical determinants of the individual's fate; the disposition to think in rigid categories.

f. Power and toughness. Preoccupation with the dominance-submission, strong-weak, leader-follower dimension; identification with power figures;

---

162   T.W. Adorno, Else Frenkel-Brunswick, Daniel J. Levinson, and R. Nevitt Stanford, *The Authoritarian Personality*, abridged ed. (New York: W.W. Norton & Co., 1982), 1.

overemphasis upon    the conventionalized attributes of the ego; exaggerated assertion of strength and toughness.

g. Destructiveness and cynicism. Generalized hostility, vilification of the human.

h. Projectivity. The disposition to believe that wild and dangerous things go on in the world; the projection outwards of unconscious emotional impulses.

i. Sex. Exaggerated concern with sexual 'goings-on'.[163]

The dynamics of this 'F-Scale' can be understood somewhat more easily in terms of four major personality aspects, which are defective cognition, violent paranoia, an obsession with expanded and centralized authority, and a preoccupation with sexuality.

On the basis of their findings, the Berkeley group speculated that an underdeveloped personality formed the core of this cluster of personality traits. The authoritarian personality demonstrates an "inability to build up a consistent and enduring set of moral values within the personality; and it is this state of affairs, apparently, that makes it necessary for the individual to seek some organizing and coordinating agency outside of himself."[164] The group speculated that this inability was brought about in childhood, by parents who failed to take an individualized approach to childrearing, and contented themselves instead merely with imparting conventional behavioral codes.[165] The result is a person superficially well-adjusted, though emotionally constrained and unable to relate to individuals as individuals. The absence of a self-governing character structure leads him to incorporate external norms in place of individualized personality attributes, eventually drifting into a form of "'psychological totalitarianism' … which seems to be almost a microcosmic image of the totalitarian state at which he aims."[166]

The F-Scale has come in for severe criticism from other behavioral scientists since its release.[167] For a start, it was pointed out that the questions

---

163    Ibid., 157.
164    Ibid., 163.
165    Ibid., 257.
166    Adorno et al., 324.
167    For a concise and helpful overview of the debate on the authoritarian person-ality, see John Duckitt, *The Social Psychology of Prejudice* (Westport: Praeger,

developed by the Berkeley group were phrased in such a way that a positive response to any one of them indicated authoritarianism. This meant that anyone inclined, as a general matter, to answer questions in a positive way would register as an authoritarian. Conceptually, the study was criticized for questions designed to register 'right-wing' authoritarianism, with critics noting that communists tended to score low on the F-Scale in spite of their apparent 'authoritarian' behavior. Later researchers were also unable to get the F-Scale traits to covary, with all nine appearing simultaneously in individuals on a consistent basis. The current verdict on the authoritarian personality seems to be 'unproven,'[168] suggesting that the basic model retains considerable intuitive allure in spite of its deficiencies. It does stand up very well as a basic if incomplete description of the personalities discussed herein, whether coming from the left or right side of the traditional political spectrum.

By way of its defense, it may be noted that the failure of F-Scale criteria to covary consistently may possibly be explained by the fact that the totalitarian personality is only one of a number of personality types that might be termed authoritarian. It is possible that there are differences, in degree or in kind, as far as the personality types that will respond to measures and messages which tend to favor authority in some general way. Without a clear conceptual framework and a clear identification of the precise phenomenon to be explained, the danger will always exist that one is casting the net too wide and finding nothing but inconsistencies as a result. By way of a critique, if the Berkeley team was concerned with identifying an individual predisposed to embrace 'fascistic' concepts based on their own underlying 'psychological totalitarianism,' the 'Authoritarian Personality' was an especially poor term for their construct. Totalitarians have absolutely no respect for authority that stands in defiance of their ideological system. The idea trumps virtually everything else in the ideological mass movement, something plainly evident at the inception of the movement, when the idea is virtually all the movement has to offer. Simple group loyalty or an unquestioning adherence to authority may

---

1994), 193-207.

168    Ibid., 204-7. Note also Karen Stenner: "The idea that there is a readily rec-
       ognizable disposition that somehow brings together certain traits -- obedience
       to authority, moral absolutism and conformity, intolerance and punitiveness
       toward dissidents and deviants, animosity against racial and ethnic out-groups
       -- remains widespread." Karen Stenner, *The Authoritarian Dynamic* (New
       York: Cambridge University Press, 2005), 3.

explain why someone became a Nazi in the mid-to-late 1930s or a Bolshevik in the 1920s. They provide no possible explanation for why someone became a Bolshevik in Romanov Russia or a Nazi in early Weimar Germany, in defiance of prevailing authority and given a myriad of other options in terms of political allegiance.

One researcher attempting to improve on the authoritarian model, Milton Rokeach, concentrated his inquiry on the cognitive processes of the authoritarian personality. He noted several consistent dynamics in the thought processes of those who demonstrated authoritarian characteristics. These included a propensity for rigid problem-solving behavior, premature closing of perceptual processes, distortions in memory, and intolerance of ambiguity.[169] Rokeach put forward the idea of logical systems of thought as a subset of psychological systems of thought generally. In logical systems, the beliefs which make up the system (substructures) are interrelated according to the rules of logic, whereas in psychological systems the beliefs may be interrelated for other reasons, and logically isolated from one another. According to this model, the essence of authoritarianism is to be found in the absence of logical connections in one's belief system.

The presence or absence of logically isolated beliefs is in turn the product of a basic disposition toward information, and the use of authority in accepting information as valid. On the one hand, there are 'open systems,' characterized by a belief that the world is generally unthreatening, a belief that information should not be accepted from authorities uncritically, and the existence of logical interrelationships between substructures of the system. On the other hand, 'closed systems' are characterized by the belief that the world is a threatening place, that "authority is absolute and people are to be accepted and rejected according to their agreement or disagreement with such authority"[170] (belief congruence theory), and substructures of the system that are in isolation from one another. The psychological dividing line rests between the basic need for an accurate understanding of the world and the need to insulate oneself from the more threatening aspects of reality.[171] The closed system

169  Milton Rokeach, *The Open and Close Mind: Investigations into the Nature of Belief Systems and Personality Systems* (New York: Basic Books, 1960), 16.
170  Ibid., 56.
171  Rokeach, citing Erich Fromm, speculates as to the precise cause of anxiety: "To varying degrees, individuals may become disposed to accept or to form closed systems of thinking and believing in proportion to the degree to which they are made to feel alone, isolated, and helpless in the world in which they live

is a defense against cognitive anxiety; the higher the anxiety, the more likely a closed system will result. The most basic way to differentiate the authoritarian personality from the nonauthoritarian is then "the extent to which the person can receive, evaluate, and act on relevant information received from the outside on its own intrinsic merits...."[172]

The thought processes of the totalitarian, like Rokeach's authoritarian, are characterized by logical deficiencies. The totalitarian's belief system is never the product of uncritical acceptance of authority, though. The process actually seems to work in reverse if anything, with potential authority figures measured by their adherence to the ideological system. Moreover, the defective logic and factual resistance of the totalitarian is tied specifically to his or her ideological system. This individual may be perfectly rational otherwise, and in some cases quite extraordinarily intelligent. This will tend to provide such movements with a degree of camouflage and facilitate their acceptance by non-ideological elements. As totalitarian ideologies are built out of commonly accepted ideas, anyone sympathetic to those ideas, and unfamiliar with the basic structure of a totalitarian ideology, will tend to accept their adherents and ideas at face value. The result is a compartmentalized and socially acceptable form of insanity, one thus difficult to recognize and especially dangerous for precisely that reason.[173]

---

(Fromm, 1947) and thus anxious of what the future holds in store for them. Such a state of affairs should lead to pervasive feelings of self-inadequacy and self-hate." Ibid., 69.

172 Ibid., 57.

173 Adorno and company find that "psychological treatment of prejudiced persons is problematic because of their large number as well as because they are by no means 'ill' in the usual sense, and ... at least on the surface are better adjusted than the nonprejudiced ones." Adorno et al., 350. See also Robert S. Robins and Jerrold M. Post: "In the political sphere, blatantly delusional thinking is not the main concern. Such thinking is exceptional and evident to others. Far more dangerous is when the delusional thinking is borderline and consequently not easily recognized as the product of madness. For most political paranoids the delusion is likely to involve exaggeration and distortion of genuine events and rational beliefs rather than pure psychotic invention." Robins and Post, *Political Paranoia: The Psychopolitics of Hatred* (New Haven: Yale University Press, 1997), 19. Note also Andre Haynal: "Therein lies one of the difficulties in examining fanaticism: its aspirations are human, common, often respectable and acceptable aspirations. But what characterizes them is their 'megalomaniacal' side, the desire to realize them outside the framework of realities, to deny all limits, not to accept any constraints, including those imposed by civilization (the superego)." Andre Haynal et al., *Fanaticism: A*

By way of contrast, we have the work of Robert Altemeyer, which covers a more conventional, robotic personality type. Altemeyer finds authoritarianism in the consistent covariation of three basic attitudinal clusters: (1) submission to authorities, (2) aggression against sanctioned enemies, and (3) endorsement of conventional values endorsed by authorities.[174] For the conventional authoritarian, each of these three psychological propensities is built around a fundamental disposition toward authority and authority figures. It is thus right-wing in the sense of being pro-authority and not, as Altemeyer clarifies, in terms of a substantive political program.[175] Conventional authoritarianism is simply the product of learning and experience, a disposition picked up through upbringing and imitation. It has no deeper aspect.[176] Altemeyer specifically differentiates it from more radical political tendencies, noting that left-wing terrorists could hardly be called submissive to authority. He adds that the attitudes he discusses "can create a climate of public opinion which promotes totalitarian movements," and further that while authoritarianism threatens from the right, "totalitarianism threatens democratic institutions on either side."[177]

Altemeyer was criticized by John Duckitt for the absence of a conceptual aspect to his model, simply forming his construct out of the covariation of the elements listed above. Duckitt attempted to improve on the model by tying these elements together in terms of an underlying need for group identification and demand for cohesion. Where this is greater:

1. Then first, the greater will be the emphasis on behavioral and attitudinal conformity with ingroup norms and rules of conduct -- that is, conventionalism.

2. Second, the greater the emphasis will be on respect and unconditional obedience to ingroup leaders and authorities -- that is, authoritarian submission.

*Historical and Analytical Study*, trans. Linda Butler Kezdoglou (New York; Shocken Books, 1983), 64-65.

174   Robert Altemeyer, *Right-Wing Authoritarianism* (Manitoba: University of Manitoba Press, 1981), 147-48.

175   Robert Altemeyer, *The Authoritarian Specter* (Cambridge: Harvard University Press, 1996), 10.

176   Ibid., 78.

177   Altemeyer, *Right-Wing Authoritarianism*, 151.

3. And third, the greater will be the intolerance of and punitiveness toward persons not conforming to ingroup norms and rules -- that is, authoritarian aggression.[178]

In sum, "authoritarianism is simply the individual or group's conception of the relationship which should exist ... between the group and its individual members."[179] The authoritarian will, of course, prefer that the group define the individual to whatever extent possible. At the opposite end of the extreme, one finds libertarianism, the idea that the individual should, to the greatest extent possible, be self-regulated. Duckitt gets very much to the heart of the matter when he notes that the latter seems to cause the former a great deal of distress. The need for group cohesion will actually lead the authoritarian to rebel against a social and political order characterized by libertarianism. As to this phenomenon, which Duckitt labels 'authoritarian rebellion,' he notes that "violent rebellion against a social and political order which does not express the 'true' needs of the identification group ... tends to be characteristic of most highly authoritarian and fascist social movements."[180]

Karen Stenner advances the 'group cohesion' model by identifying its sociological trigger. She begins by noting, on the one hand, the strange similarity in 'authoritarian' theories across time and space, and at the same time the varying reactions of individuals within particular cultures to those same theories. The notion of authoritarianism simply as a learned phenomenon was thus rejected. In its place, she puts forward the idea of authoritarianism as a common psychological predisposition which remains a constant, but expresses itself in different ways depending on social-environmental factors. She explains, following Duckitt, that "authoritarianism is an individual predisposition concerned with the appropriate balance between group authority and uniformity, on the one hand, and individual autonomy on the other."[181] The obsession with authority is largely instrumental, though, to an underlying desire for oneness and sameness, for unity and uniformity. As expressed, authoritarianism "inclines one towards attitudes and behaviors variously

---

178   John Duckitt, "Authoritarianism and Group Identification: A New View of an Old Construct", Political Psychology, Vol. 10, No. 1 (1989), 70.
179   Ibid., 71.
180   Ibid., 75.
181   Karen Stenner, *The Authoritarian Dynamic* (Cambridge: Cambridge University Press, 2005), 14.

concerned with structuring society and social interactions in ways that enhance sameness and minimize diversity of people, beliefs, and behaviors."[182]

Stenner structured her research by dividing her subjects into libertarians and authoritarians, using a basic disposition to authority as a marker.[183] She was able to demonstrate a general similarity between the two groups in response to questions on a wide range of subjects. The differences appeared with the introduction of 'normative threat', or inquiries which challenged the subject's sense of collectivity by suggesting a lack of consensus on values, lack of validity of values, disobedience to authorities, and general cultural disarray.[184] Libertarians showed little difference in their responses, but those identified as authoritarians began to display heightened levels of intolerance when so prompted. Transposing this to the world at large, cultures that feature diversity, in terms of morality or values in particular, are those likely to activate the authoritarian predisposition.

Totalitarian movements are invariably to be found in environments in which social norms are in flux or decay, the historical record thus lending strong support to Stenner's concept of normative threat. She, in turn, provides an empirically-based explanation for a phenomenon readily observable to anyone interested in ideological mass movements, namely a violent reaction on the part of some to an increase in freedom. The deeper causes of this need for unity and uniformity, frequently taken to the point of genocide, still remain unexplained. Why exactly is it that normative

---

182  Ibid., 17.

183  "Childrearing values ... can effectively and unobtrusively reflect one's fundamental orientations toward authority/uniformity versus autonomy and difference. And they can do so without implicating specific social and political arrangements, by simply querying in the context of the social microcosm of the family the trade-off deemed appropriate between the two: between parental authority and children's autonomy, between conforming to the rules and thinking for oneself." Ibid., 24.

184  Stenner's authoritarian subjects apparently tended to gravitate toward discussion of the normative order rather than avoid it: "Finally, we come to the issue domain that appeared to exercise authoritarians more than any other, and to which they seemed to return persistently irrespective of the question actually put to them. It is no exaggeration to report that fears regarding immorality and crime, claims about the critical need to reestablish some normative order, and elaboration of plans for accomplishing this reversal occupied the bulk of authoritarians' 'psychic space', consuming a vastly disproportionate share of their time and energy in these discussions." Stenner, 256.

threat should be quite so threatening? Why also the remarkable similarity in ideological elements that emerge, in spite of their cross-cultural origins? To go deeper into the problem, a shift will be taken from empirical models of authoritarianism to observational models of totalitarianism, which, though lacking in scientific rigor, have the advantage of direct applicability, as well as a basis in the 'revealed preferences' or actual behavior of totalitarians themselves.

## *Totalitarian Psychology — Observational Models*

**Even prior to the development** of the authoritarian personality, Erich Fromm reasoned that forces both psychological and sociological in nature were at work in the formation of the totalitarian personality. According to the theory, a person begins life with 'primary ties', or relationships which "connect the child with its mother, the member of a primitive community with his clan and nature, or the medieval man with the Church and his social caste."[185] These are very basic, spontaneous, 'organic' relationships that operate to orient the individual to his or her place in the world, offering a sense of security and a feeling of belonging. They provide a kind of personal definition without the need for an individualized self; one is defined almost entirely in terms of a matrix of limited possibilities and predetermined choices. In certain social environments, the individual might never move beyond these basic relationships. The family, the church, the community, the occupational guild, etc., would never release their holds on the individual, fate becomes a very real sociological phenomenon, and one lives out the life one was always destined to live. There is no tension and no sense of conflict for those who fail to develop as individuals, though, because there is no conflict between personality and social constructs. While the development of the self is constrained, the development of self-awareness is inhibited as well. In this context, the individual remains underdeveloped personally but stable politically.

In more dynamic, atomized social environments, the process of 'individuation' operates to destroy these primary ties, and the individual develops a stronger sense of his or her own individual existence. This process of individuation has two aspects.[186] The first is the development and integration of the self physically, intellectually, and emotionally, or the

---

185    Erich Fromm, *Escape From Freedom* (New York: Henry Holt, 1994), 24.
186    Ibid., 24-36.

growth of 'self-strength'. The second aspect is the growing sense of isolation and aloneness. The development of self-strength allows for the development of genuine interpersonal relationships, which in turn offsets the feeling of isolation and aloneness. If the development of the individual keeps pace with the sense of isolation and aloneness, there is again no conflict for the individual in terms of leading an independent existence. The problem, Fromm explains, is that the process of individuation in terms of isolation tends to work automatically in dynamic societies, whereas the process of self-growth does not. The underdeveloped individual is then forced to confront "a world, which in comparison with one's own individual existence is overwhelmingly strong and powerful, and often threatening and dangerous, [creating] a feeling of powerlessness and anxiety."[187]

The possibility then exists that this individual will attempt to 'escape' the freedom of an individualized society, by attempting to link oneself with a power that is seen as 'unshakably strong, eternal, and glamorous' (a totalitarian movement, perhaps), substituting 'secondary ties' for the primary ties that have been lost. The individual attempts to reduce his or her individual self to nothing in an effort to eliminate the awareness of oneself as individual. Yet there can never be a return to the state that existed prior to individuation, nor can the process of self-renunciation and merger ever completely wipe away the consciousness of one's own self.

> This course of escape … is characterized by its compulsive character, like every escape from threatening panic…. It assuages an unbearable anxiety and makes life possible by avoiding panic; yet it does not solve the underlying problem and is paid for by a kind of life that often consists only of automatic or compulsive activities.[188]

This insoluble conflict causes a kind of political psychosis, which finds it outlet in three external phenomena: (1) masochism combined with sadism, a simultaneous urge to dominate and be dominated; (2) a general tendency toward destructiveness, which in its most severe form is rationalized either as self-defense or a preventative strike; and (3) automaton conformity.

As noted previously, the totalitarian ideology sees the true human will in terms of a natural and irresistible law. The movement following or enforcing this law is, in a sense, omnipotent, as are all who participate.

---

187    Ibid., 28.
188    Ibid., 139-40.

Thus for the adherent, "One surrenders one's own self and renounces all strength and pride connected with it, one loses one's integrity as an individual and surrenders freedom; but one gains a new security and a new pride in the participation in the power in which one submerges."[189] Every aspect of the totalitarian ideology can be traced back to some foundational 'law of nature,' including its campaign of bloodletting. The totalitarian, notes Arendt, merely carries out a death sentence decreed by nature: "Liquidation is fitted into a historical process in which man only does or suffers what, according to immutable laws, is bound to happen anyway."[190] The totalitarian ideology claims omnipotence, even power over life and death, as a compensation for the fear of powerlessness.

Eric Hoffer's study of the fanatical mass movement, and its 'true believer,' analyzes a very broad range of movements and generates an almost identical theoretical model. Sociologically, "The milieu most favorable for the rise and propagation of mass movements is one in which a once compact corporate structure is, for one reason or another, in a state of disintegration."[191] It is here we find the individual who, for whatever reason, cannot cope with the dynamics of an individualized society. Yet where Fromm posited a sense of powerlessness as the impetus for self-renunciation, Hoffer sees it more as a product of a sense of imperfection (the 'plague of individual frustration') brought on by the competitive society. The individual who feels he cannot compete, having become self-aware in an atomized society, begins to hate himself: "Unless a man has the talents to make something of himself, freedom is an irksome burden. Of what avail is freedom to choose if the self be ineffectual?"[192] The individual then seeks a merger with some outside force, turning "into a highly reactive

---

189 Ibid., 154. Note also Andre Haynal on the fanatic: "In his illusion of having found the absolute and superhuman, the fanatic believes himself to be in possession of the truth, which confers upon him omniscience, omnipotence, and invulnerability -- all superhuman conditions. The omnipotence is accompanied by a narcissistic thrill at the idea of being among the elect of God or history. This elation could heal the anxiety of individuals injured by life, who have not been given enough security." Andre Haynal et al., *Fanaticism: A Historical and Analytical Study*, trans. Linda Butler Kezdoglou (New York; Shocken Books, 1983), 36.

190 Hannah Arendt, *The Origins of Totalitarianism* (New York: Harcourt, 1973), 349.

191 Eric Hoffer, *The True Believer: Thoughts on the Nature of Mass Movements* (New York: Harper & Row, 1966), 45.

192 Ibid., 35.

entity. Like an unstable chemical radical he hungers to combine with whatever comes within his reach."[193] The successful mass movement is, first and foremost, the one that provides the greatest possibility for self-renunciation.

In Hoffer's model, the driving force behind the urge for self-renunciation is an anxiety generated through individuation and a subsequent measuring of oneself against others. Self-renunciation is then to be accomplished most directly through equality and uniformity. Conceptually, the great mass of true believers are treated as an undifferentiated whole, one interchangeable with any other. The possibility of comparison is eliminated in this way. As Hoffer explains, "The passion for equality is partly a passion for anonymity: to be one thread of the many which make up a tunic.... No one can then point us out, measure us against others and expose our inferiority."[194] Hoffer also cites this desire for anonymity through equality as part of the reason these movements become so violent. The overturn of the existing order, downfall of the powerful, and destruction of one's entire reality are all aimed at facilitating a sense of unity and conformity between true believers, and an equivalence with, if not superiority over, those one resents. In the end, "Chaos, like the grave, is a haven of equality."[195] It might be added that the totalitarian ideology not only renders individuals indistinguishable from one another, but makes them perfect (in conformity with the laws of nature) as well.

Hannah Arendt confines her analysis to twentieth century movements, yet she identifies the same basic pattern observed by Hoffer and Fromm. This would be widespread social atomization leading to some form of individual disturbance, which leads individuals to seek self-renunciation and collective merger. Rather than a sense of powerlessness or imperfection, the triggering factor for Arendt's totalitarian is social isolation (or loneliness) brought on by an inability to relate to individuals as individuals. "The chief characteristic of the mass man is not brutality and backwardness," she writes, "but his isolation and lack of normal social relationships."[196]

---

193  Ibid., 80.
194  Ibid., 37.
195  Ibid., 91.
196  Hannah Arendt, *The Origins of Totalitarianism* (New York: Harcourt Inc., 1973), 317. Other studies have reached similar conclusions. Robert S. Robins and Jerrold M. Post, in their study on 'political paranoia', note that "The paranoid tends to be a loner, averse to association," and further that, "Socially isolated who are experiencing isolation are especially drawn to mass move-

This social isolation, "once a borderline experience usually suffered in certain marginal social conditions like old age [and now] an everyday experience of the evergrowing masses of our century,"[197] begins to undermine the very concept of a self, which, she suggests, is "realized in solitude, but confirmed in its identity only by the trusting and trustworthy company of my equals."[198]

This sense of isolation is thought by Arendt to be held in check by membership in and strong identification with a political and economic class. The gravitational pull of totalitarianism thus acts first on those outside class system, the resentful and disaffected 'residue' of all economic and political classes (the 'mob'). It is within this group that the movement finds its leaders, individuals characterized similarly by "failure in professional and social life, perversion and disaster in private life."[199] Isolation then becomes a mass phenomenon with the complete breakdown of the class system, the whole of society now having been robbed of its sociological 'protective walls'. The palliative comes in the form of a mass movement demanding complete and unconditional loyalty from each of its members. "Such loyalty can be expected only from the completely isolated human being who, without any other social ties to family, friends, comrades, or even mere acquaintances, derives his sense of having a place in the world only from his belonging to a movement, his membership in the party."[200]

This need to avoid social isolation would go a long way in explaining the prominence, in fact dominance, of collective themes in the ideological systems discussed herein. The totalitarian ideology is designed to promote universal connection, though in a completely non-interpersonal way. Every individual is linked to every other individual through the ideology, and in fact ideological thinking presupposes that there are no true idiosyncratic characteristics in the individual in any case. One connects to the collective through an act of will, and this connection requires no specific reciprocal act on the part of the collective. The hope is that so long as one remains ideologically pure, one will never be abandoned by the collective, never be made to feel alone ever again. This leads in some cases to a rather interesting

---

ments. ...such individuals experience a 'merger hunger.'" Robert S. Robins & Jerrold M. Post, *Political Paranoia: The Psychopolitics of Hatred* (New Haven: Yale University Press, 1997), 94-96.

197 Arendt, 478.
198 Ibid., 477.
199 Ibid., 327.
200 Ibid., 323-34.

phenomenon, noted by Arendt and Hoffer, wherein a member of the movement will assist in his own investigation, condemnation, and execution by the movement.[201] This is done not in the hope of saving one's own life but rather in the hope of remaining a member of the movement in death as in life.

This leaves one major source of personal anxiety untouched, and the one perhaps most responsible for giving the totalitarian movement its destructive and genocidal qualities. This would be the fear of death, which Robert Jay Lifton finds at the core of the Chinese Cultural Revolution. The fear of death, he explains, results in a tendency to rationalize one's own existence in such a way that one becomes immortal in some sense.[202] There are several ways to do this, including biological immortality (living on through one's children), theological immortality (belief in an afterlife), creative immortality (living on through one's own works), identification with natural forces, and experiential immortality which involves a feeling state so intense it removes awareness of the biological process of living and dying. All five are to be found in the totalitarian ideology. The foundation of the immortality system of the Cultural Revolution involved the formation of a vast and eternally enduring 'family,' which eventually became linked, in quasi-biological fashion, to cultural, national, and racial identifications. To the revolutionary, moreover, "works are all important, and only to the extent that he can perceive them as enduring can he achieve a measure of acceptance of his own eventual death."[203] Completing the list of five, he notes that the secular utopia sought by the movement appears similar to a religious afterlife, the natural order is to be overturned yet guide and constrain the movement, and the revolutionary himself may achieve an experiential transcendence like that of a religious mystic. "What all this suggests," Lifton concludes, "is that the essence of the 'power struggle' taking place in China, as of all such 'power struggles', is power over death."[204]

The desire for immortality is the fourth and final totalitarian theme that can be traced directly to some form of personal anxiety. Most movements mention it explicitly, though it is always assumed that the movement will continue on forever. As one might expect, immortality for

201  Arendt, 307; Hoffer, 62-63.
202  Robert Jay Lifton, *Revolutionary Immortality: Mao Tse-Tung and the Chinese Cultural Revolution* (New York: Random House, 1968), 7-8.
203  Ibid., 8.
204  Ibid.

the totalitarian is of a collective nature. Ideologically, each individual member of the collective is essentially the same, which means that the life or death of any particular individual within the collective is irrelevant. People die; the organization (or organism) continues on forever. The collective persona enables one to escape death metaphysically, to render biological death unimportant. The individual lives on both through the works of the movement which are everlasting, as well as through the indefinite continuation of the quasi-genetic code which renders each individual identical in all relevant respects.

Far from being life-affirming, the immortality system of the movement is tied directly to its campaign of mass extermination. Psychologist Otto Rank traces the immortality systems of modern totalitarian movements down into the most primordial forms of human society. Over the course of history, the universal desire for an individualized immortality, being inherently uncertain, has given way "to a collective immortality originally embracing small units, such as the clan or tribe, and eventually extending to the conception of a nation."[205] Even primitive societies, though, were known to express their immortality through their king, with the incoming regent being required to kill the one outgoing as a prerequisite for accession. The immortality of the collective continues unabated, as immortality is transferred from the one king to the other at the moment of death. A similar practice is found in the ancient ritual of killing one of two twins, the rationale being that if it was not done, both twins would die. As Rank explains, "in twin mythology the typical motif of fratricide turns out to be a symbolic gesture on the part of the immortal self by which it rids itself of the mortal ego."[206]

The significance becomes clearer in light of the work of sociologist Gordon Allport, who notes the frequent connection between prejudice and scapegoating, the tendency to assign (or project) some unwanted characteristic of the prejudiced individual onto another.[207]

---

205   Otto Rank, *Beyond Psychology* (New York: Dover Publications, 1958), 40.
206   Ibid., 92.
207   According to Allport: "Whenever anxiety increases, accompanied by a loss of predictability in life, people tend to define their deteriorated situation in terms of scapegoats. Anomie is a sociological concept representing the accelerated disruption of social structure and of social values such as mark most nations today." Gordon Allport, *The Nature of Prejudice* (Massachusetts: Addison-Wesley Pub. Co., 1954), 224-25.

The term scapegoat originated in the famous ritual of the Hebrews, described in the Book of Leviticus (16:20-22). On the Day of Atonement a live goat was chosen by lot. The high priest ... laid both his hands on the goat's head, and confessed over it the iniquities of the children of Israel. The sins of the people were thus symbolically transferred to the beast, it was taken out into the wilderness and let go. The people felt purged, and for the time being, guiltless.[208]

The import is that there seems to be some very primitive instinct that leads one to the idea that human attributes of all varieties can be transferred and situated in some designated biological entity. To then eliminate that entity is to eliminate the attributes transferred. As Rank demonstrates, this process of expurgation would apply to mortality; to destroy the bearer of mortality is then to destroy death itself. Recalling the three basic principles of totalitarian violence outlined at the end of chapter 2.1, the act is thought of in terms of self-defense, the killer gains only at the expense of his victim, and the two are closely connected in some way. Totalitarians are also quite consistent in comparing their victims to biological impurities, diseases, decay, and inevitably death itself. Given the collective nature of the totalitarian movement, the nature of totalitarian violence comes clear. Totalitarian 'self-defense' refers to the threat of mortality in general, and the process of defending the collective from it. It requires the in-group and out-group to be in proximity in order for the destruction of the out-group to facilitate the metaphysical transference of mortality from the collective to the out-group. In sum, the totalitarian collective is immortal, and this immortality is achieved by the continual removal and elimination of those elements most closely associated with mortality.

## *The Totalitarian Personality*

**The most basic principle to** be derived from each of these models is that of fear brought on by individuation, leading to a desperate and compulsive quest for alleviation through the totalitarian movement and its ideology. The totalitarian fears, and what he fears most are the basic limitations inherent in human existence. The movement itself is thus aimed not merely at some program of reform within the context of this reality, but rather at a wholesale

---

208    Ibid., 245.

exchange of realities. This latent totalitarian reality, waiting to be made extant, can be traced directly to the fears which generate such movements, given that each of the four fears just identified matches up with one of the four dominant themes of the totalitarian ideology. The fears of isolation, imperfection, powerlessness, and mortality correspond with the traditional totalitarian themes of anti-individualism and collectivity, perfection, omnipotence, and immortality. These fears are primordial, thus constant, and thus the totalitarian movement and its ideology will tend to look the same regardless of the particular social, cultural, or national context in which it emerges.

The sociology of the totalitarian movement follows a fairly standard pattern, consistent with the one identified by the scholars above. Every totalitarian movement is preceded by a trend of modernization and liberalization in a society previously exhibiting a stable and stultifying quality. These are precisely the conditions found in 11th century France just prior to the First Crusade, in Renaissance Europe prior to the demonological movement of the 16th and 17th centuries, in 18th century France, in 19th century India prior to the advent of Hindutva, in NEP Russia (1921-28) giving way to Stalinism, in Weimar Germany, and in early 20th century China. The totalitarian personality does not rebel against the presence of political and social repression, but rather their absence. It is a sense of individuation, of being disconnected, that triggers this particular complex, and this sense increases as a society grows, modernizes, urbanizes, and becomes advanced, liberal, and tolerant.

Societal atomization tends to mass-produce the four fears identified earlier. As these fears cannot be alleviated through a rational, tangible political program, the totalitarian movement becomes a rebellion against reality itself. There is a very desperate need on the part of the ideologist to have some compelling and plausible delusion set between himself and the reality which terrifies him. The ideologist responds to authority, though authority that serves the purpose of reinforcing his delusional thinking. Successful totalitarian leaders generate and expound a system of thought that addresses these ideological fears specifically, and those that have been successful often are so because they are plagued by precisely the same phobias as their followers. The apparent deference to authority, refusal to think for oneself, impulse to proselytize, and the severe or even savage violence against those who challenge the validity of the totalitarian system of thought can all be traced back to this need for an alternate reality.

This leaves only the sexual aspects of the totalitarian ideology to be explained.

## 2.4 Into the Dark Heart of Utopia

**Totalitarian movements are created by** the introduction of sexual individualism into sexually-corporate societies. This is strongly implied by the character of the totalitarian ideology, which is directed above all else to the eradication of sexuality apart from purely collective and reproductive objectives. One need not rely on implications in this area, though. Sexual atomization is a readily-observed phenomenon preceding every ideological mass movement discussed herein. Each of the four basic fears identified previously (isolation, imperfection, powerlessness, and mortality) is triggered by sexual atomism, and each one plays out in the sexual realm with particular intensity. The totalitarian ideology, and the movement which makes it operational, are compensation for these specific fears.

The pre-totalitarian society is always characterized by a marked increase in sexual individualism, particularly as it involves the selection and retention of a partner. The prospect of selection is increased relative to a smaller pool, which, if small enough, may actually push two people together simply by virtue of the fact that they come of age at roughly the same time. One common individuating force is the shift from a system of strict family control over the choice of marital partner to a system of individual choice. Totalitarian movements are also found in periods of rapid population increase, urbanization, and migration into cities, factors which tend to introduce a pronounced degree of anonymity into the selection process. Individual choice tends to lead to an increase in age at first marriage, which increases the overall pool of potential lovers. The upshot of all this is that the relationship that might have been formed by circumstance or outside agency would now have to be formed through the initiative and abilities of the partners themselves. The legalization of divorce, particularly when combined with the economic independence of women, means that a choice is never final and even those in marital relationships are never entirely secure in their status.

For the ideologist, the difficulty seems less a matter of being able to secure a relationship than it is the simple fact of having to do it independently. The idea of initiating a relationship based on personal characteristics, rather than some highly idealized conception of what men and women are and how they relate, usually gives them pause and frequently stops them outright. Totalitarians are renowned for their inability to form interpersonal relationships and tendency to use ideological alliances as a substitute. In a number of cases, we find them turning to protean ideological concepts on the heels of some failed attempt at a sexual relationship. Often we find them rejecting sexual relationships altogether, and those that do show interest tend to lose their virginity late and marry late. Most importantly, ideologists find no comfort even when they are in a relationship with another person. As indicated earlier, they condemn erotic love precisely for its 'isolating' quality, taking them away from the stable and all-embracing love of the collective. Totalitarians relate to one another through this love, ideologically, not in terms of their respective idiosyncrasies and emotions.

In addition to social individuation, more complex and sexually liberal societies tend to feature a kind of normative individuation as well. If there is one constant in the 'traditional society', it is the presence of rigidly-defined, comprehensive gender roles which correspond firmly with biological sex. One is born a man or a woman, and one refers to this basic dichotomy to answer the most fundamental questions in life: whether to work, take control of marital finances, take control of one's spouse, marry a man or a woman, determine where to live, maintain a home, go to war, or raise children. Courtship rituals, also a mainstay of the traditional society, are heavily dependent on gender as well, with prospective bride and groom playing out pre-arranged roles at pre-arranged meetings. Even further removed from the modern world of dating, courtship may be eliminated altogether, with spouses selected by their relatives. Traditional sexual norms range from moderately restrictive to entirely prohibitive, with the sexual act itself cause for penance even within marriage. In these societies, sexual identity is suppressed or even nonexistent insofar one relates to sexual partners, approaches prospective sexual partners, or engages in sexual activity. There are few opportunities for choice, and there is thus no sexual individual in any real sense. This is not to say that deviance or iconoclasm are entirely absent, but that one typically measures and is measured normatively in terms of conformity with a uniform standard, not as an individual.

In periods of massive population increase and urbanization, the social pressure behind these social constructs begins to fade, and soon the constructs themselves begin to disappear. Gender roles no longer correspond to biological sex or anything else, and adherence to them becomes a largely voluntary matter. Sexual norms, both as to partners and specific behaviors, become more ambiguous. Where these constructs begin to dissolve, the range of possible sexual identity is increased, and the possibility, and perhaps even the necessity, of sexual self-definition presented. The individual now decides whether to be masculine, feminine, passive, aggressive, homosexual, heterosexual, bisexual, transsexual, family man, libertine, vixen, or ingenue; the individual decides what to do, when to do it, how often, and with whom. In short, sexuality exists more at the level of personal definition rather than societal norm.

Sex and power are closely intertwined in a multitude of ways, though for present purposes the concentration will be on the question of sexual agency. In this context, we begin with an individual with a conscious, deliberate mind mediating between purely rational thoughts and bodily urges. In certain circumstances, one freely submits to these desires, and in others one tries to resist them, with varying degrees of success. In those situations in which one is called upon to exercise sound judgment contrary to desire, one's control is at least tested, and on occasion one may see it fail. Thus where sexual desire exists, agency is imperfect or incomplete. Desire can be induced externally, and the 'object' of that desire, typically, is another live, sentient individual. As individuals are endowed with the capacity to make themselves more or less desirable, the control of one's own mind and body may be partially externalized in another person, and the question of sexual agency becomes ever more complex. The totalitarian finds this state of affairs entirely unacceptable. Passion is to stand in diametric opposition to reason, and reason (ideology) is to win out over passion at all times. One yields no control to bodily desires, and certainly not to some other individual through those desires.

The idea of being controlled through sexual desire is a central theme of the totalitarian ideology. Ideologists are absolutely horrified at the prospect, so horrified in fact that they will subject themselves to any and all forms of control known to man if only they are granted some measure of freedom in this one respect. Ideological freedom means controlling sexual desire externally, thus controlling the objects of desire, which traditionally means men desexualizing women. Certainly pornography is out, though anything even slightly suggestive, even down to the undulating rhythms of a Shostokovich opera, will be suppressed as well.[209] Clothing often becomes

---

209   Shostakovich's opera *Lady Macbeth of the Mtsensk District* was condemned by close associates of Joseph Stalin, with editorials complaining that it sounded like sex and attributing its international success to the 'perverted' tastes of the

an issue, with totalitarian movements favoring women either in more traditional forms of dress (Germany) or androgynous clothing (China) — in either case clothing that signals an absence of erotic interest on the part of the woman wearing it. The underlying issue of control is never really addressed, though. The ideologist actually then conceives a second level of threat coming from the out-group member, who intends to control him via the sexualization of the culture at large. On a societal level, the out-group member creates a sensual atmosphere which, as explained previously, will tend to inhibit the development of the collective instincts of the in-group member. Cultural desexualization is, at a minimum, thought to require total cultural control and dominance over loose and/or defiant women, and those sinister forces which control them.

Sex and death form two opposite ends of the life cycle, beginning and end, and thus the connection between sex and issues of mortality is fairly straightforward. The physical sensations of sexual activity are as suggestive of new life as they are of its inevitable termination. For the individual who has come to terms with his or her own mortality, the sexual act is predominantly, if not entirely, pleasurable. For the totalitarian, such congress is simply a reminder that one is inhabiting an individual, organic body, thus fated to die, and thus the act is often a source of existential terror rather than pleasure. In the totalitarian mind, in his or her utopia, reproduction does not lead to the eventual replacement and termination of the self, because there is no real individual self to begin with. The individual is the living embodiment of the collective, and engages in the reproductive act only to produce new generations of indistinguishable 'cells' for the collective. The act of sexual intercourse is intended to be automatic, businesslike, disgusting certainly but tolerated because it guarantees collective immortality. The guarantor of this collective immortality is that the cells of the organism replicate spontaneously and continuously, and in no way try to limit their own fecundity. If sex for pleasure is to be tolerated, the continuity of the collective is put in doubt, however slight that doubt may be. Ideological anxiety always requires absolute certainty for its alleviation, and thus one arrives at the most fundamental of totalitarian postulates: Reproduction is everlasting life, and sexual pleasure is death.

In the totalitarian context, anything or anyone linked to sexual pleasure is quickly linked to individualism, and eventually death. Homosexuality,

---

west. Sheila Fitzpatrick, *The Cultural Front: Power and Culture in Revolutionary Russia* (Ithaca: Cornell University Press, 1992), 188.

lacking reproductive possibility, will always be viewed as problematic in this regard, though for reasons similar to the totalitarian's hostility to contraception and abortion. Abortion is an especially interesting issue here, with concern for human life in the reproductive context increasing as concern for human life in all other contexts decreases and reaches zero. Totalitarians will bemoan the destruction of life due to abortions in one breath, and call for war, mass slaughter, and even genocide in the next. The apparent contradiction is easy to resolve if one understands the particulars of the totalitarian's 'pro-life' sentiment, life in this case referring to the life of the collective and its properly-functioning cells. One kills off harmful 'cells' (members of the out-group) within the collective organism in the interest of collective life. Members of the ideological out-group will, with regularity, be accused of non-procreative practices including homosexuality, the use and dissemination of pornography, engaging in sexual slavery, providing contraception to women, facilitating and performing abortions, engaging in deviant sexual behavior, and of having sex for selfish and individualistic purposes. The association of this group with sexuality is a very strong indicator that the group has been slated for extermination.

In sum, totalitarian sociology follows a basic pattern built around sexual destabilization: The pre-totalitarian society is characterized by what would generally be called sexual conservatism. The family is the dominant institution in society. Individual loyalty to family and father is expected, a loyalty which generally mirrors the loyalty citizens are expected to show to their ruler. Individualism in sexual matters is largely nonexistent. At some point, there is an increase in the population, followed by urbanization and migration into cities. Relationships and normative structures break down and early signs of anxiety appear. Ideologies are developed, and movements built around them begin to form. Individuals of varying dispositions gravitate to them, though the core members of the movement will tend to exhibit sexual phobias almost uniformly. The movement will grow at a slow but steady pace, eventually constituting a substantial minority of the relevant population. At some point, a political event or breakdown will occur which allows this impassioned and intense minority to take the levers of power and institute its program of reproductive collectivism and extermination. China's Cultural Revolution (1966-76) will be taken as a brief example.

## Sexual Atomism in China

**For two millennia, the political** system of Imperial China remained unchanged and unchallenged. A dynasty might be overthrown, but only to be replaced by another, and there was never any question as to the form of government that would follow. China was subject to occasional 'rebellion but never revolution'. During these same two millennia, the family structure of Imperial China remained unchanged and unchallenged, and this was very much by design. Domestic relations were structured around Confucian ideals of regimentation in relationships and absolute patriarchal control, which were intended to maintain not only the harmony of the family but also of the political order in general. The obedient son, it was hoped, would evolve into the obedient subject.

> 'The root of the Empire is in the State. The root of
> the state is in the family. The root of the family is in the
> individual', says Mencius, the greatest philosopher of the
> Confucian school. If the individual was properly brought
> up, if he was taught to respect authority within his family, he
> would also respect it outside the family and be an obedient
> subject of the empire. Out of this conviction came the
> stress put by Confucius and his disciples on the importance
> of the family. The family, a primary social unit of any social
> organization, was consciously cultivated in China perhaps
> more than in any other country in the world and achieved
> greater importance.[210]

The family rather than the individual formed the basic unit of society,[211] which was itself, according to Confucian theory, merely a "huge conglomeration of families under the Emperor."[212] The Confucian family and Confucian state complemented one another with great effect for the whole of the Imperial era, "Hence the frequent assertion that, for some two millennia, no major social revolution had successfully introduced extensive alterations in the basic pattern of Chinese society."[213]

---

210   Olga Lang, *Chinese Family and Society* (Archon Books: 1968), 9.

211   Immanuel C.Y. Hsü, *The Rise of Modern China* (New York: Oxford University Press, 2000, 6th ed.), 69.

212   M.J. Meijer, *Marriage Law and Policy in the Chinese People's Republic* (Hong Kong: Hong Kong University Press, 1971), 6.

213   C.K. Yang, *The Chinese Family in the Communist Revolution*, fwd. Talcott Parsons (Massachusetts: Technology Press, 1959), 3. Note also Paul Chao: "In

Historian Olga Lang describes the Chinese family as a 'Confucian state in miniature', governed autocratically by the eldest male.[214] The Chinese patriarch held title to all property acquired by any member of the family, could sell family members into slavery, and suffered only mild punishments for killing an adult child.[215] The entire family structure was shot through with hierarchical relationships, based on generation, age, and sex, with everyone in his place and a place for everyone. The ideal in the imperial era was the joint family, with several generations living under one roof. This would have provided economic security as far as holding an estate together was concerned, as well as political strength vis-à-vis other families; multiple generations would have also meant that there were layers of control over most household members.[216] The actuality, in most cases, was the nuclear family, perhaps five or six strong, constrained in size economically.[217] One still had the controlling influence of kin and clan, which formed concentric circles outside the nuclear family.[218] The emphasis on family loyalty was so strong that it actually seems to have frustrated the formation of national loyalties, with Imperial China remaining integrated on the village (and village cluster) level for most of its existence.[219]

Marriages were arranged via matchmakers, with the actual marriage contract being signed by the heads of the respective families rather than bride and groom. Contracts could be made prior even to the birth of either spouse. The sexes were segregated completely by the age of 10, and lessons in deportment and virtue begun for young women.[220] "The Chinese," writes Paul Chao, "having much respect for womanhood, consider feminine purity as something sacred, comparing the woman to flawless jade."[221] This purity was preserved in part by wrapping a girl's feet tighter and tighter, preventing them from developing properly, and thus rendering her unable to walk

---

fact, notwithstanding its long history, Chinese culture, which is based on the principle of filial piety, proves to be rather homogenous." Paul Chao, *Chinese Kinship* (London: Kegan Paul International, 1983), 4.

214 Lang, 16.
215 Ibid., 27.
216 Hugh D.R. Baker, *Chinese Family and Kinship* (New York: Columbia University Press, 1979), 13-14.
217 Baker, 4; Lang, 16.
218 Lang, 13; Chao, 26.
219 James E. Sheridan, *China in Disintegration: The Republican Era in Chinese History, 1912-1949* (New York: The Free Press, 1975), 14-17.
220 Chao, 50.
221 Ibid., 51.

without tremendous difficulty. Presumably this would prevent her running out of the house and having extramarital affairs. Every woman was expected to marry at some point in her life, China having no equivalent word for 'spinster', but rather 'girl not yet married'.[222] Divorce was available at the option of the family heads if the woman exhibited any of the following: (1) infertility; (2) infidelity; (3) jealousy; (4) neglect of parents-in-law; (5) incurable sickness; (6) theft; or (7) garrulousness.[223] Three defenses were available to the woman: (1) three years of mourning for her in-laws; (2) recently acquired wealth in her husband's family; or (3) there was no family to which the woman could return.[224] A rare bright spot for women in Imperial China was the possibility of acquiring rights in inheritance, if she was born into a family with no surviving sons or married to a man with no birth heirs.[225] As to sexual matters specifically, China, for the most part, was less concerned with sexual repression generally than enforcing behaviors appropriate to individuals of certain rank, or 'status performance' as Matthew H. Sommer refers to it.[226] China's last dynasty (Qing), though, is frequently accused of having introduced sexual conservatism in later centuries, particularly during the Yongzheng period (1723-35).[227]

Imperial China would eventually be undone over the course of the nineteenth century, and in part by the very stasis it worked so hard to preserve. The technological and industrial progress that characterized European nations of the time was wholly absent in the Middle Kingdom. As its trading partners began to sense the resulting disparity in military power, China found itself on the losing end of conflicts and negotiations with the United Kingdom, France, Russia, Germany, and Japan. With China divided up into foreign spheres of influence, the need to modernize became clear.

At first, there existed a consensus that the basic Confucian social order would be preserved, and that modernization would be confined to the technological realm. By the end of the nineteenth century, though, liberal intellectuals like Kang Youwei were challenging fundamental Confucian

222 Baker, 9.
223 Baker, 45; Lang, 40.
224 Lang, 41.
225 Kathryn Bernhardt, *Women and Property in China, 960-1949* (Stanford: Stanford University Press, 1999), 3.
226 Matthew H. Sommer, *Sex, Law, and Society in Late Imperial China* (Stanford: Stanford University Press, 2000), 6.
227 "The imperial chastity cult was greatly expanded over it Ming and early Qing precedents. ... Lawmakers invented new categories of chastity heroine and martyr...." Ibid., 9-10.

principles, proposing not only an end to foot binding but an end to the family itself.[228] By the late 1890s, even the Guangxu emperor was thinking along similar though less drastic lines, initiating the Hundred Days Reforms in 1898. The reforms ended with the Emperor being overthrown by the Empress Dowager the same year. Conservatives were still in the ascendant in China, and there was as yet no widespread opposition to Confucianism. Imperial China was about to reach its end in any case. A revolution against the Qing dynasty begun in 1911 yielded a republic in the year 1912.

In the republican era, the number of intellectuals attacking the Confucian system grew rapidly.[229] As scholars like Confucius and Mencius had exalted the family for its role in preserving an authoritarian political system, modern scholars like Wu Yu attacked the traditional Chinese family for precisely the same reasons, arguing that it was simply incompatible with a democratic system.[230] 'New Culture' intellectuals were able to link China's failure to develop as a nation with its failure to develop the talents of its own people, and thus to link nationalism with individualism. "Our policy must be," wrote scholar Lu Hsun, "to rely upon the individual and reject the mass. When the individual becomes fully developed and is strengthened the country as a consequence will be invigorated."[231] The popular journal New Youth became the "most important progressive force" during the period from 1915-1919, launching a direct and unequivocal assault on Chinese traditions. "They urged that the old family system be abolished and that the equality of all individuals in society, especially the equality of the sexes, become a reality in China. They asked for freedom of choice in marriage in place of parental arrangements, and they opposed the double standard of sexual morality."[232] In short, New Culture intellectuals favored the nuclear, conjugal family common to the industrialized world.[233] Joining the chorus we find a young Mao Zedong, who devoted a sympathetic

228 Ono Kazuko, *Chinese Women in a Century of Revolution, 1850-1950*, ed. Joshua A. Fogel, trans. Kathryn Bernhardt et al., (Stanford: Stanford University Press, 1989), 33-43.
229 Sheridan, 20.
230 Lang, 110.
231 Huang Sung-K'ang, *Lu Hsun and the New Culture Movement of Modern China* (Amsterdam: Djambatan, 1957), 34.
232 Sheridan, 119.
233 Susan L. Glosser, "'The Truths I Have Learned': Nationalism, Family Reform, and Male Identity in China's New Culture Movement, 1915-1923", in *Chinese Femininities, Chinese Masculinities*, ed. Susan Brownell and Jeffrey N. Wasser-

article to the suicide of a young woman forced to marry against her will.[234] In 1920, he referred privately to the marriage system as a 'rape league'.[235] Intellectuals were increasingly rejecting Confucian norms in their personal lives, though James Sheridan suggests that the intellectual attack was largely ineffectual as far as the general population went.[236]

Economic changes, on the other hand, did have an impact on the Chinese family. The demand for cheap labor will often trump the generalized desire to see women completely subordinated, and China's rapid industrialization during the period from 1914 to 1918 resulted in the formation of an extensive female working class.[237] According to Lang, by 1927 some 58.7% of Shanghai's factory workers were female.[238] Economic independence for women had the effect of loosening parental control, which, among other things, allowed for free choice in marriage,[239] and even lesbian preferences to flourish.[240] Women with bound feet were obviously unsuitable for work, and the Republican era saw official endorsement of the campaign against foot binding.[241] The new century also brought in educational opportunities for young Chinese women, which, according to Elizabeth Croll, "introduced them to Western ideas, literature and institutions based on the ideals of 'freedom', 'individualism', 'self-fulfillment', and 'equality of the sexes', which came to have popular appeal among students in the first decades of the twentieth century."[242] Women were by now also active in political and military affairs, having taking part in the 1911 revolution,[243] and were also beginning to participate in the emergent labor movement.[244]

strom, fwd. Thomas Laqueur (Berkeley: University of California Press, 2002), 121.

234 Kazuko, 100.
235 Jung Chang and Jon Halliday, *Mao: The Unknown Story* (New York: Alfred A. Knopf, 2005), 23.
236 Sheridan, 115-122.
237 Kazuko, 112-13.
238 Lang, 103.
239 Elizabeth Croll, *Changing Identities of Chinese Women: Rhetoric, Experience, and Self-Perception in Twentieth-Century China* (Hong Kong: Hong Kong University Press, 1995), 46; Lang, 102.
240 Kazuko, 122-23.
241 Lang, 103.
242 Croll, 46.
243 Kazuko, 75.
244 Ibid., 124.

Even at this point, the waters were clouded by the ostensibly progressive, though collective and asexual, disposition of many intellectuals. Anarchists returned to republican China and founded a 'Society to Advance Morality', which posited individual purity (e.g., giving up prostitutes, and gambling) as a prerequisite for social reform.[245] Colleen She finds the Peking intelligentsia of the 1920s and 30s rejecting the idea of romantic love for the sake of individual fulfillment, arguing instead that love was a matter of social concern.[246] Ono Kazuko notes that the exaltation of the chaste widow increased in proportion to the perceived threat against the traditional family system.[247]

Republican China never amounted to very much as a modern nation-state. The country quickly devolved into various feudal states run by warlords, with a weak central government controlled by whichever warlord happened to control Beijing. Against this backdrop, China's nationalist party (the Kuomintang) was officially formed in 1919, followed by China's communist party in 1920.[248] Before long, the two were cooperating in military ventures against warlords, though the 'United Front' broke apart in 1927 after nationalist leader Chiang Kai-shek attacked striking workers in Shanghai. The conflict would go unresolved over the next two decades, with warlords still commanding attention, and the Japanese invading Manchuria. The Sino-Japanese War began in earnest in 1937 and lasted for eight years, putting the communist-nationalist battle on hold yet again. With Japan expelled from China in 1945, the communists and nationalists were able to begin a proper civil war free of distractions. The communists won control of the Chinese mainland in 1949, leaving the nationalists confined to the island of Taiwan. The People's Republic of China was then formed by the communists, electing Mao Zedong as its chairman.

During the same period of time, additional strains were being placed on family norms and gender constructs. In 1930-31, the republican government of China issued a new marriage code, which explicitly guaranteed free choice in marriage.[249] The right of women to inherit and possess property was also guaranteed, as was the right to stand as head of

245 Sheridan, 112.
246 Colleen She, "Toward Ideology", Issues and Studies 27, no.2: 104-32 (1991).
247 Kazuko, 147.
248 The Party began to take on a 'Leninist' or 'Bolshevik' quality around 1924 or 1925. Michael Y.L. Luk, *The Origins of Chinese Bolshevism: An Ideology in the Making* (Hong Kong: Oxford University Press, 1990), 203-4.
249 Lang, 116.

the family.[250] The code would have revolutionized Chinese society if it had been enforced strictly, though it never was, existing only as a statement of principle. Principles were certainly changing for the urban intelligentsia, who espoused the idea of sexual equality from the late 1920s on.[251] More tangible changes came during the republican era as well. The trend was toward later marriage, typically in the twenties rather than in the teen years as previously.[252] Women gained an increasingly high profile, being utilized in agricultural production during the civil war, with perhaps as many as 70% of them beginning to work outside the home.[253] Educational opportunities were on the rise for women as well. Coeducation was the norm by the end of the republican era, and this introduced opportunities for romantic love on an unprecedented scale.[254] Individualism in domestic relations was on the rise generally, according to Marion J. Levy Jr.: "Parents to a degree never before true in China are coming to live for their children as individuals rather than having children who will live for the family."[255]

With the foundation of the PRC, the traditional Chinese family broke down definitively. Land reform became one of the first initiatives of the new communist government. Citizens were encouraged to form tribunals which, under communist guidance, held public trials for landlord 'evildoers'. The landlord in question would typically be sentenced to death and his property expropriated.[256] The distribution of land took on an increasingly collective character over the 1950s, beginning with the sharing of tools, labor, and land, and ending with the formation of super-massive property-owning communes.[257] Property rights, such as they were, were enjoyed equally by men and women and had at pleasure of the state. Paternal and marital authority were severely compromised, having lost their economic foundations.[258] In the wake of land reform, gender roles began to vanish, with new, androgynous, unisex modes of address and clothing.[259] Women

---

250   Bernhardt, 119.
251   Yang, 119.
252   Ibid., 41.
253   Kazuko, 174.
254   Marion J. Levy Jr., *The Family Revolution in Modern China* (Cambridge: Harvard University Press, 1949), 295.
255   Ibid., 294.
256   O. Edmund Clubb, *20ᵗʰ Century China* (New York: Columbia University Press, 1978, 3rd ed.), 319.
257   Baker, 185.
258   Baker, 184; Kazuko, 173.
259   Croll, *Changing Identities of Chinese Women*, 70-71.

were now depicted in Chinese propaganda in the role of workers or farmers rather than mothers.[260]

In 1950, the PRC issued a new marriage law, which declared in its first article that "the feudal marriage system based on arbitrary and compulsory arrangements and the supremacy of man over woman, and in disregard of the interests of the children, is abolished."[261] The code guaranteed free choice in marriage, divorce, equal rights for women, monogamy, and the right of widows to remarry.[262] Unlike the republican civil code of the early 1930s, the PRC both promoted and enforced its new measures quite vigorously. Divorces skyrocketed in the early years of communist rule, going from roughly 200,000 in 1950 to 400,000 in 1951, and on pace for 800,000 by mid-1952.[263] Women found themselves subjected to a proportional increase in violence as a result of domestic disputes. According to Ono Kazuko, "During the two or three years following the law's enactment some 70,000 - 80,000 people per year were killed over marriage-related issues throughout the country. The majority of the dead were young women who had boldly resisted conventions."[264] Early signs of ideological patterns begin to emerge. The PRC supported its marriage law with a nationwide publicity campaign, which involved house-to-house investigations and show trials for men accused of murdering their wives.[265] One such series of trials actually included separate charges of 'seducing women' and 'messing around with women'.[266] While men convicted of murder were typically given death sentences, men charged with seduction or messing around with women were given only 2 to 4 years of hard labor or prison.

Thus during the early years of the PRC, the traditional Chinese family

---

260   Ibid., 71.
261   Baker, 26. M. J. Meijer notes an interesting progression in communist commentary on the new marriage law. Early discussion focused on the concrete aspects of the Law itself, while later commentary, especially leading into the Cultural Revolution, involved "moral discussions on how to be a good married Communist and Communist parent or child, and how to educate people in that direction. There is a reminder here of the Great Learning with a variation: when you turn to yourself and transform yourself into a good Communist then your family will be in order; when your family is in order your work will benefit; when your work is in order..., etc." Meijer, 272.
262   Baker, 26.
263   Kazuko, 179.
264   Ibid., 181.
265   Diamant, 43.
266   Ibid.

begins to disappear, replaced by an atomistic system of individual choice, romantic love, and the formation of nuclear families. Sociologically, China was now a giant lake of gasoline, set to explode if anyone threw a match into it.[267] At first, no one did. Mao's objective in the 1950s was to make China a superpower, and to do so virtually overnight. Less than fully utopian in nature, he did combine a lack of realism with spectacular incompetence as an administrator, and both of these with a complete disregard for the value of human life. This combination would prove lethal for tens of millions of people. Forced collectivization in the 1950s led to Mao's 'Great Leap Forward', which called for massive, indeed impossible, increases in food production. Bureaucrats falsely reported having achieved these goals, and Mao exported the 'excess' food to countries in Europe as tens of millions of his own people were starving to death. Conflicts came with top officials like Defense Minister Peng Dehuai and President Liu Shaoqi, who had actually bothered to visit areas afflicted by famine. At the 1962 party congress, Liu openly challenged Mao's account of China's food production, and found support amongst the participants. Mao was furious. His revenge came four years later in the Great Proletarian Cultural Revolution (GPCR), which was essentially a massive purge against disloyal officials and bureaucrats at every level.

## The Great Proletarian Cultural Revolution

**In June of 1966, the** People's Daily issued a call to the students of China to reject the 'bourgeois' ideas disseminated by their teachers and to 'safeguard' Chairman Mao. Work teams fanned out across the country encouraging students at middle schools and colleges to set up their own Cultural Revolution committees. Of these 'Red Guards', elite members were made privy to a classified politburo report calling for a movement against "revisionist opinions and views ... [those] who are deeply influenced by bourgeois thinking, severely individualistic, and have a strikingly erroneous stand and viewpoints."[268] Violence was largely spontaneous and sporadic as summer came to a close, though certainly of a high level of severity where

---

267  "That an explosive mix of repressed anger and violence was brewing under the surface, waiting to explode at the first crack in the veneer of socialist order, was something the [Central Committee] leadership had long been aware of but rarely discussed." Roderick Macfarquhar and Michael Schoenhals, *Mao's Last Revolution* (Cambridge: Harvard/Belknap Press, 2006), 103.
268  Macfarquhar and Schoenhals, 41, 106.

it occurred. On August 5, for example, a school headmistress was tortured to death by Red Guards, being kicked, trampled, doused with boiling water, beaten with belt buckles, and sticks studded with nails.[269]  On August 8, the Central Committee publicly issued the 'Sixteen Points', which explicitly called for struggle against bourgeois influences:

> Although the bourgeoisie has been overthrown, it is still trying to use the old ideas, culture, customs, and habits of the exploiting classes to corrupt the masses, capture their minds and endeavor to stage a comeback. The proletariat must ... change the mental outlook of the whole of society. At present our objective is struggle against and overthrow those persons in authority who are taking the capitalist road....[270]

On August 18, in the first of a series of massive rallies in Beijing,[271] Mao himself reviewed a formation of red guards, encouraging one young woman to change her name to 'seeking violence'. In honor of the event, her school was thereafter renamed the 'Red Seeking-Violence Middle School for Girls'. Students got the hint and violence now became systemic, spreading across the country as the Red Guards returned home from Beijing. Mao then encouraged his Red Guards to attack culture in general, to sweep away the 'four olds', and ordered his police and army to stay out of the way. Soon lists of specific targets were being drawn up for the guards to attack. By January of 1967, students were encouraged to overthrow high-ranking party members (like Liu Shaoqi), getting underway the purge which had always been his real intention.

Mao provided very little in the way of ideological guidance for this popular uprising, apparently needing only to order his police not to interfere with the Red Guards, and letting events take their course. The movement seems to have been animated by a very simple 'us' versus 'them' mentality, the Red Guards dividing those backing Chairman Mao from everyone else. A spontaneous and widespread concordance emerged among red guards and certain officials, which held that 'they' were characterized by their sexual desire. "As in France or Germany," writes Neil Diamant, "highly polarized images for good and evil, sexually pure and impure, led

---

269   Chang and Halliday, 517.
270   Macfarquhar and Schoenhals, 92.
271   Altogether, 12 million Red Guards had heard Mao speak by the last rally in November. Mac Farquhar and Schoenhals, 110.

urban youth … to look toward sexual behavior, and how people conducted their private lives generally, as criteria for participation in, or exclusion from, the new community."[272]   Red guards rendered themselves largely asexual in dress and behavior. According to Harriet Evans, "the slightest suggestion of sexual interest was considered so ideologically unsound that gendered tastes in hairstyle and dress were coerced into a monotonous uniformity of shape and colour."[273]  Hair was to be cut short and clothing was to be loose fitting. One test devised by the guards was to drop a soda bottle down the pant legs of young women, and if the bottle failed to make it to the bottom, the pants would be slit on the sides.[274]  Femininity in general was rejected, and Chinese propaganda posters displayed women doing jobs traditionally done by men.[275]

On the other hand, any sort of sexual indiscretion would push one toward the 'bourgeois' or 'reactionary' side. Zhimei Zhang explains that an affair would be sufficient to harm one's career during this era. "If our relationship became public," she writes, "we would share the disgrace. The words 'immoral person' would go into both our files. Even years later, we could be denied promotions because of it."[276]  The individual who only lost a promotion could count him or herself lucky at that point. Jung Chang notes a teacher beaten ostensibly for having met her husband at random on a bus. "Love arising out of a chance meeting was regarded as a sign of immorality. The boys took her to an office and 'took revolutionary acts over her'— the euphemism for beating someone up."[277]  And in the climate of the time, being labeled reactionary or bourgeois could get one killed very easily.[278]  By 1968, Mao had what he wanted and simply turned the valve

272   Diamant, 286.

273   Harriet Evans, *Women and Sexuality in China: Female Sexuality and Gender Since 1949* (New York: Continuum, 1997), 2.

274   Gao Yuan, *Born Red: A Chronicle of the Cultural Revolution* (Stanford: Stanford University Press, 1987), 95.

275   Emily Honig, "Maoist Mappings of Gender: Reassessing the Red Guards," in *Chinese Femininities, Chinese Masculinities*, ed. Susan Brownell and Jeffrey N. Wasserstrom, fwd. Thomas Laqueuer (Berkeley: University of California Press, 2002), 255.

276   Zhimei Zhang, *Foxspirit: A Woman in Mao's China* (Montreal: Vehicule Press, 1992), 127.

277   Jung Chang, *Wild Swans: Three Daughters of China* (New York: Doubleday, 1992), 294.

278   Anchee Min describes an instance as late as 1974 of a man being killed for consensual sexual intercourse with a woman on a segregated collective farm.

off, sending young urbanites out into the countryside on the pretext of their learning from the peasantry.

# 3.1 Lust Raging Crosswise Through the City

**The modern religious system often** comprises a vast collection of ideas, founded in some basic text and amplified exponentially via exegesis over the course of many centuries. It can be all things to all people, and to say that someone is a Muslim or a Christian is to say very little as to that person's nature and character. The liberal humanist approaches Christianity as a liberal humanist, and, conversely, the totalitarian approaches Christianity as a totalitarian. Now lying within the overall structure of Christian thought are all the essential elements required to form a totalitarian ideology. These elements were set in place and promoted by church theorists who were quite uniformly hostile to sexuality. Foremost among these would be St. Augustine, who details his own discomfort with sexuality at length in his *Confessions*. Augustine's entire theological system is predicated on the idea of achieving religious transcendence through the rejection of sexual pleasure, which is in fact how he describes his own religious transformation to God: "You converted me to yourself, so that I no longer desired a wife or placed any hope in this world...."

Augustinian theology posits a basic division between two realities, one good and the other evil, one true and the other false, and, critically, one setting ideology and community against the individualism of the other. "The two cities then were created by two kinds of love: the earthly city by a love of self carried even to the point of contempt for God, the heavenly city by a love of God carried even to the point of contempt for self."[279] In fact, the very first sin ever committed was individualism, and by no less an individualist than the Devil himself. "For the devil too, chose to live according to his own self when he did not adhere to the truth.... Therefore, when man lives according to man and not according to God, he is like the

---

Anchee Min, *Red Azalea* (New York: Pantheon Books, 1994),58-61.

279    Saint Augustine, *The City of God Against the Pagans Vol. 4*, ed. T.E. Page et al., trans. Philip Levine (Cambridge: Harvard University Press, 1966, 7 Vol.), 405.

devil...."[280] God favors community, as evidenced by the creation of the entire human race out of a single man, "to ensure that unity of fellowship itself and ties of harmony might be more strongly impressed on him, if men were bound to one another not only by their similar nature but also by their feeling of kinship."[281] To whatever extent man conforms to God's vision, he also favors community, for "there is a city of God, and its Founder has inspired us with a love that makes us covet its citizenship."[282]

Pride is the beginning of all sin, though not necessarily pride in the sense of excessive vanity, but rather any attempt at individual differentiation. As Augustine explains, "Where pride ... seeks to excel, there it is cast down into want and destitution, turning from the pursuit of the common good to one's own individual good out of a destructive self-love."[283] True love is directed toward the collective according to Origen; it is created by God and implanted in the human heart so "that it might love God and what God wills. Therefore ... whoever loves anything other than God and what God wills is said to have a love that is false and with pretense."[284] Aquinas adds that the love of one person for another is only meritorious to the extent that the love exists for God's sake.[285]

This ideological form of love is engendered by God and exerts a certain gravitational pull, and yet it remains ultimately subordinate to the power of the free will of the individual.[286] As Augustine writes, "The right will is ... well-directed love, and the wrong will is ill-directed love."[287] This power is to be construed in a very narrow sense, however. Luther explains that free will is not "a power of freely turning in any direction, yielding to none and

280 Augustine, *The City of God*, Levine trans., 274-75.
281 Augustine, *The City of God*, Levine trans., 111.
282 Augustine, *The City of God*, trans. Marcus Dods, intro. Thomas Merton (New York: Random House, 1950), 345.
283 Saint Augustine, *On Genesis Against the Manichees*, trans. Roland J. Teske (District of Columbia: Catholic University of America Press, 1990), 146-47.
284 Origen, *Spirit and Fire: A Thematic Anthology of His Writings*, trans. Robert J. Daly, ed. Hans Urs von Balthasar (District of Columbia: Catholic University of America Press, 1984), 202.
285 Saint Thomas Aquinas, *Summa Theologica Vol. II*, trans. Father Laurence Shapcote, rev. Daniel J. Sullivan (Chicago: Encyclopedia Britannica, 2d ed., 1990), 526.
286 Saint Thomas Aquinas, *Summa Theologica Vol. I*, trans. Father Laurence Shapcote, rev. Daniel J. Sullivan (Chicago: Encyclopedia Britannica, 2d ed., 1990), 734, 739.
287 Augustine, *The City of God*, Dods trans., 449.

subject to none ... in all that bears on salvation or damnation, [a man] has no 'free-will', but is a captive, prisoner and bondslave, either to the will of God, or to the will of Satan."[288] This basic ability to mediate between good and evil is not only limited in its nature, but is also subject to various external influences which compromise even the freedom inherent in this basic choice. As Augustine recalls his younger years to God, "all that you asked of me was to deny my own will and accept yours. But, during all those years, where was my free will?"[289] The true freedom of the Christian consists not in the power to choose but rather in the choice itself, the correct choice being to embrace the will of God.[290]

In its ideological form, Christianity places particular emphasis on singularity and unity, relying directly or indirectly on the existence of a single 'spiritual' entity which transcends mere common belief or shared feeling. We learn from the Book of Corinthians that "for as the body is one, and hath many members, and all the members of that one body, being many, are one body: so also is Christ. For by one Spirit are we all baptized into one body...."[291] Sin is contrary to this collectivity, according to Origen: "He who is one, when he sins, becomes many, cut off from God and divided into parts, and fallen away from the unity."[292] One cannot truly know God without merging into the one, a merger Origen analogizes to the union of flesh between a man and a woman.[293] Aquinas does note that separation may be in the interest of the collective organism when some part of it begins to decay. The agent of decay is the heretic, and Aquinas quotes with approval a passage from Jerome advising the faithful to "cut off the decayed flesh, expel the mangy sheep from the fold, lest the whole house, the whole dough, the whole body, the whole flock burn, perish, rot, die."[294]

Pride is the beginning of all sin and heresy its primary manifestation; it is a love of self and untruth and rejection of the Christian unity which embodies truth itself. Aquinas explains that a thing may be said to be true if it conforms either to the divine purpose established for that thing, or if

288 Martin Luther, *Bondage of the Will*, trans. J. I. Packer and O. R. Johnston (New Jersey: Revell, 1957), 105-07.
289 Augustine, *Confessions*, trans. R.S. Pine-Coffin (New York: Penguin Books, 1961), 181.
290 Origen, *Spirit and Fire*, 342.
291 1 Corinthians 12:12-13.
292 Origen, *Spirit and Fire*, 43.
293 Ibid., 247.
294 Saint Thomas Aquinas, *On Law, Morality, and Politics*, ed. William P. Baumgarth and Richard J. Regan (Indianapolis: Hackett Publishing, 1988), 256.

the thing is such that it leads the human intellect to an accurate assessment as to the nature of the thing. Divine truth is true reality, and human truth the recognition of conformity and nonconformity of something in this reality relative to divine reality.[295] Only the human reality allows for the possibility of falsehood, and the presence of falsehood in this reality serves to obscure the true nature of God's reality. Tertullian explains that "divine reason is in the marrow, not on the surface, and is frequently in opposition to things as they seem."[296] Origen has similar ideas on the subject, noting that "there is, next to this visible and sensible world ... another world of things not seen ... where the clean of heart will look upon its aspect and beauty...."[297]

These two realities are in motion. In the beginning, God created everything and everything was perfect, though as Augustine explains, there really is no beginning or end from God's perspective. "He does not pass from this to that by transition of thought, but beholds all things with absolute unchangeableness...."[298] Anything set in motion by God moves inexorably toward a fixed and certain outcome, with no possibility of reconsideration or deviation: "For certainly He would not be the perfect worker He is, unless His Knowledge were so perfect as to receive no addition from His finished works."[299] Thus from a real-time perspective, God works very much a law of physics. This is important because it means that whatever God sets in motion continues in motion, and will not be called off at the last minute due to a divine change of mind.

The future history of Christianity is the Apocalypse, the end of reality as it stands and the beginning of a new heaven and a new earth. The new reality, the City of God, is the natural world, the true reality which exists at all times regardless of its presence in this reality. St. John Chrysostom writes that "the temporal world is as far removed from the other world as dreams are from the truth, no even more...."[300] The world of truth is also the world of good, and a world set in diametric opposition to the world of

---

295  Saint Thomas Aquinas, *Truth*, 3 Vols. (Indianapolis : Hackett Pub. Co., 1994), 11.

296  Tertullian, *Treatise on the Resurrection*, ed. trans. Ernest Evans (London: S.P.C.K., 1960), 13.

297  Origen, *Spirit and Fire*, 44.

298  Augustine, *The City of God*, Dods trans., 364.

299  Augustine, *The City of God*, Dods trans., 364.

300  Saint John Chrysostom, *On Virginity, Against Remarriage*, trans. Sally Rieger Shore, intro. Elizabeth A. Clark (New York: Edwin Mellen, 1983), 96.

falsity and evil. Augustine posits that "no nature at all is evil"[301] and further that "if sin be natural, it is not sin at all."[302] While the two realities are conceptually distinct, for various reasons "the two cities ... are in this present world commingled, and as it were entangled together."[303] The one world, moreover, can only exist at the expense of the other: "Vice ... is so contrary to nature, that it cannot but damage it."[304] Tertullian advises one to "meditate on the things of Heaven and you will despise the things of earth."[305]

The division between the true reality created by God and the reality which confronts us today was initially brought about by the Devil, working in conjunction with the first man (Adam) and first woman (Eve) created by God. God first formed man in his own image on the sixth and final day of creation, then placed him in the Garden of Eden to act as its custodian. Eve was formed later out of Adam's rib and brought to Adam to be a 'help meet' for him. "Therefore," explains the Book of Genesis, "shall a man leave his father and his mother, and shall cleave unto his wife; and they shall be one flesh. And they were both naked, the man and his wife, and were not ashamed."[306] The second verse is intended to establish that the nature of male-female relations were initially such that men and women had no reason to be ashamed of their own bodies. In Paradise, there was neither lust nor involuntary desire nor passion even in the sexual act itself.[307] "Why ... may we not assume," queries Augustine, "that the first couple before they sinned could have given a command to their genital organs for the purpose of procreation as they did the other members [of their bodies] ... without any craving for pleasure?"[308] This control, according to Augustine, is the reason that neither Eve nor Adam experienced shame while in Paradise, for "why would they be ashamed, since they did not perceive in their members any law at war with the law of their mind?"[309]

God left Adam and Eve in the Garden of Eden with exactly one command, which was to refrain from eating the fruit of the tree of

301  Augustine, *The City of God*, Dods trans., 365.
302  Augustine, *The City of God*, Dods trans., 359.
303  Augustine, *The City of God*, Dods trans., 346.
304  Augustine, *The City of God*, Dods trans., 361.
305  Tertullian, *Treatises on Marriage and Remarriage*, trans. ann. William P. Le Saint (Westminster: Newman Press, 1956), 16.
306  Genesis 2:24-25.
307  Augustine, *On Genesis*, 74.
308  Ibid., 81.
309  Ibid., 135.

knowledge of good and evil, warning them that "in the day thou eatest thereof, thou shalt surely die."[310] Enter the serpent, the most 'subtle' of all creatures according to the Bible, though subtle owing to the control of the Devil, according to Augustine. The serpent approaches Eve and convinces her that she will not really die if she partakes of the forbidden fruit, so she promptly does, then offers some to her husband who also indulges. In this pivotal moment, man chooses to separate his will from the will of God, thus committing the transgression that will lead God to expel man from Paradise. The first effect of this original sin, however, is the removal of God's grace which had heretofore protected Adam and Eve from sexual desire. As Genesis continues, "And the eyes of both of them were opened, and they knew that they were naked ... and Adam and his wife hid themselves from the presence of the Lord God amongst the trees of the garden."[311] (Gen 3:17) As Augustine interprets this passage, the reason Adam and Eve hid from God was the experience of shame resulting from the inability to control their own bodies, "an unprecedented movement of their own disobedient flesh as punishment in kind ... for their own disobedience. The soul ... was stripped of the former subjection of the body, and ... no longer kept its lower servant responsive to its will."[312]

The punishment for the transgression of turning away from God's will is then twofold, namely sexual desire and death. These biological defects are transmitted to each member of the human race in the first moment of existence, the 'vitiated origin' or original sin of all humanity. Origen suggests that human existence is a sufficient condition for sin, that "those first movements of the soul, borne forward according to the desires of the flesh, fall into sin."[313] Aquinas explains that the sins of Adam and Eve are imputed to humanity as a single entity with a single moral nature, and that "we should consider the whole population of human beings receiving their nature from our first parent as one community, or rather as the one body of one human being."[314] The mere fact of existence is thus a sufficient condition for original sin, though not actual sin which requires a voluntary act from the individual.[315] The two are linked through sexual desire, which

---

310   Genesis 2:17.
311   Genesis 3:17.
312   Augustine, *The City of God*, Levine trans., 179.
313   Origen, *Spirit and Fire*, 63.
314   Saint Thomas Aquinas, *On Evil*, trans. Richard Regan, ed. Brian Davies (Oxford: Oxford University Press, 2003), 196.
315   Ibid., 198.

is the punishment for original sin and frequently the cause of actual sin.

Sexuality is by its very nature a part of the Devil's reality, and is perhaps even the distinguishing characteristic of the false reality of this world. Though all truth is derived from God, notes Aquinas, "when we say that fornicating is true, we do not imply that the defect involved in the act of fornication is included in the notion of truth. True predicates merely the conformity of that act to an intellect. Hence, one cannot conclude that fornicating is from God, but merely that its truth is from God."[316] According to Tertullian, one can distinguish between those who embrace the truth and those who embrace falsehood by their sexual behavior. As he writes:

> For after chastity and sanctity of the spirit there followed purity of the flesh. This, therefore, it immediately safeguarded by outlawing adultery which is its enemy. Nothing second is far from first... so adultery, since it is the next thing to idolatry -- for idolatry is often made a matter of reproach to the people under the name of adultery and fornication -- will share its fate as it does its rank, and be joined with it in punishment as it is in position.[317]

**Sexual desire and experience serve** to inhibit one's ability to distinguish between the two realities, or as Tertullian explains, "virgins, because of their perfect integrity and inviolate purity, will look upon the face of God most closely...."[318] According to Luther, "our whole purpose is to be directed only toward the driving out of lusts. Since by faith the soul is cleansed and made to love God, it desires that all things, and especially its own body, shall be purified so that all things may join with it in loving and praising God."[319]

Sexuality is contrary to reason generally, with Augustine explaining that "so possessing indeed is this pleasure, that at the moment of time in which it is consummated all mental activity is suspended."[320] Luther describes sexual intercourse as "so hideous and frightful a pleasure that physicians compare it with epilepsy or falling sickness."[321] Reason, though,

---

316  Aquinas, *Truth*, 39.
317  Tertullian, *On Penitence and On Purity*, trans. ann. William P. Le Saint (Westminster: Newman Press, 1959), 63.
318  Tertullian, *Marriage and Remarriage*, 21.
319  Martin Luther, *Christian Liberty*, ed. by Harold J. Grimm, trans. by W. A. Lambert, rev. by Harold J. Grimm (Philadelphia : Fortress Press, 1967), 22.
320  Augustine, *The City of God*, Dods trans., 464.
321  Martin Luther, *Luther on Women : A Sourcebook*, ed. trans. Susan C. Karant-Nunn and Merry E. Wiesner-Hanks (Cambridge: Cambridge University Press,

is here to be understood in a very limited sense, as ideological uniformity and never unrestrained intellectualism. As Luther explains, "Prior to faith and a knowledge of God, reason is darkness, but in believers it's an excellent instrument. ... Enlightened reason, taken captive by faith, receives life from faith, for it is slain and given life again."[322] Augustine condemns the inquisitive mind in no uncertain terms, referring to intellectualism as a self-indulgence roughly comparable to the search for physical pleasure.[323] He explains that a man of great temporal knowledge "is not happy unless he knows [God]; but the man who knows [God] is happy even if he knows none of these things."[324] The two seem to travel together, with Luther noting that "whenever faith and the word of God are absent, it is unthinkable that one could resist evil desire and love. Inquisitiveness is present as well as vain, sinful affection."[325]

As sexuality is contrary to the proper cognitive state of the Christian, it is, perhaps in much the same way, contrary to the proper emotional state of the Christian. More specifically, sexual desire leads to the misdirection of Christian love. As Aquinas writes:

> And we should note two things regarding the disorder of desire in sexual lust. The first is that there is a desire for pleasure toward which the will is borne as one's end. And in this regard, we designate sexual lust self-love, namely, that one inordinately desires pleasure for self. And by contrast, one has hatred for God, namely, inasmuch as God forbids the desired pleasure. And the second thing to be noted is the desire of the means whereby one attains the end of pleasure. And in this regard, we designate sexual lust love of this world, that is, of all the things whereby those who belong to this world attain the end they strive for. And we by contrast designate sexual lust despair of the next world, since the more one desires pleasures of the flesh, the more one despises spiritual pleasures.[326]

**Sensual pleasure thus presents the** Devil with an opportunity to disengage

---

2003) 147.

322  Luther, *Works Vol. 54*, ed. trans. Theodore G. Tappert (Philadelphia: Fortress Press, 1966), 183.

323  Augustine, *Confessions*, 239-40.

324  Ibid., 94-95.

325  Luther, *On Women*, 21.

326  Aquinas, *On Evil*, 432.

the individual Christian from his or her faith, though faith itself remains the best defense against sexual desire. Luther writes that where faith is absent, "there is no defense against evil lust and desire.... We are similar to our father and mother and bring the same disease and illness with us. The devil deals with us today in the same way: he leads us into the main temptation touching on faith."[327] Chrysostom explains that "day and night we must stand armed with arguments and appear formidable to these shameful passions. When they arouse us just a little, the devil stands by with fire in hand ready to burn down the temple of God."[328]

Chrysostom implies that the sexuality of one Christian is the concern of all, as it provides the Devil a gateway into the metaphysical Christian collective. Origen explains that "he who defiles his own body seems to sin against the whole church, because the stain is spread through one member to the whole body."[329] Tertullian refers to the 'poison of lust and infecting filth' of sexual desire, cautioning that "fornication [is not] an act committed against something which is your own and not the Lord's, he dispossesses you of yourself and ... gives you over to Christ."[330] Heresy is comparable to sexual deviance and heresy spreads like an infection, though heresy may itself be spread sexually. Tertullian explains that Christians are "defiled by contact with unbelievers," and further that "Christians who enter into a marriage with pagans commit a sin of fornication and are to be cut off completely from communion with the brethren...."[331]

Marriage is thought to create a barrier between men and lust, "For like a dam," writes Chrysostom, "marriage gives us an opportunity for legitimate intercourse and in this way contains the flood of sexual desire."[332] According to Luther, "a man gives himself into captivity, such that all other carnal outlets are closed off and each one is satisfied with one sleeping companion, God therefore regards the flesh as subdued, so that lust does not rage crosswise through the city."[333] Having been bound to one another, and, according to Chrysostom, "By forcing one spouse to endure the baseness of the other, this servitude is sufficient to obscure every joy."[334] Marriage is

327 Luther, *On Women*, 21-22.
328 Chrysostom, *On Virginity, Against Remarriage*, 36.
329 Origen, *Spirit and Fire*, 306.
330 Tertullian, *On Purity*, 99-100.
331 Tertullian, *Marriage and Remarriage*, 27.
332 Chrysostom, *On Virginity, Against Remarriage*, 12.
333 Luther, *On Women*, 91.
334 Chrysostom, *On Virginity*, 62.

merely a best-case scenario in this reality, a remedy for the evil of lust, and certainly not something to be celebrated in Tertullian's opinion: "Marriage and fornication are different only because laws appear to make them so; they are not intrinsically different, but only in the degree of illegitimacy. For what is it that all men and women do in both marriage and fornication? They have sexual relations, of course; and the very desire to do this, our Lord says, is the same thing as fornication."[335]

Marriage will, however, serve to control women, which gives Origen some small measure of comfort: "Every woman is either under a man and subject to the laws of a man or is a whore and makes use of liberty to sin."[336] Tertullian would also appreciate some self-control on the part of women as well: "You must know that perfect modesty, that is, Christian modesty, requires not only that you never desire to be an object of desire on the part of others, but that you even hate to be one.... Since beauty we know to be naturally the exciter of lust."[337]

Augustine's view on marriage does vary somewhat from other scholars, though. First, he considers marriage and continence two goods, the latter simply being more desirable than the former.[338] Marriage dulls the sex drive not through personality conflicts between man and woman, but through a change of roles from husband and wife to mother and father. For a kind of dignity prevails when, as husband and wife they unite in the marriage act, they think of themselves as mother and father."[339] Moreover, marriage is the basic building block of society, the relationship between man and wife being the "first natural tie of human society...."[340] It is also the foundation of the political order according to Augustine, who explains that it is "a duty of virtue to live for one's country, and for its sake to beget children...."[341] Further, family relationships should be structured with the political order in mind: "The father of the family ought to frame his domestic rule in accordance with the law of the city, so that the household may be in harmony with the civic order."[342]

---

335  Tertullian, *On Marriage*, 57.
336  Origen, *Spirit and Fire*, 271.
337  Tertullian, *Disciplinary, Moral, and Ascetical Works*, trans. Rudolph Arbesmann, Sister Emily Joseph Daly, and Edwin A. Quain (New York, Fathers of the Church, 1959), 131.
338  Augustine, *On Marriage*, 20.
339  Ibid., 13.
340  Ibid., 9.
341  Augustine, *The City of God*, Dods trans., 670.
342  Augustine, *The City of God*, Dods trans., 695.

To the benefit of those able to control their desires, the City of God becomes forcibly disentangled from the world of human reality during the Apocalypse, an event which will feature the return of Christ and the final battle between good and evil. The forces of truth are victorious, as we learn from the symbolism-heavy Book of Revelations, but not before the unrepentant lovers of this world are tormented for some period of time. There are firstly the Four Horsemen of the Apocalypse, with the rider of the white horse representing Christian militancy, red martyrdom, gray economic instability, and the pale (green) horse ridden by death. "And power was given unto them over the fourth part of the earth, to kill with sword, and with hunger, and with death, and with the beasts of the earth."[343] The Devil is later given a key to a bottomless pit housing a cloud of smoke and a swarm of malevolent locusts. The Devil opens the pit, and the cloud, which represents the corruption of the moral atmosphere, darkens the sun. Once released, the locusts, representing decay, will begin to torture those who do not have the mark of God upon them. "And in those days shall men seek death, and shall not find it; and shall desire to die, and death shall flee from them."[344] Soon after, the Four Angels of the Euphrates are to be released and, leading an army of several hundred thousand, directed to kill one-third of the lovers of this world. In spite of all this, those who survive remain unrepentant. "Neither repented they of their murders, nor of their sorceries, nor of their fornication, nor of their thefts."[345]

A great battle in heaven follows, with the Archangel Michael casting the Devil out of heaven forever. The Devil responds by raising up two beasts, one of the sea and one of the land, the former representing the political and military power of those opposed to the church and the latter representing rival religions. There is one last opportunity to repent, as an angel urges those who worship the beast to repent. In the next moment, God's wrath is poured out upon the earth and the 'great city Babylon' is destroyed, Babylon being the symbolic city of worldly cares and physical pleasures. Jesus then returns with a sword in his mouth and fire in his eyes, destroying the 'beasts' of temporal opposition. The Devil is then cast down into the bottomless pit for 1000 years, and set loose once again when the term expires. Then comes a final battle, a final judgment, those whose names are found in the 'book of life' will enter the new Jerusalem, and everyone else is cast into a lake of fire. "And I saw a new heaven and a new

343  Revelations 6:8.
344  Revelations 9:6.
345  Revelations 9:21.

earth; for the first heaven and the first earth were passed away ... and there shall be no more death, neither sorrow, nor crying, neither shall there be any more pain, for the former things are passed away."[346]

The arrival of the new Jerusalem is an absolute certainty, and yet the specific character of life in the City of God remains something of a mystery. Thus the need for an apocalypse, according to Origen: "He calls it 'revealing' (apocalypse), thus indicating that not everything that is and is present is seen."[347] No amount of prayer or scriptural analysis will ever allow one to comprehend fully the reality behind the reality. Augustine asks, "And we shall see all those things which we do not see now; but even now, because we believe, we imagine them, up to the poor capacity of our human minds; though our idea of them falls incomparably short of the reality."[348] Luther explains that "it isn't given to us here to know what the creation of the next world is like, for we can't fathom this first creation of the world and its creatures."[349] According to Origen, one can manage only a glimpse into the true reality that lies beyond, for "it is impossible to find the origin of God. ... for the last things cannot be related as they are. ... What we see — admitting that we do see something — are the things in between."[350]

In spite of human fallibility and the distortion of perception inherent to this false reality, certain aspects of the future life are clear to theologians. Most broadly, there will be endless ecstasy in the true reality to come. Augustine explains that "after the hardships of our anxieties and worries in this mortal state we shall be comforted like little children carried on the mother's shoulders and nursed in her lap. For that unaccustomed bliss will lift us up, untrained and immature as we are, and support us with tenderest caresses."[351] Origen focuses on the collective quality of the future life: "God gathers together the just, but the sinners he scatters ... punished by the fact that they cannot be with each other...."[352] There will be perfect transparency of thought among the righteous, and perfect uniformity of thought according to Augustine: "Since from many souls there is to be one City of those having one soul and one heart in regard to God, this perfection

---

346   Revelations 21:1-4.
347   Origen, *Spirit and Fire*, 320.
348   Augustine, *Concerning The City of God Against the Pagans*, trans. Henry Bettenson, intro. David Knowles (London: Penguin, 1972), 939.
349   Luther, *Works Vol. 54*, 297.
350   Origen, *Spirit and Fire*, 318.
351   Augustine, *The City of God*, Dods trans., 939.
352   Origen, *Spirit and Fire*, 334.

of our unity is to be after this peregrination, when the thoughts of all will not be hidden from one another nor in any way opposed to one another....."[353] There will be no deviant sex of any kind, as Tertullian explains that "adulterers and fornicators and the effeminate and sodomites will not possess the kingdom of God,"[354] and further that "we must conclude that those who wish to enter Paradise ought, at long last, to put an end to a way of life which is not found in paradise."[355]

In point of fact, there will be no sex of any kind in heaven. Physical incorruption and perfection will be universal,[356] thus the defects inherent to man's animal nature will be left behind with the resurrection. "And since to eat, drink, sleep, beget, pertain to the animal life ... it follows that they will not be in the resurrection," writes Aquinas.[357] Even the desire to have sex will disappear altogether, and this actually seems to be the prime attraction of heaven for many theologians. Augustine writes that "virginal integrity and freedom from all carnal relation through holy chastity is an angelic lot, and a foretaste in the corruptible flesh of perpetual incorruption."[358] There is no marriage in heaven, writes Tertullian, "no promise given Christians who have departed this life that on the day of their resurrection they will be restored once more to the married state. They will, it is clear, be changed to the state of holy angels. For this reason they will remain undisturbed by feelings of carnal jealousy."[359] Luther, articulating a minority position, once remarked that "in the future life we'll have enjoyment of every kind.... I don't believe that we shall all be of the same stature, and there will be no marriage; otherwise everybody will want to be a woman or a man."[360] Augustine, in contrast, explains that the preservation of sexes will be preserved in heaven, and that the vagina, once loathed and reviled, will now be celebrated: "The female members shall remain adapted not to the old uses, but to a new beauty, which, so far from

---

353 Augustine, *Treatises on Marriage*, 35.
354 Tertullian, *On Purity*, 98.
355 Tertullian, *Marriage and Remarriage*, 64.
356 Aquinas and Augustine both suggest that everyone will be resurrected in a state of perfection relative to their own genetic codes, at the moment they would have been their most physically perfect. Everyone will thus be resurrected as their 30-year-old selves. Aquinas, *Summa Theologica Vol. 2*, 965; Augustine, *City of God*, 838.
357 Aquinas, *Summa Theologica Vol. 2*, 967.
358 Augustine, *Treatises on Marriage*, 155.
359 Tertullian, *Marriage and Remarriage*, 11.
360 Luther, *Works Vol. 54*, 41.

provoking lust, now extinct, shall excite praise to the wisdom and clemency of God...."[361]

As noted previously, the totalitarian ideology is built up from a non-ideological system of thought, with a specific pattern of absorption, distortion, and addition. The process can be reversed. That is, ideological precepts can be developed by scholars in a given religion, those precepts can then be folded into the overall theoretical scheme of that religion and deemphasized, and then passed along as a matter of doctrine rather than embraced as a matter of psychological need. One then finds a totalitarian ideology, or at least the better part of it, sitting dormant within the overall doctrinal scheme of that religion. When sociological conditions mass-produce the anxieties discussed previously, the generation of a totalitarian ideology is largely a matter of emphasizing certain elements of the religious system over others. The totalitarian variant will require two major modifications, though. First, the battle between good and evil is brought onto the temporal plane, and becomes prescriptive rather than purely predictive. The apocalypse is to be brought about by men acting accord with a divine plan; one defeats evil rather than waiting for evil to be defeated. Second, some group is clearly identified as the agent of evil. This group will be associated with mortality and sexuality, deemed a threat to collective purity, and then targeted for destruction. We will observe this development twice, first in the First Crusade (1096-99), and later in the witch hunts of the early modern period (1450-1750).

## 3.2 Vapor Trail

**The First Crusade (1096-99) would** not traditionally be thought of as a totalitarian movement, but the commonalities with unquestionably totalitarian movements are many and glaring. It was preceded by a sociological milieu virtually identical to those of the totalitarian movements of the nineteenth and twentieth centuries, specifically a trend towards sexual liberalism against a strong background of sexual conservatism. This led in turn to a trend toward ideological thinking and sexual utopianism. All of the basic themes of the totalitarian ideology are adapted to fit Christian religious doctrine, and crusading millennialism is thus structurally identical to the totalitarian ideologies of the twentieth century. And like the totalitarians who followed centuries later, the crusaders designated an out-group whose

---

361   Augustine, *The City of God*, Dods trans., 839.

destruction became prerequisite to the manifestation of utopia, in this case the transformation of Jerusalem into Augustine's City of God.

## Sexual Atomism in 11ᵗʰ Century Europe

**In the years after the** fall of the Roman Empire, the fortunes of the Catholic Church vacillated with the political and military fortunes (and benevolence) of its sponsoring kingdoms. The Visigothic kingdom in Spain was the ecclesiastical favorite prior to its being overrun in the eighth century, at which point the Carolingian kingdom in Gaul became the citadel of the Catholic faith. Charlemagne converted much of continental Europe to Christianity by force of arms late in the eighth century, though his empire would be broken apart with the Partition of Verdun in 843. The rise and expansion of the Saxon Empire in the tenth century continued this imperial and evangelical campaign. The Empire united the duchies of Thuringia, Franconia, Swabia, Bavaria, Lotharingia, annexed Italy, and would later be referred to as the Holy Roman Empire. The Empire became the Church's official protector, though the emperor soon asserted his own right to appoint the pontiff and to extract oaths of loyalty prior to consecration.

Aside from ensuring its own physical security, the Church was especially interested in socializing people in its sexual mores during the Dark Ages. In the fifth and sixth centuries, Germanic marriage was a social arrangement with no legal status, entered into on a trial basis, terminable at will for the man, and occasionally polygamous if the man was wealthy enough to support multiple wives.[362] Men were generally free to do as they wished sexually regardless of marital status, though women were held to a strict code of monogamy. The Church's first attempts at reforming Germanic marriage involved the promotion of exogamy and monogamy, thus, according to David Herlihy, forcing "a freer, wider circulation of women throughout society. The poorer, less powerful male improved his chances of finding a mate."[363] The patterns that emerge in the early Middles Ages are those of uniformity in the character of the medieval family, and marriage becoming widespread to the point that the family becomes the core component of, and basic unit of measurement for,

---

362  James A. Brundage, *Law, Sex, and Christian Society in Medieval Europe* (Chicago: University of Chicago Press, 1987), 127-132.

363  David Herlihy, *Medieval Households* (Cambridge: Harvard University Press, 1985), 61.

the medieval community.[364] By the year 800, the family as 'coresidential descent group' emerged and began to exert a pull on the sexuality of its individual members: "The sexual foibles of each member," writes James Brundage, "reflected upon the whole family, and marriage was a matter of family policy, not of individual choice."[365]

The church supplemented family pressure with other attempts at normative reform. These were made primarily through the use of the penitential, a confessional manual listing sins and the corresponding penance for each. Sexual sins were the dominant category, as one might expect. Most of these sins related to intercourse between marital partners, and the level of detail regarding these specific sexual behaviors is quite striking. The penitentials covered impermissible intentions for sex, impermissible days of the week and year, and impermissible positions; they forbade nudity, fondling, and lewd kissing; they also specifically advised the couple to refrain from enjoying sex.[366] Whether the penitentials had any effect on sexual behavior is unclear, though there is speculation that many people were following the guidelines by the end of the tenth century.[367] The overall sexual climate of the Dark Ages seems to have been rather morbid and morose, appropriate perhaps for a society expecting the end of the world, though this is more or less what Europe was coming into the end of the first millennium.[368]

Of course, anyone seriously expecting or hoping for the apocalypse in or around the year 1000 would have been terribly disappointed. The eleventh century turned out to be a relatively tranquil period in western Europe, the threat to Christendom having been lessened substantially with the recent conversions of prominent Vikings and Magyars.[369] The second millennium C.E. would feature three major periods of population growth in Europe, the first of these lasting roughly from 1000 to 1250.[370] It was

---

364    Ibid., 62.

365    Brundage, *Law, Sex, and Christian Society*, 135.

366    Brundage, *Law, Sex, and Christian Society*, 152-69; G. Rattray Taylor, *Sex in History* (New York: Vanguard Press, 1954), 52-55.

367    Brundage, *Law, Sex, and Christian Society*, 160.

368    Though not, we are cautioned, necessarily fearing the end of the world. See generally Richard Landes, Andrew Gow, and David C. Van Meter ed., *The Apocalyptic Year 1000: Religious Expectation and Social Change, 950-1050* (Oxford: Oxford University Press, 2003).

369    James Reston, Jr., *The Last Apocalypse: Europe at the Year 1000 A.D.* (New York: Doubleday, 1998), 276-77.

370    Herlihy, 79.

during this time that Europe first began its urban development, most of its cities having been established by the year 1300.[371] The economy was becoming specialized, adding simple manufacturing to its agricultural base. Migration increased, as did trade in goods and ideas. An intellectual revival took place in Gaul, described by one scholar as the 'renaissance of the twelfth century'. The political culture of the cities was trending toward individualism, freedom, and self-rule.[372]

The new millennium also brought in dramatic changes in the characteristics of medieval sexuality, these changes stemming in part from a shift in the nature of inheritance and property rights. For landholding classes, the rule had been partible inheritance, with each family member having full ownership of some separate portion of the family estate. Partible inheritance meant a certain degree of independence for each heir, women included, though alienation of property by individual members fractured estates to the point where prominent families were dropping down into the lower classes.[373] The situation stabilized somewhat in the eleventh century with the adoption of impartible systems of estate ownership, such as the *frérèche* (joint ownership between brothers) and later primogeniture (full ownership vested in the eldest male heir).[374] This socioeconomic stability was had, however, at the expense of sexual stability. The *frérèche* system usually involved the designation of one brother as an estate manager, and limited marriage to this sibling and possibly one other.[375] Primogeniture similarly took young men out of the marriage pool by depriving them of any means of an independent subsistence.[376] In either case, young men were being converted into 'rootless adventurers' *en masse*, thus leaving their female counterparts with grim prospects for marriage as well.[377]

A lifetime of chastity, however, seems to have been the exception rather than the rule for men of the nobility. As James Brundage explains:

371 Paul M. Hohenberg and Lynn Hollen Lees, *The Making of Urban Europe 1000-1994* (Cambridge: Harvard University Press, 1995), 1.

372 John Boswell, *Christianity, Social Tolerance, and Homosexuality: Gay People in Western Europe from the Beginning of the Christian Era to the Fourteenth Century* (Chicago: University of Chicago Press, 1980), 208.

373 Frances Gies and Joseph Gies, *Marriage and Family in the Middle Ages* (New York: Harper and Row, 1987), 123-24.

374 Ibid., 124.

375 Ibid., 125.

376 Primogeniture rules would be circumvented by property-law innovations in the thirteenth and fourteenth centuries. Ibid., 188-89.

377 Gies and Gies 134; Duby 14.

They had sexual access to servant girls, peasant women, bastard daughters of their relatives, and staggering numbers of harlots. The more presentable and ambitious of these young men might also offer consolation, sexual and social, to widows, possibly in the hope of marrying into wealth. Daring or foolhardy young men sometimes became involved with married women as well. The idealized dalliance that modern scholars depict as innocent or platonic courtly love masks the more fleshly reality of sexual mores among young men of good families.[378]

The sexual standards of the lower classes were quite similar. Social and economic pressures forced many such men to remain unmarried. The women of these classes were often placed in a very difficult position, having no marketable skills and often lacking the connections to enter a convent.[379] The combination of population increase, urbanization, migration into cities, resulting anonymity and excess female population fueled a rapid growth in prostitution.[380] Western Europe seems also to have discovered erotic love, heterosexual and homosexual, sometime between the tenth and twelfth centuries.[381] According to historian John Boswell, "erotic passion -- which had been almost totally absent from Western literature since the fall of Rome -- suddenly became the subject of a large proportion of literature and seemingly the major preoccupation of feudal society."[382] The connection between erotic love and marriage was by no means self-evident to people of the time. As Georges Duby encapsulates the eroticism of the High Middle Ages, "fine amour was a game whose territory should not be that of obligations and debts, but that of carefree adventure."[383]

## Sexuality and the Rise of Christian Ideology

**During the same time period,** the Church was fighting to wrest jurisdiction over marriage away from secular authorities. It was during this period that the Church renewed its interest in canon law and brought marriage within

---

378  Brundage, *Law, Sex, and Christian Society*, 204-5.
379  Ibid.
380  Ibid., 211. The increase in prostitution led to a corresponding renewal of interest in Mary Magdalene and the rehabilitation of prostitutes.
381  Boswell, 208.
382  Ibid., 208-9.
383  Duby, 33.

the jurisdiction of ecclesiastical courts.[384] The institution as found at the time was designed primarily to consolidate property rights and political power. Marriages were arranged at a very early age by family members,[385] tended to be endogamous, and might subsequently be rearranged where a more advantageous union could be found.[386] For ecclesiastical officials, controlling sexuality was the primary objective, and marriage was desirable only to the extent that it was instrumental to that objective.[387] This 'lesser evil' approach designated marriage the only legally protected sexual union, and mandated that the union be monogamous, indissoluble, and freely contracted by parties in permitted categories.[388] A marriage thus contracted was not to be construed as a license to enjoy sex, and church officials were adamant that a couple's only thought during intercourse should be procreation.[389] The campaign for ecclesiastical control of marriage met with an increasing level of popular acceptance and even changes in attitudes regarding the sexual behavior of the laity.[390] By the year 1100, canonical courts had sole jurisdiction over marriage.

The eleventh century also witnessed a revitalization of the debate on clerical marriage, concubinage, and celibacy. Church policy on the contours of clerical marriage fluctuated throughout the early middle ages, though the basic normative prescriptions presented at the Councils of Nicea and Elvira (a priest should abstain from his wife) were a constant in Catholic

---

384   Brundage, *Law, Sex, and Christian Society*, 180; Duby 15.
385   Duby, 26.
386   Duby, 37. Marriages could also be contracted secretly and casually, and the church would endeavor to eliminate both possibilities. Brundage, *Law, Sex, and Christian Society*, 189.
387   Duby 10.
388   Brundage, 183. Gratian's *Decretum* initially proposed that the essential elements of marriage were consent and sexual union, though the view ultimately adopted was that of Peter Lombard's *Sentences* which required only consent. The problem with Gratian's approach was that it could not account for the marriage of Mary and Joseph which, the critics insisted, was both legitimate and asexual. Penny S. Gold, "The Marriage of Mary and Joseph in the Twelfth-Century Ideology of Marriage," in *Sexual Practices & the Medieval Church*, Vern L. Bullough & James A. Brundage ed. (Buffalo: Prometheus Books, 1982), 102-117.
389   Brundage, 182, 199; Duby 10. Those incapable of procreation could be divorced and denied the right to remarry. Brundage, 202.
390   Brundage, 184; Gies and Gies, 134.

doctrine.[391] Nevertheless, clerical marriage continued unabated into the tenth century, a period when the majority of rural priests were married and many urban priests were raising children with their wives.[392] In 1049, Pope Leo IX initiated an era of official reform when he anathematized married clergy and condemned them to damnation.[393] Pro-conjugal elements reacted violently, and Leo was forced to turn back during a trip to Mantau when his army was attacked by forces loyal to the local bishop. Anti-conjugal elements returned the favor soon after, driving married clergy out of Milan by force in 1056-57.[394] In 1054, one Cardinal Humbert traveled to Constantinople as a papal legate and informed the eastern church that priestly marriage was heretical. Humbert also informed them that there was no room for compromise, anathematized the entire eastern church, and, for good measure, excommunicated its ruler.[395] For these and other reasons, the eastern and western churches separated in the Great Schism of 1054.[396] For anyone who still found the western church too undisciplined and worldly, a whole series of ascetic and eremitical orders were springing up in order to provide men with yet a further escape.[397]

The campaign to separate clerics from their wives and lovers was justified partly in terms of the economic impact (i.e., diversion of church property, inheritance rights of children), and also in part on the idea that marriage engendered loyalties that prevented total devotion to the Church. The primary reason for some, however, was the need to keep the physicality of Christ free from the pollution of sex, or in Peter Damian's formulation, "the hands that touch the body and blood of Christ must not have touched

---

391  On the sporadic attempts to eliminate clerical sexuality in the interim, see Brundage, 150-52.

392  Anne Llewellyn Barstow, *Married Priests and the Reforming Papacy: The Eleventh Century Debates* (New York: E. Mellen Press, 1982), 37.

393  Ibid., 53.

394  Brundage, 216.

395  Barstow, 54; Uta Ranke-Heinemann, *Eunuchs for the Kingdom of Heaven: Women, Sexuality, and the Catholic Church*, trans. Peter Heinegg (New York: Doubleday, 1990), 107.

396  Ibid.

397  Jean Richard, *The Crusades 1071-1291*, trans. Jean Birrell (Cambridge: Cambridge University Press, 1999), 9. The trend continued well into the twelfth century, by which time the Cluniacs, Carthusians, Cistercians, and the Military Orders, the Templars and Hospitallers, were all going concerns. Giles Constable, *The Reformation of the Twelfth Century* (Cambridge: Cambridge University Press, 1996), 49.

the genitals of a whore...."[398] This notion of the preservation of Christ's purity through clerical purity formed the leitmotif of Pope Gregory VII's attack on clerical sexuality.[399] At the Synod of Mainz in 1074, he declared that all priests would have to take a vow of celibacy before being admitted to orders, and instructed the laity not to attend services of priests living with women. Gregory distinguished himself less in the originality of his thought and more in the fanatical enforcement of these ascetic measures, threatening and even excommunicating those who defied him.[400] Canon law still allowed for the ordination of married men and a priest could still contract a marriage at the cost of his position, though marriage and priesthood would be made mutually exclusive at the Second Lateran Council of 1139.[401] Yet even in Gregory's time, the notion of clerical celibacy was gaining some measure of popular acceptance.[402]

The period was also marked by a renewal of interest in the precise origin of the Virgin Mary's purity.[403] Leading Mariologists such as St. Anselm of Canterbury insisted that Mary was born with original sin and purified by God later, for "his Mother's purity, by which he is pure, was only from him, whereas he was pure through and from himself."[404] A student of St. Anselm's named Eadmer put forward the first detailed theory of the Immaculate Conception, which held that Mary was conceived sexually, though free of original sin by divine exception.[405] Popular devotion to Mary was on the rise as well, and increasingly she came to be seen as an intercessor who might facilitate salvation where Christ alone would not grant it.[406] The Virgin Mary was also beginning her long association with crusading and violence, "which was to be a particular characteristic of devotion to her in the central Middle Ages," according to Jonathan Riley-Smith.[407]

---

398   Barstow, 59-60.
399   Ibid., 70.
400   Ibid., 67-75.
401   Ranke-Heinemann, 108-110.
402   Barstow, 76.
403   One author sets the 'Golden Age of Mariology' in this century. Hilda Graef, *Mary: A History of Doctrine and Devotion Vol. 1* (New York: Sheed and Ward, 1963), 210.
404   Ibid., 210-11.
405   Graef, 218.
406   Ibid., 217-18.
407   Jonathan Riley-Smith, *The First Crusade and the Idea of Crusading* (London: Athlone, 1986), 104.

Mary's power of virginal childbirth, along with the virginity of her child, formed part of the *casus belli* for the crusade again Cathar heretics in southern France in the beginning of the thirteenth century. Catharism was a dualist modification of Christianity equating the material world with hell and the spiritual world with heaven.[408] The objective was to escape this physical reality altogether, and sexual relations resulting in conception, thus bringing new souls into the physical world, were as evil as sex for pleasure if not more so. The specific doctrines varied somewhat, but Catharism generally held that Jesus Christ had never assumed physical form, that the Virgin Birth was therefore an illusion, and/or that Christ had taken Mary Magdalene as his concubine.[409] The Roman Catholic Church's military campaign against this particular heresy lasted from June of 1209 until the fall of the Cathar stronghold at Montségur in March of 1244. It was during the initial campaign of 1209 that the crusading army stormed the city of Béziers, killing perhaps fifteen or twenty thousand people, regardless of age, sex, or religious affiliation.[410] It was here that Arnold Amaury was supposed to have uttered the immortal words, "Kill them all. God will know his own."[411] In his *Historia Albigensis*, Peter of les Vaux-de-Cernay deemed it fitting that the massacre took place on a day dedicated to Mary Magdalene, "that these shameless dogs should be captured and destroyed on the feast day of the woman they had so insulted and whose church they had defiled with the blood of their lord...."[412]

## Origins of the First Crusade

**Sexuality, though, had already become** a justification for violence by the time of the First Crusade in 1096. Christianity found a highly aggressive rival in the religion of Islam, which, from the seventh century to the tenth,

408 Walter L. Wakenfield, *Heresy, Crusade, and Inquisition in Southern France 1100-1250* (Berkeley: University of California Press, 1974), 27-30.

409 Zoe Oldenbourg, *Massacre at Montségur: A History of the Albigensian Crusade* (New York: Wiedenfeld and Nicholson, 1962), 37.

410 Stephen O'Shea, *The Perfect Heresy: The Revolutionary Life and Death of the Medieval Cathars* (New York: Walker and Co., 2000), 86.

411 There is some controversy as to whether Amaury actually made the infamous comment, though he certainly embraced the sentiment. In a letter to Pope Innocent III, he later explained that "nearly twenty-thousand of the citizens were put to the sword, regardless of age or sex. The workings of divine vengeance have been wondrous." O'Shea, 87.

412 Peter of les Vaux-de-Cernay, *Historia Albigensis*, ed. trans. W.A. and M.D. Sibly (Woodbridge: Boydell Press, 1998), 51.

had conquered several expansive regions around the Mediterranean and taken control of the city of Jerusalem. Islam, even more so than Christianity, was divided internally, with the Sunnite-controlled Abbasid caliphate in Baghdad and the Shi'ite-controlled Fatimid caliphate based in Cairo. In 1055, the Abbasid caliphate was taken over by the Seldjuk Turks, whose imperial ambitions soon led them to invade the eastern regions of the Byzantine Empire as well. The reign of Seldjuk sultan Malik Shah, which lasted from 1077 until 1092, oversaw the expulsion of Byzantium from Anatolia and even threatened Constantinople itself.

The possibility of European Christendom offering a united response was limited by a number of factors. There was, first and foremost, the split between eastern and western churches. The aforementioned sex-reformer Gregory VII had hoped to arrange an expedition against the Seldjuks, then backed out in 1078 when his attempts to arrange a marriage between a Byzantine princess and Norman ruler fell through in a palace coup. Gregory, keeping up a tradition, excommunicated the new ruler. The Church and the Holy Roman Empire were at odds over the appointment of church officials by secular authorities (the Investiture Contest), and the excommunication of Emperor Henry VI who had installed his own personal pope in Ravenna. In keeping with the western church's newfound obsession with moral rigorism, King Phillip I of Gaul was excommunicated in 1094 for abandoning his wife. Europe's rulers were, meanwhile, going to war with one another with regularity for purely temporal reasons. Apparently no one in the west was thinking in terms of fighting a defensive war against Islam.

In any case, Christendom had in fact little reason to go to war for Jerusalem specifically, and its interest, once aroused at the end of the eleventh century, was based on ideological rather than strategic considerations. One of the major themes of crusade ideology was the increasing difficulties encountered by Christians, whether pilgrim or resident, in the Holy Land. While Jerusalem and its environs were under Islamic control, pilgrimages to the city continued up until the time of the First Crusade. In 1064-65, an expedition led by four German bishops came under attack from forces unknown in Palestine, though the group was then rescued by the emir of Ramla.[413] There seems to have been very little in the way of institutional persecution of Christians living in Muslim-

---

413   Richard, 18.

controlled territories,[414] excepting Jerusalem under the reign of the 'mad caliph' Hakim. Hakim achieved notoriety with the destruction of the Holy Sepulchre in 1009, though no calls for a crusade were issued even then. Historian Hans Eberhard Mayer points out that no call for help ever came from the Christians living in Islamic territories.[415]

In terms of proximate cause, the holy war for Jerusalem seems to have been initiated inadvertently by the strategic designs of Byzantine emperor Alexius Comnenus. Alexius had taken the throne of Byzantium by force in 1081, thus joining his predecessor in excommunication by order of Gregory VII. Unlike his predecessors, Alexius proved to be a highly capable military commander, turning back an assault by Norman invaders in 1081 as an encore to his conquest of Constantinople. In 1091, Petchenegs allied with the Seldjuks attacked Byzantium and never fully recovered from the defeat. The Seldjuk empire broke apart under its own weight with the death of Malik Shah in 1092, and Alexius negotiated a peace treaty with the relevant remainder that same year. His position temporarily solidified, he set out to reorganize the Byzantine army with an eye toward retaking Anatolia. Western mercenaries had been a key variable in Byzantium's military equation for some time, and Alexius considered an influx essential for his present purposes.

In Rome, the diplomatically-adept Urban II had acceded to the papacy in 1088. In 1089, he sent a delegation to Alexius to lift the sentence of excommunication and to discuss reconciliation. Friendly relations thus established, Alexius sent a delegation to Urban's council on church reform at Piacenza in March of 1095. The delegates there painted the picture of an eastern church under severe and constant threat, and, for maximum propaganda effect, apprised the council of the 'desperate' situation of Christians in Jerusalem. By August, Urban had made the decision to call for military intervention in the east, his concern for Jerusalem being subject to doubt. Cold logic and self-interest might have brought him to the same decision, with the prevalence of internecine warfare in Europe creating an effectively cost-free opportunity to acquire political capital with the eastern church. One author notes Urban's 'cool and calculating' character,[416] while another finds it impossible to believe that a man of his background could

414 Ibid., 21.
415 Hans Eberhard Mayer, *The Crusades*, trans. John Gillingham (Oxford: Oxford University Press, 1988, 2d ed.), 6.
416 H.E.J. Cowdrey, *The Cluniacs and the Gregorian Reform* (Oxford: Clarendon Press, 1970), 174.

have preached the crusade to Jerusalem without being caught up in the 'spiritual' side of it.[417] Whatever his specific intentions, at Clermont that November, to a crowd so large that the sermon had to be given in a nearby field, Urban called for a war of liberation in the east.[418] Those assembled erupted with a chant of *Deus lo volt*— God wills it.

Among those in attendance at the sermon was Guibert of Nogent, born in Clermont some forty years earlier.[419] He never set foot outside of France, but did go on to provide one of the literary accounts of the First Crusade early in the twelfth century. He also produced an autobiography, one modeled on Augustine's *Confessions*, with an even darker tone. He writes, for example, that the consummation of his parents' marriage was initially prevented by an evil spell which lasted seven years before being broken. His mother's chastity was preserved by the grace of God during that period, and Guibert wonders whether it wouldn't have been better if she had continued to remain chaste considering the evil son (himself) to whom she gave birth.[420] He recalls the evil thoughts and deeds of his youth, and they include disliking school and church, playing with friends, and sleeping in. He does occasionally condemn himself for lust and desire, though he connects them directly to poetry rather than to women of flesh and blood.[421] His self-descriptions frequently involve the words filth or filthy, occasionally substituting words like wretched and repulsive. Apart from the direct attacks upon his own person, he informs God at one point that what he wants "is to be made by you, not by myself."[422]

Guibert seems to have been destined for a monastic lifestyle from the moment he was born. Complications during his mother's labor had led his family to promise the Virgin Mary that Guibert's life would be dedicated to the service of God if he survived, and he would eventually be elected abbot of Nogent in 1104.[423] Guibert found monasticism prevalent in ancient times and relatively rare in his own, concluding that the world was in a state of

---

417  Riley-Smith, *The First Crusade,* 21-22.
418  Riley-Smith notes that 'liberation' was the word Urban used most frequently when supplying a rationale for the crusade. Ibid., 17.
419  Guibert of Nogent, *A Monk's Confession: The Memoirs of Guibert of Nogent,* trans. intro. Paul J. Archambault (University Park: Pennsylvania State University Press, 1996).
420  Ibid., 38.
421  Ibid., 59.
422  Ibid., 70.
423  Ibid., 104.

decline.[424] Even those who did take vows were not, he supposed, motivated by a heartfelt hatred of sin. Outside of the monastery, the sexuality of the laity was seemingly breaking down all boundaries and subject to little or no earthly restraint. "Nobody is despised for flaunting love affairs before your face…. In this and in other similar ways," he writes, "the modern world corrupts and is corrupted, pouring its evil ideas upon some, while the filth spreads to infinity like a hideous epidemic."[425] In particular, he observed that female chastity and modesty had all but disappeared within his mother's lifetime.[426] For the most part, Guibert eschews the generalized misogyny typical of Christian theologians, yet his descriptions of female contemporaries tend to be unflattering and focused on sexual indiscretions.

## Crusading Millennialism

**Guibert's interpretation of the sermon** at Clermont places heavy emphasis on the eschatological implications of a war for Jerusalem. The crusade, as Guibert has Urban conjecturing, may very well be the hand of God setting the stage for the final battle between good and evil.[427] The time of the Antichrist was coming, though prophecy stated that he would arrive in Jerusalem, attack Christians, and kill the Christian kings of Egypt, Africa, and Ethiopia. Obviously this could not take place unless Christianity was reestablished in those regions. Guibert also cites scripture which states that "Jerusalem will be trodden down by Gentiles [heathens], until the time of the nations will be fulfilled." He interprets 'time of nations' to mean either the period wherein the heathens "ruled at will over the Christians, and for their own pleasures have wallowed in the troughs of every kind of filth,"[428] or the moment before Israel is saved, when unspecified nations will join the faith. Guibert explains that the second interpretation is less important than the first, if not irrelevant altogether. The crusade, as he envisions it, is simultaneously a war of historical motion and a war of purification, "to cleanse the holiness of the city and the glory of the tomb, which has been polluted by the thick crowd of pagans…."[429]

---

424  Ibid., 24-29.
425  Ibid., 36-37.
426  Ibid., 36.
427  Guibert de Nogent, *Gesta Dei per Francos*, trans. Robert Levine (Woodbridge: Boydell Press, 1997), 43-44.
428  Ibid., 44.
429  Guibert, *Gesta Dei*, 43. Jean Richard notes that Islam was generally seen as a simplistic pagan heresy involving idol worship, and only rarely as anything

As for the pagan heresy at issue, Guibert developed an interesting theory on the nature of the Islamic faith, which, he explains, is partly sexual in its origin and predominately sexual in its object.[430] As the story goes, the death of an unnamed Alexandrian patriarch was followed by a deadlock on the question of successor. A majority of church officials were willing to support a nearby hermit until they visited him and discovered his anti-Catholic views. The disappointed hermit was then approached by the Devil, who informed him that great power could still be achieved through careful manipulation of one of his recent visitors. The young visitor's name was Mahomet, and his legend begins with an arranged marriage to a wealthy widow, convinced by the hermit that she was marrying a prophet. "And since the vessel of a single bed frequently received their sexual exchanges," explains Guibert, "the famous prophet contracted the disease of epilepsy...."[431] His subsequent epileptic fits were then mistaken for symptoms of divine visitation and his status as a prophet confirmed. With financial backing from his wife and guidance from the Devil, he began to preach a return to pagan heresy, denying Christ's divinity and challenging prevailing notions of sexual morality.

The new heresy swept across the eastern lands, masquerading as a religion and deceiving those of 'uncertain mind' according to Guibert. The effects were terrible: "As though sent from the sky, the new license for random copulation was propagated everywhere, and the more the supply of permitted filth increased, the more the grace of a God who permitted more lenient times ... was preached."[432] Guibert seems to be referring to a provision of Islamic law allowing a man to take multiple wives when he writes that "the greater opportunity to fulfill lust, and, going beyond the appetites of beasts, by resorting to multiple whores, was cloaked by the excuse of procreating children."[433] He also refers to Islamic sexual practices 'unknown even to animals' which he refuses even to discuss, though homosexuality is most likely what he has in mind. He notes also that the prospect of sexual depravity was deliberately held out for recruiting purposes, and that the technique was a great success.[434] As for the prophet

---

resembling a coherent structure of political and religious thought. Richard, 23.
430   Guibert, *Gesta Dei*, 32-36.
431   Ibid., 33.
432   Ibid., 34.
433   Ibid., 34-35.
434   Ibid., 34.

himself, he suffered an epileptic seizure one day and was devoured by pigs, "so that the master of filth appropriately died a filthy death."[435]

With Guibert, one has little trouble connecting up self-hatred with sexuality and the need for an all-encompassing theory of human destiny.[436] Whether Guibert is representative of any substantial portion of those who actually went on the First Crusade is still an open question, though the social dynamics of the era suggest an affirmative answer. During the Dark Ages, Europe undergoes a shift towards a static and deindividualized, though also highly inclusive, system of marriage, with the sexual act depleasured to whatever extent possible. During the eleventh century, this system begins to break apart as western society initiates a transition to an era of romantic love and 'carefree adventure', meaning individual freedom in the erotic realm. The same century brings in a massive campaign of ecclesiastical asceticism, marital reform, intolerance, violence, and, subtending all of the above, deindividualization.

More specifically, deindividualization was sought through an ideological system which shifted sexuality out of the Christian body and onto rival 'entities', thus allowing it to be destroyed outright. Several historians have noted a marked increase in attention given to boundaries and definitions during the eleventh and twelfth centuries, especially as they involved attempts to divide those of the true faith from unbelievers. R.I. Moore finds patterns in the emergence of perceived threats from multiple and apparently unrelated groups, specifically heretics, Jews, and lepers. Aside from chronological similarities, in each case the threat is some form of contagion which must be dealt with through the physical expulsion or extermination of the group member.[437] As Moore writes:

> The coincidence is too great to be credible. That three entirely distinct groups of people, characterized respectively by religious conviction, physical condition, and race and culture, should all have begun at the same time and by the same stages to pose the same threats, which must be dealt

---

435  Ibid., 35.
436  On even a superficial level, one may note that Guibert uses the word filth in reference to Muslims, sexuality, and himself in the singular, and that the elimination of filth is at the center of his destructive worldview.
437  R.I. Moore, *The Formation of a Persecuting Society: Power and Deviance in Western Europe, 950-1250* (Oxford: Basil Blackwell, 1987), 67. To a lesser extent, homosexuals and prostitutes also fit the pattern during this period, for reasons that will be made clear below. Ibid., 91-97.

with in the same ways, is a proposition too absurd to be taken seriously. The alternative must be that the explanation lies not with the victims but with the persecutors.[438]

Caroline Walker Bynum seconds the notion, arguing that the development of theories on heresy represented "less a quarrel with a clearly existent 'other' than a process by which groups defined themselves through the creation of an 'other'."[439] For the first time since the fall of the Roman Empire, the church began to enforce orthodoxy and silence those who challenged its doctrines.[440] This was accompanied in the eleventh century by a sudden resurgence of interest in Augustine's notion of justified warfare.[441] It was also during this era that western society came to institutionalize the punishment and extermination of people based solely on their membership in groups.[442]

Sexuality, mortality, and ideology formed overlapping lines of demarcation in this respect. Vern Bullough notes that sexuality and heresy became virtually synonymous during this period, as in "a person who engaged in forbidden kinds of sexual pleasure must be a heretic - and a heretic must engage in 'deviant' sexual activity."[443] Guibert, writing in 1114 about the persecution of heretics at Soissons, described their sexual habits as follows:

> They condemn marriage and the procreation of offspring; and indeed, wherever they are scattered throughout the Latin world one might see men living with women without taking the name of husband and wife. Nor do men and women confine themselves to the same partner: men are known to sleep with other men, women with women, for they hold intercourse of man and woman to be a crime. They eliminate any offspring issuing from their intercourse. They hold meetings in underground

---

438  Moore, 67.

439  Caroline Walker Bynum, *The Resurrection of the Body in Western Christianity, 200-1336* (New York: Columbia University Press, 1995), 215.

440  Moore, 11-27.

441  Riley-Smith, *The First Crusade*, 27.

442  Moore, 5.

443  Vern L. Bullough, "Postscript: Heresy, Witchcraft, and Sexuality", in *Sexual Practices & the Medieval Church* , Vern L. Bullough & James Brundage ed. (Buffalo: Prometheus Books, 1982), 206. Boswell notes that heretics were frequently accused of engaging in 'sodomy', heterosexual or homosexual, in spite of the fact that heretical movements were often composed of people who found Catholicism insufficiently ascetic. Boswell, 283-86.

vaults or hidden cellars, without distinction of sex. They light candles and come forward to present them from behind to a young girl who, it is reported, lies in a prone position having bared her buttocks for all to see. Soon the candles are extinguished, they shout "Chaos!" from all sides and everyone has intercourse with the first person who happens to be at hand.[444]

This seems to have been the classic heretical sex fantasy of the Middle Ages; a virtually identical version of it shows up in the *Errores Gazariorum* written in 1437, with witches standing in for dualist heretics.[445] Sexuality was viewed not simply as a behavioral phenomenon but as a virus, and a highly contagious one at that according to Moore.[446] As he continues, "The analogy between heresy and leprosy is used with great regularity and in great detail by twelfth-century writers. Heresy spreads like leprosy ... infecting the limbs of Christ as it goes."[447] Both heresy and leprosy are spread through the air by the poisoned breath of the carrier, but, it was assumed, most effectively as a virus transmitted through the seminal fluid.[448] The 'virus' was sin, and those hospitals treating the disease dealt with it primarily as a moral affliction.[449] Women were considered a prime vector of transmission, with twelfth century propagandists alleging that heretics were specifically targeting them for conversion.[450] Christian prohibitions on religious intermarriage had been on the books for some time, but the passion for strict enforcement was very much an eleventh-century invention.[451] According to David Nirenberg, "Between the eleventh and fourteenth centuries, canon lawyers elaborated an extensive literature on the impermissibility, not just of marriage, but of any sexual contact between Christian and non-Christian...."[452]

444  Guibert, *A Monk's Confession*, 196.
445  Alan Charles Kors and Edward Peters ed., *Witchcraft in Europe 400-1700: A Documentary History* (Philadelphia: University of Pennsylvania Press, 1998, 2d ed.), 160-61.
446  Moore, 100.
447  Ibid., 63.
448  Moore, 63; see also Peter Lewis Allen, *The Wages of Sin: Sex and Disease, Past and Present* (Chicago: University of Chicago Press, 2000), 34.
449  Allen, 26-32.
450  Bynum, 216.
451  David Nirenberg, *Communities of Violence: Persecution of Minorities in the Middle Ages* (Princeton: Princeton University Press, 1998), 130-31.
452  Ibid., 131.

The core concepts of the First Crusade fit comfortably within the same basic theoretical model. The idea of Islam as a kind of biological pollutant or contagion appears in various versions of Urban's sermon at Clermont. Baldric of Dol's Urban refers to the shedding of Christian blood and the "unspeakable degradation" of Christian flesh, and then notes that Jerusalem "has been reduced to the pollution of paganism...."[453] Robert the Monk refers to the beloved race of the Franks and the accursed race of the Persians, accusing the latter of destroying and defiling altars, circumcising Christians, and then pouring the blood into baptismal fonts.[454] His version of Urban's call to arms: "Let the Holy Sepulchre of the Lord, our Savior, which is possessed by unclean nations, especially move you, and likewise the holy places, which are now treated with ignominy and irreverently polluted with filthiness."[455] Fulcher's Urban has the purity of the crusaders on his mind, lamenting "people who are ignorant and panting with desire after the wantonness of the world ... rotten with sins", wondering also that "if one has dirty hands, how will he be able to wipe the filth off another one defiled?"[456] In exchange for their services, the crusaders would be purified of their pre-existing sins through papal indulgences, which, to a large extent, would have meant purification of sexual sins specifically.[457] Much of the theoretical groundwork for the crusade had already been developed by the Cluniac Order, a monastic order developed out of revulsion for all things sexual and seeking collective purity through asceticism.[458]

The specific threat Islam presented to Christianity was inevitably

453 August Krey ed. trans., *The First Crusade: Accounts of Eye-witnesses and Participants* (Gloucester: Peter Smith, 1958), 33.
454 Ibid., 30.
455 Ibid., 31.
456 Fulcher of Chartres, "Historia Hierosolymitana", in *The First Crusade: The Chronicle of Fulcher of Chartres and Other Source Materials*, ed. Edward Peters (Philadelphia: University of Pennsylvania Press, 1971), 28.
457 James A. Brundage, "Prostitution, Miscegenation, & Sexual Purity in the First Crusade," in *Crusade and Settlement*, ed. Peter W. Edbury (Cardiff: University College Cardiff Press, 1985), 57.
458 On the sexual theory of Odo of Cluny, see Raffaello Morghen, "Monastic Reform and Spirituality", in *Cluniac Monasticism in the Central Middle Ages*, ed. Noreen Hunt (London: Macmillan, 1971), 23-24; the Cluniacs were proponents of holy war in general and pilgrimage to Jerusalem, which were combined to form the concept of the armed pilgrimage or crusade as it has come to be known. H.E.J. Cowdrey, 180-87. Urban II began his career as a member of the order. Thomas Asbridge, *The First Crusade: A New History* (Oxford: Oxford University Press, 2004), 10-11.

sexual in nature. Crusade chronicles described Muslims as sexually depraved and especially interested in taking advantage of virtuous Christian women.[459] Nor were they particularly interested in preserving the virtues of their own women, according to the crusade chronicle of Raymond D'Aguilers, for "they placed youths in brothels and exchanged their sisters for wine for more lewdness."[460] One particularly effective piece of crusade propaganda was a forged letter, supposedly from Alexius requesting help from Count Robert of Flanders, which detailed the deviant character of sexuality in Middle East.[461] In his *Gesta Dei per Francos*, Guibert includes part of the letter which accuses Muslims of converting cathedrals into brothels, forcing virginal Christian girls to become prostitutes, and then raping their mothers in front of them.[462] This, according to the letter, is where things become particularly objectionable. It seems the women were insufficient to satisfy the men and they soon turned to homosexuality, "this urgent lust, worse than any insanity anywhere, which perpetually flees wisdom and modesty, and is enkindled more powerfully the more it is quenched...."[463]

Thus the collective metaphysics of the crusade, the biological threat posed by rival systems of thought, and the sexual character of the threat are all present and even prominent in crusade propaganda. Other ideological elements are turn up as well. An emphasis on singularity of thought ('so that the crusaders were of one heart and mind') runs throughout the crusade chronicles.[464] The unifying force was love of God and love of one's

---

459   Ibid., 60. As late as the Fifth Crusade, propagandist James of Vitry described Islamic sexuality in the following terms: "Sunk, dead, buried in obscene desire, pursuing like animals the lusts of the flesh, they can resist no vices but are miserably enslaved to and ruled by carnal passions, often without even being roused by desire; they consider it meritorious to stimulate the most sordid desires." Boswell, 281.

460   Raymond D'Aguilers, *Historia Francorum Qui Ceperunt Iherusalem*, trans. John Hugh Hill and Laurita L. Hill (Philadelphia: American Philosophical Society, 1968), 109.

461   Boswell, 279-80.

462   Guibert, *Gesta Dei*, 37.

463   Ibid., 37.

464   Fulcher, for example, wrote that "we who were diverse in languages, nevertheless seemed to be brothers in the love of God and very close to being of one mind." Fulcher, 49. Guibert asks "what is it that drives a whole community unless it is that simplicity and unity which compels the hearts of so many people to desire one and the same thing?" Guibert, *Gesta Dei*, 29.

fellow Christians,[465] though as Riley-Smith points out, "Love of neighbor was always treated in crusade propaganda in terms of fraternal love for fellow-Christians, never in terms of love shown for enemies as well as friends."[466] This love was in turn linked to a highly suspect rationalization of violence in the name of God and revenge on his behalf.[467] Beyond mere agent, the crusader is an instrument of God's will, and is therefore endowed with a kind of derivative omnipotence in the execution of holy orders.[468] Reality is in never allowed to intrude, disbelief is not to be tolerated, and while every victory proves that the power of God is behind the crusade, every failure merely proves the sinful nature of crusaders.[469] According to the chroniclers, the only possibility of failure on crusade lies in the power of the human will to separate from the will of God.

This separation of wills is designated the cause of every military setback and reversal on the crusade, and the source of this separation is typically sexual. As James Brundage writes:

> The vast majority of notices concerning women in the records of the First Crusade deal with the sexual temptations that they posed for male crusaders and the lamentable frequency with which the men yielded. ... The lesson was plain: the crusaders were assured of victory in this life and salvation in the next, but only so long as they avoided carnal sins.[470]

---

465 Crusade chronicles point approvingly to the tearful farewells of women left behind, and in some cases the complete absence of concern for family members on the part of the crusaders. Guibert, *Gesta Dei*, 29, 63; Fulcher, 37-38.

466 Jonathan Riley-Smith, "Crusading as an Act of Love", in Thomas Madden ed., *The Crusades: The Essential Readings* (Oxford: Blackwell, 2002), 41.

467 James A. Brundage, *The Crusades: A Documentary Survey* (Milwaukee: Marquette University Press, 1962), 2-3; note also Raymond D'Aguilers, referring to the crusades "launched in the name of vengeance against those who desecrated the land of Christ's nativity and His apostles...." D'Aguilers, 113.

468 On divine inspiration and intervention, see Jonathan Riley-Smith, *The First Crusaders 1095-1137* (Cambridge: 1997) 63, 73. Raymond D'Aguilers argues that 12,000 crusaders successfully routed 60,000 enemy combatants at Jerusalem, thus proving that "all affairs, be they great or small, undertaken in the Lord's name will succeed...." D'Aguilers, 125.

469 From a crusader's vision relayed by Raymond D'Aguilers: "Then I asked, 'What shall we do with the doubters?' The Lord answered: 'Show them no mercy, kill them; they are My betrayers, brothers of Judas Iscariot." D'Aguilers, 95.

470 Brundage, "Prostitution, Miscegenation, and Sexual Purity ", 58.

Islamic women, or 'filthy pagan women' as the chroniclers called them, appear with the specific intention of seducing the crusaders, thus rendering them combat ineffective. Desexualized Christian women occasionally turn up to offer logistical support, though at certain points, women are actually expelled from the crusader camps altogether to eliminate the possibility of sex.

The one major ideological element conspicuous for its near-absence in crusade chronicles is the intent to transform reality itself, to bring forth the City of God, through military conquest.[471] Of course, the chroniclers were working with the benefit of hindsight, the conquest of Jerusalem having yielded only temporal benefits as they completed their drafts. Contemporary historians assure us that millenarianism was very much a part of the motivation for the First Crusade. According to Jean Richard, "the announcement of this great journey with Jerusalem as its goal led large numbers of people to believe that if they reached it they would actually be present at the Second Coming of Christ."[472] Mayer notes also that the crusaders never developed a plan for the administration of Jerusalem prior to conquering the city, as if they weren't really sure they were going to have to do anything with it once they had taken control of it.[473] Riley-Smith finds eleventh-century Christian attitudes toward Jerusalem 'obsessive', though he adds the qualifier that millenarian 'hysteria' was probably limited to a handful of crusaders.[474]

## The First Crusade

**When he called for a** crusade, Urban envisioned a professional military operation, led by regional nobility and nominally under the control of the Western church.[475] It seems, though, that Urban was not the only one preaching a crusade to Jerusalem, either before or after the sermon at

---

471  Fulcher does cite the rejection of the 'beauties and pleasures of the world' and the 'desire after the wantoness of the world' as an appropriate motivation for the crusader. Fulcher, 24, 28.

472  Richard, 27.

473  Mayer, 61.

474  "Milleniarianism was certainly a subject of discussion, as is demonstrated by contemporary references to the Muslims as attendants of Antichrist and a number of allusions to the Last Days and to signs and portents of them, but the evidence is not copious enough for us to suppose that eschatological ideas were widespread." Riley-Smith, *The First Crusade*, 35.

475  Urban specifically advised women, the old, and the sick to stay home.

Clermont. Popular evangelists like Peter the Hermit were already traveling the countryside, energizing the masses with the thought of reclaiming the Holy Land. One result was the Popular Crusade of 1096, a somewhat disorganized campaign which ended up terrorizing the European countryside instead of Asia Minor. It seems that a number of these crusaders found it difficult to understand why they should travel so far to kill foreign unbelievers when there were perfectly good unbelievers to kill at home. Jews in the Rhineland suffered terribly from the campaign of Emicho of Leiningen, in what is sometimes referred to as the 'First Holocaust'. It is interesting to note that the slaughter of Jews at Mainz involved attempts by the crusaders to convert the wounded, and at Moers some were forcibly baptized rather killed.[476] Here, conversion was preferable to extermination,[477] though the principle failed to hold relative to Muslims.[478] Emicho himself never had the chance to put any principle into practice in the Holy Land, his contingent offering the Hungarians a sampling of the same treatment and being routed and dispersed in response. The other major contingent of the Popular Crusade led by Walter Sans-Avoir made it to and through Constantinople, this time being slaughtered by the Turks at Xerigordon in October of 1096. Only Peter the Hermit and a handful of others survived.

The professional or Seigneurial Crusade, meanwhile, was just beginning to take shape at this point. Urban named Adhemar, Bishop of Puy, to act as papal legate to the crusade. Adhemar accompanied the largest contingent, led by Count Raymond of Toulouse, whose objective was to demonstrate the will of God at work in the affairs of men. Bohemund of Taranto apparently had more worldly objectives in mind; he had to order his army to lift an ongoing siege of Amalfi so he could take them on the crusade. Another army of Lorrainers, northern Frenchmen, and Germans, was led by Duke Godfrey of Bouillon and his brother Baldwin of Boulogne, both of whom would eventually sit on the throne of Jerusalem. Three armies set out together, led by Count Robert II of Flanders, Duke Robert of Normandy, and Count Stephen of Blois. The first contingent to arrive in Constantinople was a smaller one led by Count Hugh of Vermandois, followed by that of Duke Godfrey in December of 1096. Bohemund reached Constantinople in early April of 1097, with Count Raymond

---

476  Robert Chazan, *European Jewry and the First Crusade* (Berkeley: University of California Press, 1987), 71, 74.

477  Chazan, 75; Richard, 39.

478  On the near-complete absence of forced conversion in Asia Minor, see Riley-Smith, *The First Crusade*, 110-11.

arriving at the end of the same month. By the time Duke Robert and Count Stephen arrived in May of 1097, the crusading armies had all reached Constantinople, though this is not to say that they were all in Constantinople at the time.

Instead of the manageable group of mercenaries for which he had hoped, Alexius found himself confronted with wave after wave of heavily-armed fanatics washing up onto the shores of his city. Anna Comnena, Alexius' daughter, would later write that "the race of Gauls is not only very passionate and impetuous in other ways, but, also, when urged on by an impulse, cannot thereafter be checked."[479] Alexius had begun to fear an assault on Constantinople itself, and perhaps with good reason given that one of the crusading nobles (Bohemund) had previously gone to war with the Byzantine Empire. He developed a four-part strategy for dealing with the armies, which involved restricting them to the suburbs of Constantinople, allowing only leaders and a handful of others to enter the city, extracting oaths that territories previously belonging to Byzantium would be restored to the empire as they were liberated from the Turks, and lastly encouraging them to cross the Bosporus quickly rather than waiting near Constantinople for all the armies to assemble. The strategy netted him few friends among the crusaders, but did manage to get rid of them without any major incidents.

The crusading armies came together for the first time at the siege of Nicea. The city was ruled by a sultan named Kilij Arslan, who happened to be fighting elsewhere when the attack began on May 14. Unable to reenter his city when he returned, he was forced to engage the crusaders head-on and then quickly forced to retreat. Orderic Vitalis would later write that, "As they fought they were pure in character, active in body, and stout-hearted. Mindful of their souls' salvation, they renounced all the illicit desires and delights of the flesh."[480] In spite of this widespread anhedonia, the city itself proved a more intractable foe, its location on the shore of a lake initially offering a safe route in and out of the city. Byzantine naval forces were called in to effect a blockade, which demoralized the residents of Nicea enough so that they were willing to surrender the city. The

---

479   Krey, 71. Crusade chronicler Peter Tudebode also mentions a 'wave of religious fervor' sweeping through Gaul prior to the crusade. Peter Tudebode, *Historia de Hierosolymitano Itinere,* trans. intro. John Hugh Hill and Laurita L. Hill (Philadelphia: American Philosophical Society, 1974), 15.

480   Orderic Vitalis, *Ecclesiastical Histories Vol. 5,* ed. trans. Marjorie Chibnall (Oxford: Clarendon Press, 1975), 55.

surrender, however, was offered not to the crusaders but to Alexius, who forbade the crusaders to enter Nicea with the city now returned to the Byzantine Empire. Some compensation was offered in lieu of plunder, but the crusaders remained disappointed. Guibert speculated that the distribution of gifts only to the very rich and very poor had bred resentment, but Peter Tudebode suggested that it was because the unjust and deceptive emperor let the Turks get away without any physical harm having been done to them.

The siege of Nicea lasted only a few weeks, and the crusaders quickly turned their attention to the next major objective, which was the city of Antioch. The march through Anatolia would take four months altogether, but it took only a few days before a division of the army led by Bohemund came into contact with Kilij Arslan's army at Dorylaeum. Sex, we learn from Fulcher of Chartres, is one of the reasons that this division was caught alone and outnumbered: "It was evident that this had befallen us because of our sins. For dissipation had polluted certain ones, and avarice or some other iniquity had corrupted others."[481] The crusade had been intended to be a male affair, though one contemporaneous estimate put the number of women on crusade at several thousand. Wives, prostitutes, and women of intermediate dispositions all made the journey, much to the dismay of those who feared divine retribution for sexual intercourse. To counteract the effects of this rampant licentiousness, a quick prayer and confession of sins followed that night, and reinforcements led by Godfrey de Bouillon and Raymond of Toulouse arrived the next day. The Turks were routed, and the victory was attributed to belief in God and in the Son of God born to a virgin mother.

The crusading armies again divided and headed south, arriving in Antioch in October of 1097. The former Roman metropolis was surrounded by a massive wall, bordered by a small mountain-range, and defended by 400 towers, thus presenting the crusaders with the prospect of an extended encounter. Raymond of Toulouse proposed storming the city immediately, though the idea was rejected in favor of a traditional siege. The surrounding areas were initially well-stocked with food, and initial engagements with enemy forces from both inside and outside the city went in favor of the crusaders. As the months wore on, though, supplies ran low and optimism faded in the absence of an apparent endgame. As the difficulties began to mount, issues of sex came to the fore once again. According to Guibert:

---

481   Fulcher, 46.

In the course of this siege the strength of Christian law flourished greatly, and, if anyone was convicted of a crime, he submitted to the severe judgment of the leaders of the army. Moreover, sexual crimes were punished with particular severity, and this was just. Those who were surrounded by atrocious deprivations, who seemed to be exposed to the swords of the enemy every day, if God were not protecting them, should not have been at the mercy of lustful thoughts. And how could pleasure enter where the fear of death was ceaselessly present? So it happened that merely speaking of a prostitute or of a brothel was considered intolerable, and they feared dying beneath the swords of the pagans if they committed such a crime.[482]

One incident involving a monk and his mistress was noted in at least two crusade accounts; the two were reportedly forced to walk around the army naked while being beaten.[483] At some point, even the temptation to have sex was eliminated. According to Fulcher, "After holding council, they drove out the women from the army, both married and unmarried, lest they, stained by the defilement of dissipation, displease the Lord."[484] All of the women, including the wives of crusaders, were sent to live in nearby camps.[485] Raymond D'Aguilers noted also that "we hope that our account of the shamelessness of our army will bring neither blame nor anger of God's servants against us, because really God on the one hand brought adulterous and pillaging crusaders to repentance and on the other cheered our army in Hispania."[486]

The siege of Antioch continued into the next year with neither side able to accomplish anything militarily significant. The crusaders were becoming demoralized and desertions were occurring as early as January of 1098. Only in March was a full blockade completed, and in the end it took help from the inside to conquer the city. At some point, Bohemund had made contact with a Turkish captain named Firouz who controlled three of the city's towers. It seems that the captain was willing to give the crusaders an opening into the city, though Bohemund was first determined to extract promises from the other leaders of the crusade that the city

---

482   Guibert, *Gesta Dei*, 88-89.
483   Brundage, "Prostitution, Miscegenation, and Sexual Purity", 61.
484   Fulcher, 54.
485   Brundage, "Prostitution, Miscegenation, and Sexual Purity," 59.
486   D'Aguilers, 15.

would be his if taken. In May, word came that Kerbogha of Mosul was bringing a massive army to relieve Antioch. The threat of being caught out in the open led Raymond to promise the city to Bohemund rather than honor a similar promise to Alexius. Early in the morning on June 3, 1098, under cover of darkness, Firouz let Bohemund and his knights into the city and the rest of the Latin army followed soon after. As they stormed the city, the crusaders killed everyone within reach, whether man, woman, or child. Some of Antioch's residents managed to reach the citadel which still held out, and others managed to escape the city altogether. The chronicles, however, would later describe streets overflowing with bodies.

The crusaders had hardly finished taking the city when Kerbogha's army arrived, leaving them trapped in a city with little food and a citadel still resisting. The situation easily could have been much worse. Fortunately for the crusaders at Antioch, Kerbogha had wasted three weeks besieging crusaders at Edessa, and had narrowly missed an opportunity to catch the rest of the army out in the open. Good fortune is a relative concept of course, and sex, Fulcher contends, is the only reason Kerbogha arrived at all. "Seeing this army, the Franks were more desolate than ever, because punishment for their sins was doubled. For when they had entered the city, many of them had sought out unlawful women without delay."[487] The crusaders lost another contingent when Stephen of Blois, who had ventured outside the city, made a discreet return and saw the size of Kerbogha's army. Stephen's wife was thought to have been displeased to see him when he returned to France, though Guibert suggests that even a coward is still to be preferred over someone engaging in the pursuit of pleasure.[488] As it happens, Kerbogha was supposed to have been something of an authority in that area. The crusade chronicles have him decidedly unimpressed with his opposition upon arrival, and telling his men to "give yourselves up to pleasures: in greater security than that to which you are accustomed, eat the finest foods; lie with multitudes of wives and concubines to propagate the race, so that the increasing number of sons may oppose the Christians… ."[489]

---

487   Fulcher, 60.
488   Guibert, *Gesta Dei*, 104.
489   Guibert, *Gesta Dei*, 96. Tudebode recalls the instruction as, "Have a good time, carouse and gourmandize … Let everyone indulge in lascivious luxury and again rejoice over siring many sons who will fight valiantly against the Christians." Tudebode, 68. The anonymous *Gesta Francorum* has the instruc-tion as "all men shall give themselves up to wantonness and lust…." *Gesta*

The Dark Heart of Utopia

Kerbogha's morale problems begin with the arrival of his mother, an apparently fictionalized character who is intended to provide independent confirmation of the veracity of the Christian ideological system. Guibert, injecting some anti-individualism, has her telling her son that "you rightly despise them as individuals, but you should know for a fact that the authority of the Christian religion is superior."[490] The Christian army is no match for her son but for the protection of God, "whose power is everywhere to be feared" she explains.[491] Kerbogha's mother is a pagan as is he, but she has somehow obtained Christian scripture foretelling the inevitable dominance of the Christian religion, and explains to her son that this scripture is confirmed in the Koran as well. She attempts to dissuade Kerbogha from engaging the crusader army, though to no avail.

Inside Antioch, meanwhile, the crusaders were having visions of their own. In this manner, Fulcher's thesis about the connection between sex and the protection of God receives independent confirmation. The *Gesta Francorum* has Jesus telling a priest named Stephen, "Behold, I gave you timely help and put you safe and sound into the city of Antioch, but you are satisfying your filthy lusts both with Christians and with loose pagan women, so that a great stench goes up to Heaven."[492] The Virgin Mary and St. Peter intervene on behalf of the crusaders, and Jesus then explains that if the crusaders return to him (i.e., take an oath, presumably involving chastity), he would return to them and send help of some kind. A second vision was offered to Peter Bartholomew by St. Andrew, who informed him that the Holy Lance that had pierced the side of Christ was buried in the Church of St. Peter. The floor of the church was dug up a few days later, and a lance was discovered buried in the ground. Holy Lance No. 1 was already sitting in a collection in Constantinople when Holy Lance No. 2 was found in Antioch, and some were incredulous. Nevertheless, morale was raised for the army as a whole, and the crusaders were now determined to break out of the blockade.

The determinative battle for Antioch took place on June 28, 1098, with Bohemund handing Kerbogha a decisive defeat. Most of the successes of

---

Francorum et Aliorum Hierosolimitanorum, ed. trans. Rosalind Hill (London: Thomas Nelson and Sons, 1962), 52.

490    Guibert, *Gesta Dei*, 96.

491    *Gesta Francorum*, 56.

492    *Gesta Francorum*, 58. Guibert only mentions sexual relations with 'filthy pagan women' in this context, noting cryptically that the crusaders had behaved badly toward Christians. Guibert, *Gesta Dei*, 100.

the First Crusade can be attributed to Islamic disunity and disorganization, and both were in evidence on this day. Kerbogha proved an inferior tactician to Bohemund and a contingent of his army from Damascus, already offended at the inclusion of a rival contingent from Aleppo, fled the battlefield in fear of their lives. The aftermath of the battle offers a few more clues as to the character of the crusade. According to Guibert:

> ...young women came with quivers full of arrows, looking like a new form of ancient Diana; they seem to have been brought here not to fight, but rather to reproduce. When the battle was over, those who were present asserted that new-born babies, born by women brought for this purpose on the expedition, were found thrown into the grass by these women, who, in their urgent flight from the Franks, could not endure the burden, and, more concerned for themselves than for the babies, heartlessly cast them away.[493]

This seems a particularly harsh judgment considering the ensuing display of chivalry described by Fulcher: "When their women were found in the tents, the Franks did nothing evil to them except pierce their bellies with lances."[494]

In a rare display of civility, Bohemund later allowed those still trapped in Antioch's citadel to convert to Christianity or leave the city in safety. With Antioch now firmly under crusader control, Jerusalem was the only major objective left to be taken. The journey south to Palestine was relatively uneventful, with the siege of Antioch convincing a number of local rulers to pay the crusaders off as they came through. The Fatimids had taken control of Palestine in 1098, which left the Seldjuk emirs with little reason to fight. The Fatimids were still trying to negotiate a settlement with the crusaders that would keep them from entering Palestine, which, notes Mayer, "shows how little the Muslims were able to understand what the crusade was all about."[495] The crusaders crossed into Palestine in May and to within sight of Jerusalem by June 7. The city's defenses left few points of vulnerability, and the Fatimid governor had expelled the Christian inhabitants and poisoned the local wells. Jerusalem was no Antioch, however. The attack began on June 13 and ended July 15, when Godfrey

---

493    Guibert, *Gesta Dei*, 103.
494    Fulcher, 64.
495    Mayer, 54.

managed to position his siege castle next to the wall of the city, allowing his knights to climb over and open the gates.

Once inside Jerusalem, the crusaders attempted to surpass their own death-dealing performance at Antioch. The inhabitants were exterminated as fast as they could be found, regardless of age, sex, or religion, "Nor did they spare ... even those pleading for mercy," according to Fulcher.[496] A large number took refuge in the Temple of Solomon which the crusaders promptly stormed, though some portion of this group was initially spared and left alive on the roof of the temple. Apparently unsatisfied, the crusaders returned the next morning and killed the rest of the survivors. According to Orderic Vitalis, "They pursued and slaughtered them with such hate because they had polluted the Temple of God and the church of the Holy Sepulchre, and had appropriated the Temple of Solomon and other churches for their own sacrilegious cult, desecrating them blasphemously."[497] Fulcher adds that "if you had been there your feet would have been stained up to the ankles with the blood of the slain. ... Not one of them was allowed to live. They did not spare the women and children."[498] It does seem that some of them were allowed to live just long enough to pile up the bodies of their fellow Muslims and then burn them. The sight of the bonfires left quite an impression on Tudebode: "Has anyone ever seen or heard of such a holocaust of infidels? God alone knows the number for no one else does."[499] A celebration was held soon after, marking the occasion of Jerusalem's newly restored purity. "Cleansed from the contagion of the heathen inhabiting it at one time or another, so long contaminated by their superstition," wrote Fulcher, "it was restored to its former rank by those believing and trusting in [God]."[500] Raymond D'Aguilers, in one of the more disturbing passages to be found in the crusade chronicles, writes that "Jerusalem was now littered with bodies and stained with blood.... A new day, new gladness, new and everlasting happiness, and the fulfillment of our toil and love brought forth new words and songs for all."[501]

Jerusalem's newly-restored purity would last a total of 88 years. In July of 1187, forces under the command of Syrian-Egyptian overlord Saladin annihilated the bulk of the Latin army at Hattin. In the months that

496   Fulcher, 78.
497   Vitalis, 173.
498   Fulcher, 77.
499   Tudebode, 120.
500   Fulcher, 78-79.
501   D'Aguilers, 128.

followed, Saladin marched through Syria and Palestine, conquering one town after another without significant opposition. In September, he turned his attention to Jerusalem. Given the dearth of armed defenders, residents attempted to defend the city by shaving the heads of their daughters, and then forcing them to undress and take cold baths in public. The tactic was unsuccessful and the city capitulated after a two-week siege. Richard Coeur de Lion led the massive Third Crusade in an unsuccessful attempt to recover the city, though some coastal areas were reclaimed. In 1204, the leaders of the Fourth Crusade, for reasons unknown, decided to forego the long trip to Jerusalem and to sack Constantinople instead. The Fifth Crusade was launched in 1217, with the crusaders taking control of Damietta in 1219, only to lose it again in 1221.

The character of the crusade shifted over time, from the mass movements of the eleventh and twelfth centuries to the thirteenth-century *passagium*, a seasonal influx of knights serving limited tours of crusading duty.[502] The Military Orders, the Knights Templar and Hospitallers, both maintained a presence in the Latin Kingdom as well. Yet as the fanaticism of the twelfth century faded, the western presence in Asia Minor became increasingly difficult to maintain. Frederick II led a crusade in 1228-29, which ended up by simply negotiating for control of Jerusalem, now stripped of all its defenses and featuring a Muslim section. The city was overrun and lost permanently in 1244, prompting yet another failed crusade in 1249-50 courtesy of St. Louis. Pope Gregory X called for plans for a crusade in 1272-74, and seems to have received more criticism than volunteers in response. The Mameluks began conquering portions of the Holy Land soon after, and when Acre fell in 1291, the Latin Kingdom was brought to an end. The 'crusades' of the fourteenth century were primarily defensive wars fought to repel Ottoman advances in Anatolia and the Balkans; Jerusalem was by now more or less forgotten as an object of conquest. The crusading impulse seems to fade away as the sexual environment becomes more static and stifling and during the thirteenth and fourteenth centuries. Christianity begins its next major ideological phase in the relatively open and dynamic sexual environment of the fifteenth century, with a new objective, new methodology, new out-group, and structurally-identical rationale.

---

502   Mayer, 219-220.

# 3.3 Burn This Mother Down

**If the crusades were something** like a comet, a large, single entity streaming across the sky every so often, the great 'witch-craze' of the early modern era was more in the nature of a meteor shower. There were sporadic flare-ups and burnouts, an outbreak in one town and then another followed by another, yet with virtually all of them following a single broad trajectory. The craze took place roughly from 1450-1750, with an especially violent period coming in the century from 1560-1660. Conservative estimates put the number of dead at 100,000, the vast majority of these women, with less reliable estimates going as high as 9,000,000. The campaign was carried out with such fanatical intensity and willful disregard for the truth that the term 'witch-hunt' is now idiomatic for "an intensive effort to discover and expose disloyalty, subversion, dishonesty, or the like, usually based on slight, doubtful, or irrelevant evidence."[503] That the idiom is apposite so frequently does itself suggest the potential benefit of a comparative approach in this area.

The basic inquiry is generally framed in terms of whether the ideas supporting the craze represent propaganda developed specifically to justify repression, or are merely a continuation of the sincerely-held superstitions of an irrational age. The answer is neither, and in actuality what we find is an ideological system of thought built out of the superstitions of the time. The system is predicated on a set of beliefs lacking a rational foundation, yet it is also irrational in very precise ways owing to the patterns of logic intersecting with its mythology. It is, for example, one thing to believe that witches exist, and quite another to believe in the validity of evidentiary principles and procedures that allow only for proof of guilt and nothing in the way of exculpatory evidence.[504] As in, a woman who fails to cry during torture is a witch, and a woman who does cry is probably a witch faking

---

503   *Webster's Encyclopedic Unabridged Dictionary* (San Diego: Thunder Bay Press, 2001).

504   Most contemporary critiques of the witch-hunting campaign, courtesy of men like Johann Weyer, Reginald Scot, and Friedrich Spee, were directed at the legal procedures employed in the witch hunts rather than the underlying belief in witches. Spee, writing anonymously in 1631, explained that for an accused witch, "it is never possible to clear herself by withstanding [torture] and thus to wash away the aspersion of crime, as is the intention of the laws. It would be a disgrace to her examiners if when once arrested she should thus go free. Guilty must she be, by fair means or foul, whom they have once but thrown into bonds." Friedrich Spee, "Cautio Criminalis", in *Witchcraft in Europe,*

tears.[505] This system was designed by the intellectual elite of the time, and its illogical character is by no means accidental. It is designed specifically to resist rational criticism, and, failing that, to support the elimination of critics. The great sixteenth century jurist, philosopher, and demonologist Jean Bodin explained that his witch-hunting treatise was written:

> partly to respond to those who in printed books try to save witches by every means, so that it seems Satan has inspired them and drawn them to his line in order to publish these fine books. One was Pietro d'Abano, a doctor who tried to teach that there are no spirits; it turned out later that he was one of the greatest witches in Italy.[506]

One is either with the witches or the witch-hunters in the early modern period, and any deviation from the general line puts one squarely in the first category.

## The Foundations of Demonology

**There is a lengthy evolution** to the set of beliefs that eventually provided the substance for witch-hunting ideology, and its ultimate ideological refinement does look considerably different from its pre-Christian origins. The one constant in witchcraft belief from the time of the Roman Empire up through the eighteenth century was the power of witchcraft to produce effects in the physical world. Yet from the time of the Roman Empire up through the Dark Ages, punishment was reserved specifically for the commission of physical harm through witchcraft, or *maleficium* as it came to be known.[507] Maleficium is still a component part of witchcraft indictments in the early modern era, but it is no longer the only reason or even the most important reason to prosecute someone for witchcraft. Prosecutions are now based on the theory of demonology, which posits a vast conspiracy of witches

---

*400-1700: A Documentary History,* ed. Alan Charles Kors and Edward Peters, (Philadelphia: University of Pennsylvania Press, 2001), 428.

505  Henry Boguet, *An Examen of Witches* (United States: John Rodker, 1929 [1590]), 121.

506  Jean Bodin, *On the Demon-Mania of Witches,* trans. Randy A. Scott, intro. Jonathan L. Pearl, (Toronto: Center for Reformation and Renaissance Studies, 1995 [1581]), 37.

507  Jeffrey Burton Russell, *Witchcraft in the Middle Ages* (Ithaca: Cornell University Press, 1972), 55.

bent on world domination and the destruction of the Christian faith.[508] The individual witch is of no consequence here, depersonalized,[509] her inevitable extermination less in the nature of a punishment and more in the nature of a 'cleansing operation'.[510] The specific character of the threat she and her fellow conspirators pose is both sexual and collective; it is an assault on the reproductive capacities of Christians effected by sexually depraved and demonically inspired women who intend to outbreed them.

The ideological modification is laid over an intermediate stage in the evolution of witchcraft theory known as diabolism. In the Medieval Christian imagination, diabolism is a conspiratorial form of witchcraft, complete with demonic invocation, group sex, ritual sacrifice, and flight through the air to secret locations where all of this would take place. Certain aspects of diabolism were adapted from pagan mythology, most notably the night flights of worshippers of the goddess Diana. During the early Middle Ages, as Christianity was first spreading across Europe, the Church assimilated elements of pagan mythology into its own belief system rather than attempt to destroy them outright. Doctrinal difficulties were resolved with a syllogism asserting that all supernatural powers are ultimately vested in God or in the Devil, God is never subject to human compulsion, and hence the supernatural powers of humans are always derived from the Devil.[511] In this manner, pagan mythology was translated into devil worship and heresy, though heresy was then treated with considerable leniency. Charlemagne specifically forbade the burning of suspected witches in the eighth century, condemning it as a pagan custom.[512] The first executions of heretics in the Middle Ages do not take place until early in the eleventh century, and the practice remained a rarity for some time even after the precedent had been set.[513]

---

508   Richard Kieckhefer, *European Witch Trials: Their Foundations in Popular and Learned Culture, 1300-1500* (Berkeley: University of California Press, 1976), 6.
509   Ibid., 76.
510   Christina Larner, *Enemies of God: The Witch-Hunt in Scotland,* intro. Norman Cohn (Baltimore: Johns Hopkins University Press, 1981), 8.
511   Russell, 46. The represents a more official position on the nature of magic. A popular distinction between white (beneficial) and black (demonic or harmful) magic did hold up in places as late as the early modern period.
512   Trevor-Roper, 92.
513   Norman Cohn, *Europe's Inner Demons: An Enquiry Inspired by the Great Witch-Hunt* (New York: Basic Books, 1975), 18, 22. Russell notes also that "usually

This general absence of urgency in the early and high Middle Ages was accompanied by a degree of skepticism as to essential elements of early modern demonology. The *Canon Episcopi*, issued around the turn of the ninth century, specifically denied the reality of night flights even as it called for officials to expel witches from their parishes.[514] The massive nighttime congregations of witches described later in the sixteenth century would have been particularly implausible without the power of air travel, and they do not appear to have played a role in witchcraft theory at this point in time. In the eleventh century, though, the classic heretical sex fantasy of the Middle Ages emerges in roughly the same time and place as the Church begins to execute heretics.[515] Sorcery, heresy, and sex orgies are here beginning their long association with one another, and it is here that the basic template for diabolism is first formed.[516] Yet whether the Church was persecuting Reformists, Cathars, or Waldensians, allegations of sorcery were generally added onto charges of heresy leveled against actual, existing heretical sects. Diabolism had not yet come into its own as a form of heretical conspiracy.

Prosecutions for specific acts of witchcraft were very rare during the high Middle Ages, in part because the accusatorial system of criminal law still predominated. Under this system, ordinary citizens were expected not only to bring the complaint but to conduct the entire prosecution themselves. Failure to obtain a conviction exposed the accusing party to severe penalties, and the difficulty in proving *maleficium* would have acted as a serious deterrent for potential accusers.[517] The rise of the inquisitorial system early in the thirteenth century brought criminal investigation and adjudication under the control of the church, opening the door for widespread persecution under the aegis of ecclesiastical law. Conrad of Marburg was appointed official inquisitor of Germany in 1231, and immediately set about terrorizing his jurisdiction with a Stalinist system of denunciations and executions.[518] After a brief reign of terror, Conrad was murdered in 1233, bringing relief to

---

heretics were corrected and reprimanded many times before receiving even the lightest punishment." Russell, 71.

514    Ibid., 76.

515    Cohn, 21. The very first was in Orleans in 1022.

516    Russell, 95.

517    Cohn, 160-63.

518    Conrad's investigative technique was to accuse people of heresy, threaten them with immediate execution if they failed to recant, and then extort the names of other 'heretics' as a condition of release. His acolytes let it be known that they "would gladly burn a hundred, if just one among them were guilty." Ibid., 26.

The Dark Heart of Utopia

potential suspects and alarmed church officials alike. One exception was Pope Gregory IX, who subsequently issued a proclamation on the secret meetings of heretics (*Vox in Rama*), basing his conclusions on Conrad's investigations. He describes a congregation led by the Devil, initiates being forced to kiss the Devil on the mouth or anus (perhaps depending on which animal form he has assumed), a ceremony with a short liturgy followed by the extinguishing of lights, and then a bisexual orgy. The classic heretical sex fantasy of the Middle Ages, expanded to include ritual sex with the Devil, now had papal legitimacy.[519]

As of the fourteenth century, prosecutions for witchcraft become a steady occurrence, though not necessarily due to a growing fear of witchcraft itself. Many of the witchcraft trials of the early fourteenth century appear to have been motivated in part or in whole by political considerations.[520] Invocation of the devil appears only sporadically in these trials, and diabolism even less frequently.[521] Even the casting of spells does not seem to have been a major concern during this period.

A significant shift in intensity occurs at the end of the Middle Ages, evidenced in both an increase in witchcraft trials and in the quantity of ideological literature devoted to the subject.[522] The rate of witch trials in Europe held fairly constant from 1300 until 1430, averaging around six trials per five-year period and never exceeding twelve in any such period.[523] A slight increase during the 1430s leads into a significant increase in witchcraft trials in the second half of the century, with the period from 1455-59 witnessing thirty-nine witch trials and the period from 1480-84 featuring forty-two. This upsurge in judicial activity corresponds roughly to a proliferation of texts on the subject of witch-hunting beginning in 1420s and 30s.[524] This quantitative shift corresponds in turn with a new evolutionary phase in witchcraft theory, with the emphasis shifted to diabolism and diabolism taking on a more distinctly sexual character. This shift takes place

---

519   Cohn, 30-31; Russell, 145.
520   Kieckhefer, 13-14; Russell, 194. The most obvious example would be the trial of the Knights Templar, prosecuted for witchcraft by King Phillip IV from 1305 to 1314.
521   Kieckhefer, 14; Russell, 194.
522   Kieckhefer, 18.
523   A graph showing the frequency of witchcraft trials during this period is included in Kieckhefer, 11.
524   Russell, 233.

roughly during the half-century around 1400,[525] at which point the theological literature begins, according to historian Richard Kieckhefer, to "set forth all the elements of diabolism in great, pornographic detail."[526] The diabolic conspiracy also seems to be growing in size. According to C. Eric Midlefort, "The late Middle Ages did indeed make two fundamental contributions to the witch hunt, notably the idea that all magic involved a pact with the devil, and the idea that a massive, organized witch cult threatened Christendom."[527]

If the fifteenth century was more receptive to theories of diabolism than previous centuries, it did not exhibit the mass hysteria that would characterize the witch hunts of the centuries to follow. The inquisitors of this period were often frustrated in their efforts by authorities, secular and ecclesiastical, who were either disinterested in or actively opposed to the campaign. Two of the most notorious witch hunters of all time, Dominicans Heinrich Kramer and Jacob Sprenger, were forced out of Innsbruck by the local bishop mid-prosecution.[528] In their time off, they penned the *Malleus Maleficarum* (Hammer of Witches), a fully worked-up ideological system of witchcraft theory complete with legal procedures, reality-proofing, and seemingly endless discussions of demonic sexual practices. First published in 1487, the *Malleus* turned out to be enormously popular, undergoing thirty-five printings altogether during the witch hunts and thirteen by the year 1520.[529] It was largely a summation and systematization of fifteenth century ideas about witchcraft, though it featured one very important innovation. For the first time ever, a witch-hunting treatise declared that witches were predominately female.[530] And not at all for the first time ever, a witch-

---

525 Kieckhefer, 18; Russell, 199. In the period from 1384-90, two women were prosecuted for actually following Diana on a nighttime ride, a sign that even the limited skepticism of the Canon Episcopi had faded out. Cohn, 217-28.

526 Kieckhefer, 22.

527 C. Eric Midelfort, *Witch Hunting in Southwestern Germany 1562-1684: The Social and Intellectual Foundations* (Stanford: Stanford University Press, 1972), 20.

528 Sigrid Brauner, *Fearless Wives and Frightened Shrews: The Construction of the Witch in Early Modern Germany*, ed. intro. Robert H. Brown, fwd. Sarah Lennox (Amherst: University of Massachusetts Press, 1995), 7.

529 The Malleus does not seem to have been reprinted between 1520 and 1563, which Brauner suspects is due to the high number of copies in circulation by 1520. Brauner, 11, 32.

530 Brauner, 31. Sprenger and Kramer seem to have part of a broader trend at the end of the 15th century, though for exceptions see Monter, 23-24.

hunting treatise declared that witches were sexually depraved. Kramer in particular was convinced that the giveaway for these women was promiscuity, and this, according to Sigrid Brauner, is what led to his expulsion from Innsbruck: "Kramer based his case against [Helena Scheuberin] primarily on her sexual behavior. During her initial interrogation, he asked such detailed questions about her sex life that the bishop's representative was appalled and ordered him to stop."[531]

Coming out of the fifteenth century, the fires of demonology had been lit but were not yet burning out of control. There is a lull early in the sixteenth century, a kind of dormant phase when the energy and desire for transformation were perhaps being channeled into the Reformation and Counter-Reformation. Neither movement had any significant reservations about prevailing theories of witchcraft, though both seem to have inadvertently dampened the enthusiasm for prosecution. The explosion of witch trials in the early modern period comes only as the Counter-Reformation winds down early in the 1560s. As Hugh Trevor-Roper describes the emergence of demonology:

> All of Christendom, it seems, is at the mercy of these horrifying creatures. Countries in which they had previously been unknown are now suddenly found to be swarming with them, and the closer we look, the more of them we find. All contemporary observers agree that they are multiplying at an incredible rate. They have acquired powers hitherto unknown, a complex international organization and social habits of indecent sophistication.[532]

Where the fifteenth century witch-hunter often found himself a distinctly unwelcome individual, the sixteenth and seventeenth century demonologist found virtually no obstructions to his homicidal ambitions.

With regard to these men, E. William Monter writes that "if we examine their biographies, we find that the writers were men of exemplary erudition and blameless lives, the upright voices of conventional wisdom and common sense, certainly not 'fanatics'."[533] That is, aside from setting innocent women on fire they were honorable, decent men, the pillars of their communities, beyond reproach. Which is to say that they differ in no

---

531    Brauner, 46.
532    Trevor-Roper, 93.
533    E. William Monter, *Witchcraft in France and Switzerland: The Borderlands During the Reformation* (Ithaca: Cornell University Press, 1976), 35.

way from other prominent totalitarians, being men of moderate to high intelligence, obsessed with sexual matters, possessed of a curious inability to apply simple rules of logic, and unexceptional in behavior outside of their ideological framework. Their destructive impulses are the product of selflessness, as demonologist Nicholas Remy assures his readers, and their expression therefore moral.[534]

## European Sexuality in the 15th and 16th Centuries

**The evolution of demonology finds** a close parallel in the evolution of European sexuality during the same period. For example, we find heretical diabolism first beginning to emerge in the eleventh and twelfth centuries, relatively unstable periods sexually, though crusading millennialism was the dominant ideological system of the time. The crusades take on a distinctly pragmatic character in the late thirteenth and fourteenth centuries, precisely the same time witchcraft theory is being put primarily to political use. The sexual dynamics of western society are largely static and repressive during these two centuries, with John Boswell describing them as "ages of less tolerance, adventurousness, acceptance - epochs in which European societies seem to have been bent on restraining, contracting, protecting, limiting, and excluding."[535] Similarly, James Brundage explains that "this was an age not of innovation but of consolidation and refinement in the canon law about sex. Canonists during the late thirteenth and early fourteenth centuries were far more concerned with enforcing the existing sex laws of the Church than with creating new law."[536] This stasis begins to break apart in the fifteenth century, a period of relative freedom and tolerance in sexual matters, at the same time as diabolism is evolving into demonology. Demonology is ascendant by the second half of the sixteenth century, with the ideological system coming as part of a much broader social reaction against the sexual freedom of the time. We can trace this shift from stability and repression to instability and freedom, and then to sexophobic reaction, in several different areas.

Clerical celibacy seems never to have taken hold in practice during the Middle Ages, though the Gregorian reforms of the eleventh century still

534 Nicholas Remy, *Demonolatry*, trans. E.A. Ashwin (New York: Barnes and Noble, 1970)[1595], 128.
535 John Boswell, 271.
536 James A. Brundage, *Law, Sex, and Christian Society in Medieval Europe* (Chicago: University of Chicago Press, 1987), 419.

reflected the church's position in principle. Occasional complaints were raised over concubinage during the thirteenth and fourteenth centuries, and clerics living in sin were liable to suspension if caught by some particularly intrepid reformer.[537] A priest, though, could generally maintain a relationship if he kept it quiet, and if caught could generally count on the support of colleagues to keep him out of serious trouble.[538] As the Middle Ages waned, the church more or less gave up trying to enforce celibacy.[539] During the fifteenth and sixteenth centuries, priests were pursuing erotic relationships quite openly, even living in public concubinage, and seemed to have little or no fear of reprisal.[540] As late as the Council of Trent (1545-1563), a representative of the Duke of Bavaria noted a survey showing that 96% to 97% of the priests in his jurisdiction had concubines.[541] Steve Ozment notes that the church did find a way to make the best of the situation: "Bishops regularly fined priests for whoring and forced those living in concubinage to pay annual penitential fees and 'cradle taxes' when children arrived."[542]

Overseeing and even expanding the Catholic Church's sexual pay-for-play system was one Giuliani de Medici, Pope Leo X as of 1513. Leo's predecessor, Julius II, had been a fiscal disciplinarian with a penchant for violence, an unpleasant man who had won the respect of his cardinals but nothing in the way of personal affinity. The cardinals were looking to replace him with an anti-Julius when he died, and they turned out to be tremendously successful in that regard. Leo was charming, easygoing, unpretentious, intelligent, and in possession of a singularly welcome vision for the character of his nascent pontificate: "God has given us the papacy - let us enjoy it," he wrote to his brother soon after his election.[543] Leo was tremendously fond of classical scholarship, and devoted so much time to it that people questioned his interest in Christian scriptures. He was also quite fond of classical courtesans, the *hetarae*, and included a number of them in his entourage. These women were, according to E.R. Chamberlin, "ideal companions for a man such as Leo who delighted in feminine

---

537   Ibid., 474.
538   Ibid., 474-75.
539   Ibid., 537.
540   Steve Ozment, *When Fathers Ruled: Family Life in Reformation Europe* (Cambridge: Harvard University Press, 1983), 5.
541   Brundage, 568.
542   Ozment, 5.
543   E.R. Chamberlin, *The Bad Popes* (New York: Barnes and Noble, 1993), 210.

company but had no desire to become entangled with a demanding mistress."[544]

The one thing Leo X seemed to enjoy most of all, though, was spending money. In particular, the restoration of the basilica at St. Peters was fast becoming a financial black hole, and in 1515 Leo hit on the idea of funding the project with revenues from sales of papal indulgences.[545] Two years later, an Augustinian monk named Martin Luther offered his reaction in the form of the *Ninety-five Theses*, which pointed out the virtues of self-hatred and explained that true contrition loves *real* punishment. The resulting dispute eventually turned into the Reformation, and sex quickly became a central issue. Luther considered clerical celibacy little more than a masquerade, noting that the saints might have resisted temptation but "the rest of these celibates can only desire that kind of will; they cannot produce it."[546] All manner of sexual improprieties (fornication, adultery, incest, etc.) followed with the inevitable failure of will.[547] Sexual depravity was thus a particular feature of the Roman clergy, and even of the Italians in general according to Luther: "We have come so far that it is often doubted and disputed whether having a relationship with a whore outside marriage is also a sin. Actually now in Italy it is considered an honor among reasonable people...."[548] And then there was homosexuality, which Luther hesitated even to discuss given his belief that most of his fellow Germans were as yet 'uncontaminated' with the knowledge of its existence. "The Carthusian monks deserve to be hated because they were the first to

544  Ibid., 221.
545  For discussion on the particulars of indulgences, see Scott H. Hendrix, *Luther and the Papacy: Stages in a Reformation Conflict* (Philadelphia: Fortress Press, 1981), 23-26.
546  Martin Luther, *Works Vol. 44* (ed. trans. James Atkinson) (Philadelphia: Fortress Press, 1966), 341.
547  Martin Luther, *Works Vol. 54*, ed. trans. Theodore G. Tappert (Philadelphia: Fortress Press, 1966), 335.
548  Martin Luther, *Luther on Women: A Sourcebook*, eds. trans. Merry Wiesner and Susan Karant-Nunn (Cambridge: Cambridge University Press, 2003), 142. He writes also that "desire for a woman is the creation of God, as long as its nature is pure and not corrupted as it has been by the Italians and Turks." Ibid. 148. Luther visited Rome in 1510 or 1511, and was apparently shocked by the hedonism and irreligion of the city. Rumors were floating that Pope Julius II was homosexual and that his predecessor, Alexander VI, had committed incest with his daughter. This may account for some of his anti-Italian sentiment. Richard Marius, *Martin Luther: The Christian Between God and Death* (Cambridge: Belknap/ Harvard University Press, 1999), 80-82.

bring this terrible pollution into Germany from the monasteries of Italy," he explained. "Of course, they were trained and educated in such a praiseworthy manner in Rome...."[549]

The actual status of homosexuality in the late Middle Ages is a bit difficult to decipher. Authorities had become progressively more hostile to it from the middle of the twelfth century onward; in the period from 1250 to 1300, homosexuality went from a permissible activity to a capital offense in most parts of Europe.[550] Those convicted were generally sentenced to be burned alive, even for a first offense, with castration also used as a punishment.[551] In the fifteenth century, Florence made various attempts to make its penalties more severe, though authorities there found that denunciations tended to decrease in number as they did.[552] The hostility to homosexuality continued to escalate even in places where sexual norms were otherwise becoming more relaxed, as in fifteenth century Venice. Guido Ruggiero describes the emergence of a faintly visible homosexual subculture in Venice at the time, which was apparently sufficient to trigger a panic comparable to the witch-craze of the early modern period.[553] The analogy appears especially apt given that, as we learn from Louis Crompton, "more men and women fell victim to homophobia in the three centuries from 1400 to 1700 than in the Middle Ages, as Protestants and Catholics competed in enforcing harsh laws."[554]

The art of the Italian Renaissance brought a kind of restrained and enigmatic sensuality into vogue, in works from Donatello's statue of David to Botticelli's Birth of Venus to Titian's Venus of Urbino.[555] Michelangelo offered much the same with his 4-meter-high statute of David, "the largest and most widely admired sculpture of the male nude in the history of post-classical art."[556] The statue brought him to the attention of Pope Julius II, who then commissioned him to paint the ceiling of the Sistine Chapel.

---

549   Luther, *Luther On Women*, 162.
550   Boswell, 293; Brundage, 472.
551   Louis Crompton, *Homosexuality & Civilization* (Cambridge: Belknap/Harvard University Press, 2003), 246.
552   Ibid., 255-58.
553   Guido Ruggiero, *The Boundaries of Eros: Sex Crime and Sexuality in Renaissance Venice* (New York: Oxford University Press, 1985), 137-40.
554   Crompton, 245.
555   Andrew Graham-Dixon, *Renaissance* (Berkeley: University of California Press, 1999), 151, 252.
556   Ibid., 193.

Michelangelo was very fond of the nude male form,[557] and decided to include several, without apparent religious significance,[558] in each of the frames depicting the book of Genesis. Within a decade of its completion, Pope Hadrian VI condemned it as a 'bathroom of nudes', and he was far from alone in his sentiments. The growing intolerance of sexual expression in the sixteenth century quickly led to a campaign of censorship: "Pope Paul IV ... ordered that the nude paintings by Michelangelo in the Sistine Chapel be clothed with decent draperies, and for the next century several painters, nicknamed breeches-makers, spent their time painting clothes on unclothed old masterpieces."[559] Michelangelo's works were chief among those targeted, his Last Judgment being declared obscene and painted over in 1539.[560] Bronze underwear was added to his previously nude Risen Christ, with every sixteenth century reproduction featuring a similar alteration.[561]

As a general rule, ages at first marriage began to rise in Europe from the end of the fourteenth century through the early modern period.[562] People were marrying quite young in the two centuries previous. In Prato at the end of the thirteenth century, average ages at first marriage were around 40 for men and 24 for women; by 1371, the average ages were 24 for men and 16 for women.[563] David Herlihy finds women marrying at an average age of twelve in thirteenth-century Italy and in Toulouse in the fourteenth and fifteenth centuries at an average of sixteen, noting also that early marriage "seems not to have been exclusively a Mediterranean pattern, but marked the careers of medieval women wherever we can trace them."[564] Men are more ambiguous during the same period, though by the 1400s, economic pressures were pushing the ages for both sexes higher and higher, if not excluding

---

557   Robert J. Clements, *Michelangelo's Theory of Art* (New York: Gramercy Publishing, 1961), 170.

558   Graham-Dixon, 201.

559   Vern L. Bullough, *The History of Prostitution* (New York: University Books, 1964), 130.

560   Allen, 47.

561   Leo Steinberg, *The Sexuality of Christ in Renaissance Art and in Modern Oblivion* (London: Faber Limited, 1983), 18.

562   Brundage, 494; Ozment, 38.

563   Frances and Joseph Gies, *Marriage and the Family in the Middle Ages* (New York: Harper and Row, 1987), 233.

564   David Herlihy, *Medieval Households* (Cambridge: Harvard University Press, 1985), 103-7.

people altogether.[565] James Brundage finds that in Florence in 1427, 43% of households consisted of single women with or without children, and that less than half of the men aged 28 to 32 were married.[566] In Italy, the 1400s were a period of relatively open sexuality for men, though also a period of danger for women lacking male protection, given the frequency of rape during the period.[567]

It is in the sixteenth century that the distinctive 'European pattern' becomes the norm, a pattern distinguished by a high age at first marriage and a high rate of people who never marry.[568] One study finds the average age at first marriage shifting from sixteen to twenty-three for women and from twenty-seven to thirty for men.[569] The normative view of sex was changing as well. "Sex," writes historian Reay Tannahill, "or, more accurately talking about sex -- was one of the most popular outlets for self expression in the fifteenth as in the late twentieth century."[570] Historian John Noonan also finds that "between 1450 and 1750 there was a substantial rejection of the Augustinian view that intercourse may be initiated only for procreation. A broad range of values in intercourse, from health to pleasure, had been defended by some authorities."[571] Clandestine marriages, allowing the bride and groom to avoid parental selection, were on the rise. Remarriage was also becoming more common, with men having slightly better odds, but both sexes enjoying a substantial possibility of finding a new partner.[572]

565 Paul M. Hohenberg and Lynn Hollen Lees, *The Making of Urban Europe 1000-1994* (Cambridge: Harvard University Press, 1995), 79-80; Peter Lewis Allen, *The Wages of Sin: Sex and Disease, Past and Present* (Chicago: University of Chicago Press, 2000), 45

566 Brundage, 494.

567 Allen, 46.

568 J. Hajnal, "European Marriage Patterns in Perspective", in *Population in History: Essays in Historical Demography*, ed. D.V. Glass and D.E.C. Eversley (London: Edward Arnold, 1965), 101. Hajnal finds the following ages at first marriage for ruling families in Geneva: 1550-99 (men 27.2 / women 21.4); 1600-49 (men 29.1 / women 24.6); 1650-1700 (men 32.6 / women 25.7). Page 114. He traces the European model only as far back as the seventeenth century 'with fair confidence' among the general population, though Ozment finds a "widespread 'late marriage pattern' reflected in both law and practice..." during the sixteenth century. Ozment, 38.

569 Riddle, 163.

570 Reay Tannahill, *Sex in History* (New York: Stein and Day, 1980), 283.

571 John T. Noonan, Jr., *Contraception: A History of Its Treatment by the Catholic Theologians and Canonists* (Cambridge: Harvard University Press, 1966), 339.

572 Friedrichs, 173.

Reformers were of the opinion that the family was in a state of crisis, with Luther in particular pushing for earlier ages at marriage.[573] They rejected the idea of marriage by present consent alone and clandestine marriages, favoring public marriage and parental control.[574] External controls were deemed necessary because the stability of marital and family relations were thought to be essential to the stability of society as a whole.[575] Further, the patriarchal nature of the family was thought to mirror God's patriarchal relationship to humanity, hence spiritual chaos would erupt where the family and its attendant gender roles were disrupted.[576] Women were expected to marry and to submit, the expectation becoming so strong that, according to Lyndal Roper, "the discourse of wifehood began to displace that of womanhood altogether."[577] Theories of gender were quickly tied to theories about witchcraft, reformers viewing the witch less as someone sexually depraved than a woman who defied prevailing gender expectations. Later witch hunters would add the one to the other and arrive at the following:

> Older widows were believed to have the power to ruin young men sexually, and youths were warned against marrying such women because they were sexually ravenous, and would suck out their seed, weakening them with their insatiable hunger for seminal fluid and contaminating them with their own impurities. The old witch's fluids did not flow outward.[578]

Sigrid Brauner finds that the trial records of the period suggest that 'inappropriate' or 'assertive and aggressive' behavior on the part of suspected witches often led to their convictions.[579] The obsession with gender is curious because, with few exceptions, the status of women changed very little during the Renaissance and early modern period.[580] The real damage

573  Ozment, 38.
574  Brundage, 552.
575  Margaret R. Sommerville, *Sex and Subjection: Attitudes to Women in Early Modern Society* (New York: St. Martin's Press, 1995), 123.
576  Brauner, 64.
577  Lyndal Roper, *Oedipus and the Devil: Witchcraft, Sexuality and Religion in Early Modern Europe* (London: Routledge, 1994), 40.
578  Roper, 208.
579  Brauner, 113-117.
580  See generally Joan Kelly-Gadol, "Did Women Have a Renaissance", in *Becoming Visible: Women in European History*, ed. Renate Bridenthal, Claudia Koonz, and Susan Stuard (Boston: Houghton Mifflin, 1987, 2d ed.) 175-97. On the

was being done elsewhere.

The sixteenth century witnessed the rise of 'protoindustrial' Europe, which featured increases in population, economic specialization, and, in particular, urbanization. This rapid growth would level off by the end of the seventeenth century as the witch hunts were winding down. Cities with at least 10,000 inhabitants rose from 154 in 1500 to 220 in 1600, rising only to 224 in the year 1700.[581] Cities with populations of 50-100,000 increased from 21 in 1500 to 24 in 1600, the number being unchanged by 1700; cities with populations of 100-200,000 increased from 3 in 1500 to 10 in 1600 compared with 9 by 1700.[582] The percentage of the overall population in urban areas stood at 7.4% in 1500, rose to 7.8% in 1550, 8.8% in 1600, 10.0% in 1650, 10.5% in 1700 and then fell slightly back down to 10.4% in 1750.[583] The increase was primarily the result of massive immigration from rural to urban areas rather than a relative increase in urban birth rates.[584] The pattern of migration into cities was 'stepwise', with people moving into smaller towns closer to home prior to braving the move to a metropolis.[585] Paul Hohenberg and Lynn Lees note that "larger centers and county towns gained at the expense of small ones, notably in the half century after 1570."[586]

At the same time, some percentage of urban dwellers would have migrated out to rural areas. Migration within and out of cities would mean that even the total percentage of urban dwellers at any given point in time would fail to give a complete picture of the atomization resulting from early modern urbanization. Jan de Vries speculates that the social and cultural influence of the cities on rural areas would have been significant during this period: "If, say, 8 per cent of a rural population cohort moves to a sizeable city for at least a few years, most rural-dwellers will be likely to have some personal contact with a compatriot living in, or having lived in, a city."[587]

---

controversy surrounding the legitimacy of female rule in England under Mary and Elizabeth Tudor , see Sommerville, 51-55.
581  De Vries, 29.
582  Hohenberg, 109.
583  De Vries, 50.
584  Jan de Vries, *European Urbanization 1500-1800* (Cambridge: Harvard University Press, 1984), 199.
585  Ibid., 201.
586  Hohenberg and Lees, 111.
587  De Vries, 206.

These patterns of migration would have introduced a high degree of anonymity into European courtship. One study of marriage contracts in late-sixteenth-century Aix-en-Provence found that "among brides and grooms for whom a place of origin is specified, roughly half came from outside the city."[588] The impact was felt even where migration was limited. Some towns had actually taken to preventing women from marrying men who lived outside city limits, though the prohibition could be avoided with a secret marriage.[589]

As for sex outside of marriage, prostitution was flourishing openly in the late Middle Ages. Peter Allen describes the profession as "not exceptionally shameful" at the time, while James Brundage finds a "recognized, if not honored, trade," and E.R. Chamberlin writes that the courtesans of the day "did not disdain to have their profession inscribed upon their graves."[590] By the end of the fourteenth century, prostitution was actually becoming a public utility, with various governmental entities establishing and operating their own brothels.[591] Prostitutes were still to be found in the private sector, of course, working in bathhouses, bordellos, and on the streets. Regulations on prostitution were typically designed to limit the places where prostitution could take place, and cities would occasionally mandate residence in a public brothel so as to achieve a monopoly in the sex trade.[592] Prostitution was so widespread during the fifteenth century that one author actually felt compelled to address the question of property ownership in the case of a nun doubling as a prostitute.[593] Some town councils provided women in the sex industry with legal protection from physical assault, and court records suggest that the rules were being enforced.[594] Church officials supported the sex trade in their own way; Peter Allen finds that clerical patronage of bordellos in the fifteenth century could account for as much as 20% of total visits depending on time and place.[595]

---

588  Christopher R. Friedrichs, *The Early Modern City 1450-1750* (New York: Longman Group, 1995), 133.
589  Brundage, 499.
590  Allen, 46; Brundage, 569; Chamberlin, 221. One estimate put 1,500 prostitutes in Rome in 1527, when the total population of the city was only 55,000. Noonan, 363n.
591  Brundage, 521.
592  Ibid., 524.
593  Ibid., 523.
594  Ibid., 529.
595  Allen, 47.

Syphilis had made an entrance by the end of the fifteenth century, afflicting soldiers and prostitutes first and thus lending itself well to theories about divine retribution for the sin of lust.[596] As with leprosy, theories about contagion involved some ambiguous combination of biology and morality, and syphilis victims were divided by guilt and innocence.[597] Prostitutes were routinely condemned for the spread of the disease, and, if afflicted, were sometimes expelled from cities or locked in away in prisons masquerading as hospital wards.[598] More broadly, the sixteenth century brought in a massive campaign to do away with prostitution altogether, or at least severely restrict it. London closed its houses of prostitution in 1546, Paris in 1560, and Rome attempted the same in July of 1566. In Rome, however, "When 25,000 persons, including the women and their dependents, started preparations to leave, the city was thrown into a panic, and the pope was convinced to rescind the ordinance on August 17 of the same year."[599] The reformers in Germany were quite hostile to prostitution as well, closing down brothels in Lutheran-controlled territories in order to preserve 'sexual fidelity and family unity'.[600] Some were left open owing to a fear that something worse would take the place of prostitution, though they were sometimes supervised by an officer charged with denying entry to married men.[601]

Midwives, perhaps the only other substantial group of female professionals of the time, were subjected to many of the same regulatory abuses as prostitutes and more besides. As the profession first developed in the late Middle Ages, an aspiring midwife undertook an apprenticeship (generally one year) in which she would accompany an established midwife on all of her deliveries.[602] She would then decide on her own whether to go into private practice or undertake an exam and become a licensed midwife working for a city council.[603] Toward the end of the fifteenth century, city councils began to establish licensing requirements for all

---

596  Ibid., 43.
597  Ibid., 50.
598  Ibid., 42-43. The idea of branding afflicted prostitutes on the cheek was also thrown out on occasion.
599  Bullough, 131.
600  Ozment, 55; Brundage, 569.
601  Bullough, 131.
602  Merry E. Wiesner, "The Midwives of South Germany and the Public/Private Dichotomy", in *The Art of Midwifery: Early Modern Midwives in Europe*, ed. Hilary Marland (New York: Routledge 1993), 82.
603  Ibid., 82.

midwives and brought in university-trained doctors (all men) to assist in developing the exam.[604] The practice is noteworthy given that European universities were actually taking gynecology and other women's health issues out of their curricula.[605] The city councils soon grew disenchanted with having to meet with midwives in person given their lower-class status, and women of the upper classes were soon appointed to act both as supervisors and liaisons to the councils. The reaction to the professionalization of midwifery in the sixteenth and seventeenth centuries was anything but positive.

Midwifery and witchcraft were closely linked in the minds of many during this period, the nexus being the focus on reproductive matters, and the control of fertility in particular. As to prosecutions for witchcraft, Barbara Ehrenreich and Dierdre English write that "women were accused, in effect, of giving contraceptive aid and of performing abortion."[606] John Riddle suggests similarly that "the primary reason witches were persecuted was the same as that for which a woman in Hamburg was burnt to death in 1477: 'because she had instructed young females how to use abortion medicines'."[607] Contraception and abortion were in fact becoming deadly serious issues in their own right during the early modern period. In 1532, the Holy Roman Empire issued the *Carolina* which mandated a penalty of death for either one.[608] In 1588, Pope Sixtus V issued a bull entitled *Effraenatuam*, declaring that "the most severe punishments [should go to those] who procure poisons to extinguish and destroy the fetus within the womb ... [and those] who by poisons, potions and maleficia induce sterility in women, or impede by cursed medicines their conceiving or bearing... ."[609]

---

604    Wiesner, 83; John M. Riddle, *Eve's Herbs: A History of Abortion and Contraception in the West* (Cambridge: Harvard University Press, 1997), 132.

605    Riddle, 108-09. Barbara Ehrenreich and Deirdre English suggest that, "In the persecution of the witch, the anti-empiricist and the misogynist, anti-sexual obsessions of the Church coincide: Empiricism and sexuality both represent a surrender to the senses, a betrayal of faith." Barbara Ehrenreich and Deirdre English, *Witches, Midwives, and Nurses: A History of Women Healers* (New York: The Feminist Press, 1973), 15. This is very much in line with the association of sexuality and intellectualism found in other mass movements.

606    Barbara Ehrenreich and Deirdre English, *Witches, Midwives, and Nurses: A History of Women Healers* (New York: The Feminist Press, 1973), 11.

607    Riddle, 112.

608    Ibid., 126-27.

609    Ibid., 157.

The issue of infanticide took on the same degree of disturbing urgency in the sixteenth century. In 1557, Henri II declared that a concealed pregnancy would raise a presumption of infanticide if the child died.[610] Merry Wiesner notes that in the early to mid-sixteenth century, German midwives were tasked with a new public function: "This was the reporting of illegitimate births, with as many details as the midwife could supply… ."[611] Midwives were even required to assist with the prosecution if a woman was suspected of infanticide.[612] According to E. William Monter, "trials and executions for infanticide multiplied in the late sixteenth and seventeenth centuries, exactly when witch-hunting reached its peak in Europe."[613] As to the practice itself, Angus McLaren finds "no good evidence of increasing neglect or infanticide," merely a change in prosecutorial zeal.[614] Single women were targeted exclusively for such prosecutions, which in itself highlights the specific character of the anxiety driving these measures. Infanticide, abortion, and contraception were all associated with sexual pleasure and, worse yet, the sexual freedom of women. Noonan points out that, at the time, "The use of potions is more often connected with contraception outside of marriage. [James] Marchant says that 'frequently' girls who fornicate use 'herbs or other poisons' 'lest they conceive'."[615] Similarly, a Nuremberg law of the late sixteenth century stated "that those women who live in sin and adultery have illegitimate children and, during birth or before, purposefully attempt to kill them by taking harmful, abortion-causing drugs or through other notorious means."[616]

## Demonology

**The sixteenth century is often** described as one of the most misogynistic periods in the history of western civilization, which is an especially dubious

---

610 Angus McLaren, *A History of Contraception: From Antiquity to Present Day* (Cambridge: Basil Blackwell, 1990), 159.

611 Wiesner, 86.

612 Ibid., 87.

613 E. William Monter, "Women in the Age of the Reformations", in *Becoming Visible: Women in European History*, ed. Renate Bridenthal, Claudia Koonz, and Susan Stuard, (Boston: Houghton Mifflin, 1987, 2d ed.), 216.

614 McLaren, 159.

615 Noonan, 344.

616 Wiesner, 87.

distinction in light of the competition. The difference, though, is one of kind as well as degree. This is misogyny with a purpose, with a specific character, and rooted in the sexual instability of the period. The *Malleus* asserts, in an oft-cited passage, that "all witchcraft comes from carnal lust, which is in woman insatiable."[617] As the *Malleus* elaborates, the responsibility for this unparalleled threat to Christendom lies with wanton women, for the "mouth of the womb" is never satisfied, and thus "for the sake of fulfilling their lusts they consort even with devils."[618] Remy's fellow attorney and demonologist, Henry Boguet, also notes that "the Devil uses them so because he knows that women love carnal pleasures ... there is nothing which makes a woman more subject and loyal to a man than that he should abuse her body."[619]

Demonologists were in general agreement that witchcraft was linked to sex, and the theory translated into practice with deadly force in the early modern period. Women accounted for 80% of those accused and 85% of those executed in the early modern period;[620] in practice, witchcraft was a "sex-related but not a sex-specific crime" as Brian Levack explains.[621] Accused witches tended to be single and tended to be older, generally over 50 years of age, and in some places the median age could be as high as 60.[622] Midelfort notes a progression in the order of persecution, with witch-hunters targeting elderly, single women first and then moving on to other segments of society: "It was only during the largest hunts that the stereotype deteriorated dangerously, leaving all social classes and all types of people open to suspicion."[623] While the percentage of men would increase as a trial progressed,[624] distinctions could still be drawn between the sexes. Anne Llewellyn Barstow finds that most of the men accused were either related to women already convicted of witchcraft, or else had independent felony convictions for murder, theft, robbery, heresy, or a

---

617 Jacob Sprenger and Heinrich Kramer, *The Malleus Maleficarum*, trans. Montague Summers, intro. Dennis Wheatley (London: Arrow Books, 1971), 122. The *Malleus* actually goes on at some length on the subject of female sexuality and inferiority, noting generally that women are more emotional, credulous, impressionable, and prone to following their impulses. Ibid., 112-125.

618 Ibid., 123.

619 Boguet, 29.

620 Barstow, 23.

621 Levack, 124.

622 Ibid., 128.

623 Midelfort, 1-2.

624 Ibid., 178.

sexual offense.[625]

The women engaged in witchcraft were thought to be part of a massive conspiracy, led by the Devil and carried on in secret so as to obscure its size and strength. According to the demonologist, the Devil seeks to obscure the nature of true reality entirely, so as to seduce and subjugate humanity with his own false, demonic ideology. Remy writes that "Satan very astutely backs his sorceries with the seeming force of religion; for thus he more easily leads into superstitious error the minds of those whom he knows to be prone to his worship...."[626] Similarly, Bodin explains that "Satan's ruse is not only to dazzle the eyes and deprive men of a knowledge of the true God, but also to uproot from the human spirit all religion, all conscience and even that which everyone believes to be the true God...."[627] The battle is for consciousness, for an awareness of the true character of this false reality, with Remy noting that "many sins may be committed through ignorance of who is our adversary, and the beginning of victory is to know and understand his strength and his devices...."[628]

As to these devices, demonologists offer detailed descriptions of nighttime congregations or sabbats, which are called together, according to Martin Del Rio, "So that the witches may enjoy the association; to aggravate their sinfulness; to increase numbers by initiating new witches there; to make them bolder in wickedness; to provide them with illicit sensual pleasure; and to harden them to wicked behavior."[629] The meetings are secret and thus married women who attend them must either cast sleeping spells on their husbands, or else replace their own bodies with something similar in appearance. Remy cites the case of a husband who "said that he had for long suspected [his wife] of black magic, chiefly because, every Thursday night when he went to bed, he always felt her grow as cold as ice."[630] Witches then fly through the air to the sabbat, riding broomsticks rubbed with ointments made from the corpses of murdered children. Once there, a fire is lit and participants pay homage to their dark lord with a kiss on the buttocks or anus.[631] Celebrants are then offered a banquet featuring

625 Barstow, 24-25.
626 Ibid., 154.
627 Bodin, 139.
628 Remy, 186.
629 Martin Del Rio, *Investigations Into Magic*, ed. trans. P.G. Maxwell-Stuart, (Manchester: Manchester University Press, 2000 [1608]), 97.
630 Remy, 10.
631 Remy, 66; Bodin, 114.

repulsive food and black wine, with salt left off the table given its status as a symbol of immortality.[632] Dancing is also a part of the festivities, though as the food leaves hungry those who consume it, the dance provides no pleasure and simply leaves everyone exhausted according to demonologist Francesco Maria Guazzo.[633] Many facets of the imagined celebration appear to be distortions of Christian ritual, with Del Rio explaining that "sometime they imitate the sacrifice of the Mass (the greatest of all their crimes), as well as purifying with water and similar Catholic ceremonies. ... They behave ridiculously in every way, and in every way contrary to accepted custom. Then their demon-lovers copulate with them in the most repulsive fashion."[634]

Demons have no bodies of their own, and thus to copulate they use animated corpses or condensed vapors to give the appearance of life.[635] They are also able to change gender at will, appearing either as a male incubus or female succubus, though presumably the former incarnation is the more common one. Women, as we have seen, involve themselves in witchcraft primarily to have sex, and yet we find a split among demonologists as to whether sex with an incubus (or perhaps even the Devil) is at all pleasurable. The *Malleus* argues that the Devil does give sexual pleasure to witches, though on sacred days like Christmas and Easter to offend God.[636] Remy, in contrast, notes that "all female witches maintain that the so-called genital organs of their Demons are so huge and so excessively rigid that they cannot be admitted without the greatest pain."[637] Boguet agrees the sex is unpleasant, though he seems to have found at least one counterexample on the subject of demonic penis size, coming across one suspect witch who described her demon's 'member' "as cold as ice and a good finger's length, but not so thick as that of a man."[638] Remy agrees that the sex is cold, noting a description of the succubial vagina as an 'ice-bound cavity',[639] as well as a consensus among witches that "if the Demon emits any semen, it is so cold that they recoil with horror on receiving it."[640]

632  Boguet, 58; Remy, 57.
633  Francesco Maria Guazzo, *Compendium Maleficarum*, trans. E.A. Ashwin, (New York: Dover Publications, 1988 [1628]), 37.
634  Del Rio, 93.
635  Sprenger and Kramer, 243;  Remy, 12.
636  Sprenger and Kramer, 250.
637  Remy, 14.
638  Boguet, 31.
639  Remy, 14.
640  Ibid., 13.

Boguet suggests that the purpose of intercourse between women and demons is to commit a sin in the nature of interfaith sexuality, "For if God abominates the coupling of an infidel with a Christian, how much more shall He detest that of a man with the Devil?"[641] The issue of demonic procreation presents another split between demonologists, with Remy noting that the cold semen emitted by demons is unsuitable for reproduction.[642] In contrast, the *Malleus* asserts not only that demons can store and redistribute functional semen (by switching from succubus to incubus), but that "the devil can, by commixture of another semen, infect that which has been conceived."[643] Bodin adds that "those who originate from this are of a different nature than those who are procreated naturally..."[644]

Bodin also suggests that women themselves become physically corrupted in some way, that "by intimacy with Satan [they] become hideous, doleful ugly and stinking to an unnatural degree."[645] The association between witches and filth or pollution is quite strong in other demonological works as well, though Remy suggests that the connection is circular: "The Devil for the most part has for his servants filthy old hags whose age and poverty serve but to enhance their foulness; and these, as being of a vitiated nature most apt to his purpose, he instructs in all impurity and uncleanness."[646] Infection, like pollution, is a persistent theme in demonological treatises, and in the *Malleus* in particular. The *Malleus* explains that in terms of semen transfer, the Devil "prefers to perform this visibly as a Succubus and an Incubus, that by such filthiness he may infect body and soul of all humanity, that is, of both woman and man, there being, as it were, actual bodily contact."[647] Del Rio writes also that "philosophical or natural enchantment cannot really be called 'enchantment'. It is, rather, 'contagion' or 'infection'".[648]

Sexuality is contrary to will according to the *Malleus*, hence its status

641 Boguet, 30.
642 Remy 12, 13.
643 Sprenger and Kramer, 251.
644 Bodin, 131.
645 Ibid., 155.
646 Remy, 38. He writes also that the Devil is "impure in his nature and character ... [he] takes immoderate delight in external filth and uncleanness. ... Most often, indeed, he dwells in those parts of the body which, like the bilge of ships, harbor the excremental waste of the body." Remy, 38.
647 Sprenger and Kramer, 81.
648 Del Rio, 123.

as a weapon of first resort: "The power of the devil lies in the privy parts of men. For of all struggles those are the hardest where the fight is continuous and victory rare."[649] Bodin refers also to the "torrent of fluid nature which always flows on to corruption, which is characteristic of the Destroyer, contrary to God, Creator of all things."[650]

As the *Malleus* explains, the Devil has no power to influence the will directly, yet the will is subject to the intellect which is in turn subject to the power of imagination. The imagination is the storehouse of ideas and images received physically through the senses, and is thus subject to physical manipulation. Deception through physical manipulation is achieved most effectively through the use of emotion, with the *Malleus* citing Aristotle for the proposition that "anyone who lives in passion is moved by only a little thing, as a lover by the remotest likeness of his love, and similarly with one who feels hatred."[651] The power to generate inordinate love leads to the power to recall past images in the mind, which affects the ability of the intellect to distinguish between true and false, good and evil.[652] As the *Malleus* sums up, "since all our reasoned knowledge comes from the senses, therefore the devil can affect the inner fancy, and darken the understanding. And this is not to act immediately upon the mind ... Therefore when the understanding is darkened, the will also is darkened in its affections."[653]

None of this is to say that people are powerless to defend themselves. The power to resist this sexual assault on the will is derived from a firm grasp of the truth, given that "the intellect of man is of that condition that, the more it is enlightened, the more it knows the truth, and the more it can defend itself from deception."[654] The logic becomes somewhat circular here unless one presupposes a way of knowing the truth distinct from the thought processes subject to compromise. Boguet argues in favor of the emergence of just this type of epistemological aptitude among those favored by God.

> I know that there have before this been those who have
> not been able to believe that what is said of witches is true;
> but in these present days they are beginning to believe it,

---

649   Sprenger and Kramer, 81.
650   Bodin, 48.
651   Sprenger and Kramer, 130.
652   Ibid., 135.
653   Ibid., 132.
654   Sprenger and Kramer, 127.

owing to a special grace of God, who has opened their eyes, which had been blinded by Satan that by this means he might, as he has done, increase his kingdom.[655]

As to defending oneself against witchcraft, Bodin notes simply that "the surest and most effective way of all, is to have faith in God, and to trust in Him like a high and unassailable fortress."[656]

The concept of will as used by demonologists implies its connection to some form of collective sentiment. The destruction of this bond between Christians is the primary objective of the Devil, who "from the time of his first Fall has tried to destroy the unity of the human race."[657] The unity of Christendom is to be destroyed through a massive campaign of subversion and conversion. Witches are thus commanded to make every effort to recruit other women according to the *Malleus*,[658] and Bodin explains that "it is important to note that it takes only one witch to make five hundred. For to do what is most pleasing to the Devil, and have peace with him, when one has given oneself to him, means attracting many subjects."[659] There seems to be a consensus that the demonic campaign is highly successful coming into the early modern period. Del Rio finds that the population of witches in Europe is at an all-time high,[660] and Boguet finds nothing outlandish in the suggestion that a demonic army of 1.8 million witches could be raised. Those awakened to the truth of witchcraft thus face the daunting reality that they are as yet in the minority, opposed by a massive conspiracy that is still growing.

Everyone is a potential vector, as women infected or polluted with witchcraft never limit themselves to recruiting other women into their midst. Just as demons seduce women into witchcraft with sex, women use sex to lure unsuspecting men into the dark arts. This, according to the *Malleus*, is where the real danger to Christendom lies.

> These women satisfy their filthy lusts not only in themselves but even in the mighty ones of the age ... causing by all sorts of witchcraft the death of their souls through the excessive infatuation of carnal love, in such a way that for no shame or persuasion can they desist from

655  Boguet, xxxvi.
656  Bodin, 149.
657  Sprenger and Kramer, 250.
658  Ibid., 254.
659  Bodin, 113.
660  Del Rio, 27.

such acts. And through such men ... there arises the great
danger of the time, namely the extermination of the faith.
And in this way do witches every day increase.[661]

The *Malleus* states explicitly that loving one's wife immoderately
presents an opening for witchcraft to spread,[662] and Bodin writes that
"usually the wife attracts her husband, the mother leads her daughter, and
sometimes the whole family carries on for many centuries...."[663] In the end,
the fault remains with the woman, for "it does not appear that men thus
devilishly fornicate with the same full degree of culpability; for men, being
by nature intellectually stronger than women, are more apt to abhor such
practices...."[664]

Demonologists are in general agreement that a person descended from
a witch is properly presumed to be a witch, and daughters of witches in
particular according to Bodin.[665] There is less clarity as to whether the reason
is demonic indoctrination or some form of congenital transmission. In
another context, Bodin suggests biological transmission when he writes that
there are those "who are engendered by corruption and who attract the
poison from the earth, and the infection from the air. But well cultivated
land, purified air, and cleared trees are not so subject to this infection. And
if one lets the vermin multiply, it engenders corruption and infects
everything."[666] Remy states explicitly that the 'contagion' of witchcraft is
passed from infected parents to the children, and that witchcraft is a
'hereditary crime'.[667]

Aside from infecting the whole of humanity with heresy, the Devil's
other major objective is to depopulate and eventually exterminate the human
race by interfering with the reproductive process. The *Malleus* cites a list of
five methods used by the Devil to obstruct conception, which are: (1) his
physical presence between lovers; (2) secret methods of controlling male
desire; (3) distorting the man's perception of his wife so that she appears
unattractive; (4) preventing erection; and (5) preventing the flow of 'vital
essence'.[668] Another method is for the witch to cast a 'glamour' over a man's

---

661  Sprenger and Kramer, 124.
662  Ibid., 360.
663  Bodin, 113.
664  Sprenger and Kramer, 351.
665  Bodin, 177.
666  Ibid., 145-46.
667  Remy, 92.
668  Sprenger and Kramer, 138-39.

penis, rendering it invisible.[669] "There is no doubt," explains the *Malleus*, "that certain witches can do marvelous things with regard to male organs...."[670] A more subtle method involves the tying of the 'codpiece-string', a knot tied secretly, often during the wedding ceremony, which prevents intercourse between the couple. According to Bodin, "those who are bound go and commit wanton acts or adultery. It is therefore a hateful impiety, and one which merits death, as we shall argue in due course."[671] Any couple that does manage to conceive faces yet another threat in the form of the infanticidal witch-midwife, who either offers the child to the Devil, or kills the child and uses the corpse for magical ointments.[672]

The ultimate goal is humanity's extinction. Satan seeks "only the destruction of the human race"[673] according to Bodin, and Remy theorizes that "if he were able to do all he wished, the whole human race ... would long ago have perished."[674] Witchcraft is on the rise and an apocalyptic battle looms, a critical turning point when the future of the human race will be decided.[675] The earth is "cooling and declining to its end"[676] according to the *Malleus*, and "the evils which are perpetrated by modern witches exceed all other sin which God has ever permitted to be done...."[677]

For the demonologist, the battle against the evil of witchcraft will be fought not with the sword but rather the scales of justice, in courts secular and ecclesiastical, for however long, and by any means necessary. The purpose of an ideologically-driven legal system is to find examples of its own truth; any will do, and it is thus unimportant whether a conviction is obtained in any particular case. What is essential is that convictions are obtained with

---

669   Ibid., 146.
670   Ibid., 145.
671   Bodin, 101.
672   Sprenger and Kramer, 304-13; Boguet, 88.
673   Bodin, 120.
674   Remy, 115.
675   "The eschatological view that witchcraft flourished because the world was in a state of terminal decline was as common among French Catholic authors ... as among the writers of Lutheran Germany and Calvinist England - in this case reflecting the popularity of apocalyptic history in both Reformations." Stuart Clark, "Protestant Demonology: Sin, Superstition, and Society (c.1520 - c.1630)," in *Early Modern European Witchcraft: Centres and Peripheries*, ed. Bengt Ankarloo and Gustav Henningsen (Oxford: Clarendon Press, 1998), 47-48.
676   Sprenger and Kramer, 167.
677   Ibid., 177.

regularity and in large numbers.[678]   In the case of witchcraft, this is accomplished through confessions obtained under torture or threat of torture, and eviscerated evidentiary standards which amount to no standards at all. The accused, for example, is entitled to the benefit of the doubt, "unless this is contrary to Justice" according to the *Malleus*.[679] Confessions were taken with the use of interrogatories, or lists of leading questions designed to elicit certain responses consistent with demonological theory.[680] The conspiracy is proved by multiple confessions, with the validity of any particular confession established through its consistency with other confessions.  Confessions are reinforced with evidence of fact, though the 'facts' which establish the reality of witchcraft generally could be virtually any kind of deleterious natural phenomena, perhaps an infant dying or a hail storm destroying crops.[681] The use of fragmentary and seemingly irrelevant evidence is considered acceptable because the Devil works secretly and the broad conspiracy is well established. Bodin closes the feedback loop, noting that "since witnesses agree on the universal occurrence and general crime, singularity of evidence is not incompatible or objectionable, but it aids and strengthens the proof...."[682]

Demonological legal procedures represent a departure from the standards of the time, something demonologists freely acknowledge and discuss with regularity.[683] Witchcraft is a *crimen exceptum*, both because of the enormity of the threat and the difficulty in establishing a conspiracy conducted in

678   Midelfort suggests that the 'true acquittal rate' (people presumed guilty but found innocent against the total presumed guilty) may have been as low as 5% or 10% during the height of a witch panic. Midelfort, 149.

679   Sprenger and Kramer, 456.

680   Kieckhefer, 31, 90-91.  The Malleus even lists the order in which certain aspects are to be confessed, instructing judges that "after she has confessed the injuries done to men and animals, he shall ask for how many years she has had an Incubus devil, and how long it is since she abjured the faith.  For they never confess to these matters unless they have first confessed their other deeds; therefore they must be asked concerning these last of all." Sprenger and Kramer, 483.  Bodin instructs his fellow jurists to "appear to have pity on [suspects], and tell them that it is not they , but the Devil who forced and compelled them to cause peoples death. So for this reason they are innocent." Bodin, 178.

681   Sprenger and Kramer, 449.

682   Bodin, 184.

683   Compare to the legal procedures of the Roman Inquisition.  John Tedeschi, "Inquisitorial Law and the Witch," in *Early Modern European Witchcraft: Centres and Peripheries*, ed. Bengt Ankarloo and Gustav Henningsen, (Oxford: Clarendon Press, 1998), 83-118.

extreme secrecy.[684] The distinguished jurist/demonologist Jean Bodin writes that a trial for witchcraft must be conducted "in such a way that the iniquity and absurdity of the law is overcome, especially with the deeds of witches where the proof is so obscure and the wickedness so hidden, that out of a thousand there is hardly one punished."[685] Boguet explains that "witchcraft is a crime apart, both on account of its enormity, and because it is usually committed at night and always secretly. Therefore the trial of this crime must be conducted in an extraordinary manner; and the usual legalities and ordinary procedure cannot be strictly observed."[686] Del Rio classifies witchcraft as an offense in the nature of treason or heresy, and a composite crime combining "apostasy, heresy, sacrilege, blasphemy, murder, and not infrequently parricide, unnatural sexual intercourse with a spiritual creature, and hatred of God; and there can be no offences more dreadful than these."[687] Witchcraft is therefore a crime against the collective, and presents a collective duty to prosecute. According to the *Malleus*, a proceeding against witchcraft should open with a statement that the participants "do endeavor with all our might and strive with our whole heart to preserve the Christian people entrusted to us in unity and the happiness of the Catholic faith and to keep them far removed from every plague of abominable heresy...."[688]

A prosecution for witchcraft is initiated in one of three general ways, through a formal allegation by a private citizen, an anonymous denunciation, or an alleged accomplice's confession and denunciation extracted by an inquisitor. Witnesses are essential to begin a prosecution, and to obtain a conviction as well. At every phase, though, unreliable witnesses are not only acceptable, their testimony is actually to be encouraged according to demonologists. Even though a biased witness might be inadmissible in another proceeding, writes Bodin, in the case of witchcraft he will "make exception only for the objection of a major enmity arising from a cause other than witchcraft. For what righteous man does not hate the enemies of God and of the human race, whereas private enmity for another reason could lead to slander against the innocent."[689]

---

684   Del Rio, 195.

685   Bodin, 195. More generally, he writes that "In a criminal action, and especially this crime of witchcraft, the normal approach to charges must not be followed. On the contrary, the judge must get the truth by every means he can imagine." Ibid., 191.

686   Boguet, 212.

687   Del Rio, 189.

688   Sprenger and Kramer, 432.

689   Bodin, 188.

The *Malleus* resigns itself to the fact that "in these cases it is very seldom that anyone bears witness without enmity, because witches are always hated by everyone."[690] Those guilty of perjury or otherwise disreputable in character may testify against witches, or else one would never be able to prosecute them successfully according to Bodin.[691] Accomplices are allowed to testify for the prosecution, but never to establish the innocence of a defendant.[692] A defendant has the right to counsel in a witchcraft proceeding,[693] yet even defense counsel may be called to testify for the prosecution. While family members are generally not permitted to testify against one another, the crime of witchcraft is 'singular' according to Bodin. The daughters of witches should be arrested because "it has been found that they were taught by their mothers, and taken to the assemblies. And at a young age they will be easy to persuade and set straight with promises of impunity, which their youth and the bad influence of their mothers ought to obtain for them."[694] False promises as it turns out.

The confession remains the *sine qua non* of the convincing conviction, and thus the real work of witch-hunting is done in the torture chamber. Demonologists acknowledge that torture will compromise the validity of a confession, though it will not vitiate it entirely.[695] According to Bodin, the voluntary confession is stronger than one obtained under torture, with the latter creating a presumption of guilt rather than a definitive proof if retracted later.[696] The *Malleus* notes that "torture is often fallacious and ineffective,"[697] and that one should initiate torture only if questioning proves ineffective and there are indicators of guilt. Yet the standards for initiating torture are fairly loose and, once again, inconsistent with existing legal standards. Bodin notes that although at least two witnesses are ordinarily required for someone to be 'sentenced to the question', only a

---

690 Sprenger and Kramer, 460. The *Malleus* suggests that only a mortal hatred between accuser and accused will render testimony unreliable; see also Boguet at 230.
691 Bodin, 187.
692 Sprenger and Kramer, 439.
693 According to the *Malleus*, defense counsel is to be prohibited from 'prolix or pretentious oratory', raising legal technicalities, leveling counter-accusations against witnesses for the prosecution., or defending heresy. Ibid., 456.
694 Bodin, 177.
695 Boguet, 221.
696 Bodin, 195.
697 Sprenger and Kramer, 504.

single, reputable witness is required in a proceeding against a witch.[698] Boguet would sanction the torture of a suspect based on the confession and denunciation of a single accomplice, assuming there are other indicators.[699] Boguet would also favor torture where there is a mass of light indications, such as where the suspect has marks on the body, has family relationships with witches, looks at the ground during the examination, is unable to cry, has no cross or a defective cross, fails to deny a rumor of witchcraft, or asks to be re-baptized.[700] Bodin finds that a reputation for witchcraft creates a 'powerful presumption', as does one's status as the daughter of a witch: "One can make a rule which will not have many exceptions: that if the mother is a witch, so also is the daughter."[701] He explains further that torture *must* be applied if there are any strong presumptions or partial proofs.[702]

The methodology used to extract confessions appears especially sadistic, and, relative to women, sexually-tinged. A woman might be stripped naked and then forced to sit on a red-hot stool, a red-hot iron, or, with weights attached to her feet, on a pointed metal horse called the *chevalet*.[703] An especially sadistic form of torture and interrogation was the search for the Devil's mark, a physical mark placed on the body by the Devil which was supposed to be entirely insensate. The mark could be located anywhere, though according to Remy, "Demons more often soil and befoul with their talons those parts which the priest has in no way touched."[704] The mark could discovered with a technique known as 'pricking', which generally involved lifting a woman's skirt up over her head, and then stabbing her repeatedly with a metal pin. The vagina would be probed as a matter of routine, and a positive result for witchcraft would be declared if, due to shock, exhaustion, or some combination of the two, the woman failed to scream or at any point stopped screaming.[705]

Silence would work to the disadvantage of the defendant in all other contexts as well. Bodin writes that "if there is proof ... silence will have the

698  Bodin, 185.
699  Boguet, 221.
700  Ibid., 223-25.
701  Bodin, 198-99. Mothers and daughters were frequently executed together. Midelfort, 186.
702  Bodin, 179.
703  Camille Naish, *Death Comes to the Maiden: Sex and Execution, 1431-1933* (London: Routledge, 1991), 27-28.
704  Remy, 8.
705  Barstow, 130; Naish, 28.

effect of a confession on the part of the defendant," and further that "if he will not say anything under torture, the crime will be half confessed...."[706] The *Malleus* offers yet another one-way test here, noting that silence during torture means the defendant is bound to the devil, whereas a confession means the defendant is incompletely bound or abandoned.[707]

A confession, however obtained, will be sufficient for a sentence of death, as will the testimony of accomplices, as will evidence of 'fact', as will a 'grave suspicion' arising from threats made by the defendant.[708] The execution of the witch is always the ultimate objective for the demonologist, and something that should be carried out "on the least pretext" according to Boguet.[709] Bodin bares his fangs as well, explaining that there is "no penalty cruel enough to punish the evils of witches, since all their wickedness, blasphemies, and all their designs rise up against the majesty of God to vex and offend Him in a thousand ways...."[710] Elsewhere he suggests that the death penalty is in the nature of a cure for the witch, or else a method of purification designed to protect the innocent "from being infected and harmed by the wicked, as plague victims and lepers infect the healthy."[711] It is interesting to note that the witch can never really be cured, or at least not in any way that might save her life. Once tainted with witchcraft, the body must be destroyed, as Boguet explains that "once a person has been entangled in Satan's coils, he can never escape from them...."[712] According to the *Malleus*, a penitent witch having confessed can be sentenced to life imprisonment or excommunication, though the secular court is then free to execute the defendant for the temporal harms of *maleficium*.[713] The *Malleus* also provides for a legal fiction whereby a defendant can be deemed to have relapsed into heresy, and thus sentenced to death under ecclesiastical law.[714]

Jurists who wavered on these points or gave clemency to those accused of witchcraft might be putting their own lives in danger. Bodin actually prescribes death for judges who fail to adhere to demonological principles:

706   Bodin, 192. Bodin also holds that an 'obscure' or 'equivocal' answer is the equivalent of a confession. Ibid., 191-92.
707   Sprenger and Kramer, 467.
708   Bodin, 181-84; Sprenger and Kramer, 492-93.
709   Boguet, 171.
710   Bodin, 204.
711   Ibid., 203.
712   Boguet, 169. Boguet thus sees no reason to refrain from executing children.
713   Sprenger and Kramer, 524.
714   Ibid., 527.

"As much may be said of those who send witches away acquitted (even though they are guilty) and give as their only excuse that they cannot believe what is said of them: they deserve death. For it calls into doubt the law of God...."[715] The defendant shown mercy by a judge would still be in danger for the rest of her life in any case. According to Del Rio, "Whenever the malefice or divinatory superstition is so great that it should be considered an exceptional or horrendous crime, the accused will be subjected to repeated investigation as long as he lives."[716] And people once acquitted did often find themselves accused again years later.[717]

# 4 Good Behavior Well Chastised

**For the totalitarian movement, a** violation or infringement of individual freedom is a logical impossibility, and this is true however seemingly reactionary the ideology which animates it. In theory, nothing is forced onto the individual other than his or her own true will. Given this basic ideological precept, transforming the liberal-democratic hopes and dreams of the French Enlightenment into the nightmare of Jacobinism would have posed no great intellectual challenge. Only one important innovation is required to merge a totalitarian ideology with democratic theory; it is the deduction of a 'correct' political solution from the ideologist's intimate, in fact total, knowledge of the true nature of the human will.[718] One determines popular will rationally, scientifically, axiomatically, and then proceeds to implement it without recourse to inefficient systems involving voters, legislators, judges, debate, dissent, and counterbalancing branches of government. Those who oppose the implementation of popular will, construed thusly, are deemed to be outside the general will, hostile to it in fact, and therefore subject to extermination in the interest of collective self-defense.[719] This, in brief, is the

715  Bodin, 212.
716  Del Rio, 193.
717  Midelfort, 74.
718  J.L. Talmon, *The Origins of Totalitarian Democracy* (London: Secker and Warburg, 1955), 104.
719  As Jean Jacques Rousseau explains, "every malefactor, by attacking social rights, becomes on forfeit a rebel and a traitor to his country; by violating its laws he ceases to be a member of it; he even makes war upon it. In such a case the preservation of the State is inconsistent with his own, and one or the other must perish...." Jean-Jacques Rousseau, *The Social Contract and Discourses*, trans. G.D.H. Cole, rev'd. J.H. Brumfitt and John C. Hall, intro. Alan Ryan (New York: Knopf, 1993), 208.

theory which yielded the French Revolution's year of the Terror, from mid-1793 to mid-1794.

The basic political and economic causes of the French Revolution of 1789 are by now well-established. Massive debts incurred over the course of the late eighteenth century, particularly as a result of French participation in the Seven Years' War and the American Revolution, necessitated radical reform in the tax system. These reforms were a practical impossibility given France's system of decentralized political power (royal laws had to be approved and implemented by local *parlements*) and the disposition of those who would be subject to the additional taxes (which included members of the local *parlements*). In order to resolve the problem, finance minister Jacques Necker advised King Louis XVI to convoke the Estates-General, which would bring together the clergy (the First Estate), the nobility (the Second Estate), and representatives of the general population (the Third Estate). When the Estates-General did assemble in 1789, a functional impasse turned into a formal deadlock. Dissatisfied, the Third Estate withdrew and formed the National Assembly, with the intention of drawing up a new national constitution on its own authority. This open rebellion gave life and voice to a simmering popular discontent, bourgeois in particular, that had been building for some time.

The source of this popular discontent is much less well-established. The king himself, Louis XVI, appears to have been one of the least tyrannical monarchs in the history of monarchy. His theory on governance: "I must consult public opinion. It is never wrong."[720] The King and his wife, Queen Marie Antoinette, were fairly popular in the early years of their reign.[721] A food crisis in 1789 led the women of Paris to retrieve the King, under threat of force, from his palace at Versailles that October, though food crises had occurred previously in the eighteenth century without political consequence. William Doyle notes that disturbances over bread prices in 1775 were easily put down, "and in any case the rioters did not see themselves as opposing the government."[722] More broadly, Alexis de Tocqueville's study of pre-revolutionary France finds a political environment characterized by liberalism and leniency, with remission of taxes and relief for the poor the norm for

720 David Andress, *The Terror: The Merciless War for Freedom in Revolutionary France* (New York: Farrar, Straus, and Giroux, 2005), 12.
721 Christopher Hibbert, *The Days of the French Revolution* (New York: William and Morrow and Co., Inc., 1980), 22.
722 William Doyle, *Origins of the French Revolution* (New York: Oxford University Press, 1980), 67.

authorities dealing with those in poverty.[723] The nation as a whole was experiencing a dramatic increase in population along with unparalleled economic growth. Yet de Tocqueville notes that "it is a singular fact that this steadily increasing prosperity, far from tranquilizing the population, everywhere promoted a spirit of unrest,"[724] and further that "it was precisely in those parts of France where there had been the most improvement that popular discontent ran highest."[725]

## Sexual Atomism in 18th Century France

**France** *was* **experiencing some social** instability at the time, in the area of sexuality in particular. James Traer sums up seventeenth and early eighteenth century French sexuality with a single word: traditional.[726] Royal edicts concerning the family had begun to compete with ecclesiastical law since the Council of Trent in the mid-sixteenth century, though this seems only to have strengthened an especially repressive system of paternal control. A father enjoyed complete control over his wife, children, and property. He could discipline any of them physically, or by having any of them imprisoned through the use of *lettres de cachet*.[727] The latter constituted an invaluable tool for a father enforcing his choice of marital partner against a disobedient and/ or love-struck child, though the threat of disinheritance was often wielded as well. Authorities brought clandestine marriage within the definition of rape in the seventeenth century (Edict of Blois, Edict of 1639), in an attempt to further bolster the father's authority in matters of sexual selection.[728] Royal law even attempted to raise the age limit of parental control to 25 or 30, though the latter two measures met with resistance in terms of enforcement.[729] Lynn Hunt finds a conceptual link between the paternally-controlled family and paternally-controlled polity, with the King as father of the nation. According to Hunt, the two were so "intertwined under the old regime, [that] an attack on absolutism seemed to entail an attack on

723 Alexis de Tocqueville, *The Old Regime and the French Revolution*, trans Stuart Gilbert (New York: Doubleday/Anchor Books, 1955), 172.
724 Ibid., 175.
725 Ibid., 176.
726 James F. Traer, *Marriage and the Family in Eighteenth-Century France* (Ithaca: Cornell University Press, 1980), 15.
727 Ibid.
728 Ibid., 35.
729 Ibid., 47.

excessive paternal authority as well."[730]

Both systems broke down completely over the course of the eighteenth century. According to de Tocqueville, pre-revolutionary France had become "a nation of pleasure seekers, all for the joy of life."[731] Maurice Lever, describing the erotic climate surrounding the marriage of one Marquis de Sade, explains that "in the eighteenth century marriage was no obstacle to libertinage. ... The man who had several mistresses the night before his wedding found his way back to them the night after. ...marital fidelity and unwavering love seemed ridiculous."[732] Otto J. Scott finds that "perversion became not only acceptable but fashionable. Homosexuals held public balls to which heterosexuals were invited and the police guarded their carriages."[733] Roger Chartier concludes from his studies of age at last pregnancy that contraception was being used in increasing numbers: "This was true in Rouen, where the proportion of 'contraceptive' couples ... shifted from a range of 5 to 10 percent at the end of the seventeenth century ... to over 50 percent on the eve of the Revolution."[734] He also finds premarital intercourse on the rise, evidenced by an increase in premarital conception, in the second half of the eighteenth century.[735]

Gender roles were breaking down along with the institution of marriage. The possibility of upward social mobility came through invitation to the salons, which facilitated introductions and served as a kind of finishing school for the bourgeoisie. As Joan Landes notes, the salons were run by women, which in effect made them the arbiters of social advancement.[736] Women entered the newspaper trade, sponsored major philosophical publications, and were thought to be increasingly influential in academy selection.[737] Two European empires were already run by

---

730    Lynn Hunt, *The Family Romance of the French Revolution* (Berkeley: University of California Press, 1992), 40.

731    De Tocqueville, 118.

732    Maurice Lever, *Sade: A Biography*, trans. Arthur Goldhammer (New York: Farrar, Strauss and Giroux, 1993), 118.

733    Otto J. Scott, *Robespierre: The Voice of Virtue* (New York: Mason & Lipscomb, 1974), 8.

734    Roger Chartier, *The Cultural Origins of the French Revolution*, trans. Lydia G. Cochrane (Durham: Duke University Press, 1991), 97-98.

735    Ibid., 99.

736    Joan B. Landes, *Women and the Public Sphere in the Age of the French Revolution* (Ithaca: Cornell University Press, 1998), 24.

737    Ibid., 53-58.

women,[738] with the prospect of a third in France, *de jure* or *de facto*, inspiring a considerable amount of public dread. Up to the moment of revolution, Hunt finds that those women who attempted to influence the public sphere were accused of obscuring the natural divisions between men and women, and of overturning the sexual order.[739]

Pornographic books, known in the publishing industry as 'philosophical works', enjoyed a mid-century resurgence just as France was undergoing the intellectual revolution known as the Enlightenment.[740] According to Robert Darnton, "the double explosion was fueled by the same source: libertinism, a combination of freethinking and free living, which challenged religious doctrines as well as sexual mores."[741] In spite of its illegal status, pornography was circulating openly for the first time since the days of the Roman Empire.[742] Lever adds that "sex had never sold so well. ... It was impossible to find debauches outrageous enough, lovemaking furious enough, or perversions new enough to slake the public's lusty appetite."[743]

Not all sexually explicit works are intended as a celebration of sexual pleasure, though. Chantal Thomas finds the dark undercurrent in sexually-explicit anti-royalist propaganda: "The pamphlet literature, which, as it approached the revolutionary years, increasingly wallowed in a vulgar representation of aristocratic debauchery even while denouncing it...."[744] Once again, the turning point seems to have come in the mid-eighteenth century. As William Doyle writes, "In the years between 1748 and 1770, the society and the state which upheld the established church also came under comprehensive criticism.... Nothing was any longer sacred, nothing beyond discussion...."[745] Robert Darnton finds the same shift at roughly the same time, noting that "the royal sex life provided plenty of material for gossip, but the talk tended to be friendly. In 1729, when the queen was about to give birth, the cafes rang with jubilation. ... Twenty years later,

---

738 Chantal Thomas, *The Wicked Queen: The Origins of the Myth of Marie Antoinette*, trans. Julie Rose (New York: Zone Books, 1999), 120. These would be Russia under Catherine II and Austria under Maria Theresa.
739 Hunt, 82-90.
740 Robert Darnton, *The Forbidden Best-Sellers of Pre-Revolutionary France* (New York: W.W. Norton & Co., 1995), 87.
741 Ibid., 90.
742 Scott, 8.
743 Lever, 382.
744 Thomas, 9.
745 Doyle, 25.

the tone had changed completely."[746] Censorship had more or less ended by the reign of Louis XV, and the 'libelles' were no longer making any distinction between the personal and the political.[747]

Marie Antoinette became the prime target of these works, receiving no mercy whatsoever from the pamphleteers.[748] She was referred to as the 'agent of all vices'.[749] She supposedly had sex with anything that moved, exhausted her men, then turned to women and sex toys, which, it was thought, she preferred in any case.[750] Her thirst for blood was inseparable from her erotic appetite, deriving sexual excitement from plotting against the republic.[751] She was accused of having her guards trample the tricolor cockade during an orgy in 1789.[752] Her sexual excesses take on a distinctly demonological quality at times, even bringing her down into hell itself: "'In Olympus, In Hades, I want to fuck everywhere'" she was supposed to have exclaimed.[753] As horrible and monstrous as she was, she remained but an extreme example of royal depravity in general according to her detractors.

## Rousseau and the Rise of Jacobinism

**Within this wave of anhedonic,** anti-royalist sentiment lies a particular strain of thought known as Jacobinism, an ideological system originating in the works of Jean-Jacques Rousseau. Rousseau was born in 1712 in Geneva and migrated around Europe during the early part of his with life. He makes several stops in Paris, most notably in the late 1740s where he becomes acquainted Diderot and the ideas of the French Enlightenment. He comes to prominence in his own right in 1749 by winning the Dijon Academy's essay contest on arts and sciences, with an essay explaining that arts and sciences are actually quite destructive from a moral standpoint. In his *Confessions*, he notes that sexuality always made him uncomfortable: "Not only had I no distinct idea of the union of the sexes at the age of

746  Darnton, 235.
747  Ibid., 212.
748  Hunt, 106.
749  Thomas, 15.
750  Ibid., 112-120. Marie Antoinette was specifically accused of having affairs with Princess Therese de Lamballe and Duchess Yolande de Polignac, among others. Evidence for these relationships is lacking as yet. Antonia Fraser, *Marie Antoinette: The Journey* (New York: Anchor Books, 2002), 131.
751  Thomas, 132.
752  Hunt, 94.
753  Thomas, 20.

adolescence; but the confused idea never presented itself to me but as odious and disgustful. ... What I had seen of the coupling of dogs always struck me in thinking of others, and my stomach turned at this sole remembrance."[754] He describes his first semi-sexual experience as being spanked at a young age by a female member of his household staff. The woman soon realized corporal punishment was having the opposite effect intended, and promptly ended the regimen. Fearful of admitting his desire even to a lover, Rousseau would never again experience this particular satisfaction except in fantasy. "To fall at the feet of an imperious mistress, obey her orders, have pardons to ask her, were for me the sweetest enjoyments, and the more my lively imagination inflamed my blood, the more I had the air of a bashful lover."[755]

His first relationship takes place in Chambery in the 1730s with his benefactor, Madame de Warens, some thirteen years his senior and a woman he describes as rather dispassionate erotically. She was not altogether indifferent, apparently, as she and Rousseau developed a bond that would eventually turn sexual, much to his displeasure. "How could I see the hour approach with more pain than pleasure? How, instead of delights which should have intoxicated me, did I feel almost repugnance and fear? There is not the least doubt of my having flown from this happiness with all my heart, could I have done it with decency."[756] The sexual act itself did little to change his mind: "My heart confirmed my engagements, without wishing the reward. I obtained it nevertheless; I found myself, for the first time, in a woman's arms, and that the woman I adored. Was I happy? No, I tasted pleasure. I do not know what invincible sadness poisoned its charms. I was as if I had committed incest."[757]

In Paris in 1744, Rousseau meets Therese le Vasseur, the woman he would later marry and with whom he would father several children. She makes an impression on him as a woman of 'modesty', 'devoid of all coquetry', though simple-minded and incapable of intellectual development. He abandoned all of their children to a foundling hospital, citing their lack of educational prospects in a household in which his wife and her poorly educated family were living. The relationship seems to have been a success on some level, at the very least providing Rouseau with companionship he valued.

---

754 Jean-Jacques Rousseau, *The Confessions of Jean-Jacques Rousseau*, trans. anonymous (1783/1790), rev'd A.S.B. Glover (New York: The Heritage Press, 1955), 13-14.
755 Ibid., 15.
756 Ibid., 176-77.
757 Ibid., 178.

> The heart of my Therese was that of an angel; our
> attachment increased with out intimacy, and we were more
> and more and daily convinced how much we were made for
> each other. Could our pleasures be described, their simplicity
> would cause laughter. Our walks ... on the outside of the
> city.... Our little suppers at my window...."[758]

Lest the reader think Rousseau had found true love with this woman, he offers the following clarification: "I have never felt the least love for her ... I never desired to possess her more than I did to possess Madame de Warens, and ... the physical wants which were satisfied with her person were, for me, solely those of the sex, and by no means proceeding from the individual...."[759] That is, he preferred the woman he found inert sexually, never wanted to have sex with in the first place, and who caused him such terrible anxiety by having taken him to bed.

Rousseau did also find time to do some theoretical work on the nature of human relations, and he begins with the following first principles: 'Vice' is contrary to the natural order. Its corrective comes in the form of 'virtue', which is synonymous both with chastity and with true freedom.[760] The 'virtuous man' is one who conquers his passions and affections, and thereby becomes his own master.[761] This would have been entirely unnecessary in Rousseau's 'state of nature', man being naturally devoid of emotions and indifferent to the idiosyncrasies of his sexual partners. He was subject merely to a "blind propensity that, having nothing to do with the heart, produced a merely animal act. The want once gratified, the two sexes knew each other no more...."[762] The emergence of primitive forms of association put men in a position to make comparisons as to sexual partners, to feel desire for something beyond mere gratification. According to Rousseau, this artificial state of sexual competition induced women to make themselves more sexually alluring, thus raising the 'moral part' of love over the physical part of love, and overturning the natural supremacy of men. "It is easy to see," he writes, "that the moral part of love is a factitious feeling, born of

---

758 Ibid., 333.

759 Ibid., 396.

760 Jean-Jacques Rousseau, *Emile, or On Education*, intro. trans. Alan Bloom (New York: Basic Books, 1979), 397, 444.

761 Ibid. 444-45.

762 Jean-Jacques Rousseau, *The Social Contract and Discourses*, trans. G.D.H. Cole, rev'd. J.H. Brumfitt and John C. Hall, intro. Alan Ryan (New York: Knopf, 1993), 84.

social usage, and enhanced by women with much care and cleverness, to establish their empire, and put in power the sex which ought to obey."[763] Sexual desire in a 'moral' rather than physical sense also led to generalized chaos and bloodshed. "A tender and pleasant feeling insinuated itself in their souls, and the least opposition turned it into an impetuous fury: with love arose jealousy; discord triumphed, and human blood was sacrificed to the gentlest of all passions."[764] In desperation and despair over this state of affairs, men turned willingly and foolishly to forms of political association which would inevitably enslave them.

Rousseau does offer a solution, and, lest anyone doubt his totalitarian credentials, he begins the reconstruction of society with the following principle:

> Good social institutions are those that best know how to denature man, to take his absolute existence from him in order to give him a relative one and transport the *I* into the common unity, with the result that the individual believes himself no longer one but a part of the unity and no longer feels except within the whole.[765]

Rousseau thus proposes the 'social contract', in which a group of men of indistinguishable position and disposition prescribe laws 'to themselves'. Simply, "Each of us puts his person and all his power in common under the supreme direction of the general will, and, in our corporate capacity, we receive each member as an indivisible part of the whole."[766] Rousseau does allow for the possibility that there may be opinions held which are contrary to the general will, though "whoever refuses to obey the general will be compelled to do so by the whole body. This means nothing less than he will be forced to be free...."[767] Enforced freedom means that one's desires will be controlled through the state, "for the mere impulse of appetite is slavery, while obedience to a law which we prescribe to ourselves is liberty."[768] In the pursuit of this liberty, the state may take the life of any of its citizens simply because it is judged 'expedient' to do so.[769]

Among the chaste followers of Rousseau we find 'the Incorruptible'

---

763   Ibid., 77.
764   Ibid., 89.
765   Rousseau, *Emile*, 40.
766   Rousseau, *Social Contact and Discourses*, 191.
767   Ibid., 194.
768   Ibid., 195.
769   Ibid., 207.

Maximilian Robespierre, attorney-turned-assemblyman, Jacobin leader, and principal architect of the Terror. Ruth Scurr describes him as 'emotionally self-absorbed', and his early relations with women as 'markedly stilted and formal'.[770] Growing up in Arras, he apparently refused the attentions of several women, while unsuccessfully attempting to court the stepdaughter of an aunt in 1787. He was reportedly heartbroken when he returned to Arras in 1791 to find her married to someone else.[771] While in Paris, Robespierre did pick up a mistress for some time, though she apparently found herself an unwelcome guest on occasion and was soon abandoned altogether.[772] Otherwise, he seems to have avoided female entanglements of all varieties as a member of the National Assembly,[773] and it was even rumored that he hated women.[774] Historian Stanley Loomis suggests that "his chastity was not of the kind that depends on any exercise of the will. ... Everything in his life ... hints at a distinct distaste for that desire which is popularly believed to motivate the greater portion of the male sex."[775] Sexual pleasure, as Lever interprets Robespierre, was an aristocratic ambition: "Nothing disgusted the Incorruptible more than libertinage. There was no better token of the aristocracy's decadence, and nothing more alien to the aspirations of the people."[776]

Virtue was what interested Robespierre, and he mentioned it often. Loomis notes that his references to virtue increase in exact proportion to references to the cleansing of 'pollution' and 'impure blood'.[777] When his highly sexual Jacobin rival, George Danton, joked that 'virtue' was what he practiced with his wife every night, Robespierre recorded the comment in his notebook, and in a manner indicating some degree of trauma. In the same book he noted that 'Dantonist' Camille Desmouslins practiced a 'secret and shameful vice'. Robespierre, refusing gestures of reconciliation from both men, sent them to their deaths in the spring of 1794. For

770 Ruth Scurr, *Fatal Purity: Robespierre and the French Revolution* (New York: Metropolitan Books, 2006), 51-52.
771 Ibid., 54.
772 Scott, 8.
773 A split of opinion exists on whether Robespierre was actually engaged to be married, though a consensus does exist that he never touched the woman in any case. Scurr, 194; Hibbert, 210.
774 Hibbert, 210.
775 Stanley Loomis, *Paris in the Terror: June 1793-July 1794* (New York: Dorset Press, 1989), 274.
776 Lever, 461.
777 Loomis, 268.

reasons that remain unclear, the Incorruptible had Demouslin's wife, and the wives of several other political opponents, executed as well.[778]

Saint Just, the 'Angel of Death', seems to have been even less predisposed to female contact than his mentor Robespierre. Described as having the appearance of a statue and personality to match,[779] there is virtually nothing to suggest any real interest in erotic activity. Early in life, St. Just had maintained some kind of relationship with a young woman who would eventually go on to marry someone else. It was supposed they were having an affair because St. Just moved to Paris just after her marriage, and she moved to Paris some time later, just after her divorce and prior to his death.[780] Other than speculation based on travel habits, there appears to be nothing in the way of evidence for any kind of sexual liaison. A few years later, we find him refusing the attentions of a friend's sister while on tour as representative of the republic, and this more or less closes the book on his sex life.[781]

St. Just reserved his passion for theories about sex, beginning with a poem called 'Organt' whose "dominant themes are a particularly strident blasphemy and an obsession with sex, which usually takes the form of rape."[782] In Organt, he describes a world given to free love and devoid of law, yet also devoid of the necessity of law given the natural harmony that reigns. Self-interest is the corrupting agent which necessitates the introduction of laws into this utopia, which in turn perpetuates the corruption that spawned these laws in the first place. St. Just's later work reveals Organt as a thinly-fictionalized version of his conception of reality. Following Rousseau, he seems to have believed that man in his 'natural state' had no sexual desires, apart from a desire to breed. He sought a return to a utopia, one in which men who refused to marry would be expelled from the community.[783] The progeny of those allowed to remain would be the property of the mother until age five, and then of the republic

---

778   Scott, 222.
779   Saint-Just distinguished himself in the calm, detached, and impersonal way in which he ordered people to their deaths. Geoffrey Bruun, *Saint-Just: Apostle of the Terror* (Hamden: Archon Books, 1966), 30-34; R.R. Palmer, *Twelve Who Ruled: The Year of the Terror in the French Revolution* (Princeton: Princeton University Press, 1941), 74.
780   Norman Hampson, *Saint-Just* (Cambridge: Basil Blackwell, 1991), 5.
781   Ibid., 204.
782   Ibid., 11-12.
783   Hampson, 68.

until death.[784] Other than facilitating reproduction and breast-feeding, St. Just seems to have given no other thought to the role of women in his perfect society.[785]

## *The French Revolution*

**Robespierre and St. Just, however,** were inconsequential figures when the National Assembly formed in 1789, and the utopian insanity of the Jacobins still some ways off. The Assembly was then controlled by moderates with a more concrete political agenda. They supported the idea of a constitutional monarchy, and in the early years of the republic it appeared as though this might be a viable option. In the fall of 1789, Louis XVI, under pressure, ratified the Assembly's abolition of feudal contracts and the Declaration of the Rights of Man. He also offered promises to raise his son with republican principles. Prospects for cooperation diminished in June of 1791, when the King unsuccessfully attempted to escape to Austria via Varennes. Nevertheless, the Constitution of 1791 was issued in September of the same year, eliminating legal status for nobles, but creating a constitutional monarchy with limited powers for the King.

The constitution also formed the new Legislative Assembly, which began to divide into 'Girondin' moderates led by Jacques-Pierre Brissot, and the utopian Jacobins, with Robespierre as a rising influence and backing from popular mobs of 'sans-culottes'. The governments of Austria and Prussia were, for very different reasons, as dissatisfied with the political situation in France as the Jacobins were. In August of 1791, they threatened war if the King was harmed. Brissot, while still favoring a constitutional monarchy, convinced the Assembly to initiate a war with Austria and Prussia in April of 1792. The French suffered a humiliating defeat and were left open to counterattack and invasion. Brissot, and to an extent the Girondins as a whole, were disgraced; rationality and moderation would go into decline from here, replaced by virtue.

The Jacobin ascendancy began with the storming of the Tuileries Palace, then home to Louis XVI, on August 10 of 1792. In reaction to a threat of the total destruction for Paris should harm come to the royal family, radical elements in Paris began to militarize and march on the palace. The confrontation quickly turned violent, with sans-culottes mobs

---

784    Ibid., 233.
785    Loomis, 285.

storming the palace and, in the chaos that ensued, engaging the King's Swiss Guard. The attackers suffered several hundred casualties and the Swiss Guards were killed down to the last man, in many cases after having thrown down their weapons. Paranoia grew in Paris, and calls for the extermination of counter-revolutionary enemies were on the rise. In particular, it was suggested by revolutionary journals that the jails of Paris were filled with conspirators who would spill out onto the streets and wreak havoc if given the chance. In September, mobs began attacking prisoner transports, and quickly graduated to full-scale prison takeovers. Cells were broken into, prisoners given a brief hearing, and in most cases hacked to pieces shortly thereafter. These self-appointed executioners frequently raped the female prisoners before killing them. In all, about 1,200 prisoners were killed, most of them common criminals and prostitutes. The Jacobin reaction was largely to remain silent in the face of these horrors, and later turn to a more professional and systematic method of killing. The guillotine, which had first been put in use in April of 1792, would serve that purpose, though more creative methods would be explored as time passed.

In January of 1793, King Louis XVI was tried and executed, essentially for having been king. The Assembly then proceeded to declare war on England, Holland, and Spain, even as a number of regions within France went into open revolt against the revolution. It was here in the winter of 1793 that the seeds of totalitarian government were first sown. Committees of Surveillance were formed to monitor foreigners and a 'Revolutionary Tribunal' created, over the protestations of one Girondin (Vergniaud) who suggested the new court would be something like the Spanish Inquisition times 1,000.[786] He turned out to be wrong, but only because the Jacobins were stopped before they could prove him right. A power struggle that summer led to the downfall of the Girondins, and the accession of Robespierre, Saint-Just, and many others who favored a more violent and tightly controlled brand of freedom and democracy. The Girondin leaders were brought before the Revolutionary Tribunal and executed in October of 1793. "To be just, as Robespierre told his fellow citizens, meant to be stern, and he condemned his enemies, the Girondins, as a political sect 'which wants nothing but happiness and is dedicated only to pleasure.'"[787]

The revolution's downward political spiral also turned out the

786  Hibbert, 195.
787  George Mosse, *Nationalism and Sexuality: Respectability and Abnormal Sexuality in Modern Europe* (New York: Howard Fertig, 1985), 7.

Committee of Public Safety, the *de facto* governing body during the totalitarian phase of the revolution. Formed under threat of military collapse and civil war in April of 1793, the Committee was initially intended to be a coordinating power within the assembly, a supreme executive council able to fight counter-revolution more efficiently. With the King's flight to Varennes and revolution of August 10, the constitution of 1791 was now a dead letter. A new constitution was put forth in June of 1793, which would deprive the assembly, and its committees, of their reason for being on October 10. At the moment of truth, Saint-Just reasoned that the war was not yet won, the constitution would 'destroy itself' under current conditions, and that the government of the republic was 'revolutionary until peace'.[788] Revolutionary government meant that the new constitution was suspended, executive authority unlimited, and legality traded for ideological extermination; in short, totalitarian terror.

## *The Terror*

**Puritanical principles and homicidal paranoia** went hand in hand during the Terror. During a discussion on the organization of the Committee, one speaker offered the following observation: "Certain women, Saint-Andre said, do great harm to the Republic. 'They corrupt your young men, and instead of making them vigorous and worthy of ancient Sparta, they turn them into Sybarites incapable of serving liberty -- I mean these immodest women who make a shameless traffic of their charms'."[789] Robespierre made the connection between asceticism and mass slaughter explicit during a speech in February of 1794: "Popular government during a revolution is both virtue and terror; virtue, without which terror is destructive; terror, without which virtue is impotent."[790] The Incorruptible's de-sexualized utopia, then, could not exist unless it was preceded by large-scale killings. Saint-Just, accusing Danton of treason, explained similarly that "a man is guilty of a crime against the Republic when he takes pity on prisoners. He is guilty because he has no desire for virtue. He is guilty because he is opposed to the Terror."[791]

A 'law of suspects' followed shortly after the creation of the Committee

---

788   Bruun, 69-70.
789   R.R. Palmer, *Twelve Who Ruled: The Year of the Terror in the French Revolution* (Princeton: Princeton University Press, 1941), 54.
790   Beik, 283.
791   Quoted in Hibbert, 236.

on September 17, allowing for the detainment and execution of anyone who was found, *inter alia*, to be 'depraving public morals'.[792] The fall of 1793 would actually feature several high-profile trials predicated on the defendant's lack of virtue. First among these was the trial of Marie Antoinette, which should have been wholly unnecessary given that aristocracy was, as Saint-Just had pointed out, inherently incompatible with innocence. Nevertheless, in October of 1793, the Queen was brought before the Revolutionary Tribunal and formally charged with being a rapacious slut. The particulars were straight out of the *libelles*. She was accused of influencing the king sexually, of engaging in sexual relations with enemies of the people in furtherance of her treasonous designs, and of having orgies wherein she encouraged the political disloyalty of her officers out of hatred for all things republican.[793] For good measure, prosecutor Antoine Fouquier-Tinville added a charge of incest to the indictment:

> [T]he widow Capet, immoral in every way, the new
> Agrippina, is so perverse and so familiar with all crimes
> that, forgetting her quality of mother and the demarcation
> prescribed by the laws of nature, she has not stopped short
> of indulging herself with Louis-Charles Capet, her son --
> and on the confession of the latter -- in indecencies whose
> idea and name make us shudder.

Women cheered her execution on October 16, proclaiming 'the devil is no more'.[794] A Jacobin paper welcomed her execution as an act of 'purification'.

The eradication of the aristocratic impurity continued with the trial and execution of Mme. du Barry, the mistress of Louis XV, who was referred to as "'this barrel of infection; this drain of iniquity; this impure cloaca who not content with devouring the finances of France nourished herself on human flesh on the model of the anthropophagi'."[795] Other than continuing with her hedonistic lifestyle after the death of the former king, she seems to have been entirely irrelevant to the revolutionary drama as it played out. Sexuality had become a sufficient condition for judicially sanctioned murder, with prosecutors increasingly favoring sexual inquiries

792    Hibbert, 225-6.
793    Hunt, 94-95.
794    Thomas, 149.
795    Simon Schama, *Citizens: A Chronicle of the French Revolution* (New York: Alfred A. Knopf, 1989), 800.

during questioning.[796] Prior to her execution on November 8, prominent Girondin Mme. de Roland recounted just such a line of questioning at trial.[797]

In the progressively rarefied republic of terror, virtue flourished. By early November, women were pushed out of the public sphere, their organizations shut down, and were even forbidden to gather publicly in groups of more than five.[798] On November 4, the Jacobins went so far as to execute prominent feminist Marie-Olympe de Gouges, who had penned the 'Declaration of the Rights of Women'.[799] At the same time, Robespierre began to take specific measures designed to bring about his utopian order: "The Voice of Virtue pushed a decree that abolished prostitution. The pornographic books that had once made Paris famous were banned. Salacious paintings and nudes disappeared."[800] With the ban on prostitution in place in October of 1793, its practitioners were rounded up *en masse*, the industry making a comeback only after the fall of the Incorruptible.[801] Soldiers were forbidden to bathe in the Seine for reasons of modesty.[802] According to R.R. Palmer, "The Robespierrists set a high value on ... chastity, not alone because promiscuous sex habits might take the patriot's mind off his civic duty. They believed that these virtues were good and adequate ends in themselves."[803]

The Jacobin policy on nudity seems to have varied by river, though, or perhaps simply on the bodies in question. In the autumn of 1793, the military effort had been placed under the command of the highly capable and pragmatic Lazare Carnot. Under Carnot, France began to push back successfully against its foreign invaders and reestablish its borders. The suppression of revolt within France, though, involved two exceptionally fanatical and bloodthirsty individuals: Jean-Marie Collot d'Herbois and Jean-Baptiste Carrier. Both found the guillotine horribly inefficient and impractical in light of the very large number of people they intended to kill. In Lyon, Collot d'Herbois attempted to maximize efficiency by having

796   Higonnet, 93.
797   Schama, 802.
798   Olwen Hufton, *Women and the Limits of French Citizenship in the French Revolution*, (Toronto: University of Toronto Press, 1989), 48-49; Higonnet, 91-92.
799   Andress, 232.
800   Scott, 224.
801   Hunt, 160.
802   Palmer, 324.
803   Ibid,, 324.

prisoners tied together and shot at with cannons. An explicit policy of extermination was applied in the retaking of the Vendee, such policy applying to anyone (women and children included) in any town known to have housed insurgents. As many as 250,000 people died in the region, or roughly one-third of the population. In Nantes, Carrier hit on the idea of filling up barges with naked prisoners, taking them out into the Loire river, and then sinking them.[804] This brutality seems to have cost him nothing in the way of support from his fellow party members. With the revolt suppressed, Carrier returned to the Jacobin fold and, after an introduction from Collot d'Herbois, was met with a round of applause.

By the spring of 1794, France had secured its position militarily, the Jacobins had secured their position politically, and Robespierre had secured his position vis-à-vis the Jacobins. Opposition was virtually nonexistent. Rather than an abatement of the Terror, though, we find it increasing dramatically over the next few months. Prior to the Jacobin takeover in autumn of 1793, roughly 11 people were executed each month, with the number rising to 134 in early 1794.[805] By the early spring, it was up to approximately 350, by early summer up to 800, and on pace for over 1,000 in the last month of Robespierre's reign.[806] Whole families of aristocrats were now being sent to the guillotine, "as if the future of the Republic depended on extirpating any capacity of the old ruling class of reproducing itself" writes Simon Schama.[807] The biological impurity that necessitated the total extermination of the aristocracy had clearly spread to other social classes, though. As Christopher Hibbert notes, "Less than nine in a hundred of those guillotined in the Terror were of noble birth; about six percent were clergy. The rest, eighty-five per cent, came from that class of people once known as the Third Estate."[808]

Totalitarian legal procedures were introduced to expedite the process of purification. The law of 22 Prairial (June 1794) eliminated all defense before the Revolutionary Tribunal. The accused no longer had to be interrogated prior to trial, and defense witnesses were deemed as unnecessary as defense counsel. Prosecutor Fouquier-Tinville noted with satisfaction

---

804   Other ideas considered but not used included herding prisoners into mined buildings and then exploding them, and, foreshadowing the atrocities of the 20th century, using caves as gas chambers. Schama, 789-90; Palmer, 68.
805   Higonnet, 52.
806   Schama, 837.
807   Ibid., 824.
808   Hibbert, 248.

that he would now be able to 'take the tops off' three or four hundred people a week.[809] Executions were ordered with an alarming degree of offhandedness. One prisoner was sentenced to death on a charge brought against a prisoner with the same name: "Since she's here," noted the prosecutor, "we may as well take her."[810] As many as 800,000 people may have been designated 'suspects',[811] and given the incredibly arbitrary nature of the revolutionary justice system, it seems fair to wonder if any of them would have survived had the 'reign of virtue' continued for any length of time.

France's brief experiment with totalitarianism was brought to an end with the overthrow and execution of Robespierre in July of 1794. The National Assembly would then be run by the non-ideological five-member Directory. Executions dropped off dramatically in the absence of Jacobin control. Jacobinism did have one last gasp before dying out completely, though. In 1796, Gracchus Babeuf, plagued by messianic visions, was caught attempting to overthrow said Directory and reinstitute Jacobin rule. He proclaimed that his love of the revolution had killed any other love within him, and, in light of this development, told his wife to "die, if 'tis your pleasure...."[812] In 1799, the Directory would be overthrown successfully by General Napoleon Bonaparte, who promptly dissolved the assembly and reinstituted autocratic rule.

# 5 The Land of Milk and Lemon

**Totalitarianism in France was explosive,** rising suddenly, experiencing dramatic political success, and finding itself destroyed in rapid-fire sequence. India's experience with totalitarianism (Hindutva or Hindu nationalism) is the polar opposite in this respect. It emerged slowly at the end of the nineteenth century as an extremist alternative to the generally moderate membership of the Indian National Congress (INC), took on a more

809  Hibbert, 245. Simon Schama offers the following brief description of the prosecutor: "On trial, Fouquier disappointed those expecting to see the incarnation of evil dissolve in shame and fear before his judges. But twentieth-century readers will recognize an ideal instrument of mass killing in the mild-mannered family man who pleaded that he had always obeyed the law and done his duty." Schama, 851.
810  Hibbert, 227.
811  Higonnet, 51.
812  Quoted in Talmon, 174.

corporeal aspect with the formation of the Hindu Mahasaba in 1915 and the Rashtra Swayamsevak Samiti (RSS) in the mid-1920s, and entered Indian electoral politics in the 1950s with the formation of the Jana Sangh in 1951. It remains politically active to this day, through the Baratiya Janata Party (BJP), having thus far failed in its goals to purify India of its Muslim presence or to create a utopian society based on thought control and sexual control. No one seems to be giving up just yet, though.

Aside from depleting the French treasury in the mid-eighteenth century, the Seven Years' War was also a major contributing factor in the British takeover of India. The power structure in India was highly decentralized at the time, and one's prosperity thus tied to military prowess. This was true not only of native Indian rulers, but of those foreign powers, such as the British East India Company (EIC), wishing to do business there. The EIC entered India in the seventeenth century as the Mughal Empire was on the rise, and thus did so initially with permission rather than force.[813] It adopted a policy of protecting its interests with armed forces in 1660, and in spite of the occasional conflict with native rulers, continued to do so for the next century. At the outset of hostilities between Britain and France in 1757, the British attempted to fortify their position in Calcutta, the act taken as a sign of aggression by the ruler of Bengal. The Bengalis overran the British position, but were beaten easily at the battle of Plassey not long after, thus bringing Bengal under British control in the same year. In 1764, the British turned back an assault by the combined forces of the Mughal Empire and ruler of Awadh. The Company installed itself as revenue collector for the Empire, and effectively controlled the majority of east India, an area especially rich in resources. The revenues from the region would now be used to fund the Company's relentless campaign of expansion over the course of the late-eighteenth and early-nineteenth centuries. With the fall of the Marathi stronghold in central India in 1818, the British controlled most of the Indian subcontinent apart from the northwest region.

No nationalist movement appears at this time, or even for decades after. Native objections to colonial authority are generally made on religious grounds or as a result of specific local grievances.[814] There is a general

---

813   For more on the political, military, and economic ascendance of the British East India Company, see Lawrence James, *Raj: The Making and Unmaking of British India* (New York: St. Martin's Press, 1998).

814   Peter Heehs, *The Bomb in Bengal: The Rise of Revolutionary Terrorism in India, 1900-1910* (Oxford: Oxford University Press, 1993), 6.

consensus that Indian nationalism originates slowly in the late nineteenth century, the 'extremist' or Hindu nationalist variant taking shape in the 1890s.[815] Indian nationalism takes on the character of mass movement only in the 1920s, with the rise of Gandhi, as well as the paramilitary Hindu nationalist Rashtra Swayamsevak Samiti (RSS). Political repression seems a more plausible explanation for the rise of the former than the latter. The year 1919 did bring in the Rowlatt anti-terror acts, which effectively deprived native Indians of any legal rights or protections from the British government. It was in the same year that one General Rex Dyer, faced with widespread communal riots and violence in the Punjab, decided to solve the problem by massacring a group of peaceful demonstrators at Amritsar. Yet for the Hindu nationalist, as opposed to the Indian nationalist, the British threat invariably comes secondary to the Muslim threat. As Chetan Bhatt notes, Hindutva ideologues consistently refused to engage in any form of resistance against the British government.[816] Similarly, whatever its effect on Indian nationalism generally, economic misery seems irrelevant to the rise of Hindutva. Its early proponents generally come from the middle classes, and seem to multiply most quickly in relatively prosperous areas. The region of Bengal was an incubator for protean Hindu nationalist concepts,[817] and also where the practice of terrorism came into use by Hindu nationalists in the first decade of the twentieth century. As Peter Heehs notes, "Bengalis benefited more from the Raj than any other group in India. ... Bengal was the last place in India where one would expect the revolutionary impulse to arise."[818]

815  Charles H. Heimsath, *Indian Nationalism and Hindu Social Reform* (Princeton: Princeton University Press, 1964), 138; R. Suntharalingam, *Indian Nationalism: An Historical Analysis* (New Delhi: Vikas Publishing, 1983), 43. The theoretical groundwork for the extremists had been laid by the Arya Samaj, formed in 1875, which combined Hinduism and nationalism doctrinally but remained inactive politically. Sexual asceticism was also encouraged.

816  "Both [RSS leaders] Hedgewar and Golwalkar (its second leader) actively opposed joining the colonial movement in favour of 'character-building' work in the service of the Hindu Nation. Similarly, the RSS, as a matter of explicit organizational policy, refused to join the non-cooperation movement and anti-colonial satyagrahas in the 1920s and 1940s, including the anti-Rowlatt agitations, the Civil Disobedience and Quit India movements, and the Naval mutiny in Bombay." Chetan Bhatt, *Hindu Nationalism: Origins, Ideologies, and Modern Myths* (New York: Oxford/Berg, 2001), 115.

817  Thomas Blom Hansen, *The Saffron Wave: Democracy and Hindu Nationalism* (Princeton: Princeton University Press, 1999), 75.

818  Heehs, 20.

## Sexual Atomism in 19<sup>th</sup> Century India

**A different kind of revolutionary** impulse had previously taken hold in India, in Bengal in particular, directed to the reformation of domestic life. The Indian family was beginning to come in for normative critique from Indian and British reformers in the early nineteenth century. As of 1800, sexuality and gender were governed by a comprehensive set of rules, which marked out with particular rigidity the roles and responsibilities of men and women. The joint-family system was and is something of a constant in India, providing a basic framework around which other social rules are designed. The joint family itself is essentially an extended family living under a single roof, with male descendants remaining in the household throughout their lives and women coming into it by marriage. Individualism is generally discouraged: "The large joint family is family-centered, characterized by intimacy, mutuality of interest, strong primary group controls and mutual assistance in time of need," writes Aileen Ross. "In it family tradition and pride are strong, and individual members are dominated by the opinions of the group."[819] Under the stricter versions of *purdah*, the sexes were segregated during childhood, and female members of the family were confined to certain interior parts of the home (the *antahpur*).[820] Closed carriages were the norm for women allowed to travel outside the home, and even spouses were separated for the most part. As Meredith Borthwick explains, "Husbands and wives were prohibited from meeting or talking to each other during the day. The only time they had together was a few hours at night... Under such conditions there was little opportunity for anything other than sexual relations to develop."[821]

No pretense of 'separate but equal' was ever maintained. Women were denied an education. Medieval Hindu legal scholars had effectively denied women any and all property rights.[822] Marriages were arranged, and at extraordinarily young ages for girls. The girl was to be taken sexually at her first menstruation (*garbhadhan*), the minimum age of consent here being fixed at 10 in 1860.[823] Even excluding the risks of physical and emotional

---

819    Aileen D. Ross, *The Hindu Family in its Urban Setting* (Toronto: University of Toronto Press, 1961), 14.

820    Meredith Borthwick, *The Changing Role of Women in Bengal 1849-1905* (Princeton: Princeton University Press, 1984), 5.

821    Ibid., 113.

822    V.A. Narain, *Social History of Modern India* (Meerut: Meenakashi Prakashan, 1972), 5.

823    Borthwick, 127.

harm to the girl, the potential age discrepancy between groom and bride becomes all the more significant when considers the fate of widows in India. The widow was expected either to live the rest of her life as an ascetic outside the bounds of respectable society, or to take the quick and honorable way out by ascending her husband's funeral pyre (*sati*).[824] For reasons which remain unclear, the latter practice was on the rise in Bengal in the early nineteenth century.[825]

In fact *sati* was in such favor that the 'consent' of the woman was often elicited through drugs and/or direct pressure from family members. It was the forcible burning of his brother's widow that sparked the career of Bengali reformer Rammohun Roy.[826] Roy led a massive campaign which culminated in the passage of anti-*sati* legislation in 1829, though as with most early experiments in legislative social reform, public and private resistance prevented consistent enforcement. Nevertheless, there seems to have been a steady increase the number of widows surviving their husbands, providing the impetus for the first nationwide social reform movement, which focused on widow remarriage.[827] Ashkay Kumar Dutt took up the issue in the 1850s as a component of an overall campaign for marriage reform, which would have included inter-caste marriage, courtship before marriage, and raising the age of consent to 16 for girls.[828] Iswarchandra Vidysagar made widow remarriage his defining issue at around the same time, publishing a major work on the subject in 1856.[829] Legislation allowing widow remarriage was passed that same year, shocking conservatives but having little practical effect.[830] Historian Charles Heimsath argues that practical effect was never the intent, though: "The real purpose of the widow remarriage movement ... was to gain social acceptance or at least tolerance for an individual deviation, of an extreme and socially significant kind, from the normal pattern of behavior."[831] The push for widow remarriage was often the first indication of attempts at general social reform to come in any particular area, Heimsath explains,

---

824    Indira Chowdhury, *The Frail Hero and Virile History: Gender and the Politics of Culture in Colonial Bengal* (Delhi: Oxford University Press, 1998), 71.
825    Narain, 61.
826    Ibid.
827    Ibid., 73.
828    Heimsath, 78-79.
829    Narain, 78-79; Heimsath, 80.
830    Narain, 80.
831    Heimsath, 81.

"because of its uniquely individualistic and humanitarian appeal."[832] The most progressive legislation passed in the nineteenth century may actually have been the Brahmo marriage bill of 1872, which legalized divorce, raised the age at marriage to 18 for men and 14 for women, allowed intercaste marriage, and prohibited polygamy. By its terms, it applied only to Brahmos, which for the most part meant individualists who had chosen to embrace a religion newly founded by the ultra-progressive Manmohun Roy. Hindus were unaffected, but many were outraged in any case.[833]

India was becoming a more individualistic society in general in the nineteenth century, in part due to causes beyond the control of reformers or conservatives. Railroads came to India in 1853, facilitating trade and travel across long distances. Economic expansion and increased urbanization followed soon after, as did the migration of professional Indians working with the British Raj. Those who changed locales often brought their wives with them. Relations between the sexes changed somewhat outside the confines of the joint family, with men expecting a heightened degree of companionship from their wives. Indian-British social functions with mixed company and British women playing hostess further undermined the *purdah* system.[834] In particular, Bombay, Bengal, and Madras were all characterized by industrialization, economic expansion, and social mobility by the mid-nineteenth century.[835] "It is evident," writes R. Suntharalingam, "that economic activities generated by the advent of British imperialism had created a group in India that for want of a better term may be called the 'bourgeoisie'."[836]

The education of women was also on the rise during the second half of the nineteenth century. This was due in part to the increasing influence of progressive ideas in both India and the United Kingdom, but also due to a perceived need on the part of some to compete with Christian missionaries who might thereby lure women away from Hinduism. The number of girls attending missionary schools stood at around 7,000 in 1854, increasing to 127,000 by 1882.[837] Hindu education for women was limited by a lack of funding as well as a lack of educated women to handle teaching

832   Ibid., 88.
833   Ibid., 93.
834   Borthwick, 34.
835   Suntharalingam, 58-62.
836   Ibid., 65.
837   Jana Matson Everett, *Women and Social Change in India* (New York: St. Martin's Press, 1979), 31-32.

responsibilities.[838]   Nevertheless, the overall number of girls attending school in Bengal, for example, did increase from 2,500 in 1863 to over 80,000 by 1890.[839] The first Indian women to obtain college degrees did so in Calcutta in 1883, prior even to the acceptance of women by British universities.[840] The pace would increase from there, with 45 women attending college in 1891, 177 in 1901, increasing dramatically to 201,304 by 1945.[841]

Hindu nationalists condemned the education of women as 'westernizing',[842] in spite of the fact that most Hindu nationalists were themselves educated in Great Britain.[843] Colonial rule was thought to have had an 'effeminizing' effect on the Hindu collective body in general, which would be remade masculine by the reassertion of male control over women.[844] As Tanika Sarkar explains, "Conceived of as an embryonic nation, [the conjugal] relationship could also define ingrained Hindu dispositions that might mirror or criticize and overturn the values structuring colonialism."[845] That is to say that the Hindu male first positioned himself to resist colonial domination through dominance in his marital relationship.[846] Hindu nationalism holds that the only proper roles for women are as wife and mother, the mother being heavily preferred to the wife; according to Indira Chowdhury, "the elaborative strategy in idealizing the mother in preference to the wife camouflages a desire for celibacy...."[847] Women who fell into neither category (widows) were very much encouraged to set themselves on fire, and not only just to keep them from having sex: "An immense body of patriotic tracts routinely invoked

---

838   Everett, 31.
839   Partha Chatterjee, *The Nation and Its Fragments: Colonial and Postcolonial Histories* (Princeton: Princeton University Press, 1993), 128.
840   Ibid., 128.
841   Everett, 33.
842   Borthwick, 92.
843   Heimsath, 10.
844   Chowdhury, 17.
845   Tanika Sarkar, *Hindu Wife, Hindu Nation: Community, Religion, and Cultural Nationalism* (Bloomington: Indiana University Press, 2001), 39.
846   Sarkar, 39. Sarkar notes further that the dominance of the colonist over the native was contrasted with the dominance of husband over wife, based on the loving and voluntary surrender of the wife to the husband, even though marriage was an entirely involuntary arrangement. Ibid., 49, 198.
847   Chowdhury, 132.

[*sati*] as an unfailing source of nationalist inspiration and pride."[848]

It has been suggested that the basic distinction between Hindu nationalists and Indian nationalists generally is that the former preferred a nation based on 'latent', traditional Indian characteristics, while the latter favored a more European model.[849] As many others have pointed out, there is very little that is traditional about Hindu nationalism,[850] and its rejection of the west and modernity has always been highly selective.[851] This revision of traditional Hinduism ran along sexual lines as well. As Charu Gupta describes early twentieth-century attitudes:

> There was a growing fear of romance, of sexual and bodily pleasure: these were seen as a transgression of the ideals of the nation. The assertion of a nationalist Hindu identity became associated with the formation of shared notions of morality and respectability. In the process, tradition was redefined to work out a new modernity. ... In a large part of canonized high Hindi literature, embodying new aesthetic values, the image of women in late medieval literature was declared unfit for public consumption. ... the woman was gradually transformed from a figure of eroticism, sexuality, excess and playfulness to a classic, calm and perfect figure...."[852]

The ideology of Hindu nationalism does in fact revolve primarily around issues of family, sexuality, and reproduction, and its hostility to outside influence is to be found primarily in these areas.[853]

## The Rise of Hindu Nationalism

**In this respect, a line** was apparently crossed in 1891. A young girl named Phulmani had been taken sexually at the age of eleven by her adult husband, suffered internal injuries and died as a result.[854] The acquittal of her husband prompted a public outcry and calls for reform. The issue had been taken up

848 Sarkar, *Hindu Wife, Hindu Nation*, 43.
849 Heimsath, 138.
850 Sudhir Kakar, *The Colours of Violence* (Viking: New Delhi, 1995), 195.
851 Chatterjee, 121.
852 Charu Gupta, *Sexuality, Obscenity, Community: Women, Muslims, and the Hindu Public in Colonial India* (New York: Palgrave, 2002), 40.
853 Sarkar, *Hindu Wife, Hindu Nation*, 192; Chatterjee, 9, 126.
854 Borthwick, 128.

earlier by Dutt and by the Parsi reformer Behramji Malabari, both having little to show for it, but by the end of the of the 1880s it appeared that the British legislative council was seriously considering raising the age of consent from 10 to 12. The backlash was considerable in terms of scope and intensity. According to Sarkar, "Around this issue we find the beginnings of mobilisation, mass meetings, demonstrations of unprecedented scale and strength. We find the first stirrings of a modern anti-colonial agitational nationalism."[855] According to Heimsath, opposition "was fierce and rose to a level never before seen in India. ... There were even veiled references to revolt if the measure passed."[856] Largely ignoring the fact that young girls were dying as a result, those who objected to an age increase argued that it was a sin against the Hindu religion if the girl was not sexually active at first menstruation (which often came before twelve),[857] that the crime of 'feticide' was being committed thereby,[858] and that the reproductive organs of such girls would take on some sort of infectious impurity that would spread throughout future generations at an exponential rate.[859] The measure did pass, though once again its practical effect was limited. It would be followed by an additional increase in age in 1929 (the Sarda Act), which would still require even stronger enforcement provisions in 1939.

The Age of Consent debate highlighted a theoretical fracture in Indian nationalism, and in the recently formed Indian National Congress (INC) as well. The Congress was devoted to Indian nationalism generally, though two basic variants quickly emerged. Moderates like G.K. Gokhale and PM sought the formation of an independent and liberal-democratic India modeled on European institutions, nationalism here being limited to institutional and political unification. Bal Gangadar Tilak, in contrast, would lead the 'extremist' version of Indian nationalism, predicated on the religious and social unification of the Indian population. Tilak came to prominence with his outspoken opposition to the bill raising the age of consent in the early 1890s.[860] He followed this with the creation of the

855 Sarkar, *Hindu Wife, Hindu Nation*, 229-30.
856 Heimsath, 162.
857 Borthwick, 127.
858 Narain, 140-41.
859 Sarkar, *Hindu Wife, Hindu Nation*, 224.
860 According to Jim Masselos, "The Bill provoked a storm of opposition in Bengal and in western India and particularly in Poona. ... Tilak associated himself with opposition to the Bill and soon emerged as its leading opponent." Jim Masselos, *Indian Nationalism: An History* (New Delhi: Sterling Publishers, 1985), 97-87. Tilak may have simply been positioning himself in light

Shivaji festival, named for a military leader who had fought successfully against the Mughal Empire in the seventeenth century. The festival featured obvious anti-Muslim overtones, leading to Hindu-Muslim riots in the early nineties.[861] Prominent radical intellectual Aurobindo Ghose began to criticize the Congress publicly, lamented India's 'terminal' lack of unity, and later declared that "nationalism is not a political programme: Nationalism is a religion that has come from God. ...a religion by which we are trying to realize God in the nation."[862] His circle was behind the assassination attempt of Lt. Gov. Bampfylde Fuller in 1906, which inaugurated an era of rampant political terrorism in Bengal.[863] Aurobindo also claimed responsibility for a violent clash at the 1907 INC meeting, which resulted in the complete expulsion of the extremist wing.[864]

Extremism itself was more difficult to contain by this point. Outside the confines of the INC, a nationalist movement began with the formation of local Hindu Sabhas, which eventually merged in 1915 to form the nationwide Hindu Mahasaba. The Sabhas espoused a 'proto-Hindu nationalism', with theorists like Lajpat Rai explaining that the Hindus were a nation not in a purely political sense, but in terms of civilization, culture, and organic cohesion.[865] "We do not require a Herbert Spencer to tell us that the efficiency of a social organism as such," he explained, "depends upon the sense of social responsibility amongst the members of such an organism."[866]

While perhaps lacking systematization, most of the basic concepts of the ideological system later referred to as 'Hindutva' were by now in place. Owing to the deaths of influential moderates Gokhale and Perzoshah Mehta in 1915, the extremist faction was readmitted to Congress in 1917, though its time in the ascendant would be short.

---

of the political climate at the time, because according to biographer Richard Cashman, he would have supported a circular suggesting that girls should not marry until the age of 16. Richard I. Cashman, *The Myth of the Lokamanya: Tilak and Mass Politics in Maharashtra* (Berkeley: University of California Press, 1975), 53. He also opposed high school education for girls while enrolling his daughter in one. Ibid., 54.

861 Masselos, 102.
862 Quoted in Bhatt, 38.
863 Heehs, 86.
864 Suntharalingam, 167-69.
865 Christophe Jaffrelot, *The Hindu Nationalist Movement in India* (New York: Columbia University Press, 1996), 18.
866 Quoted in Bhatt, 53.

The year 1919 featured the Montagu-Chelsmford reforms which were to split India into a diarchy, beginning the transfer of regional authority to native leaders, with the intent of developing institutions which would facilitate an eventual transition to Indian self-rule. The same year also featured the massacre at Amritsar and the Rowlatt Acts, the latter depriving Indians of basic legal process when accused of terrorism. This led to the rise of Mohandas K. Gandhi, who began a relatively progressive and nationwide campaign of non-cooperation in 1920. Gandhi's campaign was non-violent, non-sectarian, and included large numbers of women, though it left India's caste system and traditional family structure largely untouched and unchallenged. In 1922, he called off the campaign when a group of policeman were killed in a confrontation with protestors. Gandhi was arrested and tried for sedition soon after. A void was left, soon to be filled by a much less tolerant version of Indian nationalism.

It was in 1923 that future Hindu Mahasaba president V.D. Savarkar released his signature treatise, entitled "Hindutva: Who is a Hindu?" In classic totalitarian form, he explains that "Hindutva embraces all the departments of thought and activity of the whole Being of our Hindu race."[867] Hindus are a single race and single nation attempting to preserve their "organic cohesion," which will only be secure when the "forces pledged to aggressive egoism" have disbanded.[868] According to Savarkar, the primary threat to the Hindu organic collective comes from the inherently aggressive Muslim race, whose invasion of India forced upon the peaceful peoples of Hindusthan an apocalyptic "conflict of life and death."[869] Hindus being of 'common blood', interbreeding with Muslims would pose a problem, as "the lion's seed alone can breed lions."[870] Conversion to Hindutva is a possibility, he explains, but should only be done as the rare exception to the rule against interbreeding.[871] His advice to Hindus:

---

867  V.D. Savarkar, *Hindutva: Who is a Hindu?* (Poona: S.P. Gokhale, 4th ed. 1949), 4.
868  Ibid., 67.
869  Ibid., 34. For Savarkar's extended discussion of the peaceful nature of the Hindu as contrasted with the demonic and aggressive Muslim, see V.D. Savarkar, *Six Glorious Epochs of Indian History* (trans. ed. S.T. Godbole) (New Delhi: Radjhani Granthagar, 1971). Savarkar refers to this disposition as 'suicidal', suggesting that the survival of the Hindu is dependent on some form of 'retaliation' against Muslims. Ibid., 179, 277.
870  Savarkar, *Hindutva*, 105.
871  Ibid., 108.

Strengthen every tie that binds you to the main organism, whether of blood or language or common festivals and feasts or culture and love you bear to the common Motherland. Let this ancient and noble stream of Hindu blood flow from vein to vein ... till at last the Hindu people get fused and welded into an indivisible whole, till our race gets consolidated and strong and sharp as steel.[872]

While Savarkar would go on to become one of the foremost theorists of Hindutva, Hindu nationalism as a mass movement had more or less died out in the early 1920s.

Enter the RSS. In 1925, Dr. Hedgewar, frustrated with a perceived inability on the part of Hindus to organize themselves effectively, decided to form an organization perhaps modeled on the terrorist societies of Bengal.[873] The intent, as with all totalitarian movements, was to create a "new man,"[874] one based on a "mechanical-algorithmic view of the human personality" as sociologist Chetan Bhatt describes it.[875] Hedgewar would run the organization until his death in 1940, when it would be taken over by his handpicked successor, and its legendary ideologue, M.S. 'Guruji' Golwalkar.[876] The RSS was and is heavy on physical development, weapons training, and ideological development, all of which are linked in the mind of Golwalkar: "The first thing is invincible physical strength. ... Even to see God, a healthy and strong body is required. God is not for the weak."[877] Sexual abstinence is another important feature of the movement, designed to de-individualize RSS members and to sublimate the libido into the work of nation-building.[878] Golwalkar posits a fundamental sameness among Hindus, one latent and waiting to be manifested in this reality.[879] He explains that "the 'I' in me, being the same as the 'I' in others, makes me react to the joys and sorrows of my fellow living beings just as I react to my own."[880] Collectivity is not something to be imposed on the Hindu, but rather a natural disposition: "Our view of the relation between individual

872  Ibid., 114.
873  Jaffrelot, 33.
874  Hansen, 93.
875  Bhatt, 141.
876  Jaffrelot, 41.
877  Golwalkar, *Bunch of Thoughts* (Mangalore: Sharada Press, 1966), 40-41.
878  Hansen, 73,97; Bhatt, 144; Jaffrelot, 36.
879  Golwalkar, *Bunch of Thoughts*, 50.
880  Ibid., 5.

and society has always been, not one of conflict but of harmony and co-operation born out of a consciousness of a single Reality running through all the individuals. The individual is a living limb of the corporate social personality."[881]

The RSS would grow rapidly in the 1940s, from 76,000 in 1943 to 600,000 in 1948,[882] up to a total of perhaps 2.5 to 6 million at present.[883] Even during the colonial era, its popularity was based more on its anti-Muslim position than an anti-British one. As noted earlier, the RSS routinely declined involvement in anti-colonial agitation, and was in fact never proscribed by the British government.[884] Golwalkar and the RSS consider the true threat to their organic unity the rival Muslim 'race', though one defined, as in Nazi Germany, more by cultural characteristics than by any serious genetic theory: "A Race is a hereditary Society having common customs, common language, common memories of glory and disaster.... We will not seek to prove this axiomatic truth, that the Race is the body of the Nation, and that with its fall, the Nation ceases to exist."[885] The stereotype of the Muslim as sexual predator, and hence threat to the collective body, was coming into vogue. Ideologists also took great pains to combat obscenity and establish the asexuality of the Indian woman. As Gupta writes, "The debate on obscenity was largely a debate on sex for pleasure and recreation versus sex for reproduction. In the discourse of the nation, non-reproductive and hedonistic sexual behavior came under extraordinary pressure."[886]

The rise of the RSS in the first half of the twentieth century took place against a social background of increasing social atomization and normative breakdown. Feminism was on the rise according to Jana Matson Everett: "The emergence of rudiments of a women's movement in India can be seen in the formation and growth of women's associations over a period of 50 years from roughly 1880 to 1930."[887] Women achieved political suffrage on a limited basis in the 1920s,[888] while the All India Women's Conference

---

881    Ibid., 20.
882    Jaffrelot, 75.
883    Bhatt, 113.
884    Ibid., 115.
885    Quoted in Bhatt, 128. Both Golwalkar and Savarkar were open admirers of National Socialism and the Third Reich. Ibid., 107-8, 133.
886    Gupta, 46.
887    Everett, 45.
888    Ibid., 107-8.

(AIWC) grew from 58 delegates and 5,000 members in 1927 to 177 delegates and 25,000 members in 1945.[889] The number of educational institutions for women increased until the late 1930s, and declined thereafter only because women were increasingly attending coeducational facilities.[890] According to Gupta, "the spread of education among women, new ideals of companionate marriage and monogamous marriages, and the increase in the number of households — seen as undermining the joint family—created a sense of disquiet and increased patriarchal insecurities."[891] The Child Marriage Restraint Act was passed in 1929, and having been found ineffective, was amended to provide for the possibility of stricter penalties.[892] India experienced massive urban expansion at this time, going from a total urban population of 25.85 million in 1901 to 78.94 million by 1961.[893] Large population centers, those over 100,000, took over an increasing share of the total urban population, going from 22.9% in 1901 to 48.4% in 1961.[894] By the mid-1950s, the normative environment had changed enough to allow for an overhaul of the marital code. The Hindu Code Bill of the mid-1950s allowed for divorce, legalized intercaste marriage, mandated monogamy, and equal succession rights for women.[895] Traditional values were apparently still strong enough, though, that women actually experienced a decrease in their overall employment rates.[896]

889   Ibid., 74.
890   Karuna Chanana, "Social Change or Social Reform: Women, Education, and Family in Pre-Independence India," in *Women, Education, & Family Structure in India*, ed. Carol Chapnick Mukhopadhyay and Susan Seymour (Boulder: Westview Press, 1994), 41-42.
891   Gupta, 23.
892   Ross, 246.
893   Ashish Bose, *India's Urbanization, 1901-2001*, with Jatinder Bhatia (New Delhi: Tata McGraw Hill, 1978, 2d ed.), 82.
894   Ibid., 83.
895   Everett, 187-88.
896   Relative to the female population as a whole, 31.7% were a part of the labor force in 1901. The figure stood at 32.6% in 1921, then dropped to 27.6% in 1931, and then to 23.3% in 1951. G.N. Ramu, *Women, Work and Marriage in Urban India: A Study of Dual- and Single-Earner Couples* (New Delhi: Sage Publications, 1989), 23; Ashok Kumar, *Indian Women Towards the 21st Century* (New Delhi: Criterion Publications, 1989), 47-48.

## *The RSS and 'Racial' Violence*

**Gandhi returned to the national** scene in 1930, with a long march to the sea and a short-lived, illicit salt-making operation on the beach. This time women were actively and publicly involved in the march, and in agitation elsewhere in the country.[897] A major breakthrough came in 1935, with the Government of India Act, which provided for regional Indian control and substantial autonomy for regional governments. Congress went from a mass movement to the largest political party in India, and quickly demonstrated an ability to govern. They were less successful and less tactful in dealing with the Muslim League and Muhammad Jinnah, which may have led to the latter to push for a separate Islamic religious state (Pakistan) when independence came about. Congress also had a falling out with British authorities at the outbreak of World War II, owing to the British assumption that India and the Congress Party would be naturally inclined to participate without even having been asked. Congress subsequently offered the suggestion that the British 'Quit India', though the British declined to follow it at that point. Nevertheless, the economic relationship between the two countries had declined throughout the interwar period, giving the British less and less of a reason to stay in India.

India's political independence was a foregone conclusion following the second world war, the only questions being when and how it would come about. The answers, unfortunately, turned out to be soon and badly. In the summer of 1946, Congress and the Muslim League appeared headed for an impasse on the formation of Pakistan, which led Jinnah to call for a 'Direct Action Day' that August. Communal violence broke out in Calcutta almost instantly, with gangs of Muslims murdering Hindus, and Hindus later responding in kind. Violence then spread with refugees to Bihar, then to Bombay, then to Agra, and continued on a sporadic basis with the British Raj making inconsistent efforts to restore order. In January of 1947, Viceroy Mountbatten was dispatched to India with the specific purpose of facilitating a peaceful withdrawal from India. Mountbatten quickly determined that a partition was necessary, which, when finally implemented, meant the division of both the Punjab and Bengal between Pakistan and India on August 15, 1947. Muslims and Hindus were spread throughout both, and the prospect of continued sectarian violence, now reinforced by the power of a religious state, led to a scramble to be on the

---

897    Barbara D. Metcalf & Thomas R. Metcalf, *A Concise History of Modern India* (Cambridge: Cambridge University Press, 2006), 192.

right side of the dividing line. Several million members of both religious communities were displaced as a result. Several hundred thousand of each were murdered in the chaos that ensued, many of them while attempting to flee one country or the other by train.

One stands on unstable ground attempting to read an operational philosophy into actions undertaken in the context of mass anarchy. It may be noted, however, that the actions of the RSS during partition appear to have been anything but spontaneous. The RSS was acting essentially as a militia by that point,[898] participating in violence as well as organizing rallies and meetings with the intent of inciting violence on the part of others.[899] The very real prospect of murder at the hands of one religious community or another did have the effect of driving loyalties hard and fast in one direction or another,[900] giving life to the polarized reality in which the ideologist lives at all times: "RSS activists found themselves in a situation corresponding to their preferred ideological fantasies," writes Thomas Blom Hansen. "In the logic of RSS ideology this was 'just' violence, acts of self defense against cruel Muslims."[901] Aside from generalized mayhem and murder, women were subjected to extreme forms of violence: "stripping; parading naked; mutilating and disfiguring; tattooing or branding of the breasts and genitalia with triumphal slogans; amputating breasts; knifing open the womb; raping…."[902] As a result of the violence, Gandhi would later call for reparations to be paid to Pakistan. This led a former RSS member and associate of V.D. Savarkar, Nathuram Ghodse, to assassinate Gandhi in January of 1948, citing his 'effeminacy' among other things. Savarkar himself went on trial for conspiracy to commit the murder, though managed to obtain an acquittal.

In the wake of the assassination, the RSS found itself banned by Prime Minister Jawaharlal Nehru and the Congress Party. The RSS, which had previously shunned politics, now formed the Bharatiya Jana Sangh in order to run candidates for political office. The Sangh added the Vishwa Hindu Parishad (VHP), or World Hindu Organization, in 1964, an organization intended to focus on religious guidance and proselytization. The VHP

---

898  Jaffrelot, 75.
899  Gyanendra Pandey, *Remembering Partition: Violence, Nationalism, and History in India* (Cambridge: Cambridge University Press, 2001), 99.
900  Metcalf and Metcalf, 221-22.
901  Hansen, 95.
902  Rita Menon and Kamla Bhasin, *Borders and Boundaries: Women in India's Partition* (New Brunswick: Rutgers University Press, 1998), 43.

later formed its own militant wing called the Bajrang Dal, an organization similar to the RSS itself though less structured. The overall organization became known as the Sangh Parivar or Sangh combine. While the Sangh grew during the second half of the twentieth century, it experienced little in the way of electoral success. Congress dominated in the decades after partition, until the Indira Gandhi declared the 1975 election invalid. The 'emergency' she declared gave an opening to the Sangh and the formation of the Janata government in 1977. The Janata government collapsed in 1979, leading to the formation of the RSS's current political wing, the Bharatiya Janata Party (BJP) in 1980. The BJP attained a degree of political power as a member of the Janata Dal coalition from 1989 to 1991, and later headed a ruling coalition from 1998 to 2004.

One of the Sangh Parivar's signature issues would turn out to be that of the Babri Masjid (mosque) in Ayodhya. The site was supposedly the birthplace of the god Ram, and had supposedly been the site of a temple dedicated to the same, which had supposedly been destroyed in 1528 by a Mughal ruler in order to build the mosque. Lacking substantiation, Hindutva ideologues noted simply that they were making faith-based rather than fact-based claims in any case.[903]

The remedy was to take place in this reality, specifically involving the building of a Ram temple on the site. In 1989, the Sangh combine took up the issue with brick consecration ceremonies across the country, with the bricks wrapped in saffron cloth, worshipped, and eventually sent to Ayodhya. Predictably, communal violence erupted, claiming the lives of several hundred Muslims in Bihar.[904] Undeterred, the BJP and VHP acquired several acres of land adjoining the mosque, ostensibly to build a tourist center. Construction volunteers began flooding into the area, tensions rose, and boiled over on December 6, 1992. Hindu nationalists tore down the mosque that day, urged on by celibate VHP ideologue Sadhvi Rithambara, whose speeches are generally credited as the proximate cause of the chaos which ensued.[905] Her themes were typically totalitarian. The building of the Ram temple, she explained, "is not the building of the temple but the building of India's national consciousness."[906] Disunity and decay of the collective body would be the consequence of failure, as Tanika Sarkar interprets her: "Rithambara's speech abounds with fissiparous,

903 Hansen, 176; Jaffrelot, 92.
904 Hansen, 162-63.
905 Sarkar, *Hindu Wife, Hindu Nation*, 268-69.
906 Sudhir Kakar, *The Colours of Violence* (Viking: New Delhi, 1995), 202.

centrifugal politics: she evokes the horror of disintegration."[907]   As with
Savarkar, she argued that the inherently peaceful Hindu is threatened by
the inherently lustful, destructive, and evil Muslim predator, and must
therefore annihilate the predator in self-defense.[908] As Hansen paraphrases
her, Muslims are "evil incarnated that had to be 'cleansed' from the national
body so the Hindus could rise from their state of weakness and lack of
self-confidence."[909]   Communal violence spread across India as a result of
the Ayodhya agitation, cleansing some 1,200 Muslims from the collective
Hindu body between December 6 and December 13.[910]

Still undeterred, or perhaps encouraged, the Sangh Parivar took up the
issue once again in 2002, with the BJP as India's ruling party. On February
27, a group of VHP activists were returning to Gujarat from Ayodhya
when their train stopped at Godhra. A number of them exited the train
and assaulted a Muslim tea vendor at the station. A mob formed, and in
the chaos that ensued, a compartment of the train was set on fire, killing 58
people. Many of the dead were VHP members, and the power structure in
Gujarat then decided that Muslims as a group would be held
accountable.[911]

The massacres that followed the next few days appear in every way to
have been the product of considerable planning that predated the incident
at Godhra. Muslims were systematically exterminated by groups of men
armed with lists of addresses indicating religious affiliation, perhaps voter
registration lists, which in some cases were actually outdated.[912] Members
of the RSS, VHP, and BJP were seen coordinating and participating in
violence,[913] with the use of guns, swords, trishuls, petrol bombs, and gas
canisters,[914] implements unlikely to be lying around the house and picked
up in a moment of rage. Picking up on a theme from Gandhi, marauders
painted slogans such as "Muslims quit India or we will f*** your mothers,"

907   Sarkar, *Hindu Wife, Hindu Nation*, 278.
908   Sarkar, *Hindu Wife, Hindu Nation*, 276; Kakar, 204.
909   Hansen, 166.
910   Jaffrelot, 463.
911   Siddharth Varadarajan, *Gujarat: The Making of a Tragedy* (India: Penguin
      Books, 2002), 10.
912   Nandini Sundar, "A License to Kill: Patterns of Violence in Gujarat," in *Guja-
      rat: The Making of a Tragedy*, ed. Siddharth Varadarajan (India: Penguin Books,
      2002) 95-96.
913   Ibid., 87.
914   Dionne Bunsha, *Scarred: Experiments with Violence in Gujarat* (India: Penguin
      Books, 2006), 8.

on the walls of charred houses.[915] Having failed to quit India in time, Muslim women and girls were raped on a systematic basis, most of them hacked to pieces or burned alive just after. Pregnant women, as is now traditional, had their wombs torn open and their babies removed before being killed.[916] The BJP defended itself by pointing out that they had done it before and no one had seemed to mind terribly: "All these sob stories being told to us, as if this is the first time this country has heard such stories — where a mother is killed and the fetus taken out of her stomach, where a daughter is raped in front of her mother, of someone being burnt. Is this the first time such things have happened?"[917]

None of this is to say that anything goes with the Sangh. Celibate VHP ideologue and Babri Masjid agitator Uma Bharati said that "there were few issues that ... enraged her more than sexual exploitation. She spoke vehemently against the exploitation of women's bodies in advertising and the media and favored strict censorship laws to control pornography."[918]

# 6.1 Hive Mind

**The key to understanding Vladimir** Ilyich Ulyanov (Lenin), as with all totalitarians, is understanding his commitment to collectivity and violent revolution. Everything else is pretext. He was entirely indifferent to the practical situation of Russia's working classes, and openly mocked their attempts to gain better conditions as indicative of 'trade union consciousness'. Lenin split the Russian Social Democratic Labor Party (RSDLP) in 1903, rather than allow in sympathizers not subject to control by a central authority.[919] He was so hostile to his fellow revolutionaries, so intolerant of dissent, and so prone to factionalism that at one point he was actually

915 Barkha Dutt et al., "Nothing New?: Women as Victims," in *Gujarat: The Making of a Tragedy,* ed. Siddharth Varadarajan (India: Penguin Books, 2002), 221.
916 Bunsha, 37.
917 Dutt, 214.
918 Amrita Basu, "Feminism Inverted: The Gendered Imagery and Real Women of Hindu Nationalism," in *Women and Right-Wing Movements: Indian Experiences,* ed. Tanika Sarkar and Urvashi Butalia (London: Zed Books, 1995), 166. She, like fellow ideologue Sadhvi Rithambara, openly advocates violence against Muslims. Ibid., 159.
919 Helene Carrere D'Encausse, *Lenin,* trans. George Holoch (New York: Holmes & Meier, 2001), 54.

receiving covert support from the Tsarist government.[920] Communism, which was ostensibly the motivation for his revolution, was jettisoned at the Tenth Party Congress in 1921, ushering in the era of the New Economic Policy (NEP). Revolution, on the other hand, was entirely non-negotiable, and violence an essential concomitant.

Writing in 1905, Lenin explained that those who were opposed to violence "must be ruthlessly dismissed from the ranks of the supporters of the revolution, sent packing to its enemies ... [subsequent events] will compel us to distinguish between enemies and friends according to this principle."[921] When someone suggested that his legally-unconstrained People's Commissariat of Justice should be called the Commissariat for Social Annihilation, he replied, "Well said! ... That's exactly how its got to be ... but it can't be stated by us."[922] According to biographer Dmitri Volkogonov, "Lenin took every opportunity to ram home the message that terror was inevitable. A dozen times a day he would fire off tirades against anyone suspected of pacifism. 'If we can't shoot a white guard saboteur, what sort of revolution is it?'"[923] Lenin wanted a revolution, centralized authority, and the power to kill without restraint, and Marxism provided him with a superficial rationale. The need for this rationale, as with all totalitarians, is sexual.

Lenin was born in 1870 to a decidedly upper-middle class family then living in the quiet and non-industrial Russian town of Simbirsk. His youth featured no substantial contact with the working masses he later claimed to represent, unless one counts the servants working in his relatively large household. His father, Ilya Ulyanov, was a well-regarded teacher who eventually rose to become the provincial school inspector. He was also awarded the Order of Stanislav, First Class, achieved the rank of State Counselor, and joined Russia's hereditary nobility. Vladmir Ilyich also received noble status as a result, a fact he would cite from time to time when it was in his interest. He was well-educated and well provided for, and his preteen years were, on the whole, prosaic and uneventful.

Lenin was an outstanding student all his life, positioning himself to receive a gold medal from his high school upon graduation in 1887. The

---

920   Robert Service, *Lenin: A Biography* (Cambridge: Harvard University Press, 2000), 205-6.

921   V.I. Lenin, *Selected Works Vol. 1*, (Moscow: Progress Publishers, 1967), 581.

922   Ibid., 322.

923   Dmitri Volkogonov, *Lenin: A Biography*, ed. trans. Harold Shukman (New York: The Free Press, 1994), 181.

award was subject to doubt only because his brother had recently confessed to masterminding an assassination plot against Tsar Alexander III. The execution of his brother is generally cited by hagiographers as the event which gave rise to Lenin's hatred of the monarchy and his burning desire to see it destroyed. This theory does tend to obscure the fact that Lenin's hatred extended very far beyond the monarchy, in the end being directed to virtually everyone who disagreed with him. One might also take note of the fact that Lenin was exhibiting a marked distaste for human contact even prior to the death of his brother.[924] In a letter of recommendation for university study, the principal of his high school, Fedor Mikhailovich Kerensky, wrote: "Looking more closely at the life and character of Ulyanov, I cannot but remark on his excessive reclusiveness and on his self-distancing from intercourse even with his acquaintances ... and generally on his unsociability."[925]

It is at this time that Lenin's revolutionary disposition emerges clearly, prior to an interest in the working classes and prior to being introduced to the works of Karl Marx. In actuality, the book that Lenin used to rationalize his revolutionary impulse was his brother's favorite work, *What is to be Done? Tales About New People* by N.G. Cherneshevsky. Lenin would later explain that the book 'ploughed' his mind. Chernyshevsky writes in the preface that "love is the subject of this novel,"[926] though love as experienced by the 'new people,' those whose lives are 'well ordered'. The first such person whose life is well-ordered is his heroine, Vera Pavlovna. She is distinguished by the fact that she distributes all the profits from her dressmaking shop to her workers, and also by the fact that she is largely asexual. She apparently never has sex with her first husband, though she does produce a child with her second.[927] Pavlovna's attitudes about sex seem to mirror those of her creator, who declared elsewhere: "Away with erotic problems. The modern reader has no interest in them. He is concerned with the question of perfecting the administration and the

---

924   Service, 40.
925   Quoted in Service, 62.
926   N.G. Chernyshevsky, *What is to be Done? Tales About New People*, intro. E.H. Carr, trans. Benjamin R. Tucker (New York: Vintage Books, 1961), 11.
927   Chernyshevsky goes on at length assuring the reader that Pavlovna and her first husband sleep in separate quarters, and never see each other unless fully dressed. One infers sexual contact with her second husband only from the birth of their child, which is brought up as an afterthought and mentioned post-pregnancy and post-delivery.

judicial system ... with the problem of liberating the peasant."[928]

As a cautionary example, Chernyshevsky offers his readers the life of Julie, one of the 'fast set'. At one point, she explains to Pavlovna that "they call me an immoral woman, my body has been polluted ... but that is not what I consider my depravity. My depravity consists in being habituated to luxury and idleness; in not being able to live without others...."[929] Erotic love, as it involves emotional dependency, is considered contrary to true freedom, hence the new people order their lives by avoiding it. While the new people are now a minority, explains Chernyshevsky, they are soon to be a majority. "In time, even, they will be the totality; then all will be well in the world."[930] Lenin would later take the title of the novel for his first major treatise on revolution, and also declared it 'inadmissible' to criticize the artistic merits of the work.[931] As he explained, Chernyshevsky's "great service was not only that he showed that every right-thinking and really decent person must be a revolutionary, but ... what kind of revolutionary, what his principles ought to be, how he should aim for his goal...."[932]

Thusly, Lenin entered Kazan University in August of 1787, and exited in December after being arrested and expelled for involvement in student demonstrations. He would later take up the study of ecclesiastical law and police law as an external student at the University of St. Petersburg, graduating at the top of each of his classes in 1891. It was in the interim that Lenin finally discovered the works of Karl Marx and leading Russian socialist Georgi Plekhanov. In 1893, Lenin moved to St. Petersburg and began to associate with the local Marxist intelligentsia. His social life seems to have revolved almost entirely around socialist ideology and discussion groups. He did confess to falling in love — though with Marx and Plekhanov. According to biographer Robert Service, "This young

---

928    Ibid., xiv.
929    Ibid., 40.
930    Ibid., 56.
931    According to Nikolai Valentinov, Lenin, upon being told that the work was primitive and displayed an evident lack of talent, responded: "How can anyone get the monstrous and absurd idea in his head to describe as primitive and untalented the work of Chernyshevsky, who was the greatest and most talented representative of socialism before Marx? ... I declare that it is inadmissible to call What is to be Done? primitive and untalented. Under its influence, hundreds of people became revolutionaries." Quoted in Nikolai Valentinov, *The Early Years of Lenin*, ed. trans. Rolf H.W. Theen, intro. Bertram D. Wolfe (Ann Arbor: University of Michigan Press, 1969), 135.
932    Quoted in Volkogonov, 20.

heterosexual revolutionary was more excited by ideology—and its leading exponents — than by women."[933] Even in his mid-twenties, there is a surprising lack of involvement with, or even interest in, the opposite sex. As Volkogonov writes, "It appears that his preoccupation with books and revolutionary dreams left no room for the feelings that usually occupy the mind of any young man. There is no broken first marriage, no stormy romance, no love at first sight, no unhappy love affair."[934]

In December of 1895, Lenin was arrested again for his revolutionary activities in St. Petersburg, sent to prison, and then sent to administrative exile in Siberia in 1897. He did keep in touch a young woman from his St. Petersburg circle, named Nadezhda Krupskaya. Fake marriages between revolutionaries were a common practice at the time, the Tsarist regime allowing husband and wife to be exiled together. Such marriages were generally intended as, or at least idealized as, working relationships, free of sexual or emotional intercourse.[935] When Krupskaya was arrested and facing exile herself, Lenin apparently suggested the idea to her. Her response: "Well, so what — if as a wife, then as a wife."[936] By all accounts, the marriage was dispassionate and based on their shared attraction to Marxist principles and socialist revolution. Both seemed to have embraced traditional family and gender roles in practice, with Krupskaya essentially becoming Lenin's housekeeper and secretary. The marriage yielded no children, which under normal circumstances would tend to suggest that one or both partners was physiologically compromised. In the context of the Lenin-Krupskaya marriage, it does leave open the possibility that the relationship never turned sexual. One may note the advice of Lenin's first hero, Chernyshevsky, offered through his heroine by way of her husband-to-be: "Well, darling, here I am your fiancee and about to become your wife; treat me always as it is customary to treat strangers; that seems to me to be the best way of preserving harmony and love between us."[937]

The emotionless, ascetic, ideological relationship between the two would be held up as the ideal to which young Marxist lovers should aspire, the Soviet Union's answer to Romeo and Juliet according to sexologist

933 Service, 103.
934 Volgokonov, 30.
935 Robert H. McNeal, *Bride of the Revolution: Krupskaya and Lenin* (Ann Arbor: University of Michigan Press, 1972), 52.
936 Ibid., 56.
937 Chernyshevsky, 112.

Mikhail Stern.[938] Krupskaya reportedly took issue with Soviet depictions of her marriage, though if these were inaccurate, the blame is easily placed. Krupskaya's own memoir of Lenin is striking for its detached and impersonal tone. She reveals virtually nothing about the man behind the revolutionary persona, assuming there was one, nor does she delve into her own personal feelings about Lenin, assuming there were any. Her recollection of her first meeting with Lenin after becoming engaged: "We had a good long talk that night."[939] On life in Siberia: "That night Ilyich and I could not fall asleep for thinking of the huge workers' demonstrations in which we would someday take part."[940] On life in western Europe: "I will never forget those sleepless nights. It was Vladimir Ilyich's passionate desire to create a united solid party, merging into one all the detached groups...."[941] Their wedding day is never discussed in the memoir, and apparently neither she nor Lenin discussed it in their letters.[942]

After exile in Siberia, Lenin, along with a great many other Russian socialists, spent time in western Europe attempting to foment socialist revolution in Russia. Lenin spent time in London editing a journal called Iskra, moved back to St. Petersburg in 1905 during a revolutionary outbreak, left for Finland, and later went to Switzerland. In 1909, Lenin arrived in Paris, and sometime soon after that, something very unexpected happened to him. He fell in love— this time with a woman. The woman in question was French socialist Inessa Armand, a beautiful, intelligent polyglot, and a true believer in the revolutionary cause. Volkogonov adds that she was "an exceptional person, emotional, responsive and exciting,"[943] while biographer Michael Pearson suggests that, while perhaps trite to say, "they were made for each other...."[944] It was generally assumed by Bolshevik associates that the two were lovers. The exact character of the affair is unknown, but the letters that do survive are strongly suggestive of a deeply emotional relationship between the two.     Also suggestive is the fact that Lenin would later ask for a number of his letters to be returned, presumably so

938   Mikhail Stern, *Sex in the U.S.S.R.*, with August Stern, ed. trans. Mark Howson and Cary Ryan (New York: Times Books, 1980), 82.

939   Nadezhda Krupskaya, *Reminiscences of Lenin*, trans. Bernard Isaacs (New York: International Publishers, 1970), 32.

940   Ibid., 37.

941   Ibid., 85.

942   McNeal, 65.

943   Volkogonov, 37.

944   Michael Pearson, *Lenin's Mistress: The Life of Inessa Armand* (New York: Random House, 2001), 82.

that he could destroy them.[945] Krupskaya, suffering from Graves' disease when the affair began, apparently offered to leave and allow Lenin to pursue the relationship openly. Lenin, confronted with a choice between true love and an essentially fictional marriage contracted for revolutionary purposes, chose the fiction. He and Krupskaya left Paris in June of 1912.

Lenin and Armand continued to correspond in the years that followed. Armand decided to take up the subject of free love in a pamphlet, which would have involved a condemnation of loveless bourgeois marriage, contrasted with relationships of whatever legal character based on genuine emotional affinity. Lenin was clearly distressed by the idea. The tone of his replies are confrontational and dismissive, perhaps even demeaning; he tells her that he is "anxious that the pamphlet should be a good one" and that a revised plan for the pamphlet is "very important." The deficiency, as he explained it, was that Armand had taken up the subject of love without pointing to its intrinsic class character. Logically, it would be better "to contrast the base and vile marriage of the bourgeoisie-intelligentsia-peasantry … with a proletarian civil marriage with love (adding, *if you must have it*, that a fleeting passion-liaison can be vile but can also be pure)."[946] Some of his agitation may have been personal, having contracted something like a loveless, bourgeois marriage himself, then committing adultery.

The exchange does also highlight the difference between romantic, emotional critics of bourgeois marriage like Armand, and totalitarian critics like Chernyshevsky and Lenin. The latter critiqued the institution because it led, as Lenin details, to sex without love, sex without childbearing intention, and sex without restrictions against adultery. Armand was clearly stung by the criticism, a fact reflected in the changed timbre of her future communiqués. Her pamphlet was never published in any form, Lenin presumably not seeing this as an appropriate way to honor his former lover.

In early 1917, the Tsarist regime collapsed as revolution broke out across Russia. In October, Lenin would overthrow the provisional government that had formed and take over as head of government. The two ex-lovers continued their low-intensity feud that year, with Armand refusing to translate certain parts of one of Lenin's pieces because they made her "blood boil." Lenin replied with sarcastic thanks for the censorship, and suggested elsewhere that she was hysterical. Nevertheless,

---

945    Service, 198.

946    V.I. Lenin, *On the Emancipation of Women*, fwd. Nadezhda Krupskaya (New York: International Publishers, 1966).

a failed assassination attempt in 1918 left him severely injured, and he asked to see Armand while recovering. Krupskaya, for reasons unstated, chose to move out of the Kremlin at that time, even though her own health problems were more easily treated there.

Armand fell ill in 1920 doing missionary work in France, and Lenin sent her to recover in the Caucasus. She died of cholera there, having converted from romantic love to ideological love at some point prior to her death: "The importance of love, compared to social life, is becoming altogether small ... love and personal relationships are nothing compared to the needs of the struggle...."[947] Lenin suffered a number of strokes in 1922-23, which left him barely able to communicate, and Krupskaya would help nurse him until his death in January of 1924.

## 6.2 Ghost in the Pleasure Machine

**Marxism, according to Leninism, is** a scientific, all-encompassing, and thoroughly unassailable system of thought. According to Nikolai Bukharin, Marxism correctly predicted World War I while bourgeois 'science' did not, and "it is therefore clear that Marxists have a perfect right to regard proletarian science as true and to demand that it be generally accepted."[948] Scientific socialism, according to Trotsky, has proven that the proletariat "can find its salvation only in socialism, that the entire position of the proletariat drives it toward socialism and that the doctrine of socialism cannot but become in the long run the ideology of the proletariat."[949] There are only two possible modes of thinking, bourgeois and proletariat, and hence, as Lenin writes, "to belittle socialist ideology *in any way, to turn aside from it in the slightest degree* means to strengthen bourgeois ideology."[950]

Proletarian science, or ideology, is the key to a wide-scale transformation of Russian society. "Without revolutionary theory," notes Lenin, "there can be no revolutionary movement."[951] The revolution, "living reality" itself according to Lenin,[952] will, through a process of 'natural selection', eventually

947 Quoted in Volkogonov, 47-48.
948 Nikolai Bukharin, *Historical Materialism: A System of Sociology*, intro. Alfred G. Meyer (Ann Arbor: University of Michigan Press, 1969), 12.
949 Leon Trotsky, *The Permanent Revolution and Results and Prospects* (New York: Merit Publishers, 1969), 92.
950 Lenin, *Selected Works, Vol. 1*, (Moscow: Progress Publishers, 1967), 130.
951 Lenin, *Selected Works Vol. 1*, 117.
952 Lenin, *Selected Works, Vol 2*, 47.

result in the extinction of all rival systems of thought.[953] "It is only the inner connection between Darwinism and Marxism," writes Leon Trotsky, "that makes it possible to grasp the living flow of existence in its initial connection with inorganic nature...."[954] Revolutionary science has the added benefit of being supported by otherworldly, mystical forces which are also driving the world toward socialist transformation. According to Lenin, "The history of our proletarian revolution is full of ... miracles. They will lead, surely and inevitably ... to the full victory of the world Soviet republic."[955]

Leninism is based on Marxism, or more accurately, takes Marxism as its superficial rationale. In Leninism, the works of Karl Marx are interpreted in precisely the same way a religious fanatic interprets religious doctrines (e.g., selective literalism). Where Marxist theory can be fit into a totalitarian system, his postulates are held axiomatically, the inviolable dictates of a dark and angry God. Contradictions between Marxism and Leninism are generally ignored.

Marxist theory, highly simplified, is concerned with the fate of workers in a capitalist society, the latter divided into capitalists who pay wages for labor, and workers who receive wages for work. In the course of this ongoing exchange, surplus is created, of which capitalists, owing to a superior bargaining position, take a disproportionate share. Workers accept this state of affairs because capitalists control not only the means of production, but the instruments of thought control as well, 'doping' the masses with religion among other things. "The class which has the means of material production at its disposal, consequently also controls the means of mental production...."[956] Over time, though, the disparity becomes greater and greater as capital is concentrated in the hands of fewer and fewer people. The system becomes increasingly unsustainable as the proportion of workers grows relative to a shrinking class of capitalists. And then comes the communist apocalypse: "The centralization of the means of production and the socialization of labour reach a point at which

---

953   "What two or three years ago was or seemed *possible*, approached to the *probable*, and everything points to the fact that it is on the brink of becoming *inevitable*." Trotsky, *Results and Prospects*, 106.

954   Leon Trotsky, *Problems of Everyday Life: And Other Writings on Culture and Science* (New York: Monad Press, 1973), 113.

955   Lenin, *Selected Works Vol. 3*, 271.

956   Karl Marx & Friedrich Engels, *The German Ideology* (New York: Prometheus Books, 1998), 67.

they become incompatible with their capitalist integument. This integument is burst asunder. The knell of capitalist private property sounds. The expropriators are expropriated."[957]

Though Marx gave his ideological followers less to work with than an Augustine or a Rousseau, he does drift toward the totalitarian in places. Capitalist thought control, for example, is intended to explain the seemingly irrational behavior on the part of workers who fail to revolt, which presupposes an underlying rational individual in need of said thought control. Marx, though, does make stronger claims elsewhere as to the nature of proletarian thought. "As individuals express their life, so they are. What they are, therefore, coincides with their production, both with *what* they produce and with *how* they produce."[958] Consciousness, mental production, is a product of material production, he writes. "The phantoms formed in the brains of men are also, necessarily, sublimates of their material life-process, which is empirically verifiable and bound to material premises. ... It is not consciousness that determines life, but life that determines consciousness."[959] The nature of thought, then, is predicted on the nature of the structural environment, and yet Marx seems to presuppose that one structure produces truer thought than another. "Communism is not for us a *state of affairs* which is to be established, an *ideal* to which reality [will] have to adjust itself. We call communism the *real* movement which abolishes the present state of things."[960]

Leninism goes a bit further, holding explicitly that the proletariat is instinctually proletarian and instinctually collective. In *What is to be Done?*, Lenin cites industrial strikes at the turn of the century as evidence of "consciousness in *embryonic form*. ... I shall not say to understand, but to sense the necessity for collective resistance...."[961] Trotsky, looking to the Reformation, Renaissance, and October Revolution, finds the latter merely the most recent instance of a pattern. "The masses, with their invincible social instinct, always participate in these movements. In the individual this instinct attains the level of a generalizing reason."[962] Not only are the

---

957 Marx, 1977, p.929.
958 Marx, *The German Ideology*, 37.
959 Ibid., 42.
960 Ibid., 57.
961 V.I. Lenin, *Selected Works Vol. 1* (Moscow: Progress Publishers, 1967), 121-22.
962 Leon Trotsky, *Literature and Revolution*, ed. William Keach, trans. Rose Strunsky (Chicago: Haymarket Books, 2007), 78.

masses instinctually collective, but, according to Lenin, "instinctively, spontaneously Social-Democratic...."[963] According to Kollontai, "a sound class instinct and a deep distrust of ladies saved the working women from being diverted into feminism...."[964] Krupskaya explains that "class instinct, which among workers coincides with a social one, is a necessary condition for being a communist. Necessary, but not sufficient."[965]

If human behavior is governed by nature and instinct, then human behavior should be predictable for anyone who understands the nature of those instincts. As Bukharin writes, "Everything in nature ... from the movements of the planets down to the little grain or mushroom, is subject to a certain uniformity ... a certain natural law. We observe the same condition in social life...."[966] If everything in social life were purely a matter of causation, then Marxism would come or not come of its own accord, and there would be no need to engage actively in revolution. One critic of Marxism suggested simply waiting, as one might do for an eclipse. Bukharin's answer: "An eclipse of the sun does not depend either directly or indirectly on human desires; in fact it does not depend on men at all. ... The case with social phenomena is entirely different for they are accomplished *through* the will of men."[967] One must, it seems, still choose to do what one is naturally inclined to do.[968]

Thus being instinctively collective and revolutionary is insufficient to achieve full revolutionary consciousness, the latter requiring social development. Lenin says very clearly that "there could not have been Social-Democratic consciousness among the workers. It would have to be brought to them from without."[969] One of the initial tasks of the communist vanguard is, according to Trotsky, to form "the real human beings of our epoch, who still have to fight to create the conditions out of which the harmonious citizen of the commune may emerge."[970] In the interim, man

---

963 Lenin, *Selected Works Vol. 1*, 570.

964 Kollontai, *Selected Writings*, trans. Alix Holt (Westport: Lawrence Hill & Co., 1977), 44.

965 Nadezhda Krupskaya, "What a Communist Ought to be Like," in William G. Rosenberg, ed., *Bolshevik Visions: First Phase of the Cultural Revolution in Soviet Russia Part 1* (Ann Arbor: University of Michigan Press, 1990, 2d ed.), 27.

966 Bukharin, *Historical Materialism*, 19.

967 Ibid., 51.

968 "Our revolution will be invincible if it is not afraid of itself, if it transfers all power to the proletariat...." Lenin, *Selected Works, Vol. 2*, 416.

969 Lenin, *Selected Works Vol. 1*, 122.

970 Trotsky, *Everyday Problems*, 108.

can still be lured into falsehood despite his instinct. Trotsky finds the 'awakened' but not yet developed personality falling into vice during the transition to socialism, resorting to "'dissipation', 'wickedness', and all the sins denounced in the Moscow conference."[971] Lenin cites the example of the masses handing power to the 'bourgeois' Kerensky government, "… owing to insufficient class consciousness and organization of the proletariat…"[972]

The solution to this problem involves complete political, social, and cultural control by an enlightened communist vanguard. This would be the 'dictatorship of the proletariat' which Marx mentions in passing, and over which Lenin spends much of his adult life obsessing. The dictatorship rests "not on law … but on direct, open force,"[973] and is "revolutionarily bold, swift and ruthless in suppressing exploiters and hooligans."[974] Not only is the dictatorship essential to the formation of a classless, Bolshevik utopia, support for the dictatorship is indicative of proper Marxist understanding, in fact "the touchstone on which the *real* understanding and recognition of Marxism should be tested."[975] The task of the dictatorship, writes Trotsky, is to help man realize his own true self, "the nature of man himself [being] hidden in the deepest darkest corner of the unconscious, of the elemental, of the subsoil."[976]

Comprehensive social control and political exposure will help the individual man transform into his true superhuman self. "Man will make it his purpose to master his own feelings, to raise his instincts to the heights of consciousness, to make them transparent, to extend the wires of his will into hidden recesses, and thereby to raise himself to a new plane, to create a higher social biologic type, or, if you please, a superman."[977] The true nature of man is to act in a spontaneously collective manner, according to the Bolsheviks, and hence the dictatorship will lead to a society of perfect harmony devoid of the necessity of force. In this society, writes Bukharin, "The general resolution does not differ by a hair's breadth from the desire of each individual. … In such a society, all the relations between men will be obvious to each, and the social volition will be the organization of all

971 Trotsky, *Women & Family*, 23.
972 Lenin, *Selected Works Vol. 2*, 14.
973 Lenin, *Selected Works Vol. 2*, 72.
974 Lenin, *Selected Works Vol. 2*, 670.
975 Lenin, *Selected Works, Vol. 2*, 292.
976 Trotsky, *Literature and Revolution*, 207.
977 Ibid., 207.

their wills."[978]  At this point, the state will 'wither away' because it is no longer necessary.[979]  Of course, as Lenin explained in 1920, one should not expect this to happen anytime in the near future:

> The dictatorship of the proletariat means a most determined and ruthless war waged by the new class against a *more powerful* enemy, the bourgeoisie, whose resistance is increased *tenfold* by their overthrow (even if only in a single country) … victory over the bourgeoisie is impossible without a long, stubborn and desperate life-and-death struggle which calls for tenacity, discipline, and a single and inflexible will.[980]

Sexuality and ideology are closely intertwined in Leninism.  Sexual control is actually a prerequisite to ideological development.  According to Trotsky, one is incapable of revolutionary consciousness "if he has not thought through the conditions of his private life and family and domestic relationships from all angles, in their unbreakable connection with social relations, i.e., with the conditions and perspectives of the epoch of social revolution."[981]  A dialectical relationship exists between sexuality and ideology, the former certainly not to be dealt with by an ideological novice.  Lenin wonders whether "questions of sex and marriage are dealt with from the point of view of mature, vital historical materialism?  This presupposes wide-ranging, profound knowledge, and the fullest Marxist mastery of a vast amount of material."[982]

The spontaneous collectivity of the communist stands in stark contrast with the instinctive individualism of the bourgeoisie.[983]  In the early Soviet era, sexuality was virtually synonymous with individualism.  As Kollontai explains, "The 'crude individualism' that adorns our era is perhaps nowhere as blatant as in the organization of sexual relationships."[984]  Lenin sees

---

978  Bukharin, *Historical Materialism*, 41.

979  Lenin, *Selected Works Vol. 2*, 329-330.

980  Lenin, *Selected Works Vol. 3*, 339.

981  Trotsky, *Problems of Everyday Life*, 131.

982  Lenin, *On the Emancipation of Women*, 102.

983  Bukharin explains that the bourgeoisie are highly individualistic even though they ostensibly constitute a class acting in concert against the interests of the proletariat.  "As a class the bourgeoisie came our against the proletariat.  But internally, within the limits of the class itself, each member stood opposed to the other."  Bukharin, *Selected Writings*, 17.

984  Kollontai, *Selected Writings*, 241.

individualism here as well, noting that "this superabundance of sex theories, which for the most part are mere hypotheses, and often quite arbitrary ones, stems from a personal need. It springs from the desire to justify one's own abnormal or excessive sex life before bourgeois morality and to plead for tolerance for oneself."[985] Sexuality is, nevertheless, inherently bourgeois according to Lenin. He upbraided Inessa Armand for writing a pamphlet in favor of free love, explaining that, according to the "*objective logic* of class relations in affairs of love," free love will be taken to mean freedom from seriousness in love, freedom from childbirth, and freedom to commit adultery. As he cautioned her, "the proletarian view must be clearly distinguished from and contrasted from" this idea.

Sexuality actually became the basis for identity politics in Bolshevik Russia, as scholars have noted. According to Gregory Carleton, "Ideological sin and sexual deviance were the result of bourgeois influence. In a pure environment, the working class would never exhibit unhealthy, degenerate sexual activity. In fact, the indigenous sexual identity of the proletariat was diametrically opposed to that of the bourgeoisie."[986] According to Eric Naiman, "Asceticism became a means of self-identification, an affirmation of ideological purity in an environment increasingly affected by capitalism."[987]

The singular nature of the true, collective, communist man results in a metaphysical, quasi-biological, collectively-reproducing organism. Lenin refers occasionally to the "...social organism of Russia...."[988] and the "... social and economic organism...."[989] Bukharin is hesitant to ascribe a distinctly organic character to the communist collective, though he concedes the similarities. "No doubt society has much in common with an organism; but it also has much in common with a mechanism. These traits, precisely, are the traits of any totality, any system."[990] He gives up nothing in terms of singularity of consciousness or biological interdependence. Party historian Martin Liadov envisions a collective organism with sensory linkage between component organisms, so that in the society of the future each person "will feel pain, will feel burdened, if his personal interests in any way contradict the interests of the collective...."[991]

985 Lenin, *Emancipation*, 101.
986 Carleton, 57.
987 Naiman, 131.
988 Lenin, *Selected Works Vol. 2*, 646.
989 Lenin, *Selected Works Vol. 2*, 695.
990 Bukharin, *Historical Materialism*, 88.
991 Quoted in Naiman, 93.

Trotsky favors a colony model of communist collectivity, explaining that society, and the press specifically, has "no right to ignore the occurrences that justly agitate our human beehive."[992] Kollontai also favored the beehive model for communist reproduction, entitling a novel *The Love of Worker Bees*. Trotsky also explains that "communist life will not be formed blindly, like coral islands, but will be built consciously, will be tested by thought, will be directed and corrected."[993] Worker bees are asexual and coral can reproduce asexually, though bees, unlike coral, are dependent on a centralized reproduction system. Clearly Trotsky has some sort of centralized reproduction program in mind when he explains that "the human race will not have ceased to crawl on all fours before God, kings, and capital, in order to submit humbly before the dark laws of heredity and a blind sexual selection!"[994]

In the future, love will take on new and unknowable forms according to Trotsky and Kollontai, though it will be collective at a minimum.[995] Kollontai explains that in the communist society to come, "'sympathetic ties' between all the members of the new society will have grown and strengthened. ... Collectivism of spirit can then defeat individualist self-sufficiency...."[996] In order to get from here to there, Trotsky writes, "the problem of marriage has ceased to be a matter of uncritical tradition and the blind force of circumstance; it has been posed as a task of collective reason."[997] He outlines a number of conflict situations, destructive relationships doomed to failure because one or the other party to the marriage is not a member of the communist party.[998] In order to avoid these situations, Zalkind proposes explicitly that "sexual selection should only take place in line with class, revolutionary-proletarian purposes."[999] Kollontai is disturbed at the prospect of two people falling in love, and then withdrawing from the collective. "The old ideal was 'all for the loved one'; communist morality demands all for the collective," she writes.[1000] Kollontai actually proposes a list of five requirements for sexual intercourse

992   Trotsky, *Problems of Everyday Life*, 68.
993   Trotsky , *Literature and Revolution*, 206.
994   Trotsky, *Literature and Revolution*, 207.
995   Ibid., 199.
996   Kollontai, *Selected Writings*, 290.
997   Trotsky, *Women and the Family*, 53.
998   Ibid., 23-24.
999   Quoted in Carleton, 77.
1000  Kollontai, *Selected Writings*, 231.

to occur, finishing with: "The bonds between the members of the collective must be strengthened."[1001]  While generally hostile to the idea of sex for pleasure, she differentiates between 'wingless Eros', or spontaneous and casual sex, and 'winged Eros', involving sexual intercourse which may or may not involve exclusivity. Thus Kollontai allows for the possibility of non-monogamous sexuality only insofar as it increases the emotional bonds between members of the collective. This led Bolshevik Aron Zalkind to suggest that the Soviet Union would, as a consequence, no longer be able to build airplanes.   Another, P. Vinogradskaya, suggested that Kollontai's prioritization of love and sex over reproduction indicate that she "lacks the logic to think out what her current intensified statements about a new period in the area of Eros mean politically. She lacks a Marxist and communist intuition...."[1002]  She queries: "Is love really, taken in a social and biological connection, some sort of art for art's sake? Is it really not the prelude to reproduction, to the bearing of children?"[1003]

As one might expect, the Bolsheviks were rather conflicted about the institutions of marriage and the family. Lenin was especially troubled by the "decay, putrescence, and filth of bourgeois marriage with its difficult dissolution, its license for the husband and bondage for the wife, and its disgustingly false sexual morality...."[1004]  Lenin also suggests, not coincidentally, that the nuclear family is characterized by individualism: "Women's incipient social life and activities must be promoted, so that they can outgrow the narrowness of their philistine, individualistic psychology centered on home and family."[1005]  Kollontai similarly suggests that the "bonds of family and marriage must be weakened, and ... men and women need to be educated on solidarity and the subordination of the will of the individual to the collective."[1006]

A general consensus existed that the communist family in the future would be collective in some way, and at the very least things like cooking and child-rearing would be taken over by the state.[1007]  Trotsky sees the

---

1001 Ibid.
1002 P. Vinogradskaya, "The Winged Eros of Comrade Kollontai," in William G. Rosenberg, ed., *Bolshevik Visions: First Phase of the Cultural Revolution in Soviet Russia Part 1* (Ann Arbor: University of Michigan Press, 1990, 2d ed.), 116.
1003 Ibid., 119.
1004 Lenin, *On the Emancipation of Women*, 105.
1005 Ibid., 104.
1006 Kollontai, *Selected Writings*, 230.
1007 Trotsky, *Women and the Family*, 29.

family enduring otherwise, in a form somewhat difficult to distinguish from the bourgeois family Bolshevism had just 'destroyed ... from the roots up'. "A long and permanent marriage, based on mutual love and cooperation -- that is the ideal standard. ... Freed from the chains of police and clergy, later also from those of economic necessity, the tie between man and woman will find its own way, determined by physiology, psychology, and care for the welfare of the human race."[1008] The new family will in any case be markedly different from the bourgeois family in terms of psychology, "and the very idea of laws about abortion and divorce will sound no better within its walls than the recollection of houses of prostitution or human sacrifices."[1009] For Kollontai, on the contrary, the family is based entirely on economics, and, like the state, withers away with the introduction of a capitalist economy.[1010] "The external economic functions of the old family disappear," she writes, "and consumption ceases to be organized on an individual family basis.... the family economic unit should be recognized as being, from the point of view of the national economy, not only useless but harmful."[1011]

Individualized sexuality results in an energy drain on the collective organism, though collective 'energy' seems to come in two different forms. There is firstly revolutionary 'energy', the desire to engage with the collective, and labor energy, or the ability to work to build communism. Kollontai's discussion of wingless Eros is helpful here: "In the first place it inevitably involved excesses and therefore physical exhaustion, which lower the resources of labor energy available to society. In the second place, it impoverishes the soul, hindering the development and strengthening of inner bonds...."[1012] Lenin looks more toward revolutionary energy, when he explains that "the revolution calls for concentration and rallying of every nerve by the masses and the individual. It does not tolerate orgiastic conditions.... It does not need an intoxicant to stupefy or stimulate it, neither the intoxicant of sexual laxity or of alcohol."[1013] Dr. Timofeev compares the human body to a machine which, "Just like the machine ... does not store reserves of energy, but seeks to expend it in some kind of labor."[1014] People lacking 'technological self-control' in the early Soviet era,

---

1008  Ibid., 53.
1009  Ibid., 72.
1010  Kollontai, *Selected Writings*, 225.
1011  Ibid., 226.
1012  Kollontai, *Selected Writings*, 289.
1013  Lenin, *On the Emancipation of Women*, 107-8.
1014  Quoted in Carleton, 64

energy is often expended on sexual gratification which comes at the direct expense of labor energy.[1015] Zalkind, in contrast, finds sexual energy being stored after having been stolen from other areas, though these reserves of energy might still be converted to cultural work.[1016]

The individual organism will be perpetuated not only through the conservation of energy, but also through biological reengineering. As Trotsky explains, the goal will be to "perfect man's organism, using the most varied of combinations of methods, to regulate the circulation of blood, to refine the nervous system, and at the same time to temper and strengthen it, make it more flexible and hardier -- what a gigantic and fascinating task!"[1017] As the individual organism goes, so goes the collective organism:

> Even purely physiologic life will be subject to collective experiments. The human species, the coagulated Homo Sapiens, will once more enter into a state of radical transformation, and, in his own hands, will become an object of the most complicated methods of artificial selection and psychophysical training. This is entirely in accord with evolution.[1018]

According to Kollontai, the biological health of the collective will necessitate sexual intercourse based on correct levels and types of emotional involvement.[1019] In the communist society of the future, physiological changes will take place over the course of a lifetime depending on one's sexual and ideological condition. According to one commentator, "[in the future] healthy bodies will not be carriers of hidden infection; human selection will take its proper course. The exhausted debauchee will scare others off with the appearance of his body, whereas the healthy, normal person will only attract."[1020]

The collective body of communism is, in the early Soviet era, still composed of proletarian and bourgeois elements. The former are the embodiment of life and vitality while the latter are the embodiment of dissolution and decay, the 'dying class'. Trotsky discusses the difference in terms of art, noting that Communist art is "realistic, active, vitally collectivist,

1015  Ibid.
1016  Naiman, 56, 73-74.
1017  Trotsky, *Problems of Everyday Life*, 140.
1018  Trotsky, *Literature and Revolution*, 206.
1019  Kollontai, *Selected Writings*, 230.
1020  Carleton, 80.

and filled with a limitless creative faith in the future."[1021]  On the other hand, he notes the 'death-like disintegration' of émigré artists, and explains further that "non-October art is struck by a deathly impotence...."[1022] Bourgeois equals sex and bourgeois equals death, and hence sex equals death.  As Lenin explains, "it is hardly a good thing that sex, already strongly felt in the physical sense, should at such time assume so much prominence in the psychology of young people.  The consequences are nothing short of fatal."[1023]

That the elements of life, purity, collectivity are trapped within the same body as the elements of death, sexuality, and individualism presents a problem for the collective body as a whole. "When the old society dies," Lenin once explained, "its corpse cannot be shut up in a coffin and placed in the grave. It decomposes in our midst; the corpse rots and infects us."[1024] Certainly the bourgeoisie were compromising the class instincts of the proletariat, "constantly caus[ing] among the proletariat relapses into petty-bourgeois spinelessness, disunity, individualism, and alternating moods of exaltation and dejection."[1025]

The bourgeoisie were also infecting the proletariat with sexuality, according to Kollontai: "The sexual crisis does not spare even the peasantry. Like an infectious disease it 'knows neither rank nor status'."[1026]  Zalkind suggested that sexuality had come to replace religion as the opiate of the masses: 'The striving for social interaction -- for class organization and class struggle — weakens if deflected by sexual hypnosis...."[1027] Capitalists had injected the "revolutionary laboring masses with a sexual narcotic... "[1028]  Zalkind suggested that capitalism had actually changed mankind physiologically: "Under capitalism, man's sexual life had 'swollen' to an unnatural size, and his disorganized body now responded sexually to symbols that previously had not aroused him."[1029]  According to Liadov, women only menstruated once a year under normal conditions, but the rise of a capitalist economy forced them to become sexual year-round.[1030]

---

1021  Trotsky, *Literature and Revolution*, 33.
1022  Ibid., 65.
1023  Lenin, Emancipation, 105.
1024  Quoted in Naiman, 160.
1025  Lenin, *Selected Works Vol. 3*, 357.
1026  Kollontai, *Selected Writings*, 239.
1027  Naiman, 127.
1028  Carleton, 57.
1029  Naiman, 127.
1030  Naiman, 3, 182.

Sexuality is thus an infectious and virulent disease which results in the decay and decomposition of the collective organism. Lenin offers the obvious solution: "The way of reform is one of delay, procrastination, and the painfully slow decomposition of the national organism. It is the proletariat and the peasantry that suffer first of all and most of all from that putrefaction. The revolutionary path is one of rapid amputation…"[1031]

## 6.3  Everyone Pays For It

**Russia came late to many** things, not least of these legitimate statehood. Kievan Rus' rose and fell during the middle ages, followed by Muscovite rule ascendant in the early modern era. Power radiated outward from the center and diffused quickly, Muscovite rulers having very little control in fact over the Russian hinterlands. In the early 18th century, Peter the Great attempted to expand the control of the Tsar through centralized ministries, and in the late 18th century Catherine the Great attempted the same with a more generalized and geographically diffuse form of control.[1032]  Both attempts met with considerable resistance, and were limited in their effect.

In the early 19th century, a bureaucratic realignment initiated by Alexander I was followed by a bureaucratic buildup by Nicholas I, which finally gave Russia the organizational infrastructure to match its vaunted military capabilities. Which is to say that both proved themselves horribly ineffectual in the Crimean War of 1854, the defeat causing Russia to rethink her entire social and political enterprise. What followed was the era of the 'Great Reforms', led unevenly by Alexander II, which resulted in the formation of an actual working legal system, limited local self-government, and the emancipation of the serfs in 1861.[1033]  Par for the course for reformist monarchs, Alexander would later be assassinated by a group of asexual terrorists in 1881. Nineteenth century Russia, as it turns out, had come first to sexual revolution.

---

1031  Lenin, *Selected Works, Vol. 1*, 487.

1032  Marc Raeff, *Understanding Imperial Russia: State and Society in the Old Regime*, trans. Arthur Goldhammer, fwd. John Keep (New York: Columbia University Press, 1984).

1033  W. Bruce Lincoln, *The Great Reforms: Autocracy, Bureaucracy, and the Politics of Change in Imperial Russia* (Dekalb: Northern Illinois University Press, 1990); W. Bruce Lincoln, *In the Vanguard of Reform: Russia's Enlightened Bureaucrats* (Dekalb: Northern Illinois University Press, 1982).

# Sexual Atomism in 19ᵗʰ Century Russia

**The traditional, patriarchal family was,** in actuality, relatively untraditional and nonpatriarchal in ancient Russia, at least compared to the one found in the early modern period. Though the man was still dominant, society took a much more positive view of the woman. Joanna Hubbs, for example, has devoted an entire work to the feminine strain in ancient Russian mythology, the tendency to create female deities, protagonists, and antagonists.[1034] On a more practical level, Elaine Elnett points to evidence indicating the existence of a matriarchal society, with women capable of holding property and acting as the head of the family or even the tribe.[1035] A woman stood in for her husband when the latter was absent, and a widow was acknowledged as the head of her household.[1036] There is a difference of opinion as to whether there was freedom of choice in marital relationships, though if it ever existed, it disappeared sometime in the Middle Ages.[1037] Even in ancient Russia, though, there was very little in the way of independence, sexual or otherwise, with the individual bound closely to the family and the family bound closely to the tribe. Even then, women were expected to marry, the expectation being so strong that there was no Russian word for woman other than 'wife'.[1038] There was, however, very little in the way of existential terror at the thought of people having sex,[1039] and there were even various Slavic religious rituals that included sexual acts.[1040]

---

1034 Joanna Hubbs, *Mother Russia: The Feminine Myth in Russian Culture* (Bloomington: Indiana University Press, 1988).

1035 Elaine Elnett, *Historic Origin and Social Development of Family Life in Russia,* fwd. Franklin H. Giddings (New York: AMS Press, 1926), 1.

1036 Ibid., 20.

1037 Arguing no: Eve Levin, *Sex and Society in the World of Orthodox Slavs, 900-1700* (Ithaca: Cornell University Press, 1989), 38. Arguing yes: Elnett, 1. Arguing yes and no: N.L. Pushkareva, "Women in the Medieval Russian Family of the Tenth Through the Fifteenth Centuries," in Russia's Women: Accomodation, Resistance, Transformation, ed. Barbara Evans Clements, Barbara Alpern Engel, and Christine D. Worobec (Berkeley: University of California Press 1991), 30. Pushkareva cites the dual practices of 'bride capture' in which the woman had free choice, and of the formal marriage contract in which parents selected the spouse.

1038 Dorothy Atkinson, "Society and the Sexes in the Russian Past," in *Women in Russia,* ed. Dorothy Atkinson, Alexander Dallin, and Gail Warshofsky Lapidus (Stanford: Stanford University Press, 1977), 6.

1039 Ibid., 6.

1040 Levin, *Sex and Society,* 39.

Russia seems to have imported its fear of sex from the Byzantine Church, having named Christianity as its official religion in 988. This is generally cited as the moment when the status of women begins to decline, though certainly it declined much faster as church and state strengthened their ties in the early days of Muscovite rule.[1041] Byzantine proscriptions on sexual conduct were very comprehensive and detailed, though guided by one single principle, namely that one should never do anything sexual unless absolutely necessary. "The three requirements for licit sex were procreation, vaginal penetration, and the missionary position," as Eve Levin explains. Even procreative sex was viewed with extreme suspicion: "High value was placed on chastity," writes Igor Kon, "and retention of virginity, even within marriage."[1042] Though all sex was considered Satanic, couples were still encouraged to have children, with non-procreative sex considered a "double outrage" according to N.L. Pushkareva.[1043] More formal arrangements were also utilized to prevent sex for pleasure. Arranged marriages were the norm at this point, and upper class women found themselves locked up permanently in a special section of the house called the *terem*.[1044] Separation of the sexes may have worked to the advantage of women in some respects, with marriages now guided by a manual called the *domostroi*. This popular 16th century work advised men as to proper wife-beating technique, among other things: "Should a wife disregard her husband's wishes, it was his responsibility to discipline her physically. If the problem was serious, she was to be lashed, blouse removed; but this was to be done privately, 'politely', and without anger."[1045]

The arranged marriage came under attack in the early 18th century by

---

1041 Atkinson, 12-23. "Although there is evidence that many Russian women of the pre-Kievan and Kievan periods had possessed a certain amount of prestige, power, and even equality in a number of endeavors, including military ones, all this had disappeared in the centuries of Muscovite rule." Richard Stites, *The Women's Liberation Movement in Russia: Feminism, Nihilism, and Bolshevism, 1860-1930* (Princeton: Princeton University Press, 1978), 11.

1042 Igor S. Kon, *The Sexual Revolution in Russia: From the Age of the Czars to Today*, trans. James Riordan (New York: The Free Press, 1995), 14.

1043 Pushkareva, 39.

1044 "The terem was a special addition the house, either on top or behind the house, far away from the reception rooms. The windows of the terems usually faced either the garden or a fence so high that no strange eye could penetrate it. The husband and the father kept the key to the terem. Even brothers and near relatives could not always gain entrance into the women's rooms." Elnett, 27.

1045 Atkinson, 15.

Tsar Peter the Great, who apparently found his own arranged marriage less than satisfactory. In 1702, he introduced the rite of betrothal, a six-week period of acquaintance for prospective bride and groom, accompanied by a right of refusal for both parties.[1046] Women were also ordered to be brought out of the terems and forced to mix socially with members of both sexes.[1047] The impact of these reforms seems to have been minimal.

By the end of the 18th century, Russian sexuality begins to diverge into two different directions, with authors pointing both to an increase in sexual liberalism among the aristocracy,[1048] and a tightening of marital bonds by the church.[1049] Romanticism had a definitive emergence in the early part of the 19th century, perhaps due in part to an influx of western literature and ideas.[1050] It has also been proposed that the rise of the autocratic Tsar Nicholas I (1825-55) left men no room for expression in the public sphere, and hence subjective experience and 'true love' became the order of the day.[1051] As for women, the influential writer George Sand engaged in an open attack on the traditional family in the 1830s, striking a responsive chord with a number of women in Russia. According to Elnett, the George Sand-inspired woman of the 1840s and 50s considered "love as the aim of her whole existence and the only way out of harsh reality. ... She wanted to love freely first of all, and her choice coincided with the cultural movement of that period."[1052]

The Russian family had for some time been linked conceptually (and normatively) to the Russian political order. Conservatives saw the absolute subservience of the wife to her husband mirrored by the absolute subservience of the Russian subject to the Tsar, the one reinforcing the other. Reformers agreed, and felt therefore that the emancipation of

---

1046  Elnett, 46.

1047  Atkinson, 26.

1048  "The Russian gentleman of the XVIIIc was proud of his depravity.... Loose morals gave the tone to the whole social life." Elnett, 53.

1049  Barbara Alpern Engel, *Women in Russia, 1700-2000* (Cambridge: Cambridge University Press, 2004), 21.

1050  "Western literature, which had filtered into the country even earlier, gained increasing influence.... From these literary sources came a new notion of women as partners in love relationships that extended beyond the physiological bond between the sexes." Ibid.

1051  Barbara Alpern Engel, *Mothers and Daughters: Women of the Intelligentsia in Nineteenth-Century Russia* (Cambridge: Cambridge University Press, 1983), 21.

1052  Elnett, 64.

women would be essential to the destruction of the existing social and political order.[1053] The 'woman question' was debated intensely among the Russian intelligentsia in the 1860s, with the patriarchal family condemned and disrupted to whatever extent possible. The decade saw the rise of the fictitious marriage, in which some progressive man would marry some progressive young woman, then allow her to go off on her own, enabling her to escape an arranged marriage and life of servitude. The marriages were intended to be asexual and unemotional, though some genuine love affairs did begin this way. The decade also saw the rise of the nihilist woman (*nigilistka*), who, declaring her independence and rejecting all vestiges of the past, flouted gender conventions in dress and behavior.[1054] Women who rejected traditional gender roles were frequently suspected of broader revolutionary aims, and often with good reason.

The most tangible and controversial area of reform to which the sexual revolution directed itself was the education of women, something virtually nonexistent prior to the late 1850s.[1055] During the Crimean War, women had served at the front as nurses, dealing a rather severe blow to arguments of inherent female inferiority. During the 'thaw', the relaxation of censorship which followed the death of Nicholas I, radical journals began demanding educational opportunities for women. In 1859, St. Petersburg University began allowing women to audit lectures, followed by the universities of Kiev and Kharkov.[1056] At lower levels, secondary schools for girls were opened in 1858, and a decade later some 10,000 girls were enrolled at 125 schools.[1057] The conservative reaction was swift and predictable, with women officially expelled from higher education in 1863. Women began to migrate westward, attending medical school in Zurich and elsewhere, some of them becoming involved in revolutionary circles at the same time. Conservatives were thus led to reconsider their decision, concerned not only over the potential for revolutionary conspiracy but also

1053 Engel, *Women in Russia*, 69. Engel notes that Russia, at this point, was especially conservative relative to the rest of Europe. Engel, *Mothers and Daughters*, 7.
1054 Engel, *Women in Russia*, 73; Elnett, 79.
1055 As of 1856, only .1% percent of girls even managed to attend primary school. Christine Johanson, *Women's Struggle for Higher Education, 1855-1900* (Kingston: McGill-Queen's University Press, 1987), 3.
1056 Johanson, 17-18. Women actually received the support of many university professors at the time, some of whom advocated the granting of degrees without regard to gender. Engel, *Women in Russia*, 72.
1057 Johanson, 29.

for sexual impropriety.[1058] They need not have worried as to the latter, with young female revolutionaries frequently self-governed by a strict puritanical code.[1059] "For some, the struggle for reform or revolution became an all-consuming passion," writes Christine Johanson, "which left no room for love or sexual relationships. When the attractive Mariia Kal'enkina was asked why she was indifferent to men, she replied, 'I love the movement'."[1060]

Russia's sexual revolution of the 1860s was largely an intellectual affair, affecting only the upper classes and leaving the peasant family untouched. Russia's massive industrialization drive and rapid urbanization in the late 19th century would change that quite dramatically. Russia's total urban population went from roughly 9 million people in the mid-nineteenth century to about 25 million in 1913, with the population of most of Russia's major cities increasing four- or five-fold in that span.[1061] Large-scale railway construction in the second half of the nineteenth century facilitated geographic mobility, while newly industrialized cities provided economic opportunities for skilled and unskilled workers.

Immigrants from rural areas, temporary and permanent, provided for most of the growth. The social patterns they left behind were marked by strict adherence to social norms and the complete domination of the community over the individual. "Indeed," writes Christine Worobec, "individuals cannot exist outside the collective. Only as members of a household can they enjoy rights as a community members."[1062] Marriage was very much a collective affair, as was sexual morality in general. Young men were required to marry in order to become full members of the

---

1058 Stites, 77. "The Russian women who were studying in Europe in the second half of the XIXc were likened to prostitutes and accused of studying medicine and midwifery with the special aim of producing abortions." Elnett, 84.

1059 Note Engel on the movements of the time: "The Chaikovskii circle contributed to the Russian radical movement by its ethical tone as much as by its activities. ... True to their denial of traditional feminine roles, they would tolerate no flirtation or sexual advances." Engel, *Mothers and Daughters*, 124-25. Further: "[The Fritsch group's] growing radicalism created a painful conflict for the women that the moral absolutism of the group served to exacerbate. ... At some point the women also agreed to renounce sexual relations." Ibid., 141.

1060 Johanson, 54.

1061 Michael F. Hamm, ed., *The City in Late Imperial Russia* (Bloomington: Indiana University Press, 1986), 2-3.

1062 Christine D. Worobec, *Peasant Russia: Family and Community in the Post-Emancipation Period* (Princeton: Princeton University Press, 1991), 6.

community, and promiscuous young women were considered unmarriageable because of their social instability.[1063]

The social patterns they found were generally marked by atomism and individualism, with urban pressures breaking apart existing families and preventing the formation of new ones. Joseph Bradley notes that in Moscow, "The growth in housing stock could not keep pace with population growth ... families found it difficult to live together...."[1064] As to St. Peterburg, James H. Bater notes that "the population remained predominately single, far more so than the average for the Empire as a whole, and, among European capitals, St. Petersburg had a particularly low per-capita ratio of married inhabitants."[1065] Progressive jurists proposed reforms which would have made dissolving existing marriages easier, though these were never set in place.[1066]

Women made up an increasing proportion of urban migrants as time went on. They also constituted an ever-increasing portion of the industrial workforce, with female factory workers rising from 20% of the total in 1885 to 33% by 1914, and going as high as 40% in certain locations.[1067] Female workers were represented in most industries, and eventually predominated in areas like textiles.[1068] They were generally paid less, though, and many had difficulty finding straight employment. Factoring in the economic desperation of women with the large number of men who had left wives behind in the countryside, all the elements were set in place

1063 Ibid., 7, 119.
1064 Joseph Bradley, "Moscow: From Big Village to Metropolis," in *The City in Late Imperial Russia*, ed. Michael F. Hamm (Bloomington: Indiana University Press, 1986), 16.
1065 James H. Bater, "Between Old and New: St. Petersburg in the Late Imperial Era," in *The City in Late Imperial Russia*, ed. Michael F. Hamm (Bloomington: Indiana University Press, 1986), 52.
1066 Engel, *Women in Russia*, 109.
1067 Rose L. Glickman, *Russian Factory Women: Workplace and Society, 1880-1914* (Berkeley: University of California Press, 1984), 76-84.
1068 Glickman. By the late 19th century, women were frequently employed in positions requiring education, some even practicing medicine or editing and publishing journals. Engel, *Women in Russia*, 111-12. Women were also represented in Russia's merchant class by this time, making up between 8% and 15% of registered merchants in Moscow and St. Petersburg. Catriona Kelly, "Teacups and Coffins: the Culture of Russian Merchant Women, 1850-1917," in *Women in Russia and Ukraine*, ed. trans. Rosalind Marsh (Cambridge: Cambridge University Press, 1996), 62.

for an explosion in prostitution.[1069] Russian authorities then recognized two different modes of sexual expression, which were marital and criminal.[1070] The reality was far more complex, with women often trading sex for favors on a casual basis, sometimes in an effort to acquire employment.[1071] Nevertheless, officials were known to force single women into Russia's highly regulated system of prostitution, often on slight pretexts.

Individualism was taking hold by the early 20th century, and sexual individualism in particular. Richard Stites notes that 'free sex' was the norm among urban lower classes, and that "every kind of illegal liaison flourished in all ranks of society."[1072] Personal ads were now to be found in magazines and newspapers, next to advertisements for pornography and contraceptives.[1073] Literature turned sexual, in some cases taking on themes of incest and sadism.[1074] Especially popular and controversial were Artsybashev's *Sanin* and Verbitskaia's *The Keys to Happiness*, both featuring protagonists (the latter female) who indulge their sexual urges without restraint or regret. The novel *Sanin* even inspired sex clubs, presumably formed with the intent of modeling similar behavior.[1075] Abortion rates were already rising dramatically as progressive physicians attempted to secure its decriminalization.[1076] Others fought to preserve the ban specifically to provide a restraint on female sexuality.[1077] According to less progressive elements, by 1906 or 1907 Russia had entered into a 'sexual crisis', or "a sexual question with the same rhetorical status as the more familiar 'woman question' and 'social question'."[1078] As Russia approached world war and bloody revolution, Laura Engelstein finds her physicians sounding the alarm:

> Physicians construed their scientific arguments in
> increasingly organic terms, emphasizing the physiological

1069 Laurie Bernstein, *Sonia's Daughters: Prostitutes and Their Regulation in Imperial Russia* (Berkeley: University of California Press, 1995), 91-97.
1070 Stites, 178.
1071 Glickman.
1072 Stites, 178-79.
1073 Laura Engelstein, *The Keys to Happiness: Sex and the Search for Modernity in Fin-de-Siecle Russia* (Ithaca: Cornell University Press, 1992), 360.
1074 Stites, 185.
1075 Stites, 187.
1076 Engel, *Women in Russia*, 125; Kon, 40.
1077 Engel, *Women in Russia*, 125.
1078 Engelstein, 216.

consequences of sexual vice, transmissible across generations, to the ultimate detriment of the entire social body. ... Excess sexual expenditure, it was thought, depleted the nation's energy supply; profligacy undermined public health by spreading venereal disease; masturbation had long term effects.[1079]

## Origins of the Russian Revolution

**The evolution of Russian political** thought runs a close parallel to Russia's sexual evolution over the course of the nineteenth century. The reign of Nicholas I was inaugurated in 1825 with an attempted coup, the 'Decembrist' uprising, led by Russian military leaders. The decades that followed were, not surprisingly, marked by autocratic rule and the rigorous suppression of dissent. When Nicholas I died in 1854, restrictions were relaxed, and the period came to be known as 'the thaw'.

The mid-nineteenth century saw three intellectuals come to prominence: Alexander Herzen, Michael Bakunin, and Nicholas Chernyshevsky. A vague predilection for liberal thought had been growing in Russia since the 1840s and 50s.[1080] Herzen became its primary exponent and fused it with populism, the latter involving a belief that the Russian peasant would be the key to the social and political salvation. He spent his influential years (1857-1862) in London, where he received so many important visitors that he became known as Russia's 'second government'. His journal, *The Bell*, was popular even in Russia where it had to be smuggled in.[1081] Herzen's vast influence would wane quickly, having first congratulated Tsar Alexander II for the emancipation of the serfs in 1861, and later condemning an assassination attempt against the Tsar in 1866. The revolutionary mind was by then becoming distinctly militant and intolerant.

Michael Bakunin was a better fit for the mood of the 1860s and 1870s. Bakunin was an anarchist, an advocate of the lawless society, though certainly not an advocate of generalized chaos. Quite to the contrary, in

1079 Engelstein, 245.
1080 Abbott Gleason, *Young Russia: The Genesis of Russian Radicalism in the 1860s* (New York: Viking Press, 1980), 79.
1081 Adam Ulam suggests a circulation of roughly 30,000 in Russia. Adam Ulam, *In the Name of the People: Prophets and Conspirators in Prerevolutionary Russia* (New York: Viking Press, 1977), 39.

Bakunin's utopia, the personality structure is self-regulated, and operates in a collective manner without the need for the coercive power of the state. Bakunin here prefigures Lenin's post-dictatorship society, without even the need for a dictatorship of the proletariat to facilitate the transition. The devil is in the details, of course, and "so we must begin by making a precise distinction between the official and therefore tyrannical authority of the State-organized society and the influence of non-official, natural society upon each of its members."[1082] Society is actually a much more powerful influence on the individual, according to Bakunin, as it "creates and moulds all the individuals who are born and develop within it. From the cradle to the grave, it slowly instills in them with all its material, intellectual and moral essence; we may say that it incarnates itself in every man."[1083] Society is apparently synonymous with the laws of nature, because man himself "is nothing except nature; his most sublime or monstrous feelings, the most perverted, selfish, or heroic resolves of his will...."[1084] Humanity will eventually merge into a single, perfect consciousness and perfect love, leaving temporal (and sexual) pleasures behind: "What else does society offer, apart from material wealth? Carnal, human, earthly affection, civilization and culture — vast enough from the transitory earthbound point of view, but insignificant compared with eternity, immortality and God...."[1085]

Above all, though, it was the aforementioned Nicholas Chernyshevksy who captured the spirit of the age. He first made his mark editing a literary journal called *The Contemporary*, started by Eugen Pushkin and later featuring Leo Tolstoy and Ivan Turgenev on its board. With Chernyshevsky at the helm, the journal turned to politics, and nihilism in particular. Nihilism meant different things to different people, though most generally it meant the rejection of tradition and a critical reappraisal of the political

---

1082 Michael Bakunin, *Selected Writings*, ed. Arthur Lehning, trans. Steven Cox and Olive Stevens (London: Jonathan Cape, 1973), 149.

1083 Ibid., 152.

1084 Ibid., 154.

1085 Ibid., 143. Biographer E.H. Carr suggests that Bakunin was impotent late in life, and perhaps early in life as well: "When he was in his twenties, some of his contemporaries already suspected an incapacity of that kind; and he is not known to have had sexual relations with any woman. No explicit statement on the subject, medical or other, has been preserved." E.H. Carr, *Michael Bakunin* (New York: Octagon Books, 1975), 24. If so, Bakunin's recurrent tendency to differentiate personal love from 'absolute love' suggests that lack of interest might also be a possible explanation.

and social order.[1086] The stronger version was the complete destruction of the existing political and social order. The philosophy came with a complete lifestyle attached, which most frequently included sexual abstinence rather than libertinism. Chernyshevsky's great claim to fame was his asexual love story, *What is to be Done?*, a book which scholars cite as the definitive nihilist treatise of its time. Abbott Gleason writes that "seldom has a book had so immediate (and indeed so protracted) an effect upon the audience for which it was intended. ...the novel was in fact the Bible of Russian radicals for many years...."[1087] Ronald Hingley notes also that "to many Russians of the 1860s it was a sacred text, as well as a practical handbook of New Man's etiquette. It did more to mould Nihilists' beliefs and influence their actions than any other single document."[1088]

Vera Pavlovna is the heroine of the story, and the first of the 'new people' whose lives are 'well-ordered'. She is forced to contend firstly with her avaricious mother, Maria Alexnevna, who would, according to the book, do anything to make money. Pavlovna attends an opera where she overhears comments of a sexual nature pertaining to her from a suitor named Storeshnikov, the son of her landlords. Alexnevna attempts to engineer a marriage between the two, for her own financial advantage of course. The well-meaning but sexually-depraved Julie turns up at random to discuss the question of sex with Pavlovna, again to the latter's horror and disgust. Pavlovna is eventually rescued by a young man named Lopukhov, who agrees to a 'blank' or asexual marriage, thus saving her from a marriage with Storeshnikov that would involve sexual intercourse. Chernyshevsky goes on at length describing their sleeping habits, assuring the reader that they sleep in separate rooms and only meet fully dressed.[1089] Pavlovna later falls in love with a man named Kirsanov, though as Hingley points out, "The two men are both portrayed as such monumental prigs that it is not clear why Vera should prefer one to the other, or even how she can tell them apart...."[1090] In any case, Lopukhov does the honorable thing, which is to fake his own suicide, allowing Pavlovna to marry Kirsanov, and then later returns to the social circle pretending to be an American businessman. The Pavlovna-Kirsanov marriage produces children, though Chernyshevsky

1086 Ulam, 135.
1087 Gleason, 295.
1088 Ronald Hingley, *Nihilists: Russian Radicals and Revolutionaries in the Reign of Alexander II, 1855-81* (New York: Delacorte Press, 1969), 35.
1089 Chernyshevsky, 135-36.
1090 Hingley, 37.

offers no specifics as to sleeping habits as he did previously, nor does he mention pregnancy or childbirth. A minor character, Rakhmetov, perhaps the real hero of the story, makes an appearance in the middle of the story, delivering a message to Pavlovna and then offering up the details of his own ascetic, asexual, revolutionary lifestyle. He avoids women and alcohol in particular, explaining that "we demand that men may have a complete enjoyment of their lives, and we must show by our example that we demand it ... from principle and not from passion, from conviction and not from personal desire."[1091] A planned sequel to *What is to be Done?*, perhaps with Rakhmetov as its protagonist, never materialized.

What Chernyshevsky wrote he lived. He informed his wife that, man having had the upper hand for centuries, it was time for woman to be set in a dominant position, or at least freed to do as she pleased. Chernyshevsky's wife apparently took him at his word, doing whatever and whomever she pleased, and without known complaint from her husband. Gleason writes that he maintained a "slavish and hopeless passion" for his wife, though apparently without any hope of reciprocation from her or any other woman. "His asceticism," Gleason continues, "seemed to convey not only a programmatic joylessness but the desire to deprive others of pleasure, to narrow life, to make it gray. ...love and sex were in practice a humiliation to him."[1092] Hingley finds him merely an exemplar of "the common Nihilist tendency to regard human conduct, even in the most intimate personal relationships, as something subject to mechanical *a priori* regulation on the basis of abstract principles."[1093] Even Chernyshevsky himself seems to have noticed the pattern, according to Franco Venturi: "In the capital he led an ascetic life, either through lack of means or on principle. ... When in prison ten years later he translated Rousseau's Confessions, he was struck by the similarity of his own experiences to those of Rousseau."[1094]

Russian Robespierres were soon to follow. The reforms of 1861 did not go nearly as far as many would have liked, and this put liberalism in an untenable position. Having achieved a half-victory simultaneously robbed it of vitality and urgency while making it look ineffectual. Nihilism predominated in the 1860s, and revolutionary thought became all-

---

1091  Ibid., 229.
1092  Gleason, 103.
1093  Hingley, 35.
1094  Franco Venturi, *Roots of Revolution: A History of the Populist and Socialist Move-ments in Nineteenth Century Russia*, trans. Francis Haskell, intro. Isaiah Berlin (New York: Alfred A. Knopf, 1960), 133.

encompassing and absolute for young Russian intellectuals, many of whom
were attempting to model Chernyshevsky. As Gleason writes:

> In a way that is not easy to describe, one became a
> radical in the mid-1860s and began to develop a quasi-
> tribal relationship to other radicals. Becoming a radical
> tended to be more of a total experience; at some point it
> involved a conscious repudiation of the existing order. It
> was more like a religious conversion.[1095]

The year 1861 saw the formation of the first incarnation of the
underground revolutionary group, inspired by Chernyshevsky, called Land
and Freedom, which demanded free land for former serfs in addition to
political liberty. A popular uprising was thought by its members to be
imminent. At St. Petersburg University that fall, massive student disturbances
took place which led to mass arrests. The arrests, according to Ulam, seem to
have had precisely the opposite effect of that intended: "By the time [the
students] were released in December, most of them were ready for exhilarating
political action and many of them knew where to go find it. ...the tsar's
government had helped to create revolutionary subculture in Russian
society...."[1096] The next year, mysterious fires broke out in St. Petersburg,
followed again by repressive police measures which resulted in the arrest and
imprisonment of Chernyshevksy. Battle lines were being drawn hard and
fast, with upper-class revolutionaries claiming to represent the people versus
the government and the great majority of Russian society. Revolutionary
activity in the early 1860s, though, was generally limited to protests and the
publication of manifestos.

In the mid-1860s, the revolution became proactive with the formation
of an organization aptly titled 'Organization', and its militant subset called
Hell. Organization and Hell were formed by Nicholas Ishutin and Ivan
Khudyakhov, Organization comprising roughly 50 members at its peak. The
inner circle, Hell, was to be devoted to political terrorism and assassination,
and, per Ishutin, its members were to remain unmarried and avoid personal
ties of any kind. Khudyakhov was already unhappily married, his new wife
neglecting her responsibilities as his research assistant, and, worse still
according to him, "all her energy now went into the most passionate physical
love. Farewell my moderation, farewell my health."[1097] The two found an

1095 Gleason, 298.
1096 Ulam, 104.
1097 Quoted in Ulam, 150.

apparently suicidal cousin of Khudyakhov's named Karakozov, and convinced him to assassinate the Tsar in 1866. The attempt was unsuccessful, Karakozov was executed, and Khudyakov found himself exiled to Siberia. He told his sexually-immoderate wife to stay home.[1098]

The years that followed were marked by intense crackdowns on revolutionary activity, the years of the 'White Terror' according to Herzen's *Bell*. A charismatic young man named Nechaev was nevertheless having some success putting together a revolutionary organization. His Moscow branch expanded to some 70 or 80 members, and he even managed to secure financial backing from Alexander Herzen at one point. He also collaborated with Bakunin on the 'Catechism of a Revolutionary'.

According to the Catechism, the revolutionary is a "doomed man" who has entirely wiped away all vestiges of his individual existence. He or she is devoted entirely to revolution and nothing else. "To weld the people into one single unconquerable and all-destructive force -- this is our aim, our conspiracy, and our task." Emotional attachments of any kind are suspect, as the revolutionary "is not a revolutionary if he has any sympathy for this world. … All the worse for him if he has any relations with parents, friends, or lovers; *he is no longer a revolutionary if he is swayed by these relationships.*" The revolutionary is devoted to the complete destruction of the existing order, with the aim of the "complete liberation and happiness" of the working classes. Unfortunately for the working classes, the revolutionary society "will use all its resources and energy toward increasing and intensifying the evils and miseries of the people until at last their patience is exhausted and they are driven to a general uprising." The Catechism also advises revolutionaries to create lists of those individuals who are to be executed immediately and those whose destruction can wait.

Nechaev's interest in women seems to have extended only so far as they were useful to him, these uses being entirely asexual. He would, however, frequently tell a woman that he was in love with her, apparently for the sole purpose of manipulating her. After asking future Menshevik Vera Zasulich for her address, "Nechaev stood up, abruptly walked into another room, and returned to declare that he was in love with her. …Zasulich replied that, though she could not return his love, she greatly valued his friendship. Nechaev then silently bowed and left the room."[1099] He apparently tried something similar with Alexander Herzen's daughter, Tata: "She was quite

1098 Gleason, 313.

1099 Jay Bergman, *Vera Zasulich: A Biography* (Stanford: Stanford University Press, 1983), 12.

put off by Nechaev's insistence that the end justified the means and horrified by the talk of the necessity of blackmail. What really did the trick, however, was probably Nechaev's rather passionless declarations of love...."[1100] Adolf Hitler, interestingly enough, would later exhibit the exact same tendency in Munich in the 1920s. Nechaev didn't last long as a revolutionary, finding himself arrested for murdering a disenchanted financial backer, and dying in prison soon after. The Nechaev-Bakunin Catechism would have more staying power.

The upper-class populist revolution continued with the formation of the Kornilov circle, composed entirely of women, and these generally hostile to the opposite sex. "Indeed some of its more extreme members, like [Sofia] Perovskaya, believed that one should avoid contacts with one's male contemporaries altogether.... But gradually their resistance softened when they heard of a group of young men as virtuous and serious in their pursuits as themselves — the Natanson circle."[1101]

The Kornilov circle merged with the Natanson circle to form the Chaikovsky circle, with Chaikovsky soon abandoning the group and leaving for America. "In the New World, he joined the shakers for a time, and indeed their creed, which exacts complete sexual abstinence, may have appeared to him as the logical extension of views entertained in the Natanson and Kornilov circles."[1102] The residue formed the reincarnation of Land and Freedom, under the leadership of a Mikhailov, an admirer of the Nechaev-Bakunin Catechism.[1103] Mikhailov proposed regicide in 1879, which split the organization into a nonviolent wing led by Plekhanov and the extremely violent People's Will (Narodnaya Volya) and its Executive Committee. According to committee member Vera Figner, members were required "to devote all one's mental and spiritual strength to the revolutionary work, to forget for its sake all ties of kinship, and all personal sympathies, love and friendships ... to devote oneself entirely to the secret society, to renounce one's individual desires, subordinating them to the will of the majority as expressed in the ordinances of that society...."[1104]

---

1100 Gleason, 377.
1101 Ulam, 205.
1102 Ulam, 206.
1103 Hardy, 47.
1104 Vera Figner, *Memoirs of a Revolutionist* (New York: Greenwood Press, 1968), 80.

The ascetic Sofia Perovskaya became its most infamous member.[1105] According to Figner, "there was in her nature both feminine gentleness and masculine severity. Tender, tender as a mother with the working people, she was exacting and severe towards her comrades and fellow-workers, while towards her political enemies, the government, she could be merciless...."[1106] In 1881, after several unsuccessful attempts by People's Will, Perovskaya managed to throw a bomb under the Tsar's carriage, sending him to a slow and agonizing death. She became the first Russian woman executed for a political crime.

Over time, political terrorism became a persistent fact of Russian life, so much so in fact that historian Anna Geifman writes that "whereas in the nineteenth century every act of revolutionary violence was a sensation, after 1905 terror became so widespread that many of the country's newspapers no longer bothered to publish detailed reports on every attack."[1107] Anyone wearing a uniform or holding official position might be attacked at any time, and increasingly the lives of innocent bystanders were taken in indiscriminate attacks.[1108] Terror was also put into the service of revolution in the form of 'expropriations', meaning the commission of armed robbery with the proceeds filling the coffers of socialist parties. Lenin and the Bolsheviks were among those employing the technique. Most interesting, though, is that the rise of terrorism corresponds precisely to the sexual atomism of Russia's economic classes. As Geifman writes:

> In the 1860s and 1870s radical circles consisted predominately of individuals who belonged to the privileged groups of Russian society, either by birth, or by virtue of an education that raised them socially and intellectually above their origins. In the early twentieth century, in contrast, the overwhelming majority of terrorists emerged from the first generation of artisans or unskilled laborers forced to move from the countryside to nearby cities or towns....[1109]

With the turn of the century, terrorism continued to be directed at high profile targets, and specifically those in charge of Russia's

---

1105  There are occasional and conflicting reports of relationships with men, most notably fellow revolutionary Andrei Zheliabov.
1106  Figner, 112.
1107  Anna Geifman, *Thou Shalt Kill: Revolutionary Terrorism in Russia, 1894-1917* (Princeton: Princeton University Press, 1993), 22.
1108  Ibid., 43.
1109  Ibid., 11.

counterterrorism efforts. Interior Minister Viacheslav Plehve, who initiated Russia's autocratic war on terror, was assassinated in 1904.[1110] Peter Stolypin, the counterterrorism specialist who introduced military field courts, summary judgment, and immediate execution for terrorists, was killed by terrorists in 1911. None of this is to suggest that terrorism was here motivated by a lack of political liberty, and in fact one of the most violent periods came in 1906-7, just after Russia became a constitutional monarchy. According to historian Richard Pipes, "it has been estimated that in the course of 1906 and 1907 terrorists killed or maimed in the Russian Empire 4,500 officials. If private persons are added, the total number of victims of left-wing terror in the years 1905-7 rises to over 9,000."[1111]

## The Rise of the Bolsheviks

In this chaotic milieu, Russia's Communist Party began modestly in 1898 as the Russian Social Democratic Labor Party (RSDLP), its first meeting devoted to little more than the establishment of the party itself. By the time of the infamous second party congress in 1903 in Belgium, Lenin sat on the editorial board of the socialist journal *Iskra* (Spark), along with other luminaries such as Plekhanov, Vera Zasulich, and Julius Martov. Here we find the initial split between Bolsheviks and Mensheviks, on the question of whether a party member could be anyone supporting the party or someone directly beholden to a central authority, as the Bolsheviks preferred. The theoretical split turned into a split between rival parties, a split which continued even after everyone agreed that centralization was desirable for a revolutionary party. The real issue was one's ability or inability to work with the increasingly autocratic and tempestuous Lenin, who took even the slightest disagreement as a personal and ideological betrayal. Ominously, the two sides began referring to themselves on occasion as Jacobins (Bolsheviks) and Girondins (Mensheviks). According to Lenin, "A Jacobin who wholly identifies himself with the *organization* of the proletariat ... is a *revolutionary Social-Democrat*. A Girdondist ... who yearns for the absolute value of democratic demands is an *opportunist*."[1112]

Neither faction of the RSDLP had much involvement in the events

1110 Richard Pipes, *The Russian Revolution*, 9-15.
1111 Ibid., 165.
1112 V.I. Lenin, *Selected Works Vol. 1* (Moscow: Progress Publishers, 1967), 412.

that brought down the Russian monarchy. In January 1905, large-scale, though peaceful, worker demonstrations in front of the Tsar's Winter Palace in St. Petersburg were met with police gunfire. Tsar Nicholas II was absent and learned about the incident only after it was all over, but found himself blamed in any case. Nicholas grudgingly turned Russia into a constitutional monarchy, forming a representative body called the Duma, which he then proceeded to dissolve whenever it disagreed with him. His enemies on the left, though participating in the Duma, were in no way placated and still dreamed of a violent overthrow of the Tsarist government.

The monarchy held up for the rest of the decade and most of the next, but Russia's participation in World War I put an unbearable strain on it. In February of 1917, demonstrations for 'bread and peace' led to general disorder, and the recently-dissolved Duma continued to meet in secret. Under pressure from the military and Duma, Nicholas abdicated in favor of his brother, Grand Duke Michael, who promptly turned the offer down. The power vacuum was filled by leading members of the Duma, who formed a provisional government, and the Menshevik-led St. Petersburg Soviet, featuring representatives of the working class and military. Alexander Kerensky, whose father had written Lenin's letter of recommendation for university study, emerged as the leading figure in Russia at this time.

With Russia and Germany still continuing to do battle, the German government facilitated Lenin's return to his home country in April. Upon exiting the train, Lenin immediately denounced both the provisional government and the St. Petersburg Soviet. The fall of the monarchy had done nothing to lessen his desire for dictatorship and bloodshed, and the continuation of hostilities provided the Bolsheviks with their opening. They demanded that Russia pull out of the war immediately, received a positive public response to their position, and soon took majorities in both the St. Petersburg and Moscow soviets.

A series of unsuccessful coup attempts over the summer and fall culminated in the successful Bolshevik revolution of October 24-25, 1917, which overthrew the provisional government. There followed a predictable consolidation of power, persecution of rival political parties, stifling censorship, and corruption or shutting down of democratic institutions. To Lenin's way of thinking, the Bolshevik point of view was the democratic view in any case.[1113] Russia's Constituent Assembly was elected and held its first session in January of 1918. The Bolsheviks having received only 25% of the vote and rival parties refusing to give in to them, Lenin had the Assembly disbanded. According to Lenin, "The people wanted to convene the Constituent Assembly, so we convened it. But the people at once sensed what this notorious Assembly represented. So now we have carried out the will of the people...."[1114]

As early as November, 1917, Lenin was encouraging people to identify 'scoundrels' and those resisting revolution. Citizens were to turn these people over or perhaps execute them on the spot.[1115] Lenin explained that the objective was the *"cleansing of Russia's soil of all harmful insects, of scoundrel fleas, bedbugs..."* while Trotsky noted simply that the extermination of Russia's 'dying class' presented no moral difficulties.[1116] Lenin had already made clear that a dictatorship involved the application of force without the rule of law, and thus the arbitrary nature of Soviet legality should have come as no surprise.

The slaughter of Soviet undesirables intensified with the outbreak of civil war in June of 1918, and turned into the 'Red Terror' on the heels of a failed assassination attempt on Lenin in August. Revolutionary Tribunals were formed in which neither the accused nor witnesses needed to participate, and the judges had the power to suspend proceedings and issue a death sentence at any point. This approach was apparently too slow and cumbersome for Lenin, who then turned to the 'extraordinary commission', or 'Cheka' for mass killing. Its head, Felix Dzerzhinsky was noted for his asceticism. Hostages were to be taken and shot in the event of private resistance to food requisitioning, or perhaps simply for failing to perform some task in a timely fashion. Striking workers were often the victims. As Nicholas Werth notes:

> The size of these numbers alone -- between 10,000 and 15,000 summary executions in two months -- marked a radical break with the practices of the Tsarist regime. For the whole period 1825-1917 the number of death sentences

1113 Robert Service, *Lenin: A Biography* (Cambridge: Harvard University Press, 2000), 320-21.
1114 Quoted in Dmitri Volkogonov, *Lenin: A New Biography*, ed. Trans. Harold Shukman (New York: Free Press, 1994), 72.
1115 Bertram D. Wolfe, *An Ideology in Power: Reflections on the Russian Revolution*, intro. Leonard Shapiro (New York: Stein and Day, 1969), 177.
1116 Pipes, 790-1.

passed by the tsarist courts 'relating to political matters' came to only 6,321.... Moreover, not all death sentences were carried out....[1117]

The Soviets also began to experiment with concentration camps, as well as the ethnic cleansing of Cossacks and the class extermination of kulaks. The Nazis would later take note of these techniques, and as Stephane Courtois notes, "The methods implemented by Lenin ... bring to mind the methods used by the Nazis, but most often this is because the latter adopted techniques developed by the former."[1118]

Soviet Communism, or government expropriation under threat of death, ended in 1921 with the adoption of the trade and taxation program of the New Economic Policy or NEP. Government experimentation in the social realm is kept to a minimum during this period, in large part because the Soviet government lacked the money to finance it. Moreover, those few attempts undertaken to destroy bourgeois morality and/or hypocrisy were having unintended consequences. Marriage was made a purely civil contract in 1917, a dissoluble one moreover, and women found themselves abandoned with regularity.[1119] Abortion was grudgingly legalized in 1920 as a temporary measure to combat the "moral survivals of the past and difficult economic conditions of the present,"[1120] while the women's journal Rabotnitsa explained that "the application of any means of preventing pregnancy is abnormal. ... the result of sexual intercourse must be conception."[1121] As Alix Holt notes, the Bolsheviks were attempting to protect women from sexual intercourse rather its consequences, promoting abstinence rather than contraception.[1122]

1117 Nicolas Werth, "A State Against its People: Violence, Repression, and Terror in the Soviet Union," in Stephane Courtois et al., *The Black Book of Communism: Crimes, Terror, Repression*, trans. Jonathan Murphy and Mark Kramer, consulting ed. Mark Kramer (Cambridge: Harvard University Press, 1999), 78.

1118 Stephane Courtois et al., *The Black Book of Communism: Crimes, Terror, Repression*, trans. Jonathan Murphy and Mark Kramer, consulting ed. Mark Kramer (Cambridge: Harvard University Press, 1999), 15.

1119 According to Engel, "14 percent of Soviet marriages ended in divorce in the early 1920s.... The divorce rate was twice as high as that of Germany and almost three times as high as that of France...." Engel, *Women in Russia*, 154.

1120 Alix Holt, "Marxism and Women's Oppression: Bolshevik Theory and Practice in the 1920s," in Tova Yedlin ed., *Women in Eastern Europe and the Soviet Union* (New York: Praeger, 1980), 99.

1121 Ibid., 101.

1122 Ibid., 102.

Many single women turned to prostitution during NEP, which Richard Stites explains was a "painful surprise to Soviet intellectuals...."[1123] Communists believed communists would behave as anhedonic communists when the hated monarchist-capitalist system was destroyed, which may also partly explain the relatively laissez-faire approach of the Soviet government at this time.

It was generally agreed that the triumph of communism was to result in the destruction of 'bourgeois' morality, but this was understood very differently by different elements. For those who identified the bourgeoisie with sexual conservatism rather than hypocrisy and libertinage, NEP was to be an era of sexual liberalism. The early 1920s featured experimentation in 'sexual communism', such as nude marches, group sex, and free-love leagues.[1124] The confusion apparently spread to those inside the party. "Serious sexual scandals in the ranks of the party were sometimes due to garbled interpretations of utopian theories. The resulting moral debauchery caused considerable concern at high political levels in the 1920s."[1125] The reaction was quite predictable, with Bukharin launching into a spontaneous diatribe on the subject of sexual degeneracy at the 14th Party Congress. Even Kollontai, almost entirely in line with Bolshevik sexual ideology, was publicly ridiculed for the suggestion that the communist society of the future might feature free love.

Ideological elements, kindred spirits of Chernyshevksy, equated the bourgeoisie with sexual hypocrisy, specifically the public condemnation of sexuality combined with libertinage in private. Experiments in utopian sexuality, though, were generally confined either to the private sector, and ascetic propaganda was generally the product of low-level government officials and agencies. The theoretical defense of women's rights one finds during this period generally emphasizes women's right not to have sex. According to Alix Holt, "It is significant that Bolsheviks chose to sympathize with women's needs by protecting them from sexual advances, rather than by enabling them to engage freely in sexual activity. They preached abstinence, not contraception."[1126]

The period also featured 'agitation trials' or plays set in the context of public trials, in which the audience would be indoctrinated in the finer points

1123 Stites, 371.
1124 Stern, 24.
1125 Roger Pethybridge, *The Social Prelude to Stalinism* (New York: St. Martin's Press, 1974), 55.
1126 Holt, 102.

of communist morality. Women were frequently shown overcoming backward husbands and officials, sexual harassment and sexual depravity, in order to become good communists, leave the home, and enter the public sphere. As Elizabeth Wood writes, "these trials reveal rigid new assumptions that until a woman is involved in work in the public sphere, she is not yet 'human'."[1127] Choi Chatterjee finds that women were seen primarily in collective terms in Bolshevik Russia:

> It is interesting to see that in the Bolshevik world, the 'typical woman' was perceived primarily as a wife and/or mother living within a family. ... There were few references to single women, divorced women, abandoned women, or unemployed women. Single women, without the protection of an extended family, rarely appeared, but when they did they were usually past middle age and therefore untroubled by emotional and sexual complications.[1128]

Which is not to say that female sexuality was wholly absent. "In popular propaganda in the 1920s, a sexually liberated or predatory woman was usually equated with a prostitute."[1129] Studies showed that many young students were avoiding sex on their own initiative, though as Kent Geiger writes, "it is most revealing that no good Marxist theoretical arguments immediately at hand could provide a reasoned and principled underpinning to the case for self-discipline in sex."[1130]

As the 1920s came to a close, Russia's experiments in utopianism were brought to an end with the rise of Stalinism, a system of government designed to accomplish nothing more than the preservation of one man's power and the implementation of his every whim. As Stalin differentiated his own system of government from a monarchy, "the power of an absolute monarch depends on the machinery of state power; in my plan state power is sustained by the machinery of personal power."[1131] Executive authority was to be preserved by elevating people with no real competency or claim to promotion,

---

1127 Elizabeth A. Wood, *Performing Justice: Agitation Trials in Early Soviet Russia* (Ithaca: Cornell University Press, 2005), 131.

1128 Choi Chatterjee, *Celebrating Women: Gender, Festival Culture, and Bolshevik Ideology, 1910-1939* (Pittsburgh: University of Pittsburgh Press, 2002), 88.

1129 Ibid., 89.

1130 H. Kent Geiger, *The Family in Soviet Russia* (Cambridge: Harvard University Press, ), 70.

1131 Alex de Jonge, *Stalin: And the Shaping of the Soviet Union* (New York: William Morrow and Co., Inc., 1986), 32.

thus ensuring their dependence on and loyalty to their executive benefactor. Bolsheviks of ability and prominence, Bukharin for example, were murdered during the 1930s. More broadly, societal control was achieved through a system of denunciation and summary execution, which fostered paranoia and distrust at even the most intimate levels. Personal and familial loyalties were often pitted against survival instincts during this period.

Otherwise, Stalin remained positively disposed toward the family. As historian Roger Pethybridge notes, "he realized that the family, far from presenting a danger by inducing individualist tendencies in the young, accustomed them, on the contrary, to respect the authority of the father: they would later obey the orders of the Party-State just as unquestionably."[1132] Divorce became more difficult in the 1930s and penalties were increased for nonpayment of alimony.[1133] Homosexuals were purged in the early 1930s,[1134] and homosexuality was made a criminal offense once again in 1934. Prohibitions on pornography and abortion followed in 1935 and 1936 respectively.

Most telling, though, is that unlike during NEP, sex was no longer a subject of discussion, if even to condemn it. Even sex research, notes Igor Kon, "was deemed first unnecessary, then dangerous, and was finally prohibited in the 1930s. Some scholars vanished into the Gulags, and their books were either destroyed or disappeared...."[1135] Soviet theorists explained that the socialist family had more or less arrived by 1936, society now having a communist rather than capitalist foundation, and thus the family would be strengthened rather than allowed to wither away.[1136] The sexual question having been resolved happily, silence was the prescription for the duration of the Soviet Union.

# 7.1 Die Laughing

**Adolf Hitler, prime mover of** the National Socialist movement, was born in 1889 in Branau on the Inn, Austria. He had an unexceptional childhood, and, as a youth, showed every promise of becoming an unexceptional adult.

---

1132  Pethybridge, 56.

1133  Wendy Z. Goldman, 331.

1134  Dan Healey, *Homosexual Desire in Revolutionary Russia: The Regulation of Sexual and Gender Dissent* (Chicago: University of Chicago Press, 2001), 182.

1135  Kon, 75.

1136  Rudolf Schlesinger, ed., *The Family in the U.S.S.R.: Documents and Readings* (London: Routledge & Kegan Paul Ltd., 1949), 280-347.

Even in the course of his ascension to demonic god of the Third Reich, he demonstrated little common sense and few talents. Of course, just these few talents were enough to make him perfectly suited to the leadership of a political movement; he was a gifted orator, charismatic, and surprisingly adept at organizational intrigue. Fortune smiled on him whenever his judgment and skills failed him. His sexuality is frequently discussed and explored, so much so that journalist Ron Rosenbaum divides these numerous inquiries into schools of normality, perversion, and asexuality.[1137] These categories capture the Hitler scholarship quite well, but not the man himself. Hitler was certainly normal by totalitarian standards. As with Robespierre, his relations with women were characterized by a disconcerting formality. As with Lenin, he demonstrated little interest in physical relationships over the course of his life, though asexual would be too strong a term for either. As with Nechayev, he was fond of making passionless declarations of love to women who were unlikely to reciprocate in any way. Assuming they actually occurred, secret, 'perverse' sexual activities are of little importance here, and why anyone should go looking for skeletons in the closet when there are corpses all over the front lawn is something of a mystery in and of itself. Any firsthand account of Hitler's attitude toward or interactions with women deserves scrutiny, but there does seem to be a general consensus among his contemporaries as to the fact that he dealt with women via theory and mythology rather than emotion. Hitler goes very directly from the interpersonal, sexual realm to the realm of ideology, and perhaps nowhere else can the line be drawn from an individual's sexuality to his ideological system so easily and directly.

As for the man himself, from 1905 to 1908 Hitler was living in Linz, Austria with a friend named August Kubizek. Out walking one day, Hitler caught sight of a young woman named Stefanie Jansten, a tall, attractive, sophisticated blonde from an affluent family. It was love at first sight for him. It must have been apparent from the beginning, however, that she was unattainable for him. She had an army of suitors, young officers mostly, and Hitler was unemployed at the time. She was older than he was and from a higher social class. There was a further complication in that Hitler absolutely refused to speak to her, even though he had more or less decided that she was destined to fall in love with him. As Kubizek recalled:

---

1137 Ron Rosenbaum, *Explaining Hitler: The Search for the Origins of his Evil* (New York: Random House, 1998), 117.

He used to insist that, once he met Stefanie, everything would be clear without as much as a word being exchanged. For such exceptional human beings as himself and Stefanie, he said, there was no need for the usual communication by word of mouth; extraordinary human beings would understand each other by intuition.[1138]

When Kubizek tried to explain to Hitler that Stefanie might have different ideas on the subject, or for that matter, different ideas on any subject, Hitler screamed at him: "You simply don't understand, because you can't understand the true meaning of extraordinary love. ... These things cannot be explained. What is in me, is in Stefanie too."[1139]

Kubizek suggests that it was not shyness that kept Hitler from talking to Stefanie, but rather his lofty "conception of the relation between the sexes...."[1140] Flirting, according to Hitler, was undignified, and what Stefanie really wanted was a marriage proposal or nothing at all. Kubizek noticed that Stefanie liked dancing and suggested to Hitler that he might get somewhere if he learned how. Hitler's response: "Stefanie only dances because she is forced to by society on which she unfortunately depends. Once she is my wife, she won't have the slightest desire to dance!"[1141] Even as he condemned bourgeois standards of sexual morality, he cited the lack of a formal introduction as the reason he could never approach her. So instead, he contemplated kidnapping her. He also contemplated suicide, though, and he insisted on this point, Stefanie would have to die with him.[1142] In the end, Hitler walked away without ever speaking a word to her. Stefanie would later recall an anonymous letter from someone claiming he was leaving Linz to attend the Academy of Fine Arts in Vienna, and asking her to wait until he returned to marry her. It is generally assumed the letter came from Hitler.

With women, Hitler loved the abstraction and hated the personification; he only tolerated the latter because it reassured him of the former. As Kubizek writes, "He had wanted Stefanie for his wife, for him she was the ideal of German womanhood personified."[1143] The possibility of falling in

---

1138 August Kubizek, *The Young Hitler I Knew*, trans. E.V. Anderson, intro. H.R. Trevor-Roper (Cambridge: The Riverside Press, 1955), 59.

1139 Ibid., 60.

1140 Ibid., 61.

1141 Ibid., 63.

1142 Kubizek, 63-64.

1143 Ibid., 230.

love with a woman existed only where there existed room to project an idealized version of womanhood upon her, which meant either that he would have to know virtually nothing about the woman or that there was virtually nothing to know. Living in Vienna some time later and still despairing of Stefanie, his thoughts turned to the ideal woman, to the ideal relationship between a man and a woman, and from there to the role of the state in the ideal relationship. In his highly-regimented state, safeguarding sexual purity, the "Flame of Life" as he called it repeatedly, "would be the most important task of that Ideal State with which my friend occupied himself in his lonely hours" according to Kubizek.[1144] In this manner, Hitler goes directly from sexuality to a protean totalitarian ideology.

Even a woman that did embody the ideal of Germanic womanhood was actually quite threatening to Hitler on a biological level. The Germanic hero was apparently chaste, as NSDAP (National Socialist German Workers's Party) leader Otto Strasser explains:

> [Hitler] liked to think of himself as an incarnation of the heroic conception of life, and he called my own attitude Bacchic. It was useless to explain to him that the gods of antiquity loved women and wine none the less for being heroes. This kind of reflection appalled Hitler, who always fought shy of the slightest allusion to or hint of suggestiveness.[1145]

As a youth, he ruled out the possibility of a physical relationship of any kind with a woman. In fact, he showed a marked fear of anything relating to the human body, its sexual functions in particular, and went so far as to refrain from masturbation. For some reason, he felt compelled to go on tours of Vienna's red-light district, never with any intentions of indulging, yet coming home disconcerted from the threat of seduction. "He was afraid of infection," writes Kubizek. "Now I understand that he meant, not only venereal infection, but a much more general infection, namely, the danger of being caught up in the prevailing conditions and finally being dragged down into the vortex of corruption."[1146] Otto Strasser would later refer simply to his "panic fear of giving himself, of losing himself in a tender emotion...."[1147]

---

1144  Ibid., 233.
1145  Otto Strasser, *Hitler and I*, trans. Gwenda David and Eric Mosbacher (Cambridge: The Riverside Press, 1940), 69.
1146  Kubizek, 239.
1147  Strasser, 70.

As Hitler's political stature began to grow after World War I, he became slightly more comfortable around women, at least enough to begin speaking to them. Helene Hanfstaengl, one-half of a Munich power couple and early convert to the movement, may have been the first to get a taste of the new Hitler. At some point when he was alone with Helene, he fell to his knees "describing himself as her slave and bemoaning the fate that had led him to her too late."[1148] Her impression of Hitler suggests that something was missing from this expression of unrequited love. "Putzi, I tell you he is a neuter."[1149] Husband Ernst 'Putzi' Hanfstaengl finds Hitler declaring his love, or in reality a 'theoretical passion' as he called it, to at least one other married woman: "Apparently he had taken advantage of Hermann Esser's absence on one occasion to make passionate declarations to his by no means unattractive first wife. Again it was all rhetoric...."[1150] Hanfstaengl sums up his sexuality as "purely operatic, never operative. An impotent man with tremendous nervous energy.... In his relations with women Hitler had to dramatize himself, as he had to dramatize himself in his relations with the world as a whole."[1151] Berlin society columnist Bella Fromm seconded the impotence/sublimation theory, adding that "each woman crossing his path has been frightened out of her wits by Hitler. ... He tortures the woman, treating her as if she were his personal prisoner. The case of his niece, Geli Raubal, is the perfect example."[1152]

Raubal was a charismatic and attractive young woman described kindly by Munich confederates as 'no saint' and 'no prude'. She had come to live with Hitler in 1929, *sans* mother, after he had acquired a spacious new apartment in Munich. The precise nature of their relationship remains unclear, though he apparently gave the impression of a romantic emotional attachment, which in turn fueled rumors of an incestuous, sexual relationship. The relationship was, at a minimum, maintained with an air of possessiveness that suggested a romantic attachment. Suitors, including Otto Strasser and chauffer Emile Maurice, were fiercely discouraged and

---

1148 Ian Kershaw, *Hitler 1889-1936: Hubris*, (New York: W.W. Norton & Co., 1999), 281.

1149 Ernst Hanfstaengl, *Hitler: The Missing Years* (London: Eyre & Spottiswoode, 1957), 52.

1150 Ibid., 142.

1151 Ibid., 124.

1152 Bella Fromm, *Blood and Banquets: A Berlin Social Diary* (New York: Harper & Brothers, 1942, 2d ed.), 90.

even fired by Hitler,[1153] and chaperones were assigned to her anytime she went out without him.[1154]

Raubal, on the other hand, gave the impression of being miserable under the circumstances, and reportedly told a girlfriend that her uncle was a "monster. You would never believe the things he makes me do."[1155] According to Hanfstaengl, party treasurer Franz Xaver Schwarz recounted having paid off an individual who had come into a folio of pornographic drawings done by Hitler himself, "depraved, intimate sketches of Geli Raubal, with every anatomical detail, the sort of thing only a perverted *voyeur* would commit to paper...."[1156] Hanfstaengl goes further and suggests sadomasochism:

> Hitler was back on to politics and again and emphasized some threat against his opponents by cracking the heavy dog whip he still affected. I happened to catch a glimpse of Geli's face as he did it and there was on it such a mixture of fear and contempt that I almost caught my breath. Whips as well, I thought, and felt really sorry for the girl....[1157]

The stories actually become more lurid from there, the problem with all of them being that they lack substantiation and were promulgated by men whose relationships with Hitler were or would become strained.[1158] From all accounts, he was deeply involved with Raubal on an emotional level, perhaps for the only time in his life according to biographer Ian

---

1153 Strasser, 72-73.
1154 Kershaw, 353.
1155 Hanfstaengl, 162.
1156 Ibid., 163.
1157 Ibid., 164-65.
1158 Otto Strasser, when debriefed by the OSS after World War II, claimed that Raubal had told him that Hitler had asked her to urinate on him for purposes of sexual gratification. Rosenbaum, 134. Hitler had had Otto's brother, Gregor, killed during the 'Night of the Long Knives' in 1934, making Otto a rather unreliable witness. According to the OSS report prepared by Dr. Walter C. Langer and colleagues, Hitler probably engaged in these activities based on their "clinical experience and knowledge of Hitler's character." Walter C. Langer, *The Mind of Adolf Hitler: The Secret Wartime Report*, aftwd. Robert G.L. Waite (New York: Basic Books, Inc., 1972), 149. According to the report, the tendency to engage in sexual behaviors involving feces and urine springs from a desire to return to the womb, coupled with latent childhood confusion as to the correct point of exit for birth. Ibid., 188-89.

Kershaw,[1159] and genuinely distraught when he heard that she had been found dead of a gunshot wound in 1931. The gun in question was Hitler's, and rumors now flew that he had murdered the girl, or alternatively had forced her to commit suicide to prevent her engagement to a Jewish man.[1160] Psychoanalysis aside, and even assuming the truth of every allegation, this is probably Hitler's least revealing relationship. Virtually everything here is *sui generis*. Nothing adds up to a pattern for National Socialists in general, ideologists in general, or even for Hitler over the course of his relationships. The one exception would be Hitler's tendency to date much younger women.

Magda Goebbels, in the course of a highly ambiguous and faintly sexual (though never physical) relationship with Hitler, once commented simply that "he is not enough of a man to be able to stand a real woman near him."[1161] Hitler's assessment of his own sexuality seems to match up closely with that of Mrs. Goebbels. As he described his target female companion, she was "a cute, cuddly, naive little thing - tender, sweet, and stupid."[1162] It appears from his choice of women that he was quite serious. Eva Braun, his mistress for more than a decade, was often referred to as "the stupid cow" by relatives of both Hitler and Braun.[1163] Next to her lack of intelligence, Braun's unassuming nature was probably her best feature from Hitler's perspective. Perhaps keeping his obeisant mistress in mind, Hitler would later philosophize about the elasticity of the female personality. "A girl of eighteen to twenty is as malleable as wax. It should be possible for a man, whoever the chosen woman may be, to stamp his own imprint on her. That's all the woman asks for, by the way."[1164] Braun was around nineteen when the relationship began.

Braun was perhaps also attractive to Hitler for the simple reason that she had no one else going at the time. Sexual competition did not interest him in the least so far as participation went, though the idea did seem to intrigue him on a philosophical level. He subscribed to a Darwinist

1159 Kershaw, 352.
1160 Hanfstaengl, 168.
1161 Hans Otto Meissner, *Magda Goebbels: The First Lady of the Third Reich*, trans. Gwendolyn Mary Keeble (New York: Dial Press, 1980), 223.
1162 Kershaw, 45.
1163 Nerin Gun, *Eva Braun: Hitler's Mistress* (New York: Meredith Press, 1968), 110, 143.
1164 Adolf Hitler, *The Secret Conversations, 1941-1944*, trans. Norman Cameron and R.H. Stevens, intro. H.R. Trevor Roper (New York: Farrar, Strauss & Young), 202.

conception of courtship very similar to his theories on the battle between races. "It's a fact that women love real men. It's their instinct that tells them. … When two men fight for the possession of a woman, the latter waits to let her heart speak until she knows which of the two will be victorious. Tarts adore poachers."[1165] Elsewhere, he postulated that women are actually more prone to battling each other for the attention of the opposite sex than men are. "It's a form of the spirit of conservation, a law of the species. The gentlest woman is transformed into a wild beast when another woman tries to take away her man. The bigger the element of femininity in a woman, the further is this instinct developed."[1166]

Hitler had already made the acquaintance of his future wife, Eva Braun, by the time of the Raubal affair, the relationship solidifying after Braun attempted suicide in 1932. Assuming no previous sexual activity, and there is little or no evidence to suggest any, Hitler may (or may not) have lost his virginity to Eva Braun some time around 1932.[1167] She hinted at some kind of an affair while looking at a picture of Hitler sitting on a couch in his apartment with British prime minister Neville Chamberlain. "If only he knew the history of that sofa!" she is supposed to have exclaimed. The affair was kept secret from everyone but a handful of close confederates, ostensibly to maintain Hitler's sex appeal, which was actually quite considerable. Yet even within his intimate circle, Hitler never let his guard down about the affair. Mostly he ignored Braun, though occasionally he took to humiliating her in front of the confederates aware of her existence, so that even they were not entirely sure he was actually having an affair with her. As Hans Peter Bleuel writes, "his behavior toward Eva Braun was too indifferent and his private life too unfathomable to convey the certainty of a sexual relationship. In Hitler's case, not even the most natural thing in the world could be taken for granted."[1168]

Braun accompanied Hitler virtually everywhere he went, though there seems to have been little in the way of emotional involvement on Hitler's

---

1165 Ibid., 141.
1166 Ibid., 286.
1167 A woman named Mimi Reiter claims to have had sex with Hitler in his Munich apartment in 1931. Rosenbaum finds the liaison possible, while Kershaw finds it highly improbable given the timing, coming either at the height of the Hitler-Raubal affair or just after her death. Rosenbaum, 117; Kershaw, 285. Hitler was also linked to actress Renate Müller in the early 1930s, the latter also committing suicide.
1168 Hans Peter Bleuel, *Sex and Society in Nazi Germany*, ed. Heinrich Fraenkel, trans. J. Maxwell Brownjohn (Philadelphia: J.B. Lipincott, 1973), 51.

side. As Eva herself once wrote in her diary: "He needs me for special reasons. It can't be otherwise.... When he says he loves me, he thinks it is only for the time being. ... Why doesn't he have done with me instead of tormenting me?"[1169] He married her on April 28 or 29 of 1945, only when his fate had been sealed with the advance of the Soviet army into Berlin. His final thoughts on his wife:

> Although I did not think I could undertake the responsibility of contracting a marriage during these past years of conflict, I have resolved, before terminating my mortal existence, to take as my wife the woman who, after many years of loyal friendship, of her own free will entered this city when it was virtually besieged in order to share my fate. At her own wish, she accompanies me into death as my wife. This will compensate us for what we have both been deprived of by my labors in the service of my people.[1170]

At this point, it would have cost Hitler nothing to express some measure of affection for Braun, this woman who was about to commit suicide on his behalf and on account of his rather severe lapses in judgment (moral and military). On the other hand, he could have simply sent her away. Eva's biographer, Nerin Gun, suggests that Hitler let her commit suicide so as to present for posterity the image of "an Adolf Hitler who was so madly loved by a woman that she took part in his Viking funeral."[1171] Bleuel, similarly, finds any hint of gratitude "overlaid by a melodramatic assumption of self-sacrifice and rectitude which fails to conceal the cynicism of Hitler's conduct. It was not a woman with whom he wished to be united at the eleventh hour; it was a last loyal retainer, obediently escorting him into the hereafter."[1172]

With his Thousand-Year Reich coming to a premature end, Hitler's thoughts turned to sex. Not having it, as far as anyone knows, even though parts of his bunker system in Berlin had more or less degenerated into a sexual free-for-all. Rather, in his political testament, Hitler attempted to ensure that future generations would continue to have sex in accordance with the basic principles of National Socialism. "Above all, I charge the leadership of the nation and their subjects with the meticulous observance

---

1169 Gun, 87.
1170 Quoted in Bleuel, 53.
1171 Gun, 292.
1172 Bleuel, 53.

of the race-laws and the merciless resistance to the universal poisoner of all peoples, International Jewry."[1173] On April 30, 1945, Eva Braun and Adolf Hitler committed suicide.

## 7.2 Antisocial Darwinism

**National Socialism finds its starting** point in the evolutionary theories of Charles Darwin and Alfred Russell Wallace. It doesn't stay long. The Darwin/Wallace theory of evolution is that all modern species are ultimately descended from common and more simplified ancestors. Differentiation comes through the process of natural selection, the 'survival of the fittest', which operates on naturally occurring variations among organisms. Advantageous variations are preserved as organisms survive and reproduce, and disadvantageous variations are eliminated as organisms die off and fail to reproduce. Differentiation becomes pronounced over time, leading to the formation of species which are then subject to the same process of natural selection as a group. In sum:

> Owing to [the struggle for life], variations, however slight and from whatever cause proceeding, if they be in any degree profitable to the individuals of a species, in their infinitely complex relations to other organic beings and to their physical conditions of life, will tend to the preservation of such individuals, and will generally be inherited by the offspring. The offspring, also, will thus have a better chance of surviving....[1174]

The process works continuously, imperceptibly, and dispassionately. An organism or species survives or it does not, and environmental changes can shift the probabilities of survival at any time. There is no sentient force, benevolent or malevolent, guiding the process, ensuring that intrinsically superior organisms survive while intrinsically inferior organisms are destroyed. There is no grand teleological design. As Darwin himself explains, "I mean by Nature, only the aggregate action and product of many natural laws, and by laws the sequence of events as ascertained by us."[1175]

The human race was formed through the same process, evolving from some less-developed form, with man still bearing 'the indelible stamp of his

---

1173 Kershaw, 823.
1174 Charles Darwin, *The Origin of the Species and the Descent of Man* (Chicago: Encyclopedia Britannica, 1990, 2d ed.), 32.
1175 Ibid., 40.

lowly origins' as Darwin puts it. As to racial differentiation between men, Darwin is distinctly hesitant to attribute these differences to natural selection. In fact, he considers most of these differences trivial, "for if important, they would long ago have been either fixed and preserved, or eliminated."[1176] Humans of every race constitute a single species, something evidenced both by a strong tendency toward interbreeding, as well as the strong tendency toward physical variation with a given race.[1177] "It may be doubted," writes Darwin, "whether any character can be named which is distinctive of a race and is constant."[1178] These variations within races blur the line between one race and another, leading Darwin to explain that "the most weighty of all the arguments against treating the races of man as distinct species, is that they graduate into each other, independently in many cases ... of their having intercrossed."[1179]

Darwin thus provided a unifying, foundational theory for the biological sciences, but those who followed him were often more interested in practical applications for evolutionary theory. Namely, the conscious and deliberate continuation of human evolution. Francis Galton, a relative of Darwin's, developed the idea of improving mankind through selective breeding, coining the term 'eugenics' (well-born). Under Galton's program, only the middle and upper classes would be allowed to reproduce. Around the turn of the century, German zoologist Ernst Haeckel began to propagate the idea of killing off the sick in the interests of racial hegemony, taking ancient Sparta as his model.[1180] Haeckel's ideas began to gain currency in respectable scientific circles, influencing physician and award-winning essayist Wilhelm Schallmeyer, who proposed limiting the reproduction of those judged wanting according to the standards of 'socio-biological' science.[1181]

Race became increasingly the basis for historical and anthropological analysis, as in the works of Count Joseph Arthur de Gobineau, which filtered into Germany in the 1880s or 90s. Gobineau argued that all culture was created by the Aryan race, which was the natural ruler of all other races whenever it happened to migrate out of central Europe. Intermixture and a decline in the racial purity of the Aryan segment of the population would

---

1176  Ibid., 359.
1177  Ibid., 346.
1178  Ibid.
1179  Ibid.
1180  Michael Burleigh and Wolfgang Wipperman, *The Racial State: Germany 1933-1945* (Cambridge: Cambridge University Press, 1991), 30-31.
1181  Ibid., 31.

then lead inevitably to the decline of any given culture.[1182] Above all, though, it was the prominent intellectual and war-propagandist Houston Stewart Chamberlain who generated the ideas that would provide the foundation for National Socialism.

In the first part of his *Foundations of the Nineteenth Century*, Chamberlain, following Gobineau, proposed distinct biological differences between various races, and then attempted to explain the whole of human history since the birth of Christ in terms of those differences. "As if all history," writes Chamberlain, "were not there to show us how personality and race are most closely connected...."[1183] Thus racial purity leads to race consciousness, which is the prerequisite to individual development. "Race lifts a man above himself: it endows him with extraordinary — I might also say supernatural — powers, so entirely does it distinguish him from the individual who springs from the chaotic jumble of peoples drawn from all parts of the world...."[1184] As Chamberlain continues, blood mixture led to the downfall of the Roman Empire, particularly as it involved the 'transfusion' of Semitic blood into the Roman organism.[1185] He cites a natural repulsion at blood mixture for the rise of Christian asceticism during the same era.[1186] The Germanic Teutons are then distinguished from the Jewish race, the latter unable to be improved by mixture with Teutons and who will, through interbreeding, completely absorb the Teutonic race.[1187] In this model, 'real' Jews are biologically different even from the rest of the Israelites, the product of a gradual physical separation, "not the result of a normal national life, but in a way an artificial product...."[1188] In addition to physical differences, Jews are characterized by materialism and egoism, and the absence of a genuinely spiritual aspect. Teutons, conversely, are characterized by a nation-building impulse, creativity, and, above all, loyalty; loyalty to the creative impulse is freedom for the German.[1189] Europe's Middle Ages and early modern period were then defined primarily by the battle between Jewish Rome and Teutonic Germany. Chamberlain never finished the *Foundations*, though according to

1182 Ibid., 28.
1183 Houston Stewart Chamberlain, *Foundations of the Nineteenth Century Vol.1*, trans. John Lees, intro. Lord Redesdale (London: Ballantyne Press, 1914), 260.
1184 Ibid., 269.
1185 Ibid., 271, 301.
1186 Ibid., 314.
1187 Ibid., 331-333.
1188 Ibid., 359.
1189 Ibid., 542.

Field, "his plans are clear. Chamberlain intended to show the closing nineteenth century as a critical age of transition, one in which the forces of Teutonism met new dangers from an emancipated Jewry...."[1190]

Chamberlain thus fuses garden-variety anti-Semitism with slipshod historical analysis, and, post-Darwin, adds a veneer of scientific legitimacy by discussing everything in terms of a kind of pseudo-naturalistic analysis. The theoretical influence on Hitler and NSDAP theoretician Alfred Rosenberg is obvious, though a very direct connection existed between them as well.[1191] Hitler met with Chamberlain during a visit to Bayreuth in 1923, and received a very complimentary letter from Chamberlain following the encounter. "You are not at all, as you have been described to me, a fanatic.... The fanatic inflames the mind, you warm the heart," Chamberlain explained to Hitler. He also assures Hitler, not really violent in Chamberlain's mind, that he is in possession of the "force which shapes the universe" rather than the force which leads to chaos.[1192] "With this letter," explains Field, "Chamberlain became the first person of national and even international reputation as a writer to align himself with the Nazi movement: it brought elation at party headquarters at Munich."[1193]

Where Darwin developed his theories based on years of travel and observation, National Socialism proceeds axiomatically, and does so without apology. According to Dr. Walter Gross, director of the Third Reich's Office of Racial Policy, "race stands as the new controlling value in the picture of history before us — not as a controversial scientific concept, but rather as an inviolable fact of all historical life...."[1194] National Socialism is scientific as long the science proves the ideology, otherwise not, and this is considered rational because National Socialism is 'true'. According to Dr. Gerhard Wagner, medical chief of the Third Reich, "fully independent of ... scientific considerations that have never been the decisive factor for National Socialism, the objective of racial hygiene and the elimination of the genetically

---

1190 Geoffrey G. Field, *Evangelist of Race: The Germanic Vision of Houston Stewart Chamberlain* (New York: Columbia University Press, 1981), 198.

1191 Rosenberg cited Chamberlain's *Foundations of the Nineteenth Century* as a major influence for his own *Myth of the Twentieth Century*. Alfred Rosenberg, *Race and Race History: And Other Essays*, ed. intro. Robert Pois (New York: Harper & Row, 1970), 11.

1192 The text of the letter is available in Field, 436-37.

1193 Field, 438.

1194 Speech of Walter Gross, *Reichstagung in Nürnberg 1933*, ed. Julius Streicher, (Berlin: Vaterländischer Verlag C.A. Weller, 1934), 147.

incompetent from the reproductive pool is self-evidently justified."[1195] Alfred Rosenberg writes that "today, in the midst of a collapsing atomistic epoch, this true, organic *Weltanschauung* (worldview or ideology) demands its right…. The individualistic dogma whereby each individual being exists *for itself* … has been finally excluded from serious consideration."[1196] As one Nazi educator summed things up, "National Socialism is an ideology which makes a total claim to validity and refuses to be a matter for random opinion-formation."[1197] National Socialists will, according to Wagner, "help a newer, better truth to victory."[1198] Rosenberg elaborates on the nature of this truth, which "for us … does not mean that which is *logical* and that which is false; rather it demands an organic answer to the question…."[1199]

National Socialism is, to its own way of thinking, the political and social application of the laws of nature. According to Dr. Wagner:

> Where a Volk becomes unfaithful to the laws of nature, where it abandons its will to live and voluntarily decides to decline, it will inevitably suffer nature's revenge in the form of a reduction of its political power and in the weakening of its economic opportunities. The endeavor to protect our *Volk* from both of these dangers is called the National Socialist movement.[1200]

The laws of nature are apparently the product of some cosmic, teleological design. Dr. Gross, explaining the need to prevent mixture between races, cites the "great laws of nature. We have neither created the world nor prescribed its course. A greater power has done so, knowing their necessity and the ends to which they are directed. It is only proper for man to learn and implement these great laws of the world respectfully."[1201] We have also Hitler: "Eternal Nature inexorably avenges the infringement of her commands. Hence today I believe that I am acting in accordance with the will of the Almighty Creator: by defending myself against the Jew, I am

1195 Speech of Gerhard Wagner, *Reichstagung in Nürnberg 1934*, ed. Julius Streicher, (Berlin: Vaterländischer Verlag C.A. Weller, 1935), 264.

1196 Rosenberg, *Race and Race History*, 92-93.

1197 Quoted in Hans Peter Bleuel, *Sex and Society in Nazi Germany*, ed. Heinrich Fraenkel, trans. J. Maxwell Brownjohn, (Philadelphia: J.B. Lippincott, 1973), 103.

1198 Speech of Gerhard Wagner, *Reichstagung in Nürnberg 1934*, 284.

1199 Rosenberg, *Race and Race History*, 88.

1200 Speech of Gerhard Wagner, *Reichstagung in Nürnberg 1934*, 255-56.

1201 Speech of Walter Gross, *Reichstagung in Nürnberg 1933*, 158.

fighting for the work of the Lord."[1202]

With a bit of theoretical legerdemain, National Socialism takes the principle of natural selection and applies it between races, Jews and Aryans, ignoring the fact that conscious 'selection' (i.e., genocide) is no longer natural in a Darwinian sense. That a racial difference exists between Jews and Aryans living in the same country, moreover, and who have no doubt been 'interbreeding' and converting back and forth for centuries, is taken axiomatically. As Hitler contradicts Darwin, "The consequence of this racial purity, universally valid in Nature, is not only the sharp outward delimitation of the various races, but their uniform character in themselves. The fox is always a fox, the goose a goose, the tiger a tiger, etc...."[1203] Aryans are the superior race and species, while Jews are inferior, in fact 'life unworthy of life', having a parasitic relationship to the Aryan collective body. Jews would be unable to survive outside it: "If the Jews were alone in this world they would stifle in filth and offal...."[1204] Interbreeding between superior and inferior organisms produces offspring at a level between the two, frustrating nature's intention to see superior organisms survive and evolve while inferior organisms die off. "No more than Nature desires the mating of weaker with stronger individuals, even less does she desire the blending of a higher with a lower race, since, if she did, her whole work of higher breeding, over perhaps hundreds of thousands of years, might be ruined with one blow."[1205]

'Blood mixture' is a mortal threat to the Aryan race. According to Hitler, "all great cultures of the past perished only because the originally creative race died out from blood poisoning ... [the] preservation [of blood] is bound up with the rigid law of necessity and the right to victory of the best and stronger in this world."[1206] It is, however, merely one of three mortal threats, the other two being a drop in the overall Aryan population, and improper reproductive selection within the race.[1207] Population decline is frequently discussed, though measures in this area were typically in the area of inducements to German citizens to procreate. By 1936, Dr. Gross seemed

---

1202  Adolf Hitler, *Mein Kampf*, trans. Ralph Mannheim (Boston: Houghton Mifflin, 1999), 65.
1203  Ibid., 285.
1204  Ibid., 302.
1205  Ibid., 286.
1206  Ibid., 289.
1207  Walter Gross discusses all three at length in 'Racial Policy Education'. Walter Gross, *Rassenpolitische Erziehung* (Berlin: Junker and Dünnhaupt Verlag, 1936).

*Kirk Rodby*

to be contemplating some form of state compulsion in this area, though concluded happily that "for the moment, where we seek to proceed only with moralistic compulsion, in every individual (the woman stronger than in the man) there rises up some healthier instinct" toward procreation.[1208] A drop in population leads to a weakening of national power, he explains, "setting off new threats that will lead all too easily to the final downfall."[1209]

Incorrect selection refers to the tendency of Aryans to select other Aryans who are genetically unfit for reproduction. Commandment six of the Third Reich's Ten Commandments for Selecting a Spouse advises one to ask about the forefathers of any potential spouse, even if Aryan: "You do not marry your spouse alone, but rather, in a sense, his ancestors with him. ... A good man can bear in his cells that which creates misfortune in the children. Never marry the one good man from a bad family."[1210] Drs. Gross and Wagner both go on at length as to the resources which must be committed to the care of the offspring of those with genetic illnesses, and the terrible damage this does to the strength of the nation.[1211] This is contrary to the will of nature according to Wagner:

> The divine power that created the world and gave it its laws set the laws of selection in the battle for existence, that is to say the often brutal annihilation of the unfit and the less than fully capable.... And while we lost our way for some time, and gave validity to more humane methodologies, in truth we serve the real will of the creator, namely the rise and health of the human race, that a false, sick, and sentimental humanitarianism has thwarted and betrayed.[1212]

The future survival of the Germanic race thus depends on correct behavior in the reproductive area specifically. As noted by Dr. Gross, the Germanic race does enjoy, in this respect, the advantage of latent instincts in its people, which push them toward proper reproductive choices. The Aryan 'racial instinct' favors intraracial reproduction, consistent with "one of the most patent principles of Nature's rule: the inner segregation of the species

---

1208  Ibid., 21.
1209  Speech of Walter Gross, *Reichstagung in Nürnberg 1933*, 148.
1210  Arthur Gütt, Herbert Linden, and Franz Maßfeller, *Blutschutz und Ehegesund-heitsgesetz* (München: J.S. Lehmanns Verlag, 1936), 13.
1211  Speech of Walter Gross, *Reichstagung in Nürnberg 1933*, 153-54; Speech of Gerhard Wagner, *Reichstagung in Nürnberg 1934*, 260-64.
1212  Speech of Gerhard Wagner, *Reichstagung in Nürnberg 1934*, 272-73.

246

of all living beings on this earth."[1213]

Alfred Rosenberg makes reference to the ideological instinct, which first began to show itself as Germany struggled to recover from World War I. "This elementary instinct was perhaps not always the Germanic consciousness we would have liked, but it was in existence, and decisive in the great test of character in that the German Volk saw itself standing up."[1214] The Germanic racial instinct is the source of all real knowledge, and allows one to understand the cosmic forces which control all things:

> The ultimate wisdom is always the understanding of the instinct — that is: a man must never fall into the lunacy of believing that he has really risen to be lord and master of Nature — which is so easily induced by the conceit of half-education; he must understand the fundamental necessity of Nature's rule, and realize how much his existence is subjected to these laws of eternal fight and upward struggle. Then he will feel that in a universe where planets revolve around suns, and moons turn about planets, where force alone forever masters weakness, compelling it to be an obedient slave or else crushing it, there can be no special laws for man. For him, too, the eternal principles of this ultimate wisdom hold sway.[1215]

Of course, as Rosenberg intimates, the existence of racial instincts is not the same as their full development into racial consciousness, a "racially-nordically determined ideology"[1216] which is based in Germanic biology, but requiring educational work to manifest itself. One is born with a racial instinct, though the National Socialist movement will triumph, according to Wagner, on the basis of "our racial consciousness taught to us by the Führer."[1217]

National Socialism is though to be the product of a great awakening among the Germanic vanguard, which will in turn leading others to the

---

1213 Hitler, 284.

1214 Speech of Alfred Rosenberg, *Reichstagung in Nürnberg 1937: Der Parteitag der Arbeit*, ed. Hanns Kerrl (Berlin: Vaterländlischer Verlag C.A. Weller, 1938), 94-95.

1215 Hitler, 244-45.

1216 Speech of Gerhard Wagner, *Reichstagung in Nürnberg 1934*, 280.

1217 Speech of Gerhard Wagner, *Reichstagung in Nürnberg 1937: Der Parteitag der Arbeit*, ed. Hanns Kerrl (Berlin: Vaterländlischer Verlag C.A. Weller, 1938), 122.

development of their racial consciousness. According to Wagner, "Where other ideological schools of thought are devoted to a fully passive and idle acceptance of destiny as their final truth, National Socialism has awoken, through a deep respect and humility before the great powers of history, a relentless will to live and to self-mastery in the face of difficulties."[1218] The development of race consciousness is a prerequisite to the totalistic political transformation sought by National Socialists. In 1933, Gross explained that "Germany never could have experienced the turnaround of this spring ... [without] the insight gained from historical analysis, accompanied by a newfound feeling and confirmed by the latest science...."[1219] On the other hand, racial consciousness can be compromised, sickened even according to Gross, a kind of "spiritual sickness, in a loss of connection between man and nature, between man and life, between men and the great laws of existence, of the cosmos...."[1220] National Socialist 'political health' must therefore be proactive, according to Dr. Wagner: "We will not wait until the injury and the sickness have set in. Rather we will act preventatively, identifying deviation from the norm before it has come as a sickness of the consciousness of the person affected."[1221]

The healthy Aryan is naturally and instinctually collective, possessed of dormant intellectual and organizational capacities which are supposedly absent in lesser races, capacities which, if developed, allow the Aryan race to develop its culture. These organizational instincts are essential to cultural development.

> The Aryan is not greatest in his mental qualities as such, but in the extent of his willingness to put all his abilities in the service of the community. In him the instinct of self-preservation has reached the noblest form, since he willingly subordinates his own ego to the life of the community and, if the hour demands it, even sacrifices it.[1222]

The Aryan thinks in centuries and exists for the community; he is an idealist rather than an individualist. "This state of mind, which subordinates the interests of the ego to the conservation of the community," writes Hitler,

1218 Speech of Gerhard Wagner, *Reichstagung in Nürnberg 1935: Der Parteitag der Freiheit*, ed. Hanns Kerrl (Berlin: Vaterländischer Verlag C.A. Weller, 1936), 112-13.
1219 Speech of Walter Gross, *Reichstagung in Nürnberg 1933*, 146.
1220 Gross, *Rassenpolitische Erziehung*, 22-23.
1221 Speech of Gerhard Wagner, *Reichstagung in Nürnberg 1937*, 130.
1222 Hitler, 297.

"is really the first premise for every truly human culture. ... It is this alone that prevents what human hands have built from being overthrown by nature."[1223] Rosenberg adds that "the will must be grasped in its original purity as a principle of freedom working against egoistic impulses if one wishes to clearly re-establish a foundation for a Nordic feeling."[1224] Freedom here would be the exact opposite of doing what one wishes, or at least doing what one thinks one wishes. The truly free individual is "someone who is the embodiment and culmination of national tradition. Personality and Volk therefore stand in organic interrelation to one another. And their head is therefore no tyrant, but a leader."[1225] Individualism is false, according to Gross: "As the man became ever more unilateral in his thinking, and learned to forget the flow of blood through the sequence of generations, out of such a spirit he sets the destiny of the individual higher than the thoughts of the totality, and did so out of a virtually fatal, and false and unnatural, viewpoint."[1226]

The Aryan totality, having linked its will to the forces of the universe, becomes omnipotent, and by extension all those who are a part of it share in that omnipotence. As Hitler explains, true idealism "corresponds in its innermost depths to the will of nature. It alone leads men to voluntary recognition of the privilege of force and strength, and thus makes them a dust particle of that order which shapes and forms the whole universe."[1227] The Aryan also experiences a measure of immortality through the collective organism, being merely the continuation of the 'eternal line of descent' or 'blood legacy'. According to the explanation for Commandment Two of the Third Reich's Ten Commandments:

> Everything that exists in you, all qualities of mind and body, are transitory. You are a legacy, a gift of your forefathers. The unbroken chain lives on in you. Those who remain single without compelling grounds break this chain of generations. Your life is only a passing manifestation;

1223 Ibid., 298.
1224 Alfred Rosenberg, *Myth of the Twentieth Century: An Evaluation of the Spiritual-Intellectual Confrontations of Our Age*, trans. Vivian Bird (Newport Beach: Noontide Press, 1993), 218.
1225 Speech of Alfred Rosenberg, *Reichstagung in Nürnberg 1937*, 111.
1226 Speech of Walter Gross, *Reichstagung in Nürnberg 1933*, 154.
1227 Hitler, 299.

family (extended) and *Volk* continue on. Physical and mental genetic qualities are resurrected in the children.

The genotype, the legacy of blood, is all of the physical, mental, and spiritual gifts that have been conveyed to the man through the procreation of his ancestors. With the great amount of these gifts, only a part can come to expression during his life. Given that it does come to expression over and over in descendants, it is eternal. The genetic form is reflected in the physical form of the individual man.[1228]

Gross also explains the individual is judged "as a link in the chain of life, and as a drop in the great stream of blood that flows through history from eternity to eternity."[1229] Wagner makes reference to "eternal Germany,"[1230] the last words of Reich Minister of the Interior Wilhelm Frick prior to execution being "long live eternal Germany." Frick and Wagner were both co-authors of the Nuremberg laws, banning sexual contact between German Jews and other Germans.

National Socialism holds that the Jew, in contrast to the Aryan, thinks only of himself and of the present, hence the capacity to create and develop culture is wholly absent. Aryan consciousness is eternal where Jewish consciousness is temporal. "In the most primitive living creatures the instinct of self-preservation does not go beyond concern for their own ego. Egoism, as we designate this urge, goes so far that it even embraces time; the moment itself claims everything, granting nothing to the coming hours."[1231] The Jew has a "naked" instinct for self-preservation, his collective impulse developing rapidly in response to a threat or basic survival need, and fading just as quickly when circumstances no longer require it. Hitler provides the following analogy, *inter alia*: "The same pack of wolves which has just fallen on its prey together disintegrates when hunger abates into its individual beasts."[1232] Jews take on a distinctly demonological character at times, in the cartoons of *Der Stürmer* in particular, though they are more frequently compared to diseases and parasites, and (as seen) linked with decay and 'filth'.

1228 Gütt et al.,12.
1229 Speech of Walter Gross, *Reichstagung in Nürnberg 1933*, 154.
1230 Speech of Gerhard Wagner, *Reichstagung in Nürnberg 1937*, 134.
1231 Hitler, 296-97.
1232 Ibid., 301.

Jews are virtually synonymous with sexuality according to the postulates of National Socialism. As Hitler explains: "The fact that nine tenths of all literary filth, artistic trash, and theatrical idiocy can be set to the account of a people, constituting hardly one hundredth of all the country's inhabitants, could simply not be talked away; it was the plain truth."[1233] In addition to pornography, Jews also controlled prostitution and sex slavery according to Hitler: "The relation of the Jews to prostitution and, even more, to the white-slave traffic, could be studied in Vienna as perhaps in no other city of Western Europe...."[1234] Jews are also responsible for homosexuality, feminism, and abortions, according to Wagner.[1235] Jews are also intrinsically false, according to Hitler: "Only the Jew can praise an institution [democracy] which is as dirty and false as he himself."[1236]

The most direct effect of a blood mixture between Germans and German Jews, according to Gross, is a decline in racial consciousness:

> One can certainly wipe out the spirit of decomposition, one can overcome dangerous theories, and incinerate destructive books; but if the blood of a foreign race penetrates into the body of the Volk and the womb of the family, then consider it given away eternally, ever giving birth to new generations of more disunited and conflicted men, that stand with uncertain character between nations and their values, and therefore fail in the hour the state and Volk will tip the scales of history.[1237]

Blood mixture also leads to sexual degeneracy: "Today, we observe with shock how far foreign blood has penetrated into our *Volkskörper*, and suddenly we understand with deeper fear how the decline of the value of character was possible, as the past 14 years [1919-1933] have revealed to us with their filth and their shame."[1238] Elsewhere, Gross finds "a deeper intrinsic connection between the growing decay of sexual morality, traditions in general, and the leading edge of physical decay and decomposition...."[1239] Wagner explains simply that "the corrosive effect of racial mixture is disastrous for the bodily, spiritual, and moral health of the

1233 Ibid., 58.
1234 Ibid., 59.
1235 Speech of Gerhard Wagner, *Reichstagung in Nürnberg 1935*, 118-19, 126-27.
1236 Hitler, 91.
1237 Speech of Walter Gross, *Reichstagung in Nürnberg 1933*, 157.
1238 Ibid.
1239 Gross, *Rassenpolitische Erziehung*, 10-11.

individual man. ...hybridization is a terrible injustice against nations and against the polluted products of such mixture...."[1240] Blood mixture, in short, is harmful both to individual and national health, and, as Hitler explains, "if the power to fight for one's own health is no longer present, the right to live in this world of struggle ends."[1241] As he continues, the Jew, being harmful to national health, maintains merely a parasitic relationship to the collective body. "He is and remains the typical parasite, a sponger who like a noxious bacillus keeps spreading as soon as a favorable medium invites him. And the effect of his existence is ... [that] the host people dies out after a shorter or longer period."[1242]

Interracial reproduction, blood mixture, is thought to be a sufficient condition for genetic harm and ideo-biological disunity, though not a necessary one. Interracial sexual intercourse destroys the genetic integrity and of the Aryan female partner directly. As Hitler cautions, "With satanic joy in his face, the black-haired Jewish youth lurks in wait for the unsuspecting girl whom he defiles with his blood, thus stealing her from her people."[1243] According to Julius Streicher and *Der Stürmer*, a woman absorbs the soul of a man along with his semen, and interracial sexual intercourse with a Jew will turn an Aryan woman into a Jew both physically and spiritually.[1244] A woman violated even once would never again be able to bear healthy Aryan children.[1245] Exactly what she would give birth to remains unclear as well, though the descriptions (eternally cursed, predisposed to criminality) match up well with that other great enemy of the Third Reich, the genetically damaged Aryan 'asocial'. Eugenics, it should be noted, was actually a cutting-edge science by the standards of the day; genetic damage through sexual defilement had no corresponding claim to scientific validity.

Syphilis, a disease 'poisoning the health of the national body', had always been an object of fascination and horror for Hitler. A distinct parallel existed in Hitler's mind between the spread of syphilis and the

---

1240 Speech of Gerhard Wagner, *Reichstagung in Nürnberg 1935*, 120.
1241 Hitler, 257.
1242 Ibid., 305.
1243 Ibid., 325.
1244 Randal Bytwerk, *Julius Streicher* (New York: Stein and Day, 1983), 144-45.
1245 Ibid., 144. Der Stürmer also claimed that a woman could defend herself from Jews by wearing an iron cross around her neck, thus implicitly equating Jews with vampires. Dennis Showalter, *Little Man, What Now?: Der Stürmer in the Weimar Republic* (Connecticut: Archon Press, 1982), 100.

Jewish 'disease' also spreading through the national body. The Jewish impact on German sexuality was to blame in either case.

The cause lies, primarily, in our prostitution of love. Even if its results were not this frightful plague, it would nevertheless be profoundly injurious to man, since the moral devastations which accompany this degeneracy suffice to destroy a people slowly but surely. This Jewification of our spiritual life and mammonization of our mating instinct will sooner or later destroy our entire offspring, for the powerful children of a natural emotion will be replaced by the miserable creatures of financial expediency which is becoming more and more the basis and sole prerequisite of our marriages. Love finds its outlet elsewhere.[1246]

The biological inferiority of the child in these cases has nothing to do with interracial sexual contact of any kind, but rather Aryan sexual relationships which take place under the aegis of modern bourgeois standards. Presumably the "mammonization of the mating instinct" refers to a desire to marry later in life, having first achieved some measure of financial comfort and stability. As Hitler queries, "Isn't [late] marriage exactly the same as prostitution itself? Hasn't duty toward posterity passed completely out of the picture?"[1247] The primary danger inherent in late marriage is that it presents the opportunity for sexual adventure *sans* reproductive intent. Sex for pleasure, from a 'racial-hereditary' standpoint, seems to be every bit as dangerous as sex with a Jew. The resulting loss of physical integrity and strength are then passed on to the children, who "are the sad product of the irresistibly spreading contamination of our sexual life...."[1248]

The threat of sexual-ideological contamination via reproduction or sexual intercourse is dealt with through laws against interracial sex, though the threat of ideo-biological contamination is dealt with through ideological control directly. As in any ideological system, sexuality and intellectualism were mortal sins under National Socialism. Germany's youth were in imminent danger on both fronts, from the erotic culture of the Weimar Republic, and from an educational system which taught young men to think rather than fight. According to Hitler, "Our whole public life today

1246  Hitler, 247.
1247  Ibid., 252.
1248  Ibid., 248.

is like a hothouse for sexual ideas and stimulations. ... This sensual, sultry atmosphere leads to ideas and stimulations at a time when a boy should have no understanding of such things."[1249] He lists several reasons why youth should avoid sex, including premature aging, the tendency to visit prostitutes, and, whether involving the latter, a tendency to spread syphilis. As anyone might have guessed, the Jew is ultimately responsible. "Culturally he contaminates art, literature, the theatre, makes a mockery of natural feeling, overthrows all concepts of beauty and sublimity, of the noble and the good, and instead drags men down into the sphere of his own base nature."[1250]

Intellectualism, like sexuality, could do nothing but harm to Germany's youth. Jews engaged in intellectualism, and through their disproportionate influence on Germany's educational system, encouraged Aryans to do the same. The result, according to Hitler, was an increase in sexual desire.

> The excessive emphasis on purely intellectual instruction and the neglect of physical training also encourage the emergence of sexual ideas at a much too early age. The youth who achieves the hardness of iron by sports and gymnastics succumbs to the need of sexual satisfaction less than the stay-at-home fed exclusively on intellectual fare. And a sensible system of education must bear this in mind. It must, moreover, not fail to consider that the healthy young man will expect different things from the woman than a prematurely corrupted weakling.[1251]

This is a 'Jewish disease' according to Hitler, one the Aryan intelligentsia failed to stop because they were already suffering its effects. According to Rosenberg, intellectualism leads quickly to blood mixture: "Torn loose from the bonds of blood and racial order, the individual being sacrifices his absolute, unrepresentable spiritual form; he tears himself farther and farther away from his natural milieu, mixing enemy blood with his own. And it is this blood crime which causes the death of personality, *Volk*, race and civilization."[1252] The solution is total and complete thought control, thought suppression even, under the control of the state.

In sum, Jews are intrinsically sexual and individualistic, the Aryan

---

1249  Ibid., 254.
1250  Ibid., 326.
1251  Ibid., 253.
1252  Rosenberg, *Race and Race History*, 37.

intrinsically procreative and collective. The latter are something in the nature of a single organism, a single genetic code producing a single instinct, which can then be developed into collective consciousness. Jewish individualism and hedonism threaten to contaminate this collective, and frustrate the development of racial consciousness which is a prerequisite to the continued survival of the collective. This contamination can come in a directly sexual form, or via ideo-biological transmission. This 'infection' represents a mortal threat to the Germanic organism, which must be eliminated. The only question is how.

# 7.3 Love is a Battlefield

## *Sexual Atomism in 19^{th} and 20^{th} Century Germany*

**Changes in German sexuality over** the course of the nineteenth century were less pronounced and abrupt than those covered in previous chapters. The German family, while conservative, was perhaps less authoritarian than it could have been, and certainly less so than that of contemporaneous Russia, China, and India. Nevertheless, Ute Frevert describes the German family during this time as 'bourgeois', characterized by nuclear families, rigid gender definitions, arranged and typically loveless marriages, such marriages being distinctly unerotic and for the purpose of procreation.[1253]

Germany industrialized on a massive scale during the nineteenth century, going from some 85,000 workers in 1800 to 900,000 in 1848.[1254] Growth during this period was primarily in consumer goods, but from 1870 to 1900, industries like iron, steel, metalworking and machine building expanded rapidly.[1255] The percentage of women in industry was increasing rapidly as well by the late 1880s, particularly in textiles.[1256] As always, industrialization led to urbanization, which fueled a massive panic

---

1253 Ute Frevert, *Women in German History: From Bourgeois History to Sexual Liberation*, trans. Stuart McKinnon-Evans with Terry Bond and Barbara Norden (New York: Oxford/Berg, 1990).

1254 Werner Thönnesen, *The Emancipation of Women: The Rise and Decline of the Women's Movement in German Social Democracy*, trans. Joris de Bres (Bristol: Pluto Press, 1973), 13.

1255 Kathleen Canning, Languages of Labor and Gender: Female Factory Work in Germany, 1850-1914 (Ithaca: Cornell University Press, 1996), 19-20.

1256 Ibid., 31-33.

about prostitution, if not an increase in the practice itself.[1257] The increase in women's employment caused a bit of panic even within leftist circles, leading no less a distinguished figure than August Bebel to suggest that caution was in order because long hours of work promoted sexual excitement.[1258] The increase in women's employment, combined with agitation from social democrats, was enough to lead to the creation of a substantial women's movement in the early nineteenth century.[1259] Germany's nuclear family remained relatively stable, however, given that most working women were unable to achieve financial independence at this time.[1260]

German anti-Semitism, certainly nothing new by this point, was beginning to take on an apocalyptic character by the end of the nineteenth century, gaining a 'redemptive' aspect as Saul Friedländer calls it.[1261] Friedländer traces this aspect back to the Bayreuth Circle, formed in the 1880s, which was devoted to the mythical operas of composer Richard Wagner. The Bayreuth Circle would later give Hitler critical support during the 1920s. The intensity level of German anti-Semitism was rising as well as the nineteenth century ended. Lucy Davidowicz describes 1880 as "a watershed year, the start of a torrent of Anti-Semitism that did not abate for nearly twenty years."[1262] It was around this time also that anti-Semitism took on a distinctly racial aspect, Wilhelm Marr's *The Victory of the Jews Over the Germans*, published in 1879, being, according to John Weiss, "the first popular book to declare that the 'antisocial' traits of the Jews were determined by blood...."[1263] And as noted in the previous chapter, anti-Semitism was by now being linked to eugenics, most notably in the works of Houston Stewart Chamberlain. Weimar was the breaking point, both for sexual norms and anti-Semitism. By this time, one found,

1257 Lynn Abrams, "Prostitutes in Imperial Germany, 1870-1918: Working Girls or Social Outcasts?" in Richard J. Evans, ed., *The German Underworld: Deviants and Outcasts in German History* (London: Routledge, 1988), 189.

1258 Canning, 105.

1259 Thönnesen, 58.

1260 Barbara Franzoi, *At the Very Least She Pays the Rent: Women and German Industrialization, 1871-1914* (Westport: Greenwood Press, 1985), 40.

1261 Saul Friedländer, *Nazi Germany and the Jews Vol. 1: The Years of Persecution , 1933-1939* (New York: Harper Collins, 1997), 73-112.

1262 Lucy S. Dawidowicz, *The War Against the Jews, 1933-1945* (New York: Holt, Rhinehart and Winston, 1975), 36.

1263 John Weiss, *Ideology of Death: Why the Holocaust Happened in Germany* (Chicago: Ivan R. Dee, 1997), 79.

according to Davidowicz, "a world intoxicated with hate, driven by paranoia, enemies everywhere, the Jew lurking behind each one. The Germans were in search of a mysterious wholeness that would restore them to primeval happiness, destroying the hostile milieu of urban industrial civilization that the Jewish conspiracy had foisted on them."[1264]

## Weimar

**Following Germany's defeat in the** first world war, the Weimar Republic was conceived via *sua sponte* declaration on the part of Germany's Social Democratic Party in late 1918. Without significant support from the military, monarchy, or even bureaucracy, the authority of the new republic would rest primarily on its democratic foundations. Elections were held in January of 1919 for the German National Assembly, a body charged with the task of drafting a new German constitution. Life, liberty, and the pursuit of happiness, by no means a priority, were apparently considered by some to be a national threat. In April of 1919, a seemingly innocuous discussion on the subject of summer time, setting the clocks forward one hour so as to save coal and electricity, exploded into a series of impassioned diatribes on the subject of pleasure. One delegate received 'stormy applause' for the following:

> What then would happen if the working day really ended somewhat earlier? An increase in *pleasure-seeking* would set in, the workers would not go to bed any earlier and therefore would be less refreshed than if they had really made the most of the day with proper work. We are witnessing what has come to pass after this disastrous war. The pleasure-frenzy, the dancing-mania, the cinema attendance, is downright sinister, and I feel that if summer time really is reintroduced, there would be no check whatsoever on pleasure-seeking. On the contrary, people would have even more time with which to satisfy the desire for dancing and playing, in short, for enjoying life.[1265]

Nevertheless, the National Assembly turned out a prototypical liberal-

---

1264 Davidowicz, 47.
1265 Richard Bessel, *Germany After the First World War* (Oxford: Clarendon Press, 1993), 221.

democratic constitution.[1266]  It declared that all political authority was
vested in the people, and delegated legislative authority to the popularly
elected *Reichstag*. Personal liberty and private property were declared
inviolable in the absence of legal process. Of course, the saying went that
Weimar was a republic without republicans.

The Weimar Constitution also provided for the formal equality of the
sexes, though its practical impact on the position of women, for better or
worse, was virtually nil. The actual advancement of women (such as it was)
had come primarily during the war, and primarily for the purpose of waging
war more efficiently. The Hindenburg program of 1916 conscripted men
into industrial production, and encouraged women to fill the positions
thus vacated.  Some 3,000,000 women were employed in munitions
factories during the war; 700,000 were employed the mining, chemical,
metallurgical, and engineering industries by 1917.[1267]  As Ute Frevert
points out, the overall rate of women entering the workforce never increased
dramatically because women were losing jobs in non-essential industries.
The real difference was that women were now doing jobs traditionally
reserved for men.[1268]  Moreover, with young men otherwise occupied,
women were allowed to matriculate to German universities with increasing
frequency. The percentage of women in the student body rose from roughly
6% in 1914 to 9.5% in 1916.[1269]

On the other hand, certain provisions of the Imperial Civil Code
carried over into the new republic, including some designed specifically to
preserve the inequality of the sexes. A single woman was generally equal
to a man under the law, but a married woman was legally subservient to her
husband in a number of ways. The husband had control over the wife's
employment status and most of her assets, had the power to choose the
place of residence, and had decision-making authority regarding the
children's names, religion, and education.[1270]  Certain sexual restrictions
carried over into the new republic as well. The Imperial prohibition on
abortion (§218) survived, as did the prohibition on homosexuality (§175),

---

1266 Anton Kaes et al., ed., *The Weimar Republic Sourcebook* (Berkeley: University of
California Press, 1995), 46-51.
1267 Frevert, 156.
1268 Ibid., 157.
1269 Jill Stephenson, *Women in Nazi Society* (New York: Barnes & Noble Books,
1975), 15.
1270 Ibid., 13.

as did the prohibition on obscene publications (§184.3).[1271] The question, though, was to what effect.

As the Constitution failed to abrogate the Imperial Civil Code, the Civil Code was in turn powerless to prevent the decline and fall of the Imperial moral code. Sexual taboos were fading fast among those who reacted to the war with cynicism and nihilism.[1272] Demobilized soldiers were being greeted with 'homecoming divorces' from women who had perhaps married in haste and thought better of it, or simply those that had seen the city and were disinclined to return home. The birthrate had already been falling and, with 2.8 million more women than men after the war, would continue to do so. A common refrain was that women were selfishly refusing to procreate, thinking only of their own pleasure in life when they should be thinking about repopulating the nation.[1273] Abortion became a particularly sensitive issue as well; though ostensibly still illegal, the procedure was widely available.

Sexual freedom was itself the real issue, though the control of sexuality was always passed off as a means to a different end. For example, the wartime separation of the sexes had, it was assumed, led to immoral conduct by soldiers in foreign lands and immoral conduct by the women left behind. German officials then imagined that an epidemic of syphilis was spreading between the six million soldiers returning from the front and the multitude of now-immoral German women who were, they supposed, turning to prostitution in the absence of respectable financial support. No one could substantiate this epidemiological theory, however. As Richard Bessel writes:

> The problem was not that venereal disease had reached this or that particular level, but that social and sexual behavior, particularly of women, appeared out of control.... It is more than coincidental that at this time women were so often assumed both publicly and in government policy-discussions to be frivolous, pleasure-seeking, easily seduced, and to be actual or potential prostitutes.[1274]

1271 Atina Grossman, *Reforming Sex: The German Movement for Birth Control & Abortion Reform, 1920-1950* (New York: Oxford University Press, 1995), 33.
1272 Claudia Koonz, *Mothers in the Fatherland: Women, the Family, and Nazi Politics* (New York: St. Martin's Press, 1987), 43.
1273 Lisa Pine, *Nazi Family Policy, 1933-1945* (New York: Oxford/Berg, 1997), 9.
1274 Bessel, 238-39.

Kirk Rodby

## The Freikorps

**Demobilized soldiers had their own** concerns about female sexuality, especially those involved with the paramilitary *Freikorps* units. They were equipped by the regular German army, the *Reichswehr*, and authorized by the republican government now led by President Ebert. Their initial task was to secure disputed territories in the east against Polish and Baltic forces, though they were also active in the suppression of leftist uprisings throughout Germany. Most notably, they crushed the pro-Soviet Spartacist movement and murdered its leaders, Rosa Luxemburg and Karl Liebknecht, in Berlin in January of 1919. Soon after, they were openly attempting to overthrow the republic, occupying Berlin in March of 1920 and declaring right-wing politician Dr. Wolfgang Kapp chancellor of Germany. Though the Kapp putsch was unsuccessful, the *Reichswehr* overthrew the socialist government (the *Raterepublik*) in Munich and installed its own right-wing regime, providing the *Freikorps* with a safe haven from which to strike out at their enemies.

In the absence of a coherent ideology, bloodlust provided much of the *esprit de corps* for these units, composed of men who seemed to take particular pleasure in committing acts of violence against women. Klaus Theweleit's survey of Freikorps writing highlights a central division between the asexual, nurturing 'white' woman and the sexually-charged, threatening 'red' woman or she-devil. The red woman was often imagined to be a prostitute who reveled in her own sexuality, an animal devoid of human emotions, and in many cases a combatant who intended to castrate and/or kill the Freikorps member. Acts of violence against red women were viewed as self-defense, and in this area the threat of seduction always rivaled the threat of physical harm. A wave of indescribable horror washed over these men when confronted with the prospect of an erotic encounter. As Freikorp officer Ernst von Salomon explained, "It wasn't their whispered propositions that seemed so intolerable; it was the easy, matter-of-fact manner in which they groped at our bodies, bodies that had just been exposed to the ravages of machine-gun fire."[1275] An interesting association, particularly in light of the fact that von Salomon seems to prefer the machine gun. As for the overall aim of the movement: "With their screams and filthy giggling, vulgar women excite men's urges. Let our revulsion

1275 Klaus Theweleit, *Male Fantasies Vol. 1: Women, Floods, Bodies, History*, trans. Stephen Conway with Erica Carter and Chris Turner, fwd. Barbara Ehrenreich (Minneapolis: University of Minnesota Press, 1987), 64-65.

260

flow into a single river of destruction. A destruction which will be incomplete if it does not also trample their hearts and souls."[1276]

Freikorps members committed acts of 'self-defense' against women with regularity. During the Kapp Putsch, a General Maercker explained to his unit that one certainly did not need to operate on the presumption that women were innocent, and that warning shots in their direction were quite unnecessary. "Shoot off a few flares under the women's skirts, then watch how they start running. ... It's the most harmless device you can think of!"[1277] Another example of humane Freikorps violence is found in the account of a storm-troop leader dealing with a captured Bolshevik woman. "I am presented with a slut. The typical bad girl from Schwabing. Short, stringy hair; seedy clothes; a brazen, sensuous face.... 'The riding crop, then let her go,' was all I said."[1278] Women caught hiding weapons beneath their skirts were subject to summary execution, the same punishment reserved for red women caught having sex. "One such woman lay behind the bushes," recalled a Freikorps officer, "in the most tender embrace with her lover. A grenade caught her off guard in the practice of her true profession."[1279]

Freikorps members loathed physical contact with women, and Theweleit notes specifically that even when abusing women, they almost always employed some sort of instrument rather than use a bare hand. Their fantasies all existed on a "historical-political-social" level, avoiding "the private, the intimate, the individual, or, more precisely perhaps, the singular."[1280] They set love of women against love of the nation, and confined their sexuality to the latter. As Theweleit notes, "these men claimed to 'love' the very things that *protect* them against real love-object relations!"[1281] The National Socialists would later claim the Freikorps as ideological brethren, a slight inaccuracy given that the Freikorps never really developed an ideology. The *susceptibility* to ideology was certainly there, and Freikorps members would go on to fill out the ranks of the National Socialist movement in large numbers. Many gravitated toward the storm-trooper section of the movement, or Sturmabteilung (SA). Hundreds of Freikorps alumni went on to positions of prominence in the

1276  Ibid., 180.
1277  Ibid., 174.
1278  Ibid., 173.
1279  Ibid., 82.
1280  Ibid., 88.
1281  Ibid., 61.

Third Reich, including Hitler adjutant Martin Bormann, Deputy Führer Rudolf Hess, Auschwitz Commandant Rudolph Höss, SD Chief Reinhard Heydrich, Minister of the Interior (Saxony) Karl Fritsch, National Minister of the Interior Helmut Nicolai, and Himmler adjutant Karl Wolff.

## *The Rise of National Socialism*

**As for the NSDAP itself,** Adolf Hitler had managed to keep himself from being demobilized after WWI and ended up stationed in Munich, then under the control of the *Raterepublik*. The *Reichswehr* takeover initially left the army with complete control of the city, which they set out to preserve through the surveillance of local political groups and the political indoctrination of their own troops. Hitler was recruited as an informant and sent to spy on the German Worker's Party (DAP), founded by a locksmith named Anton Drexler. Hitler attended a meeting and ended up screaming at an invited speaker who was advocating Bavarian separatism. Drexler, suitably impressed, invited Hitler to join the movement. Hitler would later claim to have agonized over the decision, approving of the organization's political aims but taking issue with the quality of the organization itself. His commanding officer would later recall ordering Hitler to join, and paying him a salary to help build up the movement.[1282] In either case, Hitler signed on in September of 1919 and became member No. 555.

As a public speaker, Hitler was second to none, throwing out simple and repetitive ideas in an explosive, virtually orgasmic, fashion. He quickly became the party's public face and primary draw, packing crowds into Munich's beer halls. As a result of his efforts and abilities, the DAP (eventually adding the National Socialist prefix) grew rapidly in spite of competition from a number of other *völkisch* movements. By August of 1921, the party had some 3,300 members. Future SA Chief Ernst Röhm joined the DAP soon after Hitler, though he remained somewhat noncommittal until the movement picked up momentum. Röhm put Hitler in touch with a number of wealthy contacts who provided the cash-strapped party with funding at several points. He was also instrumental in building up the movement's paramilitary capabilities, and it was through Röhm's paramilitary organization of the time that Heinrich Himmler found his way into the Nazi party in August of 1923 as member No.

---

1282  Ian Kershaw, *Hitler 1889-1936: Hubris*, (New York: W.W. Norton & Co., 1999), 127.

42,404.

In October of 1922, Julius Streicher, head of the Nuremberg branch of the Deutsche Werkgemeinschaft, offered to fold his organization and his newspaper of the time (the *Deutscher Volkswille*) into the NSDAP. In an instant, the NSDAP grew from 6,000 strong to 20,000. Under Streicher's command, the intensely anti-Semitic and sexually explicit *Der Stürmer* began publication in 1923. The paper's continuing storyline was the Jew as sexual predator, brought to life in tales (both factual and fictional) of Aryan women being sexually assaulted by racial aliens. Der Stürmer's signature element was its cartoons, which featured exceptionally repulsive caricatures of Jewish men doing all sorts of interesting things to less than fully-clothed German women, breasts prominently displayed. One has Jewish doctors dissecting an Aryan woman's corpse during the course of an unspecified (and presumably unnecessary) medical experiment. Another has a naked woman chained in front of a copy of the Talmud, and covered in snakes bearing the names of Jewish sex criminals as well as sex reformer Magnus Hirschfeld. Circulation of the paper was generally estimated at around 6,000 in the early years, though Dennis Showalter estimates it may have been closer to 13,000. Casual readership was extended by posting the paper in showcases, which put National Socialist ideology on display for every passerby to see.

In 1923, the NSDAP unsuccessfully attempted to overthrow the republic, though with little bloodshed on either side. In the long term, the putsch attempt did the NSDAP more good than harm. Hitler received a very light sentence, and even then served very little of it. He became a national celebrity, a dangerous lunatic to some, but to others a heroic rebel fighting the evil 'system-state' of Weimar Germany. The NSDAP gained instant credibility with anti-republican forces across Germany, and nothing so drastic had been done to check the movement that the portals of power could not be reopened. In the short term, though, anti-republican sentiment waned as the nation entered a period of relative political stability and economic prosperity. The very popular Hindenburg assumed the Presidency in 1925, adding a certain aura of legitimacy to the republic. The very capable Gustav Stresemann retained his position as Foreign Minister, and managed to secure Germany a position in the League of Nations in 1926. Germany emerged as a cultural powerhouse, turning out luminaries in virtually every field of artistic endeavor. Crime went down and wages went up.

## Sexuality in Weimar

**As the NSDAP faded from** view, the sexual revolution was hitting its stride and provoking hostile reactions all the while. In 1924, author Hugo Bettauer declared quite confidently that "the erotic revolution is underway; it is not to be stopped...."[1283] Bettauer was killed the next year by a fanatical anti-Semite. Unquestionably, though, the institution of marriage was commanding less respect. Germany's experience with hyperinflation had rendered dowries worthless, in turn putting the value of female chastity in question. Promiscuity was no longer beyond the pale of civilized behavior, nor were adultery and divorce.[1284] In Berlin, a teenager might be taunted for lack of sexual experience, and at least one commentator felt compelled to issue a "Call for Sexual Tolerance" on behalf of women who were derided for refusing a sexual encounter. The 'companiate' or trial marriage was proposed, as was bigamy, as was marriage for a term. The trend toward mixed marriages between Jews and non-Jews continued, an assault on the institution depending on one's viewpoint. In the last years of the republic (1930-33), the percentages of Jews intermarrying reached 27% in Berlin and 39% in Hamburg.[1285]

Women continued to make gains in various employment sectors, constituting one-third of Germany's workforce by 1925.[1286] Sexual tensions eased with men and women in close contact, and the ritual of seduction became a more casual and direct affair. The 'New Woman' emerged, fashion conscious, prone to flirting, and sexually independent, "oriented exclusively toward the present ... not that which should be or should have been according to tradition."[1287] The New Woman also became a focal point for criticism, targeted for her perceived rationality, materialism, and individualism. Pope Pius XI felt compelled to issue an encyclical on January 1, 1930, condemning the emancipation of woman and reaffirming her subordinate position within the family.[1288] Some of the fire came from

---

1283 Kaes, 700.
1284 Frevert, 186.
1285 Marion A. Kaplan, *Between Dignity and Despair: Jewish Life in Nazi Germany* (New York: Oxford University Press, 1998), 76.
1286 Hans Peter Bleuel, *Sex and Society in Nazi Germany*, ed. Heinrich Fraenkel, trans. J. Maxwell Brownjohn (Philadelphia: J.B. Lippincott, 1973), 21.
1287 Kaes, 207.
1288 Grossman, 78.

older feminists like Gertrude Baumer and Helene Stocker, who were appalled that young women were using their newfound liberation for hedonistic purposes.[1289] The New Woman's shameless quest for sexual pleasure transformed Imperial Germany into a mythical land of spiritual purity and genuine emotional eroticism, preserved by selfless women whose "passion ... magically illuminated interactions that lifted them above the duller senses of simply egoistic relations among people."[1290]

Sex reform leagues and sex counseling centers flourished during Weimar. Ads for 'rubberware' and remedies for 'women's troubles' hit the press. Contraceptives became available in vending machines, and one could purchase syringes 'warning' women not to use them if pregnant, because said pregnancy would thereby be terminated.[1291] An estimated 1,000,000 abortions per year were taking place, and the New Woman appeared to be the primary culprit. Women who resorted to abortion frequently consulted informal networks of other women in the hopes of finding a female practitioner, heightening the anxiety over the prospect of sexual anarchy brought about entirely by women.[1292] Prostitution expanded into a highly diversified industry, with as many as 100,000 women in Berlin catering to every desire imaginable.[1293] Germany also began to produce its own pornography in large quantities, and, unlike the competing product from France and Hungary, it gravitated toward particularly intense and unusual sexual practices.[1294]

The sexual dynamics of Weimar played out in the cultural arenas that made the republic legendary, namely the theater, cinema, and literature. "According to the new *Zeitgeist*, sex, like justice, had to be seen to be done."[1295] A brief foray into expressionism was followed by the rise of the 'New Objectivity', an artistic aesthetic emphasizing cold rationalism and dispassionate realism, aiming to put the artist in control of the irrational.

---

1289 Cornelie Usborne, "Wise Women, Wise Men, and Abortion in the Weimar Republic: Gender, Class, and Medicine," in *Gender Relations in German History*, ed. Lynn Abrams and Elizabeth Harvey (Durham: Duke University Press, 1997), 146.

1290 Kaes, 205.

1291 Grossman, 11-15.

1292 Usborne, 147.

1293 Mel Gordon, *Voluptuous Panic: The Erotic World of Weimar Berlin* (Los Angeles: Feral House, 2000), 28-49.

1294 Ibid., 170-89.

1295 Walter Laqueur, *Weimar: A Cultural History, 1918-1933* (New York: Putnam, 1974), 225.

The New Objectivity was in large part an exploration of sexual anxiety, with female sexuality and gender destabilization representing the forces of irrationality. In fact, the term could be applied directly to "sexual behavior that was 'modern', unconventional, sober, cynical, or simply de-sentimentalized."[1296] For the right-wing intellectual, artistic trends in Weimar were clear and convincing evidence of Germany's cultural decay at the hands of world Jewry. A true *völkisch* culture emphasized emotion over intellectualism and saw beauty in simplicity and purity; from that perspective, there may have been very little difference between sexual rationality and sexual degeneracy.[1297] In terms of frequency, conservative values still dominated artistic endeavors in Germany, and yet, as Walter Laqueur notes, "the right-wing intellectual felt himself acutely isolated. The enemy, on the other hand, was omnipresent; he dominated the scene, his voice was the only one to be heard."[1298]

Homosexuality achieved a certain level of tolerance during the Weimar years, though sex reformer Magnus Hirschfeld founded the Institute of Sexual Science in 1919 with the hope of achieving even greater acceptance. Hirschfeld was convinced that homosexuality was determined biologically, and that if people were educated as to the facts, perhaps 90% would favor the abolition of §175 (which banned homosexuality).[1299] Lesbians already enjoyed legal immunity, yet prosecutions even of gay men were rare, and for the most part §175 existed only on paper. Lesbian culture did thrive more openly, with Berlin featuring several dozen lesbian social clubs and eighty-five nightclubs, including some where heterosexual tourists could visit.[1300] For gay men, the meeting places were less formal, even mobile in some cases, and the scene was "noticeably invisible" during the daytime. A wise policy, as even in Weimar there was some degree of danger for gay men. The Nazis were attempting to murder the high-profile Hirschfeld as early as 1923, narrowly missing him once they took power in 1933. In any case, a same-sex relationship was readily available for just about anyone who wanted one.

The restoration of the sexual order became an issue of overriding

---

1296 Richard W. McCormick, *Gender and Sexuality in Weimar Modernity: Film, Literature, and 'New Objectivity'*, (New York: Palgrave, 2001), 45.
1297 Ibid., 79-80.
1298 Laqueur, 80.
1299 Richard Plant, *The Pink Triangle: The Nazi War Against Homosexuals* (New York: Henry Holt, 1986).
1300 Gordon, 108-13.

concern, one addressed in some way by virtually every major political party during the Weimar era. The spectrum of opinions tended to be narrow and right-shifted. The German National People's Party (DNVP) linked the prevailing state of sexual chaos with the system-state of Weimar, and with the rival SPD in particular. They campaigned with images of French-African troops violating German women, in addition to the obligatory references to Jewish pornography and Jewish sexual egalitarianism.[1301] The Catholic Center Party (Center) called on women to effect a moral renewal through asceticism and maternity, reminding them that Christianity had rescued them from "male passions and male abuse."[1302] The German People's Party (DVP) also campaigned as the party of sexual morality, noting that its female members were responsible for pushing a sexual censorship provision in 1926. The Center attempted to differentiate the NSDAP from traditional conservative parties, suggesting, for one, that the Nazis planned to murder anyone they felt was genetically inferior. As for sexual morality, the DVP joined the Center in highlighting the theories of NSDAP theoretician Alfred Rosenberg, who had advocated polygamy, unwed motherhood for Aryan women, and a relaxation of the rules against adultery relative to husbands of infertile women.[1303]

Moving left, the SPD had pushed for the abolition of §175 at the end of the 19th century, pushed for constitutional voting rights for women in Weimar, and campaigned as a progressive force in matters of gender. The DVP and DNVP characterized the SPD as the party of free love and sex for pleasure, and yet even the SPD was promoting socialism as a way to facilitate "positive eugenics" and limit immorality.[1304] The SPD, meanwhile, was labeling the NSDAP the homosexual party given the involvement of 'proven' homosexual Ernst Rohm. Germany's communist party (KPD) was under fire for sexual experimentation in the Soviet Union. The KPD returned fire at the parties of the right by pointing to the economic inequality subtending traditional sexual morality, and by bringing attention to a member of the NSDAP who ran a strip club and to a member of the DNVP whose newspapers ran ads for massage parlors.[1305] The KPD did initiate a campaign to have §218 abolished altogether in 1931, though

1301 Julia Sneeringer, *Winning Women's Votes: Propaganda and Politics in Weimar Germany* (Chapel Hill: University of North Carolina Press, 2002), 46.
1302 Ibid., 39.
1303 Ibid., 251-52.
1304 Ibid., 56.
1305 Ibid., 254.

even there the debate was framed entirely in terms of the collective good, not the rights of the individual woman. They were blocked by the SPD in any case.

There was thus very little to distinguish the NSDAP's "lurid discourse of perversion and disease" from the rest. Even parties that expressed concern about the NSDAP apparently did so insincerely; the Center ended up joining the NSDAP-DNVP-Center Coalition of Death in spite of its own warnings about the homicidal inclinations of the NSDAP. Only one organization, the Unity League for Proletarian Reform (EpS), had any real sense of how far the NSDAP intended to go in its invasion of the erotic realm. In a report entitled "Love in the Third Reich," the EpS predicted that "given rumors that even gratification of sexual desire cannot be allowed for everybody,... all those who have intercourse without the permission of [marital] counseling centers will be prosecuted and put in jail." Not all, as it turned out, but many.

## Origins of the Third Reich

**The NSDAP reformed in February** of 1925, after a recently released Adolf Hitler had managed to convince Bavarian officials to lift the ban on his party. With the completion of the first book of *Mein Kampf*, Hitler began to see himself as a kind of messianic figure, both the prime mover and primary exponent of National Socialism. On March 9 of 1925, Bavarian officials imposed a ban on public speaking by Hitler, thus beginning a trend among German states and putting Hitler out of commission throughout the greater part of the country. Gregor Strasser was primarily responsible for the NSDAP's resurgence at this point. Strasser was anti-Semitic, intelligent, far and away the party's most capable organizer, and someone who could provide rational ballast to Hitler's utopian ambitions.[1306] With help from brother Otto and future Propaganda Minister Joseph Goebbles (as well as secretary Heinrich Himmler), he gave the movement life in previously inhospitable northern Germany, raising the number of local organizations there from 72 in late 1923 to 262 by the end of 1925. In 1928, the NSDAP ran for national election under its own name for the first time, receiving a dismal 2.6% of the vote and sending twelve delegates to the Reichstag. German officials decided the NSDAP was no longer a threat and rescinded

---

1306  Hans Mommsen, *The Rise and Fall of Weimar Democracy* (Chapel Hill: University of North Carolina Press, 1996), 336-37.

the speaking ban. This was despite the fact that in 1928, the party boasted some 100,000 members, and its electoral foundation was spreading into new regions with minimal party presence.

Additionally, and in spite of a ban on women in leadership positions in the party, the NSDAP enjoyed support from a sizeable women's auxiliary. Elsbeth Zander founded the Order of the Red Swastika sometime in the mid-1920s, receiving official permission in 1926 to consider herself the leader of all women Nazis.[1307] The organization boasted some 13,000 members according to Zander, though only about 4,000 according to the Munich police.[1308] The distinctly sexophobic and anti-Semitic Guida Diehl once claimed, quite improbably, that her New Land movement had some 200,000 members, though the Nazis did take her seriously enough to try to recruit her. The radical women who supported the NSDAP were apparently drawn to the anti-individualism inherent in its notion of biological determinism. In the words of Lydia Gottschewski:

> The fundamental experience of the old women's movement was the individual personality, woman's freedom and her pleasure. The fundamental experience of the new movement is the Volk and its community. ... Our banners proclaim our slogan, "The Volk must live on even if we must die...!" We want nothing for ourselves and everything for the community. We want only one right — the right to be able to serve...."[1309]

Or as Zander proclaimed, "We recognize no men's and no women's rights, but accept the duty of fighting, living, and working for the nation."[1310]

Gustav Stresemann died on October 3, 1929, three weeks before the American stock-market crashed. Stresemann had cautioned that Germany's economic renaissance of the late 1920s was predicated on short-term credit from America, and that its withdrawal would lead to disaster. It was and did. Unemployment extended well into double figures in 1930, industrial output and wages went down, and a previously existing agricultural crisis was deepened. The republic took the blame for the depression, and the NSDAP's previous lack of electoral success suddenly

1307 Claudia Koonz, *Mothers in the Fatherland: Women, the Family, and Nazi Politics* (New York: St. Martin's Press, 1987), 72.
1308 Ibid., 76.
1309 Ibid., 114-15.
1310 Ibid., 74.

became an advantage. They were able to position themselves as outsiders, a radical and dynamic alternative to the existing power structure which appeared incapable of rejuvenating the economy. The movement offered no specifics on policy, only salvation through national unity. The September 1930 *Reichstag* election brought them 18.3% of the vote and 107 seats, and of the 6.5 million people who voted National Socialist, 3 million were women. "The power of instinct so clearly demonstrated its superior strength and accuracy," Hitler would later remark. "Woman proved to us in those days that her aim is sure."[1311]

In 1932, Reich President Hindenburg's seven-year term was coming to an end, with no obvious replacement and the prospect of an electoral impasse if he ran again. Hitler was approached about NSDAP support for a provision allowing Hindenburg to remain in office. Hitler decided instead to run against him in March of 1932, receiving a respectable 37% of the vote in a three-way runoff, though Hindenburg retained his office having gained 53% of the vote. A series of state elections followed on April 24, with the Nazis picking up between 26% and 41% of the vote in each state. The high-water mark for legitimate NSDAP electoral success came in the *Reichstag* elections of July, 1932, where the movement received 37.4% of the vote and 230 seats, becoming the largest party in the legislature. At this point Hitler was offered the position of Vice-Chancellor, which he refused outright, bringing Germany's various political parties to an impasse as to the formation of a government.

The November elections brought the NSDAP back down to 33.1% of the vote and left them with 196 delegates in the Reichstag. Party members were defecting in droves, and the party's finances were drained from a year of frenetic electioneering. Strasser had favored a more conciliatory approach than Hitler, with the NSDAP perhaps joining a coalition regardless of who became Reich Chancellor. With Hitler intransigent, Strasser resigned, expressing his disappointment that Hitler was attempting to fulfill his personal ambitions at the party's expense. At this point, conservatives came up with the idea of 'taming' Hitler by placing him at the head of a cabinet composed of conservatives rather than Nazis. Hitler was made Chancellor on January 30, 1933, and chaos followed immediately. A wave of state-supported violence washed across Germany, directed at the NSDAP's enemies on the left. A former communist responded by setting fire to the

---

1311 Hans Peter Bleuel, *Sex and Society in Nazi Germany*, ed. Heinrich Fraenkel, trans. J. Maxwell Brown john (Philadelphia: J.B. Lippincott, 1973), 55.

Reichstag building on February 27; the Nazis spun the act into a communist conspiracy and raised the specter of a leftist uprising. Elections took place on March 5, bringing the NSDAP 43.9% and the DNVP 8.0% of the vote. Hitler's coalition now had a majority in the *Reichstag*, and he quickly turned his attention to the acquisition of emergency powers that would allow him to govern without limitation from the legislature or even the President. The NSDAP's Enabling Act required a two-thirds majority to pass, a level of support that could only be achieved in conjunction with the Catholic Center Party. The Center was not opposed to the idea in principle, though they were understandably a bit wary about handing Hitler so much power.

Hitler seduced the Center with two basic assurances in a speech to the Reichstag on March 23. One, the government would endeavor to achieve the "political and moral purification of public life" so as to "heighten the religious experience" for Germans.[1312] Two, the government would respect the prerogatives of religious organizations in the area of education, reserving for them "the influence which is their due...." Reading substance into the second would have been terribly naive given the deliberately noncommittal language Hitler chose to use. As to the first, however, the Center was already getting everything it had ever hoped for and more besides. On February 24, the Prussian Ministry of the Interior issued a directive ordering strict enforcement of the Obscene Publications Youth Protection Act, covering printed materials "liable to produce erotic effects in the beholder."[1313] A broader ordinance covering obscene writings, illustrations, and performances was issued on March 7.[1314] Hirschfeld's institute was raided on May 6, purged of 'unGermanic' works, and vandalized.[1315] The Nazis banned nudity and cracked down on prostitution; homosexual nightclubs were shut down and even flirting was regulated in heterosexual clubs. By 1935, the Nazis grew tired of legislating piecemeal and simply prohibited any act contrary to "wholesome popular sentiment."[1316]

In exchange for initiating this campaign of sexual censorship and repression, Hitler received the support of the Center for his Enabling Act,

---

1312 Guenter Lewy, *The Catholic Church and Nazi Germany* (New York: McGraw Hill, 1964), 35.

1313 Günter Grau ed., *Hidden Holocaust?: Gay and Lesbian Persecution in Germany 1933-45*, with Claudia Schoppmann, trans. Patrick Camiller (London: Cassell, 1995), 29.

1314 Bleuel, 5.

1315 Grau, 31.

1316 Bleuel, 8.

giving him unlimited authority over the state of Germany on March 23, 1933. The assault on eroticism allowed for a convivial relationship between church and state in the early moments of National Socialist rule. As one German newspaper proudly reported:

> The Vatican welcomes the struggle of National Germany against obscene material. ... It will be recalled that Pius XI, in his recent encyclicals, has repeatedly and vigorously stressed that defensive actions against obscene material are of fundamental importance for the bodily and spiritual health of family and nation, and he most warmly welcomes the type and manner, the resolution and purposefulness with which this struggle has been undertaken in the new Germany.[1317]

The German bishops were thrilled as well. The Bishops Conference held in Fulda from May 30 to June 1 issued a pastoral letter thanking Hitler for eliminating the threat of immorality.[1318] One church official visiting New York later in the year explained that the German bishops supported Hitler because he was defending Germany against "the plague of dirty literature."[1319]

# 7.4 The SS Brünhilde's Last Pleasure

## Coordination

**Quaint notions of chivalry were** left by the wayside as the Nazis settled into power, to be replaced by National Socialist notions of chivalry. Female legislators were removed from their positions, and partly for their own protection according to Hitler. "[S]o far from ennobling parliament," he explained, "the woman who engages in parliamentary activity will be violated by that activity."[1320] Hans Peter Bleuel suggests a subconscious link in Hitler's mind between the 'Jewified' legislative system and the sexual metaphor of

1317 Grau, 30.
1318 Uta Ranke-Heinemann, Eunuchs for the Kingdom of Heaven: Women, Sexuality, and the Catholic Church, trans. Peter Heinegg (New York: Doubleday, 1990), 330.
1319 Ibid., 331.
1320 Quoted in Hans Peter Bleuel, *Sex and Society in Nazi Germany*, ed. Heinrich Fraenkel, trans. J. Maxwell Brown john (Philadelphia: J.B. Lippincott, 1973), 59.

violation. One might also detect a hint of malice in the phrase "will be violated," threatening overtones which become clearer in light of the manner in which the Gestapo and the SA actually dealt with these women. Female legislators on every level had their offices and homes searched, and were subjected to interrogations with violence as a standard adjunct.[1321] Some were sent to concentration camps and physically abused for weeks or even years until they died; others were murdered straightaway. In Gestapo custody, women were "stripped, humiliated, and assaulted in ways most likely to break them down."[1322] Strapping electrodes to genitalia was a favorite routine for the Gestapo, though they were particularly fond of lashing women as well.

Nazi 'feminists' were treated better than female legislators, though they were pushed off the stage almost as quickly.[1323] The NSDAP's tendency to keep women's organizations at arm's length and allow them to act independently during Weimar led female ideologues to believe a similar arrangement would hold in the Third Reich. Wisdom came suddenly, as Claudia Koonz explains:

> The message seemed clear: no form of women's autonomy could be tolerated - even when accompanied by the most fanatical loyalty to Hitler or Nazi ideology. Stalwart, idealistic "old-time" Nazi women leaders withdrew or were subtly expelled from the very organizations they had helped to create. They saw themselves replaced by more "respectable" and docile women - many of whom had not even supported the Nazi Party before 1933.[1324]

Formerly unknown party activist Gertrud Scholtz-Klink was the widow of an SA member, the mother of four, a former homemaker, sufficiently docile, and stereotypically Aryan in appearance. Scholtz-Klink became Reich Women's Leader in 1934, heading up the National Socialist Women's

1321 Sybil Milton, "Women and the Holocaust," in *When Biology Became Destiny: Women in Weimar and Nazi Germany*, ed. Renate Bridenthal, Atina Grossman, and Marion Kaplan (New York: Monthly Review Press, 1984), 298-99.

1322 Roger Manvell, *SS and Gestapo: Rule by Terror* (New York: Ballantine Books, 1969), 85-86.

1323 Claudia Koonz, *Mothers in the Fatherland: Women, the Family, and Nazi Politics* (New York: St. Martin's Press, 1987), 140.

1324 Claudia Koonz, "The Competition for Women's Lebensraum, 1928-1934," in *When Biology Became Destiny: Women in Weimar and Nazi Germany*, ed. Renate Bridenthal, Atina Grossman, and Marion Kaplan (New York: Monthly Review Press, 1984), 226-27.

Bureau, or NS-Frauenwerk. The process of *gleichshaltung* (coordination) folded every other women's organization in the nation into the *Frauenwerk*, bringing several million women nominally under her control. She actually held very little power in the Third Reich, and was kept at arm's length by most of the National Socialist leadership, some of whom never even bothered to learn how to spell her name. Her task was significant, namely the design and implementation of a program of ideological indoctrination designed to restore every Aryan woman in Germany to what she was in reality. Cash incentives and concentration camps were also used to help encourage National Socialist satori where indoctrination alone might fail.

Traditionally, the Germanic woman was expected to structure her life around the three Ks: *Kinder, Kirche, Küche* (kids, kirk/church, kitchen). National Socialism dropped the emphasis on religion, but seconded the idea of the true Germanic woman as mother and homemaker. In 1933, the Third Reich began offering interest-free loans (RM 1000) to newly married women who relinquished positions of employment, with the program financed in part through an income-tax increase on single persons without children.[1325] Incentives were coupled with categorical restrictions, preventing women from certain professional occupations (e.g., judge, attorney),[1326] and barring them from certain positions in heavy industry.[1327] The percentage of female students in the universities, which stood at 20% in 1932, was capped at 10% under the National Socialist regime.[1328] Yet women continued to hold and ultimately gain positions in low-end administrative work, clothing, textiles, agriculture, food-service, and even fared relatively well in manufacturing.[1329] After an initial drop, the overall percentage of women in the workforce actually increased over the first few years of the Third Reich.[1330]

Thus the realities of running an industrialized nation did impact Nazi policy somewhat, but women were kept under foot to whatever extent possible. Or, alternatively, kept on their backs. The Nazis promoted motherhood quite fanatically, though limiting their praise for the state of

---

1325 Jill Stephenson, *Women in Nazi Society* (New York: Harper & Row, 1975), 46.
1326 Bleuel, 67.
1327 Stephenson, 89.
1328 Richard Grunberger, *The 12-Year Reich: A Social History of Nazi Germany* (New York: Da Capo Press, 1995), 252.
1329 Ibid., 254-55.
1330 Bleuel, 62-63.

motherhood itself and generally leaving aside the process which makes motherhood possible. Mother's Day, initiated during Weimar, became a national celebration in 1935. The marriage-loan program mentioned earlier also provided for a credit of RM 250 for each child born, with the entire debt thus forgiven upon bearing four children.[1331] The National Socialists converted centers for birth control and sex reform into eugenics facilities, and simply eliminated those for which they had no use.[1332] In the further interest of ensuring that sex was had exclusively for purposes of procreation, a Reich Office for Combating Abortion and Homosexuality was established in 1936. In 1938, the Nazis actually provided for no-fault divorce, in the hopes that broken and unproductive relationships might be replaced by happier, procreative marriages.[1333] Also in 1938, the German mother became eligible for the *Mutterkreuz*, a medal awarded for success on the birth front and bearing the inscription, "The child ennobles the mother."[1334] Four children rated the bronze version, six the silver, and eight the gold, with the medal to be awarded on the birthday of Adolf Hitler's mother. The ultimate impact of these measures was marginal. The birth rate stood at 59 births per 1000 women in 1934 and rose to 85 by 1939, an improvement certainly, though still less than the rate of 90 in 1922 and 128 a decade prior to that.[1335]

As for acquiring a man in the first place, women were indoctrinated on the finer points of courtship during courses on 'racial science', where they were exposed to the "Ten Commandments for Choosing a Partner."[1336]

1. Remember that you are German.

---

1331 Bleuel, 150.
1332 Atina Grossman, *Reforming Sex: The German Movement for Birth Control & Abortion Reform, 1920-1950* (Oxford: Oxford University Press, 1995), 137.
1333 Stephenson, 42.
1334 "The German people and particularly the German youth must again be brought up with reverence for the mothers of the nation. The German *kinderreich* [child-rich] mother should receive a special place of honor in national society alongside the frontline soldier, as the boundaries of her love and life for nation and fatherland are the same as the frontline soldier in the thunder of battle. The Führer has therefore ordered that a decoration for the German *kinderreich* mother will be created. A decoration in bronze for the mother of 4 children, a decoration in silver for the mother of 6 children, a decoration in gold for the mother of 8 children." Speech of Gerhard Wagner, *Reichstagung in Nürnberg 1937*, ed. Hanns Kerrl, (Berlin: Vaterländischer Verlag C.A. Weller, 1938), 126.
1335 Stephenson, 50-51.
1336 Koonz, *Mothers in the Fatherland*, 189.

2. If genetically healthy, you should not remain single.

3. Keep your body pure.

4. You should keep mind and spirit pure.

5. As Germans, choose only spouses of the same or Nordic blood.

6. In choosing your spouse, ask about his or her forefathers.

7. Health is prerequisite for external beauty.

8. Marry only out of love.

9. Do not look for a playmate, but a life-partner in marriage.

10. Hope for the possibility of many children.[1337]

The injunction to "marry only out of love" coexists uncomfortably with the distinctly unemotional and impersonal criteria surrounding it. As Katherine Thomas wrote at the time, "Love as the mysterious driving power in human relationships has been replaced by a substitute called 'Rassegefuehl' — Racial Consciousness ... the first consideration in a woman's marriage [has gone] from 'Do we love each other?' to 'Do we conform to the approved public convenience?'"[1338] For the Nazis, there was very little difference between love and race consciousness, the former simply a particularized expression of the latter. Love, like race consciousness generally, was the product of biological instinct and proper ideological development. According to the supporting text of commandment nine, marriage is a bond with "significance for the life of the individual as well as the *Volk* as a whole. The purpose of marriage is procreation. Only with spiritually, physically, and racially similar men can this ideal be reached.... Every race has its own soul. Only similar souls can understand one another."[1339]

While naturally and instinctively driven to motherhood, the true Germanic woman was also supposed to be asexual, submissive, and impassive. The Nazis promoted this concept of womanhood through visual imagery, which, for some reason, necessitated female nudity whenever possible. According to George Mosse, "The Third Reich sought to strip nudity of its sexuality.... Pictures of the nude body made hard and healthy through

---

1337 Arthur Gütt, Herbert Linden, and Franz Maßfeller, *Blutschutz und Ehegesundheitsgesetz* (München: J.S. Lehmanns Verlag, 1936), 12-14.

1338 Katherine Thomas, *Women in Nazi Germany* (London: Victor Golanz, 1943), 50-51.

1339 Gütt, 14.

exercise and sport were presented as the proper stereotype."[1340]  As Bleuel describes the National Socialist art scene, "Full-bosomed and voluptuous female forms of unambivalently ambivalent character were vividly committed to canvas on the most specious of artistic pretexts."[1341]  Adolf Ziegler, president of the Reich Chamber of Art, was a master of the National Socialist genre, and his painting "The Four Elements" received a place of honor in Hitler's home in Munich.  Each of the four elements was, of course, represented by a nude woman. As for other media, drawings of the Germanic mother bare-breasted and suckling her child made the cover of *Das Schwarze Korps* and the official 1935 Farming Calendar.[1342]  Streicher's *Der Stürmer* remained in force throughout the 1930s, excepting a brief hiatus during the 1936 Olympics. Some of the more conservative elements in German society failed to appreciate the fine distinctions between the sexually charged, degenerate nudity the Nazis were destroying and the asexual, pure, and uplifting nudity they were producing.  For the Nazis, it was perfectly straightforward; the true Germanic woman had nothing whatsoever to do with sexuality, whatever her sartorial state.

The true Germanic woman was asexual by nature, but also naturally prone to having her true nature corrupted through sexuality. Thus Scholtz-Klink and the German Girl's League (BdM) set out to reinforce female asexuality through the educational system. In this respect, physical training was critical to the development of the German girl, and she was made to perform simple and repetitive exercises in the hopes of dulling her mind along with her sex-drive. The BdM actually had little to say on the subject of sex, apart from exhortations to marriage and maternity. "The satisfaction of sexual urges was regarded as shameful, reprehensible, and biologically and medically unnecessary," writes Lisa Pine. "'Fresh, clean, clear German air' was the alternative to sexual education."[1343]  It will come as no surprise to anyone familiar with this type of sexual education that BdM girls were impregnated at a steady rate.

## Creating The True Germanic Woman

**Unmarried motherhood remained a point** of instability in National Socialist

1340  George Mosse, *Nationalism and Sexuality: Respectability and Abnormal Sexuality in Modern Europe* (New York: Howard Fertig, 1985), 171.
1341  Bleuel, 184.
1342  Ibid., 58.
1343  Lisa Pine, *Nazi Family Policy: 1933-1945* (Oxford: Berg, 1997), 54.

ideology. At one point, Himmler went so far as to set up homes where unmarried mothers could rest until delivery, and perhaps even spread rumors that women could get help with conception there if they so desired.[1344] With the outbreak of war, Rudolph Hess reassured unmarried women that if their future partner was killed, they would be receive financial support as if the marriage had taken place. One is tempted to read concerns of military capacity into National Socialist reproductive policies, except that the brakes on reproduction were never really taken off. Giving a 'gift to the Fuhrer' was good form, whereas giving too many gifts to the Fuhrer was potentially lethal for the unmarried gift-giver. Any genuine concerns about military capacity were at least matched by concerns about the possibility that women might begin using reproduction as an opportunity to enjoy themselves. Nazi ideologist George Usadel sought to clarify the National Socialist tolerance for unmarried motherhood: "Where prominent figures have said this, it was always meant as an ideal requirement of the purest hue, never as an invitation to unbridled behavior."[1345]

Sexual libertinage actually became very dangerous very quickly for women in the Third Reich. Consistent with the ideological axiom that not all Aryans are equally superior, the Nazis passed the Law for the Prevention of Hereditarily Diseased Offspring on July 14, 1933. The law called for the compulsory sterilization of those suffering from hereditary defects, which included physical and mental illnesses, deafness, blindness, and physical deformities. It also covered 'congenital feeble-mindedness', an open-ended category into which virtually anyone might be placed depending on the disposition of the examiner. The determination of 'feeble-mindedness' involved a pseudo-scientific inquiry into the acquired knowledge of the subject (geography, political figures, recipes, etc.), which apparently had little or no relevance if the questions were answered correctly.[1346] Ascertaining the subject's 'conduct in life' became the critical element in the determination of feeble-mindedness, and 'deviancy from the norm' the

---

1344  Felix Kersten, *The Kersten Memoirs: 1940-1945*, intro. H.R. Trevor-Roper, trans. Constantine Fitzgibbon and James Oliver (New York: Macmillan, 1957), 181.  Studies of the homes themselves (The Lebensborn) find no systemic activity of that kind.  Catrine Clay and Michael Leapman, *Master Race: The Lebensborn Experiment in Nazi Germany* (London: Hodder & Staughton, 1995).

1345  Bleuel, 156.

1346  Henri Friedlander, *The Origins of Nazi Genocide: From Euthanasia to the Final Solution* (North Carolina: University of North Carolina Press, 1995), 30-32.

standard against which conduct in life was measured.[1347]

Women made up two-thirds of those diagnosed as feeble-minded, with 57% of all female sterilizations predicated on said diagnosis.[1348] Deviancy from the female norm was often established through sexual behavior, as in cases where a woman changed sexual partners frequently or had more than one illegitimate child.[1349] The model Germanic woman was a selfless laborer, "her antithesis was the slut, the prostitute."[1350] The second most common diagnosis resulting in sterilization for women was schizophrenia, with the determination again resting in large part on a perceived lack of sexual restraint.[1351] Schizophrenia accounted for 25% percent of all female sterilizations in 1934, and assuming the percentages stayed constant, upwards of 160,000 of the roughly 200,000 women sterilized by the Third Reich were mutilated in whole or in part for sexual reasons.[1352] Some 4,500 women were killed in the process, many of whom were physically resisting the procedure up to the last moment.[1353] Thus, as Gisela Bock explains, the sterilization program became "the first scientifically planned and bureaucratically executed massacre of the National Socialist state ... and women were its chief victims."[1354] The program was operated in full view of the German public, due largely to the publicity efforts of the Nazis themselves.[1355]

From an official standpoint, the difficulty with sterilization was that the possibility of pregnancy no longer provided a check on sexual behavior, and many women were institutionalized after sterilization specifically to

1347 Gisela Bock, "Racism and Sexism in Nazi Germany: Motherhood, Compulsory, Sterilization, and the State," in *When Biology Became Destiny: Women in Weimar and Nazi Germany*, ed. Renate Bridenthal, Atina Grossman, and Marion Kaplan (New York: Monthly Review Press, 1984), 282.

1348 Elizabeth Heinemann, *What Difference Does a Husband Make?: Women and Marital Status in Nazi and Postwar Germany* (Berkeley: University of California Press, 1999), 30.

1349 Gisela Bock, "Antinatalism, Maternity and Paternity in National Socialist Racism," in Gisela Bock and Pat Thane ed., *Maternity and Gender Policies: Women and the Rise of the European Welfare States, 1880s-1950s* (London: Routledge, 1991), 238-39.

1350 Bock, "Racism and Sexism," 282.

1351 Heinemann, 30.

1352 Friedlander, *Origins of Nazi Genocide*, 29.

1353 Bock, "Antinatalism," 237.

1354 Ibid., 237-38.

1355 Robert Gellately, *Backing Hitler: Consent and Coercion in Nazi Germany* (Oxford: Oxford University Press, 2001), 94.

keep them from having sex.[1356] In actuality, the sterilized woman found herself in a very dangerous position once released; sterilization led to a presumption of loose morals, which, combined with the inability to get pregnant, made such women frequent targets for rape.[1357] The violation of sterilized women was of little or no interest to the professionals involved in the program, though they did use the possibility of sexual assault as a justification for the sterilization of 'hereditarily sick' women who had no interest in procreation. Thus, in the end, the genetic improvement to be achieved was simply the elimination of tendencies toward sexual independence and promiscuity in women.

The Third Reich was thus much more emphatic about preventing unwanted pregnancies than promoting those it desired, and, similarly, took greater care to prevent unwanted marriages than to encourage or facilitate them. On October 18 of 1935, the Nazis passed the Marriage Health Law, which required marital hopefuls to acquire a 'Certificate of Fitness to Marry' from their local health authorities.[1358] Applicants were given physical exams and interviewed with the intent of discovering 'hereditary defects'. After December 1941, couples would have to present a "Certificate of Unobjectionability" to marry, based on an interview with health authorities but no physical exam.[1359] Either certificate or the marriage loans mentioned previously could be withheld upon a finding of 'asociability'.

A legal definition of asociability was promulgated in the 1937 Decree Concerning the Preventive Fight Against Crime, though the concept was in force from the first moments of National Socialist rule. An asocial was someone who, though having committed no criminal act, held an attitude 'adverse to the community' or refused to 'adapt to the community'.[1360] Single women of a certain temperament were particularly vulnerable to the charge. "These were," notes Elizabeth Heinemann, "prostitutes, women with sexually transmitted disease, those who had sex prior to marriage or engagement, those who relished evenings dancing or drinking with soldiers, and those who simply struck teachers or social workers as 'overly sexual.'"[1361] The longer a woman stayed single, the more likely it was that she would be

---

1356  Heinemann, 30.
1357  Bock, "Antinatalism," 238; Heinemann, 30.
1358  Pine, 16.
1359  Heinemann, 24.
1360  Gellately, 97; Heinemann, 28.
1361  Heinemann, 26.

labeled an asocial, and thus be kept single against her will. After 1941, couples that continued to live together after being denied permission to marry were automatically labeled asocial.[1362]

While ostensibly dedicated to the concept of German racial superiority, Nazi ideologists actually found most of their fellow Germans unfit to continue the eternal line of descent. A leading Nazi eugenicist, Fritz Lenz, noted that "as things are now, it is only a minority of our fellow citizens who are so endowed that their unrestricted procreation is good for the race."[1363] Other Nazis theorized that as few as 10 to 30 percent of German women were 'worthy of procreation'. The limitations on reproduction put in place by the Third Reich led Bock to write that "never in history had there been a state which in theory, propaganda and practice pursued an antinatalist policy of such dimensions."[1364]

Of course, National Socialism was a combination of pro-natalist and anti-natalist elements, pro-natalist to the extent that reproduction acted as a limit on sexuality, and anti-natalist to the extent that a ban on reproduction acted as a limit on sexuality. Even the 'genetic' improvement of the race would have involved the elimination of female 'promiscuity genes'. In the end, marriage and motherhood were meant to form the outer boundaries of female sexuality; only women who had proven their ideological purity and anhedonic disposition were allowed to go that far. The impure were sterilized, institutionalized, and prevented from marrying. Concentration camps became the final destination for tens of thousands of asocial women.

## The Nuremburg Laws

**The centerpiece of National Socialist** social legislation was one of the infamous "Nuremberg Laws," entitled the Law for the Protection of German Blood and German Honor. A prohibition on interracial sexual intercourse had been high on the movement's agenda from its earliest days, having postulated that Germans and Jews were genetically dissimilar races, and that 'interracial' reproduction would be harmful to the Germanic people. Arthur Gütt of the Reich Ministry of the Interior explained the precise harm to be avoided:

---

1362 Ibid., 24.
1363 Pine, 105.
1364 Bock, "Antinatalism," 240.

The Law for the Protection of German Blood came out of the thought that a *Volk* can only be combined into a self-contained unity, and brought to its highest level of performance, when its citizens maintain their race consciousness. Experience shows, and science confirms, that racial mixture with foreign blood types endangers the internal unity of the individual man, and that racial hybrids are, within themselves, torn and divided men.[1365]

Initial attempts to secure its passage met with resistance over legal technicalities. In September of 1933, the Minister of Justice, along with a particularly unstable undersecretary named Roland Freisler, proposed that sexual contact (marital or otherwise) between those of German blood and racial aliens be made a punishable offense. They were informed by their own ministry that they would have to take the more drastic and diplomatically suspect step of making interracial marriages illegal altogether. The ministry also warned that such a law would promote extortion and denunciations, either from participants in broken relationships or disaffected third parties, and warned that such actions would "assume a particularly repellant form."[1366]

Reich officials were disinclined to wait for anything so trivial as the passage of a law prior to applying its provisions. Those with responsibilities in the domestic sphere were already refusing to sanction interracial marriages on the grounds that they were contrary to 'general national principles'.[1367] Officials received judicial support from one county court

---

1365 Gütt, 16. Speaking at the 1937 Nuremberg rally, Dr. Gerhard Wagner reiterated that the laws were designed to protect the race consciousness of the German people. "Our racial laws are issued not only for the protection of German blood, but also German honor. They bear the honorary name of the 'City of the Reich Party Days'. They will achieve their purpose only when their administration is sustained by the racial consciousness present right now in this city. They will have fulfilled their purpose when a new generation has grown up in Germany, that out of a self-evidently pure National Socialist viewpoint instinctively rejects the Jews, and has become immune to the Jewish virus. We are delighted and proud to see just such a youth growing up." Speech of Dr. Gerhard Wagner, *Reichstagung in Nürnberg 1937*, ed. Hanns Kerrl, (Berlin: Vaterländischer Verlag C.A. Weller, 1938), 122.

1366 Ingo Müller, *Hitler's Justice: The Courts of the Third Reich*, trans. Deborah Lucas Schneider, intro. Detlev Vagts (Cambridge: Harvard University Press, 1991), 91.

1367 Ibid., 92.

which noted that legal principles should be applied not because of their enactment into law but "because they are established on the basis of generally held convictions about what is right."[1368] The analytical jurisprudence was a bit suspect, though the court correctly gauged the 'generally held convictions' of the German public at the time. Concerned citizens had already taken to publicly humiliating women suspected of having sexual relations with Jews, and in some cases were able to halt intermarriages with public pressure.[1369] In Emmerich, public pressure even forced a mixed couple to refrain from appearing in bathing suits together.[1370]

Party radicals remained fully energized about the sexual question coming into 1935, and wholly dissatisfied with the sporadic and half-hearted attempts to end the epidemic of racial defilement. Freisler continued to push for sexual restrictions at the Reich Ministry of Justice, warning his colleagues that "we are in danger of ... betraying our fundamental convictions if we fail to include this provision."[1371] The hopes and dreams of National Socialist true believers finally came true with the passage of the Nuremberg Laws on September 15, 1935. The key provisions of the Law for the Protection of German Blood and German Honor read as follows:

Section 1

1. Marriages between Jews and citizens of German of kindred blood are forbidden. Marriages concluded in defiance of this law are void, even if, for the purpose of evading this law, they were conducted abroad.

...

Section 2

2. Sexual Relations outside marriage between Jews and nationals of German or kindred blood are forbidden.

Section 3

---

1368 Ibid.
1369 Marion A. Kaplan, *Between Dignity and Despair: Jewish Life in Nazi Germany* (New York: Oxford University Press, 1998) 79.
1370 Patricia Szobar, "Telling Sexual Stories in the Nazi Courts of Law: Race Defilement in Nazi Germany, 1933-1945," Journal of the History of Sexuality Vol. 11, No. 1/2, January/April 2002, 135-36.
1371 Müller, 96.

3. Jews will not be permitted to employ female citizens of German or kindred blood as servants.

"A Jew," according to Article 5 of the Reich Citizenship Law, "is anyone who is descended from at least three grandparents who are racially full Jews." A person of mixed blood but with fewer than Jewish three grandparents would be treated as an Aryan, subject to exceptions for certain behavior (e.g., marrying a Jew). In either case, the racial status of the grandparents would be determined by religious affiliation, which does tend to undercut the notion of a racial rather than religious separation between Jews and Germans. Moreover, the limitation on those with full-blooded grandparents would produce the illogical result that a person with 4 half-Jewish grandparents would be treated as a full German, while a person with one Jewish parent would be treated as a half-breed or *Mischlinge*. Thus, writes Ingo Müller, "the first attempt to give a precise definition of the 'chief enemy' of the Third Reich revealed the totally pseudoscientific nature of its racist doctrines and the charlatinism of the 'scientists' associated with them."[1372] A theoretical division between Jews and Germans was, in the end, more important than the substance of that division.

Adding to the ambiguity and confusion, a clear definition of sexual relations was conspicuous only for its absence. Jurists of the Third Reich were hardly at a loss for it; with regard to sexuality, they were very much on the same page as those responsible for promoting and drafting the legislation in the first place. As Ingo Müller notes, "it was the 'scholarly penetration' of the meaning of these laws and their interpretation by the courts which revealed even clearer traits of sexual pathology."[1373] The critical question was whether to restrict the prohibition to sexual acts which might lead to reproduction, or to apply the law in a more expansive manner. It only took until December of 1935 for the highest criminal court in Germany, the Grand Criminal Panel, to rule in favor of the latter approach.

> A broad interpretation is ... appropriate in view of the fact that the provisions of the law are meant to protect not only German blood but also German honor. This requires that in addition to coition, all such sexual manipulations — whether actively performed or passively tolerated — that have as their aim the satisfaction of one partner's sex drive

---

1372  Müller, 98.
1373  Ibid.

in a manner other than the completion of coition, must
cease between Jews and citizens of German or related kinds
of blood.[1374]

The prohibition on sexual conduct was designed to address sexual
concerns more directly than biological and hereditary concerns. Even a
defense based on the sterilization of one or both partners was considered
and rejected by the courts. Nevertheless, the crime of sexual defilement
was considered as serious as high treason; both were classified as crimes
against the "body of the Volk," or *Volkskörper*.[1375] A subsequent law review
article explained the more expansive approach in 1936, again coming back
to 'ideo-biological' considerations:

> The German Volk should not be kept pure only in its
> blood, but rather also pure in its culture and type. It would
> thus contradict the spirit of the law if the ban on sexual
> relationships between Germans and Jews was applied
> 'mechanically', so to speak, meaning viewed purely in
> physical terms. As a rule, the German man brings a spiritual
> influencing, a more or less extensive and continuing 'self-
> belonging', to the sexually intimate relationship, even if
> things don't come to sexual relations (*Beischlaf*) as such. As
> physical self-abandonment brings with it the danger of the
> penetration of Jewish blood, so a spiritual self-abandonment
> presents the danger of the penetration of the Jewish type,
> through the influencing of one's way of thinking and
> emotional life. This point of entry must be closed, and on
> this basis relationships between Germans and Jews must
> be punished as far as the scope of the law and will of the
> legislator (thus the leadership) will allow.[1376]

Given free rein by the Supreme Court, Germany's lower courts quickly
began to engage in Streicheresque legal reasoning. They frequently relied,
explicitly or implicitly, on the assumption that all Jewish men were sexual
predators and sexual deviants. The concepts of sexual relations and sexual
satisfaction were then expanded accordingly. Sexual relations no longer

1374 Ibid., 101.
1375 Kaplan, 80.
1376 Dr. Kuhn, "Blood Defense Laws in Criminal Law Practice," in *Deutsch Justiz*
1936 Vol. II, 1005.

required physical contact or even the active participation of both partners. Masturbation constituted sexual relations if performed in the presence of another person. Kissing constituted sexual relations according to one court, given the defendant's physiological inability to have normal intercourse. One Jewish man was convicted for receiving massage therapy on his stomach, after the Gestapo forcibly extracted a confession from him explaining that he had derived sexual pleasure from the experience.[1377] In 1939, a Jewish man was convicted for glancing at an Aryan woman across the street, because, according to the court, the glance was of a clearly erotic nature.[1378] Though apparently never tried, a Jewish man was arrested for being in an elevator with an Aryan woman, in spite of the fact that she had entered the elevator when he was already inside.[1379]

Enforcement of the Nuremberg Laws came largely through the efforts of a small but very enthusiastic segment of the population, who provided the Gestapo with information on even the slightest of interactions suggestive of sexual relations. The Gestapo was a rather passive institution relative to the population at large, though it was distinctly energetic in its investigations of Jews suspected of race defilement. Jewish women in particular were interrogated at length, questioned for several days in some cases, and forced to describe sexual encounters in extremely graphic detail according to Eric Johnson.[1380] The details sought included a play-by-play on foreplay, clothing removal, body positions, and whether anyone climaxed. If no sexual act occurred, agents contented themselves with extracting confessions of sexual desires and attempts at seduction.[1381] Patricia Szobar notes that "many of the facts elicited with such vigor in the course of interrogations appear irrelevant to the assessment of guilt and to the sentencing process."[1382]

Hitler had initially suggested that the Nuremberg Laws would only be applied directly to Jewish and Aryan men, with offending women, Jewish or Aryan, left unpunished. Nevertheless, by 1937 Jewish women were being taken into protective custody for sexual offenses with Aryan men. Courts certainly had no reservations about assigning the women the lion's share of the blame in such cases. For example: "The accused was completely at the

---

1377 Müller, 103.
1378 Szobar, 160.
1379 Kaplan, 81.
1380 Eric Johnson, *Nazi Terror: The Gestapo, Jews, and Ordinary Germans* (New York: Basic Books, 1999), 111.
1381 Szobar, 160.
1382 Ibid., 155.

mercy of the Jewess's seductive wiles.... The Jewess behaved like a whore and is mainly to blame for events."[1383] Also: "The witness B. is a lascivious, morally depraved Jewess who used her unchecked sexual appetite and ruthlessness to acquire a strong influence over the defendant."[1384] Aryan men still received sentences several years long for violations of the law.

The Third Reich left existing intermarriages intact legally, though pressure was brought to bear from other directions. Aryans married to Jews found themselves restricted from employment in civil service and education.[1385] Mixed families were banned from the German Winter Relief. Courts relaxed the rules for divorce between mixed couples, and the Gestapo and other concerned citizens made efforts to encourage such couples in that direction.[1386] According to Marion Kaplan, "Whether or not a 'mixed' couple intended to be political, the mere continuation of their marriage was a form of defiance and was seen as such by the government."[1387] At the same time, Jews married to Aryans were often spared deportation to concentration camps pending the outcome of the war. Nathan Stoltzfus cites evidence pointing to a reluctance on the part of Nazi officials to antagonize already rebellious Aryans, and particularly with regard to a program (the Holocaust) they were attempting to keep quiet.[1388] The Rosenstrasse protest of 1943 actually convinced the Gestapo to release the detained spouses of Aryan women who had gathered around their headquarters for several days.

There seems to have been some hope of an eventual conversion on the part of Aryan partners. Section 1333 of the Civil Code allowed for divorce within six months of the discovery of personal qualities of a spouse that would have prevented the other spouse from entering the marriage had he or she known of those qualities.[1389] Courts designated race a personal quality within the meaning of §1333, then held that the quality could go unrecognized because even the 'instinctual racism' of the individual was not equivalent to the racial knowledge generated through national renewal.[1390] It was assumed that the acquisition of racial knowledge would translate into a change in

1383 Ibid., 154.
1384 Müller, 104.
1385 Kaplan, 79.
1386 Ibid., 88.
1387 Ibid., 89.
1388 Nathan Stoltzfus, "Social Protection of Intermarried German Jews in Nazi Germany," in Nathan Stoltzfus and Robert Gellately ed., *Social Outsiders in Nazi Germany* (Princeton: Princeton University Press, 2001), 128.
1389 Müller, 93.
1390 Ibid., 94.

sexual perceptions. Courts held that a course of interracial sex could itself kill the sex drive of the Aryan partner, thus leaving the Aryan blameless in the event of a divorce.[1391]

By early 1942, at the Wannsee Conference, the decision was taken to kill every single Jew in Europe, regardless of who specifically was taking sexual gratification from what and with whom. Some 6,000,000 Jews died as a result, along with several million people in other categories, including Soviet POWs, Poles, Gypsies, homosexuals, 'asocials' and disabled Germans, bringing the total to 11,000,000. Scholars have suggested that the Holocaust, rather than a means to military ends, was in fact the end to be achieved in part by fighting World War II. According to John Weiss:

> The Holocaust was not simply a consequence of the war. For the Nazis, the destruction of the Jews was itself a war aim of the highest priority. Just as the Nazi revolution was a racial revolution, so also the war was a racial war. ... Even when the Germans were losing the war, materials, transport, and energies were diverted from the front to complete the slaughter of the eternal enemy.[1392]

Norman Cohn sees nothing new here:

> Chiliastically minded movements are ruthless not simply in order to safeguard or further specific interests but also – and above all – in an effort to clear the way for the Millennium. What else can have induced the Nazis, in the middle of a desperate war, to allot manpower, money and materials to the wholly irrelevant enterprise of exterminating millions of Jews?[1393]

## Other Threats

**National Socialist sexophobia ran in** other directions as well. Germany's experiment with concentration camps (Dachau being the first) began because of insufficient jail space in which to hold all of the NSDAP's political opponents. Homosexual rights leaders were among the first to receive invitations from the Reichsführer-SS, Heinrich Himmler.

1391 Kaplan, 90.
1392 John Weiss, *Ideology of Death: Why the Holocaust Happened in Germany* (Chicago: Ivan R. Dee, 1997), 325-26.
1393 Norman Cohn, *The Pursuit of the Millennium* (New Jersey: Essential Books, 1957), 310.

Homosexuality was already illegal during Weimar pursuant to §175 of the criminal code, though in 1935 it underwent a revision at the hands of the National Socialists. The original code provision covered the "unnatural sex act" committed by one man with another. According to the commentary to the revision, "the defect of the previous Section 175 ... lay in the fact that ... it applied only to intercourse-like acts, so that public prosecutors and the police could not proceed against evidently homosexual practices unless they were able to prove such acts."[1394] The new code provision prohibited the commission of a male-male "sex offense," covering anything contrary to wholesome popular sentiment and/or behavior "likely to arouse sexual desires in oneself or strangers."[1395] The Ministry of Justice had already issued guidelines in December of 1934 which allowed for prosecution in cases of attempted violations.[1396] Virtually anything, even a glance of a 'clearly erotic nature', could be construed as a violation. One man was even arrested for watching a heterosexual couple having sex because, according to the report, he had been paying more attention to the man than the woman.[1397]

The revision and application of §175 thus formed a close parallel with the drafting and application of the Nuremburg Laws. In case anyone was confused about the similarity between Jews and homosexuals in National Socialist ideology, Himmler set them straight in a public speech on October 10, 1936.

> As National Socialists we are not afraid to fight against this plague within our own ranks. Just as we have readopted the ancient Germanic approach to the question of marriage, so, too, in our judgment of homosexuality -- a symptom of racial degeneracy destructive to our race -- we have returned to the guiding Nordic principle that degenerates should be exterminated.[1398]

Step one in the extermination of homosexuals meant first identifying them, then compiling lists in some central location so as to coordinate what

1394 Günter Grau ed., *Hidden Holocaust?: Gay and Lesbian Persecution in Germany 1933-45*, with Claudia Schoppmann, trans. Patrick Camiller (London: Cassell, 1995), 66.
1395 Michael Burleigh and Wolfgang Wipperman, *The Racial State: Germany 1933-1945* (Cambridge: Cambridge University Press, 1991), 190.
1396 Richard Plant, *The Pink Triangle: The Nazi War Against Homosexuals* (New York: Henry Holt, 1986), 112.
1397 Ibid., 125.
1398 Ibid., 111.

figured to be a rather large undertaking. Himmler's ascendancy in the mid-1930s allowed him to consolidate the whole of Germany's law enforcement under a central Reich Criminal Police Bureau, featuring the aforementioned Reich Office for Combating Abortion and Homosexuality. State police were required to submit special forms to this office when addressing violations of §175 depending on the race or affiliation of the offender. Lists of names and addresses had already been acquired from now-defunct homosexual rights organizations and periodicals. After the revision of §175, names were extracted under torture from those arrested. Private citizens were trained and encouraged to identify and report suspected homosexuals, and did so with so much enthusiasm that the Third Reich actually issued appeals for a slowdown in denunciations.

No one seems sure just how many homosexual men were convicted under §175, nor how many were dealt with outside the judicial system. Himmler put the number of homosexuals in Germany at 2,000,000, and his efforts at extermination came up well short of the mark by anyone's estimate. Richard Plant makes a persuasive case for between 50,000 and 63,000 convictions between 1933 and 1944.[1399] Lesbians were occasionally taken into protective custody as asocials, or, if someone was in a creative mood, charged with a Sapphically-inspired political crime.[1400] Sometime in 1945, a female Luftwaffe assistant rejected an interested air signal corps lieutenant and was arrested along with her lover, also a female Luftwaffe assistant. The latter was charged with 'subversion of military potential' and, along with several other lesbians, handed over to a group of POWs who were promised a bottle of alcohol each for raping them.[1401]

Sex trials of all varieties were generally closed, or at least temporarily closed down during 'immoral' and potentially corrupting moments. Exceptions were made in the case of the Cloister Trials, which forced Catholic clergymen to defend themselves against charges of homosexuality and child abuse. The Church had reached an agreement with the NSDAP in 1933 (the Concordat) guaranteeing certain religious freedoms and institutional privileges, and as late as 1938 one bishop expressed hope that the "totalitarianism of the State and the totalitarianism of the Church" could

---

1399   Ibid., 149.
1400   Claudia Schopmann, "National Socialist Policies Towards Female Homosexuality," in Lynn Abrams and Elizabeth Harvey ed., *Gender Relations in German History* (Durham: Duke University Press, 1997), 184.
1401   Grau, 82-83.

coexist harmoniously.[1402] The NSDAP, on the other hand, never intended to share power with anyone, least of all the Church whom they viewed as the primary bulwark against complete National Socialist indoctrination.[1403] Between 50 and 100 hearings were held in 1936 and 1937, with a set in 1937 timed for maximum propaganda effect and supported by a massive publicity campaign. Slipshod investigations resulted in few convictions, and the hoped-for mass of defections from the Catholic faith never materialized.[1404]

The outbreak of World War II came soon after. Swift victories on all fronts brought POWs and other foreign nationals within Germany's borders, and increasingly within the sphere of German sexual anxieties. The classic arguments about purity of blood were refitted for a nationalist sexual crusade, and the crime of 'national adultery' introduced into law. British and French nationals received much better treatment than their Polish and Russian counterparts, with prison sentences for the former and the latter sent to concentration camps, sentenced to death, or summarily executed. For the offending Aryan woman, it was the usual treatment: lengthy Gestapo interrogations attempting to elicit sexual minutia followed by a term in prison or a concentration camp. Sentencing depended on the usual factors: "A seeming lack of shame, a loose sexual lifestyle, and a failure to conform politically could all serve as exacerbating factors."[1405] A declaration of emotional attachment could also get the woman into trouble.[1406] On the other hand, foreign nationals might be 'capable of Germanization', which, if granted, would effectively nullify the crime. In order for the man to be eligible, the Aryan woman would have to be single and the authorities involved would have to have some reason to want to spare her punishment.[1407]

Within the German population, young jazz and swing aficionados evolved into a threat to the national order, unnerving Himmler enough to order them sent to concentration camps in 1942.[1408] The supplement to the

---

1402 Guenter Lewy, *The Catholic Church and Nazi Germany* (New York: McGraw Hill, 1964), 167.

1403 Johnson, 213.

1404 Plant, 136.

1405 Birthe Kundrus, "Forbidden Company: Romantic Relationships Between Germans and Foreigners, 1939-1945," Journal of the History of Sexuality Vol. 11, No. 1/2, January/April 2002, 212.

1406 Heinemann, 59.

1407 Ibid., 58-59.

1408 Detlev Peukert, *Inside Nazi Germany: Conformity, Opposition, and Racism in Everyday Life*, trans. Richard Deveson (New Haven: Yale University Press,

June 29, 1944 *Völkischer Beobachter* devoted a full page to bandleader Benny Goodman: "With his swing band he not only receives the top radio fees, but exerts a positively sinister influence on American youth. 'My music is more immoral than all the courtesans in history put together', he himself boasts."[1409] Special agents of the SS were sent to monitor behavior at dance halls and within swing cliques. Though noting resistance to National Socialist propaganda, the reports tended to concentrate, with the usual level of detail, on the unrestrained and perverse sexuality of the groups. Juvenile courts also noted an increase in crimes of a moral nature during the early stages of the war. It seems that for all of the Third Reich's attempts at ideological indoctrination, what they ended up with, for the most part, was the same cynicism and sexual rebellion that emerged during the first world war.

A series of dramatic military reversals from late-1942 to mid-1944 eliminated any real possibility of a Thousand-Year Reich. Priorities are priorities, and thus all throughout the war, even as the allies were landing in Normandy, National Socialists continued to issue directives on how to combat homosexuality and masturbation. The Gestapo continued to arrest suspected homosexuals until the Russian army had encircled Berlin in 1945. In spite of everything, after twelve years of sexual repression, brutality, and mass murder on a scale that would make a Bolshevik blush, the experience ended on a note of frustration for the National Socialists. As one concentration camp survivor recalled the end:

> The sadistic SS bitch stopped and faced us with her ironical smile. ... We all wished we could tell her what we truly wanted now: tear her to pieces as a farewell to this place, for all her physical and mental torments, for the extended [line-ups], for the slaps and kicks and blows with her stick, but mostly for her ironic style that elevated abuse to sublime heights of pleasure for her. This was her last chance, to torture us once more, keeping us perched on the edge of life and death. Then an SS car came careening around the corner ... and the SS Brünhilde's last pleasure was cut off before she could reach her orgasm.[1410]

1987), 200.
1409 Ibid., 201.
1410 Vera Laska ed., *Women in the Resistance and in the Holocaust: Voices of Eyewitnesses*, fwd. Simon Wiesenthal (Westport: Greenwood Press, 1983), 182.

# Conclusion

**In conclusion, the totalitarian movement** is, for those versed in its subtleties, easily identified in its incipiency. The sociological dynamics of the pre-totalitarian society are a constant. The ideological framework of the movement is a constant. What is also a constant, unfortunately, is the tendency of more rational individuals to dismiss ideological proclamations as harmless and idle rhetoric. It seems difficult for the rational mind to accept that an apparently decent and civil human being, perhaps extolling love of God, family, country etc., intends to commit or support acts of an inhuman nature, and on unimaginable scale. For totalitarians, nothing could be more straightforward; they declare the necessity of mass extermination, and, circumstances permitting, they kill. It is this disconnect between totalitarian and non-totalitarian minds that allows totalitarianism to thrive.